A Devotional

DAILY BREAD 2012

366 Days of Discipleship Formation

Editor: Lu Mountenay

2012

Community of Christ
Herald Publishing House
Independence, Missouri

Produced by Community of Christ
1001 W. Walnut St.
Independence, MO 64050-3562

Herald Publishing House
P.O. Box 390
Independence, MO 64051-0390

Printed in the United States of America
ISBN: 978-0-8309-1510-1

Cover painting by Jeanne Davis

Library of Congress has cataloged this serial publication as follows:

Daily Bread
Independence, Mo., Herald Publishing House

v. 18cm

Annual.
"A devotional guide for every day of the year."
Key Title: Daily Bread, ISSN 0092-7147
1. Devotional calendars
BV4810.D23 242'.2 74-640475 MARC-S

Library of Congress 74 [8205]

Welcome to *Daily Bread* A Familiar Friend

Daily Bread is just that—spiritual food for your *daily* walk with God. *Daily Bread* is a way to get to know the people of Community of Christ through their stories and an opportunity to share your own testimony. *Daily Bread* can be used as a devotional or for worship. *Daily Bread* is helpful for reflecting on the lectionary scripture readings. *Daily Bread* is a connection to the Daily Prayer for Peace at the Temple in Independence, Missouri, with short prayers for peace of its own. *Daily Bread* contributes to lifelong disciple formation by offering spiritual practices. Every day you also can make a peace covenant with the Creator. *Daily Bread* is a companion on your journey of shalom.

Important Features

- The New Revised Standard Version is used for all Bible references.
- You can find the daily focus countries and complete Daily Prayers for Peace at *www.CofChrist.org/PrayerPeace.*
- Spiritual practices are repeated quarterly throughout the year.

Acknowledgments

I appreciate the writers who sent their inspirational, informative, and touching stories and testimonies. I also thank those who contributed in other ways:

- Jeanne Davis, for the original cover art.
- Carolyn Brock and the Spiritual Formation Team, for the spiritual practices.
- Sandra Ferguson of the Presiding Bishopric's office, for helping with many of the stories that appear on Saturdays.
- Karen Moreland and Pam Robison, for their help with the daily scripture readings.
- And thanks to the editorial and production team, for helping with the details of placing *Daily Bread* in your hands: Greg Clark, Pam Evans, Jack Martin, Steven L. Shields, Mary Kay Speaks, Patty Wilson, and Judith Yager.

—*Lu Mountenay*
2012 *Daily Bread* Editor

Future *Daily Bread* Submissions

If you wish to submit stories for consideration in the 2013 *Daily Bread*, send them to

E-mail: *lmountenay@CofChrist.org*
Regular mail: *Daily Bread* Editor
Community of Christ
International Headquarters
1001 West Walnut Street
Independence, MO 64050-3562
USA

I'll be waiting…Lu

DAILY BREAD 2012

Daily Prayer for Peace Countries

January 2012

1–All Nations
2–Egypt
3–Syria
4–Palestine
5–Lebanon
6–Israel
7–Jordan
8–Saudi Arabia
9–Kuwait
10–Bahrain
11–Qatar
12 –United Arab Emirates
13 –Oman
14–Yemen
15–Iran
16–Iraq
17–Cyprus
18–Bolivia
19–Greece
20–Afghanistan
21–Turkey
22–Algeria
23–Tunisia
24–Libya
25–Morocco
26–India
27–Chile
28–Australia
29–Denmark
30–Finland
31–Iceland

February 2012

1–Mauritius
2–Norway
3–Sweden
4–Albania
5–Mexico
6–New Zealand
7–Ireland
8–Barbados
9–United Kingdom
10–Armenia
11–Indigenous Peoples of Europe
12–French Polynesia
13–Belgium
14–Luxembourg
15–Serbia
16–Lithuania
17–Netherlands
18–Belarus
19–Portugal
20–Democratic Republic of Congo
21–Spain
22–Italy
23–Benin
24–Estonia
25–Malta
26–France
27–Dominican Republic
28–Taiwan
29–Slovakia

March 2012

1–Bhutan
2–Germany
3–Bulgaria
4–Austria
5–Liechtenstein
6–Switzerland
7–Monaco
8–Andorra
9–San Marino
10–Bosnia and Herzegovina
11–Burkina Faso
12–Burundi
13–Myanmar
14–Cameroon
15–Hungary
16–Thailand
17–Cape Verde
18–Cambodia
19–Central African Republic
20–Laos
21–Namibia
22–Vietnam
23–Colombia
24–Argentina
25–Greece
26–Bangladesh
27–China
28–Chad
29–Hong Kong
30–Macao
31–Comoros

April 2012

1–Vatican City
2–Brunei
3–Malaysia
4–Egypt
5–Cuba
6–Singapore
7–Swaziland
8–Cyprus
9–Philippines
10–East Timor
11–Equatorial Guinea
12–Indonesia
13–Gabon
14–Gambia
15–Japan
16–Guinea
17–Korea
18–Zimbabwe
19–Guinea-Bissau
20–Taiwan
21–Kyrgyzstan
22–Djibouti
23–Iran
24–Maldives
25–Italy
26–Indigenous Peoples of Africa
27–Somalia
28–Nepal
29–Eritrea
30–Iraq

May 2012

1–Kosovo
2–Niger
3–Poland
4–Ethiopia
5–Kyrgyzstan
6–Sudan
7–Mongolia
8–Czech Republic
9–Latvia
10–Uganda
11–Bahrain
12–Côte d'Ivoire/Ivory Coast
13–Kenya
14–Liberia
15–Human Family
16–Tanzania
17–Norway
18–Ghana
19–Iceland
20–Malawi
21–Montenegro
22–Jamaica
23–Zambia
24–Kuwait
25–Libya
26–Georgia
27–Madagascar
28–Azerbaijan
29–Botswana
30–Mali
31–Morocco

June 2012

1–Zimbabwe
2–Netherlands
3–Lesotho
4–Rwanda
5–Denmark
6–Namibia
7–South Africa
8–Micronesia
9–Swaziland
10–Niger
11–Angola
12–Palestine
13–Mozambique
14–Sao Tomé and Principe
15–Turkmenistan
16–Sierra Leone
17–Qatar
18–Brazil
19–Republic of Congo
20–United Arab Emirates
21–Yemen
22–Indigenous Peoples of South America
23–Luxembourg
24–Sri Lanka
25–Croatia
26–Argentina
27–Paraguay
28–Ukraine
29–Togo
30–Uruguay

July 2012

1–Canada
2–Bolivia
3–Andorra
4–Ireland
5–Chile
6 –Peru
7–Belgium
8–Colombia
9–Algeria
10–Ecuador
11–Cambodia
12–Venezuela
13–Eritrea
14–France
15–Costa Rica
16–El Salvador
17–Korea
18–Uruguay
19–Nicaragua
20–United States
21–Panama
22–Mexico
23–Belize
24–Guatemala
25–Trinidad and Tobago
26–San Marino
27–Honduras
28–Saint Vincent and Grenadines
29–Antigua and Barbuda
30–Dominica
31–Cuba

August 2012

1–Barbados
2–Dominican Republic
3–Haiti
4–Grenada

5–Jamaica
6–Bahamas
7–Guyana
8–Suriname
9–Saint Lucia
10–Canada
11–United States
12–St. Kitts and Nevis
13–Indigenous Peoples
of North America
14–Pakistan
15–Turkey
16–New Zealand
17–Indonesia
18–Australia
19–Fiji
20–Kiribati
21–Marshall Islands
22–Micronesia
23–Nauru
24–Palau
25–Papua New Guinea
26–Solomon Islands
27–Tonga
28–Tuvalu
29–Vanuatu
30–Estonia
31–Latvia

September 2012

1–Lithuania
2–Vietnam
3–Samoa
4–New Caledonia
5–French Polynesia
6–Czech Republic
7–Poland
8–Macedonia
9–Slovakia
10–Kosovo
11–Albania
12–Bosnia and Herzegovina
13–Croatia
14–Slovenia
15–Montenegro
16–Serbia
17–Japan
18–Myanmar
19–Hungary
20–Romania
21–Belize
22–Bulgaria
23–Saudi Arabia
24–Malaysia
25–Israel
26–Belarus
27–Moldova
28–Russian Federation
29–Ukraine
30–Liechtenstein

October 2012

1–China
2–Armenia
3–Germany
4–Georgia
5–Portugal
6–Azerbaijan
7–Afghanistan
8–Fiji
9–Uganda
10–Kazakhstan
11–Mongolia
12–Kyrgyzstan
13–Tajikistan
14–Turkmenistan
15–Uzbekistan
16–Bangladesh
17–Nepal
18–Lesotho
19–Bhutan
20–Indigenous Peoples of Asia
21–Sweden
22–India
23–Pakistan
24–Zambia
25–Sri Lanka
26–Angola
27–Syria
28–Thailand
29–Comoros
30–Madagascar
31–Seychelles

November 2012

1–Indigenous Peoples
of Oceania
2–Mauritius
3–Maldives
4–Russian Federation
5–Austria
6–Rwanda
7–Bahamas
8–Burundi
9–Djibouti
10–Democratic Republic
of Congo
11–Ethiopia
12–Sao Tomé and Principe
13–Republic of Congo
14–Gabon
15–Brazil
16–Hong Kong
17–Jordan
18–Cameroon
19–Central African Republic
20–Children of the World
21–Equatorial Guinea
22–Lebanon
23–Laos
24–Macao
25–Niger
26–Burkina Faso
27–Chad
28–Mali
29–Oman
30–Mauritania

December 2012

1–Somalia
2–Sierra Leone
3–Tunisia
4–Liberia
5–Singapore
6–Finland
7–Sudan
8–Romania

9–Senegal
10–Guinea
11–Cape Verde
12–Kenya
13–Malta
14–Gambia
15–Guinea-Bissau
16–South Africa
17–Kazakhstan
18–Benin
19–Spain
20–Côte d'Ivoire/Ivory Coast
21–Togo
22–East Timor
23–Ghana
24–Monaco
25–World Peace
26–Tanzania
27–Paraguay
28–Nigeria
29–Malawi
30–Switzerland
31–Palau

1
Sunday
January

Kneel before God

By Dave Schaal, First Presidency

> *On entering the house, they saw the child with Mary his mother; and they knelt down and paid him homage. Then, opening their treasure chests, they offered him gifts of gold, frankincense, and myrrh.*
>
> —Matthew 2:11

Most of us are not good at kneeling. It's not that we object to it, but that we seldom practice it. Most of us do not "kneel before" other people.

In addition, we tend to pray while sitting, standing, walking, or laying, because kneeling is less comfortable, and we can maintain our prayer focus longer in other positions.

There are those times, though, when we simply may feel compelled to kneel. I experienced this once while cross-country skiing. The ski trail followed a crystal-clear river as it wound through woods of birch, pine, and oak trees. The sunshine glistened as it reflected off snow-covered trees.

I was alone in the woods that day, and at one point I stopped to look around. The beauty and peace of the woods moved me, but I also was deeply struck with the awareness that this peace and beauty is intended by God for all creation. I found myself dropping to my knees in the snow, overwhelmed with awe and gratitude.

As we kneel today for the sacrament of the Lord's Supper, perhaps we can be aware of God's presence and desire to grace us with beauty and peace.

Prayer for Peace:

We are blessed by your presence in our lives, God. We may not have abundant treasure, but we can offer you homage and appreciation for your grace, the beauty of your creation, and peace.

Spiritual Practice for the Week: Connecting with God as Center

Each day this week connect with God through journal writing. Use a notebook, journal, computer, or any available paper. Prayerfully center on your intent to open yourself to God's presence and share what flows from your heart and mind.

Your "letter to God" might include thoughts, questions, feelings, needs, artwork, quotes, and scriptures; or it may take the form of a prayer, psalm, or poem. Try to write at least five minutes each day. What do you experience? Is this an effective way to connect with God? What surprises you? What new images or questions from God emerge? What deepens or changes in your relationship with God, Christ, Spirit?

Peace Covenant:

Today God, I will be aware of your presence and the beauty around me.

2
Monday
January

New Challenges for a New Year

By Joann Condit of Phoenix, Arizona, USA

> *"You are the salt of the earth; but if salt has lost its taste, how can its saltiness be restored? It is no longer good for anything, but is thrown out and trampled under foot."*
> —Matthew 5:13

Cooking can be a metaphor for life. Sometimes we might omit something from a recipe or make a mistake in the measurements. It can be a temporary disaster or a learning experience.

Occasionally we leave out an ingredient or make a substitution, and suddenly the whole creation is new and exciting.

As we start the new year we need to remember that challenges need not be feared. Challenges are a part of life.

To live fully we must not move out tentatively, but rather embrace each new day. We know this, but it is easy to forget the Creator is there should we stumble. When that happens we pick ourselves up, take hold again, and go forward.

One negative, perhaps, of the aging process is an occasional reluctance to experience new challenges. I no longer am young, and I sometimes must remind myself that challenge is good for my whole outlook on life.

With most negatives in cooking or in life, there is a positive. This is where we hold fast, rise to the challenge, and discover again that God is with us. Oh yes, and we can do all through Christ, who strengthens us.

Prayer for Peace:

Thank you for being our center, God, when we know we must change. You are our rock, our pillar, our root. With our hearts fastened to you, we can try new ways to bring about your peaceable kingdom.

Spiritual Practice for the Week: Connecting with God as Center

Each day this week connect with God through journal writing. Use a notebook, journal, computer, or any available paper. Prayerfully center on your intent to open yourself to God's presence and share what flows from your heart and mind. Your "letter to God" might include thoughts, questions, feelings, needs, artwork, quotes, and scriptures, or it might take the form of a prayer, psalm, or poem.

Try to write at least five minutes each day. What do you experience? Is this an effective way to connect with God? What surprises you? What new images or questions from God emerge? What deepens or changes in your relationship with God, Christ, Spirit?

Peace Covenant:

Today, God, I will not fear my callings and challenges.

3
Tuesday
January

Renewed with Awe

By Lu Mountenay of Independence, Missouri, USA

Listen carefully to the many testimonies of those around the world who have been led into the fellowship of the Community of Christ. The richness of cultures, the poetry of language, and the breadth of human experience permit the gospel to be seen with new eyes and grasped with freshness of spirit. That gift has been given to you.

—Doctrine and Covenants 162:4a

Witness

Heard the words, but
didn't grasp the meaning.
It was like a foreign language,
not understood.
Heard mumbling of a
mouthful of marbles.
The key words being
filtered out and left forgotten,
flattened on the floor.

But then he saw.
He saw what enthused them,
what filled them.
Saw for himself the lives being lived.
Then he knew it was
how he wanted to live—
in community.
It had nothing to do with words
and everything to do with The Word.

My sister, Anita, does not actively take part in a Community of Christ congregation. I took her to see the Temple when she came to town. As soon as she entered the foyer, even before she saw the Worshiper's Path or Sanctuary, she began to cry. She was sobbing, with tears rolling down her cheeks. She was overcome with the Spirit.

I'll never forget what she said, "Oh Lu, you told me, but I just couldn't know, I couldn't imagine." I don't remember what I had said about the Temple, but it was just words to her until she saw it for herself—until she experienced it. What I had said just lay in the back of her mind until she accepted the invitation.

My other sister, Pam, was with us, too, and we all were renewed with awe at the spirit and purpose of the Temple. Thank you to all who had the vision to build that symbol of peace and that place of shalom.

Prayer for Peace:

God of shalom, plant in our hearts courage to witness in word and in deed.

Spiritual Practice for the Week: Connecting with God as Center

Connect with God through journal writing. Prayerfully center on your intent to open yourself to God's presence and share what flows from your heart and mind. Your letter to God may take the form of a prayer, psalm, or poem. What do you experience? Is this an effective way for you to connect with God?

Peace Covenant:

Today I will not take your purposes for granted, God. I will share my witness.

4
Wednesday
January

Signal Communities

By Roy Schaefer of Independence, Missouri, USA

> *Let the floods clap their hands; let the hills sing together for joy at the presence of the Lord, for he is coming to judge the earth.*
>
> —Psalm 98:8–9

Bill Higdon, then an apostle, and I were on our first trip to Nigeria. We were hosted by Gobert Edet, a minister employed by the church, at his home in Ikot Oku Mfang.

The first morning was Sunday. We noted the Edet family was having trouble getting the children ready for church. We thought it might be helpful to ask Brother Edet if we could go ahead.

Surprisingly Brother Edet said, "No, you cannot go to church." I was surprised a minister told us he didn't want us to go to church!

But in about 15 minutes we understood why. It had nothing to do with not having his children ready. It had to do with the arrangement he had made for the Ikot Oku Mfang choir to come to his home and escort us to the church.

As they came into view near Edet's home, they treated us with their rhythmic, chanting music. We heard their beautiful singing, which was in English. The song they were singing was, "We're Marching to Zion." They sang this as they escorted us to the recently completed church building.

As a faith movement we are enriched when we choose to help build signal communities in all parts of the world. Very clearly we sense the challenge to bring forth the kingdom of God as part of the Christian journey we share together.

Prayer for Peace:

Eternal Presence, we come into your presence with singing and praise, with joy and thanksgiving. We would join with signal communities all over the world in our efforts to share the peace of Christ. Let it be.

Spiritual Practice for the Week: Connecting with God as Center

Each day this week connect with God through journal writing. Use a notebook, journal, computer, or any available paper. Prayerfully center on your intent to open yourself to God's presence and share what flows from your heart and mind. Your "letter to God" might include thoughts, questions, feelings, needs, artwork, quotes, and scriptures, or it might take the form of a prayer, psalm, or poem.

Try to write at least five minutes each day. What do you experience? Is this an effective way to connect with God? What surprises you? What new images or questions from God emerge? What deepens or changes in your relationship with God, Christ, Spirit?

Peace Covenant:

God, I will join my peacemaking efforts with others and multiply our impact.

5
Thursday
January

God's Lighthouse

By Bob Fisher of Independence, Missouri, USA

> *...who made heaven and earth, the sea, and all that is in them; who keeps faith. (Happy are those)...who give food to the hungry...who lift up those who are bowed down...who watch over the strangers; God upholds the orphan and the widow....*
>
> —Psalm 146:6–9, adapted

God's love is like the beam of a lighthouse, unseen by those inside the ship. The Divine visits the lonely through the neighbor who inquires, lingers with the despised when all others leave. God sits by the bedside through the friend who, wanting to be like Jesus, holds the dying person's hand and then stands by the open grave, head bowed, with the mourners.

Whenever human kindness is expressed, God's light makes another pass over the water, reassuring those searching for safe harbor that their vessel is on course. It is on the course to peace, where we find a glacier-fed lake that begins to steam once the sun sets. Spruces no longer cast shadows across its surface, but gray-rock mountains still glow pink in the distance as a late-feeding swallow slaps the water with his chest, causing circles to expand on the surface.

With every visit to the lonely, dying, mourning; with every peace-seeking action, the circles reach the shore and erode the hardness of hearts. And peace can be seen in the beam cast from the lighthouse of God's love.

Prayer for Peace:

Loving God, as your light passes over our lives, let us catch glimpses of ways we can serve you. Let us recognize where the lonely and mourning are in need of love; where we can share the peace of Jesus Christ.

Spiritual Practice for the Week: Connecting with God as Center

Each day this week connect with God through journal writing. Use a notebook, journal, computer, or any available paper. Prayerfully center on your intent to open yourself to God's presence and share what flows from your heart and mind. Your "letter to God" might include thoughts, questions, feelings, needs, artwork, quotes, and scriptures, or it might take the form of a prayer, psalm, or poem.

Try to write at least five minutes each day. What do you experience? Is this an effective way to connect with God? What surprises you? What new images or questions from God emerge? What deepens or changes in your relationship with God, Christ, Spirit?

Peace Covenant:

Today, God, I will let my heart be penetrated by your love and your need for disciples.

6
Friday
January

Wake-up Call (Epiphany)

By Barbara Howard of Independence, Missouri, USA

God, the Eternal Creator, weeps for the poor, displaced, mistreated, and diseased of the world because of their unnecessary suffering. Such conditions are not God's will...Do not turn away from them. For in their welfare resides your welfare.

—Doctrine and Covenants 163:4a

Poet John Donne wrote, "No man is an island entire of itself...Each man's death diminishes me, because I am involved in mankind; therefore send not to know for whom the bell tolls; it tolls for thee."

Donne expressed a basic principle of life. We are part of each other. We are part of everything in our universe.

Therefore, the agony and pain in Haiti diminish me. The suffering in the Middle East diminishes me. My response to that truth is to accept that I am incapable of loving everyone and everything. But if I can love myself wisely, then I am capable of seeing that connection—my interdependence—to be as real as my own breath.

This relationship to others brings new meaning to the scripture "...for in their welfare resides your welfare." This is a foundational ethic of most major religions in the world. It is one way of saying, "Do unto others as you would have them do unto you." Buddhists, Muslims, Sikhs, Christians, ancient Celts, and other religious traditions have sayings that paraphrase this concept.

Today I spoke on the phone with my agnostic son, who said (wisely, I think), "That statement, 'in their welfare resides your welfare,' is a good reminder that we are part of others. I think we need such wake-up calls."

As I hung up the phone, I knew I needed this wake-up call. I needed to be reminded that I am connected to those I do not know. I needed to know their welfare is my own. I cannot rewrite the admonition. I have yet to truly live by it, but I believe if I can, it holds enormous promise for me and the world in which I have influence.

Prayer for Peace:

God of networks and of our blended recipe of humankind, it is good to wake up and realize we have such a great and closely connected family.

Spiritual Practice for the Week: Connecting with God as Center

Each day this week connect with God through journal writing. Prayerfully center on your intent to open yourself to God's presence and share what flows from your heart and mind. Your letter to God might take the form of a prayer, psalm, or poem. What do you experience? Is this an effective way to connect with God? What deepens or changes in your relationship with God, Christ, Spirit?

Peace Covenant:

Today, God, as I look at others, I will imagine all the ways we could be part of one another's lives. I will work to ensure our welfare.

7
Saturday
January

Seek God's Peace in the Community

By Brenda Cummins of North Fort Myers, Florida, USA

...but with righteousness God shall judge the poor, and decide with equity for the meek of the earth.

—Isaiah 11:4, adapted

We don't always know what the answer will be when we seek Christ's peace, or in what form peace will come. That was the case recently with a young mother of two. Out of work and within two weeks of eviction from her apartment, she didn't know where to turn. In despair, she asked her grandmother for help. That's where reconnection began.

The grandmother remembered being baptized as a young child by a Community of Christ minister. As years passed, she stopped attending church while she struggled with her life. But knowing her granddaughter needed more than monetary peace, the grandmother contacted Community of Christ. The mission center arranged to help the young woman pay her rent.

She found a job near her apartment. Now she rides her bicycle to work, thanking God all the way! The Fort Myers Congregation planned a blessing service for her two young children. Your generous contributions provide hope to those who seek Christ's peace. Thank you to those who respond so faithfully.

Prayer for Peace:

Faithful God, we find your peace in the blessings of community. We find hope when disciples respond. May we be ever mindful of those who need to know you through our actions of sharing the peace of Jesus Christ.

Spiritual Practice:

Begin with quiet prayer. Ask God to help you discern some "sore places" in the body of Christ and in God's creation. Become aware of people who feel separated, wounded, or left out. Reflect on or write a short journal entry of healing words to at least one person who comes to mind. Ask God for words that will touch this person's broken spirit like healing ointment. Keep this person in your heart and prayers today and act on any ideas that come to bring blessing and wholeness.

Peace Covenant:

Today, God, I will reach out to someone who needs to reconnect to you. I pray that I will be worthy to be part of that connection.

8
Sunday
January

By Water and Spirit

By Karin Peter of Adrian, Missouri, USA

In those days Jesus came from Nazareth of Galilee and was baptized by John in the Jordan. And just as he was coming up out of the water, he saw the heavens torn apart and the Spirit descending like a dove on him. And a voice came from heaven, "You are my Son, the Beloved; with you I am well pleased."

—Mark 1:9–11

My childhood memory of the first time I heard a large congregation sing the hymn, "The Spirit of God Like a Fire Is Burning," remains clear. I was at a regional conference with hundreds of people. From the loft the organist began to play the familiar tune. A flute could be heard playing the descant, the notes hovering above the chords.

There was a sense of expectation as the trumpet and French horn joined in the refrain. Then, just as the congregation took a breath, the timpani rolled, and cymbals crashed like waves of water as the congregation sang, "Hosanna, hosanna to God and the Lamb!"

I imagine this as the sound of creation. The Spirit washes over the Earth, rising and falling like the notes of the descant. Below, the waters roll and crash with the wonder of God's creation.

As we enter a new calendar year our thoughts turn to becoming new. Many of us seek to put old habits behind and resolve to begin anew.

What a wonderful time to celebrate the first Sunday after Epiphany, the revelation of Jesus Christ in the world. In Christ we celebrate the living water and sense the presence of God's Spirit. We, too, are new creations. Hosanna, hosanna! Amen and amen.

Prayer for Peace:

Eternal God, we see before us a new year and new challenges. May we see them as opportunities. May we feel your blessing on us and work for peace that you may be well pleased in us.

Spiritual Practice for the Week: Growing a Gracious, Generous Heart

Each day this week open your heart to God's grace and generosity with a "breath prayer." Let your breath slow and deepen. Be aware of God's breath moving in and out of your heart. Spend several minutes focusing on breathing in God's generosity.

With each breath, silently name one gift for which you are thankful. "God, I breathe in the gift of ____ with thanks." Let your heart expand to contain God's gracious outpouring. With each breath out, name one gift you want to share from the overflow of your heart.

Eternal joy and peace await those who grow in the grace of generosity that flows from compassionate hearts.

—Doctrine and Covenants 163:9

Peace Covenant:

Today, God, I will welcome new challenges for peace work.

9
Monday
January

Still, Small Voice

By Judy Luffman of Lee's Summit, Missouri, USA

He said (to Elijah), "Go out and stand on the mountain before the Lord, for the Lord is about to pass by." Now there was a great wind, so strong that it was splitting mountains and breaking rocks in pieces before the Lord, but the Lord was not in the wind; and after the wind an earthquake, but the Lord was not in the earthquake; and after the earthquake a fire, but the Lord was not in the fire; and after the fire the sound of a still, small voice.

—1 Kings 19:11–12, adapted

I consider myself more of a listener than a conversationalist. If you know me this might strike you as an oxymoron because I have impaired hearing. To use current terminology, I wear *assistive hearing devices*. So jumping into conversations doesn't come naturally or easily for me.

Imagine my surprise to discover that I'm actually a pretty good listener. Maybe I have learned to compensate by using visual cues, because when I listen to someone else I often can tell more about what they are communicating through nonverbal signs than through the words they speak.

You might think being a good listener would make it easy to be sensitive to the Spirit's *still, small voice*. Sadly, that's not always true. It is far too easy for me to get caught up in the busyness of doing church rather than engaging in the discipline of spending quiet time listening for the Holy Spirit's guidance before charging ahead.

Have you been practicing your spiritual listening? Let's work at it together.

Prayer for Peace:

Whispering God, tune our ears to your promptings. Let us discern your longings for us by your sighs. Let us clear away the din so we can hear, as well as see, the horizon of your peace.

Spiritual Practice for the Week: Growing a Gracious, Generous Heart

Each day this week open your heart to God's grace and generosity with a "breath prayer." Let your breath slow and deepen. Be aware of God's breath moving in and out of your heart. Spend several minutes focusing on breathing in God's generosity. With each breath, silently name one gift for which you are thankful. "God, I breathe in the gift of ____ with thanks."

Let your heart expand to contain God's gracious outpouring. With each breath out, name one gift you want to share from the overflow of your heart.

Eternal joy and peace await those who grow in the grace of generosity that flows from compassionate hearts.

—Doctrine and Covenants 163:9

Peace Covenant:

Today, God, I will keep my ears open to receive your guidance.

10
Tuesday
January

I Have Called You by Name

By Peggy Michael of Cantonment, Florida, USA

But now thus says the Lord, he who created you, O Jacob, he who formed you, O Israel: Do not fear, for I have redeemed you; I have called you by name, you are mine. When you pass through the waters, I will be with you; and through the rivers, they shall not overwhelm you; when you walk through fire you shall not be burned, and the flame shall not consume you.

—Isaiah 43:1–2

Birth and death are bookends holding the volumes of life. Some pages are written in such fiery language, its message will burn within minds for generations. On other pages the fading ink will soon become dust particles. They will be forever silent.

Some messages tell of beauty, others of heartbreak. The stories of our days will vary. Look again at the scripture. It says God will be with us when we pass through the waters, not that we will never be in deep water. God does not say we won't go through rivers of difficulty, but that we will not be overwhelmed by them. We will not be consumed when we walk through oppressive fires.

Sometimes we will sing praises or travel on roads known only to us. Then we must speak, for no other can tell our thoughts and feelings. We alone know our stories and can tell them.

So between the bookends, we must reveal what happened that formed us into the unique creation of God that bears our name.

Prayer for Peace:

Creator of the volumes of life, the diversity of life, we know we are yours. We open ourselves to the grace of your presence during the floods and flames of life. May we gather these and tell the stories of your love and peace.

Spiritual Practice for the Week: Growing a Gracious, Generous Heart

Each day this week open your heart to God's grace and generosity with a "breath prayer." Let your breath slow and deepen. Be aware of God's breath moving in and out of your heart. Spend several minutes focusing on breathing in God's generosity.

With each breath, silently name one gift for which you are thankful. "God, I breathe in the gift of ____ with thanks." Let your heart expand to contain God's gracious outpouring. With each breath out, name one gift you want to share from the overflow of your heart.

Eternal joy and peace await those who grow in the grace of generosity that flows from compassionate hearts.

—Doctrine and Covenants 163:9

Peace Covenant:

As you have called me by name, God, I will write your name on every page of my life.

11
Wednesday
January

The Whole Story

By Ramona Seeley of Leeton, Missouri, USA

> *As God's chosen ones, holy and beloved, clothe yourselves with compassion, kindness, humility, meekness, and patience. Bear with one another and, if anyone has a complaint against another, forgive each other; just as the Lord has forgiven you, so you also must forgive. Above all, clothe yourselves with love, which binds everything together in perfect harmony.*
>
> —Colossians 3:12–14

When riding the bus in Jamaica, it was customary for those who had a seat to hold the packages of those who were standing. But on one journey, the woman beside me adamantly refused to hold packages for anyone.

I had my lap full, and the people standing began to murmur and call her names. I also wondered why she was acting as she did.

Finally she turned to me and with tears explained that she used to hold packages. One time a young man asked her to hold his packages, and she gladly agreed. The police stopped the bus and came aboard, searching for drugs. They found drugs in a package she was holding, and they arrested her. The young man disclaimed any knowledge of the bags she possessed.

We never know the true story of another's actions. May we always take time to listen to others. We are not called to judge, only to love.

Prayer for Peace:

Merciful God, forgive us when we have disrobed ourselves of compassion and humility, of meekness and patience. For without these we cannot see into the hearts of people; we cannot hear their unspoken story. Let us listen to one another and share the peace of Jesus Christ.

Spiritual Practice for the Week: Growing a Gracious, Generous Heart

Each day this week open your heart to God's grace and generosity with a "breath prayer." Let your breath slow and deepen. Be aware of God's breath moving in and out of your heart. Spend several minutes focusing on breathing in God's generosity.

With each breath, silently name one gift for which you are thankful. "God, I breathe in the gift of ______ with thanks." Let your heart expand to contain God's gracious outpouring. With each breath out, name one gift you want to share from the overflow of your heart.

> *Eternal joy and peace await those who grow in the grace of generosity that flows from compassionate hearts.*
>
> —Doctrine and Covenants 163:9

Peace Covenant:

God, I will emulate your compassion and not be tempted to judge others.

12
Thursday
January

A Prickly Cucumber

By Cindy Kor[illegible] of North Platte, Nebraska, USA

> *For he is our peace; in his flesh he has made both groups into one and has broken down the dividing wall, that is, the hostility between us.*
>
> —Ephesians 2:14

When my son was helping me pick cucumbers in the garden I told him to be careful because some had prickly spines.

"Do you know why they have sharp spines?" I asked him.

Being a science person, he replied, "It's a defense mechanism to keep bugs away."

After a moment of silence, he added, "Just like some people. They're grumpy to keep others away."

I've thought about his comment and how unknowingly we often put up barriers to keep others away; how we can come across as "prickly."

It made me think of a person who I disliked and avoided because of her "prickly" nature. But once I looked beyond her sharp facade, she was kind and sweet. It is difficult to look beyond those prickly spines and to love, yet through Christ it becomes possible.

Prayer for Peace:

God of vulnerable people, may we be open to your wisdom to look beyond defenses. Help us see the hearts and souls of those to whom we might minister. Help us share the peace of Jesus Christ with them.

Spiritual Practice for the Week: Growing a Gracious, Generous Heart

Each day this week open your heart to God's grace and generosity with a "breath prayer." Let your breath slow and deepen. Be aware of God's breath moving in and out of your heart. Spend several minutes focusing on breathing in God's generosity. With each breath, silently name one gift for which you are thankful. "God, I breathe in the gift of ______ with thanks. Let your heart expand to contain God's gracious outpouring.

With each breath out, name one gift you want to share from the overflow of your heart.

Peace Covenant:

God, today I will look deeper for opportunities to share your peace with others.

13
Friday
January

Healing of the Spirit

By Lynda Lyons of Kansas City, Kansas, USA

The Temple shall be dedicated to the pursuit of peace. It shall be for reconciliation and for healing of the spirit.

—Doctrine and Covenants 156:5a

I spent the entire week with my mentor, Ethel, at the 2010 World Conference.

I was able to serve Communion to disciples from all over the world. I watched caucus meetings and saw how the legislative assembly works. I heard hymns sung with gusto and inspiration in the Auditorium and Temple. I shared meals and worshiped with other disciples. I heard speakers I had only read about. I saw faces that smiled with God's Spirit. I saw drama played out with children and young adults.

When we were going from one event to another, Ethel asked if I would like to sit in the Temple for a few minutes. We walked slowly up the Worshiper's Path, entered the Sanctuary, and were all alone. The peace candle shone with a serene setting of greenery around it. The sun's rays came in from the spiraling windows above. It was quiet and peaceful.

I gazed at the candle and reflected on the events of the week.

God's Spirit filled me. I began looking at everything in a different light. Everything reminded me of how blessed I am.

I was at peace. And I was filled with the expectation of an even deeper peace that I knew would come. I felt the presence of Christ as the embodiment of God's shalom.

Prayer for Peace:

We feel your presence, God, when we stop long enough to breathe deeply; when we rest in your Spirit; when we reflect on your word; when we gaze on your dedicated architecture. In our sanctuaries, in our communities, and in our homes, let us move toward you, and then into your world to share the peace of Christ.

Spiritual Practice for the Week: Growing a Gracious, Generous Heart

Each day this week open your heart to God's grace and generosity with a "breath prayer." Let your breath slow and deepen. Be aware of God's breath moving in and out of your heart. Spend several minutes focusing on breathing in God's generosity.

With each breath, silently name one gift for which you are thankful. "God, I breathe in the gift of ______ with thanks." Let your heart expand to contain God's gracious outpouring. With each breath out, name one gift you want to share from the overflow of your heart.

Eternal joy and peace await those who grow in the grace of generosity that flows from compassionate hearts.

—Doctrine and Covenants 163:9

Peace Covenant:

Today I will be open and mindful of your presence wherever I am, God.

14
Saturday
January

"World" Peace Candle

By Sharon Norris of Independence, Missouri, USA

"You are the light of the world. A city built on a hill cannot be hid. No one after lighting a lamp puts it under the bushel basket, but on the lampstand, and it gives light to all in the house. In the same way, let your light shine before others, so that they may see your good works and give glory to your Father in heaven."

—Matthew 5:14–16

On January 14, 2010, my husband, Larry, and I shared our "world" peace candle during the prayer for peace at the Temple. We chose this day in honor of the birth date of our son, Ryan John, who died in 1993.

Larry's sister, Linda, gave us the candle in 2009. It actually was lit from the first Eternal World Peace Flame, which collectively was lit from seven flames flown in from five continents to Snowdonia, Wales, in 2000.

The idea was inspired and put into action by several colleagues who studied peace together at Cambridge University in the 1970s. After graduating, they formed an organization teaching peace of mind, body, and spirit.

There now are two more Eternal World Peace Flames. One is at the National Civil Rights Museum in Memphis, Tennessee, and the other is at the Peace Palace in The Hague, the Netherlands. More than 10 million candles have been lit from these World Peace Flames.

Larry and I continually enjoy sharing our candle. We have given candles lit from our flame to family members, neighbors, our congregation, and our delegation at SPECTACULAR, the annual youth gathering at Graceland University in Lamoni, Iowa.

Our candles have been carried and shared with friends in India, Canada, England, Australia, China, and all over the USA. What a joy it is for us to share the much-needed message of world peace in such a beautiful and simple way.

Prayer for Peace:

Creator of light, may we bring our lives close to you and receive the flame of your Spirit. May we use that flame to light the path to peace. May we light the lives of others with your flame. May this sharing of Christ's peace continue eternally. Amen.

Spiritual Practice:

Sit quietly and let your breathing become calm and deep. Ask God's Spirit to rest on you. See or sense the Spirit anointing you in the form of light, a dove, wind, color, or other images that might come. Ask to be made aware of God's love. Listen to the ways in which God wants to flow from your heart as living water. Give thanks that your name is "beloved,' that our name is Community of Christ.

Peace Covenant:

I will hold my candle to your flame and pass it to another.

15
Sunday
January

Lord, Speak to Me

By Rick Maupin, Council of Twelve Apostles

Now the Lord came and stood there, calling as before, "Samuel! Samuel!" And Samuel said, "Speak, for your servant is listening."'

—1 Samuel 3:10

I continue to discover that hearing and responding to the Lord often involve letting go.

During the late 1970s I was struggling to decide in which church I should live out my religious life.

I no longer was attending the church in which I grew up. I had been attending what is now known as Community of Christ, where I had developed significant relationships. However, I still clung tightly to old ideas and understandings that made it difficult to embrace this community fully.

Encouraged by my wife, I attended the closing worship at the 1980 World Conference. I could not deny feeling the impress of God's Spirit, but I still clung to old understandings. Near the end of the service, as we were singing the hymn, "The Spirit of God Like a Fire Is Burning," I suddenly heard a voice speaking. It was not an audible voice around me, but it was much more than my voice in my mind.

I had never met God in this way, but I knew it was God speaking. I would have been skeptical had anyone else described such an experience, but I could not deny this personal encounter.

The words I heard clearly directed me to join this faith community. However, in those moments I experienced much tension in my mind and heart. There I stood, clinging tightly to long-held understandings that I felt were correct, but I also could not deny the voice of the Divine. I chose to listen and let go.

Expecting God to speak to us personally and to the church, we must remember that which is spoken may challenge us to let go.

Prayer for Peace:

God of enduring love, we cling to your divine grace. We can let go of anything else without fear. With your love and grace we can share the peace of Christ.

Spiritual Practice for the Week: Caring for God's Sacred Creation

Each day this week choose a way to notice, give thanks, and care for God's sacred creation. Prayerfully consider one of the following suggested practices or create your own.

Walk in nature with a spirit of gratitude and "holy attention." Write a psalm of praise for the beauty of the Earth or a prayer of healing and blessing for the wounds of the Earth. Learn about and engage in an act of Earth-keeping, such as recycling, simple living, fasting from over-consumption of resources. Notice the unique diversity of the planet's creatures and be gentle to plants, animals, trees, and people! Give thanks.

Peace Covenant:

Today, God, I will listen as a servant and respond with faith.

16
Monday
January

It Is Good to Give Thanks

By Pen Curry of Apple Valley, Minnesota, USA

It is good to give thanks to the Lord, to sing praises to your name, O Most High; to declare your steadfast love in the morning, and your faithfulness by night...

—Psalm 92:1–2

It was my first time visiting this congregation several hours from my home. The family with whom I had spent the night invited me to go to church early to help prepare lunch. I was glad to be useful and busy because I didn't know many people there.

A young woman in the congregation came into the kitchen and asked if I helped prepare the food. Hoping there wasn't a problem, I said, "Yes." She hugged me and explained, "I always like to thank the people who make our food and help." Then she spoke to others in the kitchen, one by one.

On the ride home, I reflected on how easily we take for granted the behind-the-scenes people who smooth out the wrinkles in our lives or lend a helping hand. Do I express gratefulness to the person who removed snow from the church sidewalk, played the piano after a rough work week, or maintained the church's rain garden?

There had been several deaths of family and friends in just a few years, some with special challenges. I composed more "thank you" notes in my head than I had energy to send or say to helpful people.

A wise evangelist once advised me to live each day "as if it's a prayer," but I couldn't even find time to pray in thanks for the many blessings.

The young woman who approached me in the kitchen made thanking people a habit whenever she was at a church meal. My encounter with her made a difference. I went away feeling more connected to that congregation and was inspired to be mindful always to express gratitude. What ripple effects could my new actions have?

Prayer for Peace:

Divine peace, how can we not thank you, God who has given us so much? How can we not praise you? We appreciate your blessing of those who reveal your love by their actions. We are mindful of all your expressions of peace.

Spiritual Practice for the Week: Caring for God's Sacred Creation

Choose a way to notice, give thanks, and care for God's sacred creation. Prayerfully consider one of the following practices or create your own. Walk in nature with a spirit of gratitude and "holy attention." Write a psalm of praise for the beauty of the Earth or a prayer of healing and blessing for the wounds of the Earth. Learn about and engage in an act of Earth-keeping such as recycling, simple living, fasting from over-consumption of resources. Give thanks.

Peace Covenant:

Today, Lord, I will respond to acts of kindness without hesitation.

17
Tuesday
January

Soteni Connection

By Nadine Stallbaumer of Independence, Missouri, USA

> *But the wisdom from above is first pure, then peaceable, gentle, willing to yield, full of mercy and good fruits, without a trace of partiality or hypocrisy.*
>
> —James 3:17

In 2005, my husband and I hosted two World Service Corps volunteers. One was Calvin, a young man who had a wife and two children at home in Kenya. While he was here, he shared his dreams of education. He hoped to go to university because that meant getting a job.

He completed his volunteer work here and went home. From time to time he sent updates on his family. They were subsistence farmers with little hope of bettering their lives.

He was concerned they would not be able to send their children to school. He now has three children.

Our home congregation began to pray for Calvin to find work, and every time I heard from him, he would remind us how much he needed work.

I was at the Temple reception desk one day, and I heard someone say her daughter lived in Cincinnati, Ohio, and she was doing wonderful work in Kenya with AIDS survivors. It was an agency called Soteni, and she was looking to hire someone to be the manager in the village where Calvin lived.

The mother put us in touch with her daughter. When we talked, I learned she was going to Kenya to interview Calvin. What a miracle! He has his job and has been successful. Praise God!

Prayer for Peace:

Merciful God, we praise you for your grace on us, your imperfect worshipers. Help us to learn impartiality and to rid ourselves of hypocrisy. Then we truly can bring the peace of Christ into reality.

Spiritual Practice for the Week: Caring for God's Sacred Creation

Each day this week choose a way to notice, give thanks, and care for God's sacred creation. Prayerfully consider one of the following suggested practices or create your own.

Walk in nature with a spirit of gratitude and "holy attention." Write a psalm of praise for the beauty of the Earth or a prayer of healing and blessing for the wounds of the Earth. Learn about and engage in an act of Earth-keeping such as recycling, simple living, fasting from over-consumption of resources.

Notice the unique diversity of the planet's creatures and be gentle to plants, animals, trees, and people! Fall in love with the vast, intricate wonder of God's creation and give thanks.

Peace Covenant:

Today, merciful God, I will work toward impartiality and truth.

18
Wednesday
January

A Crumpled Blessing

By Erica Blevins Nye of Troy, Michigan, USA

Let us then pursue what makes for peace and for mutual upbuilding.
—Romans 14:19

"No...no," a woman said timidly at the table next to mine in my regular coffee shop. I looked up from my laptop and saw a middle-aged man slowly turn from her.I knew he would approach me next. I tried to blend myself into the wall behind me.

Please don't ask me for money, too. I avoided eye contact as he wound between the tables toward mine. "Excuse me, ma'am." *Oh, he saw me.* I turned and hesitantly looked up. He had thick glasses, and the right lens was cracked from top to bottom. Surely he couldn't see me comfortably with a split in his vision. And I wasn't sure how to look him in the eye, either.

"I'm sorry. I've got to catch the bus," he said. "I'm a little short. Do you have a dollar to help me out?"

Assessment: He seems sincere. The bus stop really is outside the coffee shop. A dollar is doable.

"Sure. I have a dollar." I fished in my purse and actually felt good about sharing. I'm glad I am in a position where I can help when people ask. He saw my books on the table and asked about my church. "Where is it?"

As I handed him a crumpled dollar bill, I briefly introduced Community of Christ as an international church with several congregations around the Detroit area."There's one in Troy, Old Redford, Highland Park..."

"Really? That's where I live, Highland Park! Exactly where is it?"

"I don't know—never been there myself. But I would be happy to go with you sometime if you want."

I found myself hurrying to jot down contact information before the bus arrived. He seemed genuinely interested. Many people find that sharing our faith happens when we share in some other way first. What kind of good news would we be proclaiming if we were not people who are generous with our resources—even if it's just a crumpled one.

Prayer for Peace:

Creator God, we praise you for sending opportunities to include the marginal in our communities. We are blessed by their presence.

Spiritual Practice for the Week: Caring for God's Sacred Creation

Choose a way to notice, give thanks, and care for God's sacred creation. Prayerfully consider one of the following suggested practices or create your own. Walk in nature with a spirit of gratitude and "holy attention." Write a psalm of praise for the beauty of the Earth or a prayer of healing and blessing for the wounds of the Earth. Learn about and engage in an act of Earth-keeping such as recycling, simple living, fasting from over-consumption of resources. Fall in love with the vast, intricate wonder of God's creation and give thanks.

Peace Covenant:

Today God, I will not turn away from need when you present it to me.

19
Thursday
January

World Service Corps (Part I)

By Cory Upson of Independence, Missouri, USA

> *Keep on doing the things that you have learned and received and heard and seen in me, and the God of peace will be with you.*
>
> —Philippians 4:9

Our lives are made of stories, past and present events that form the ongoing, day-to-day grind of life. A story may be unique, but it is never a monologue. Key players always make the story a shared experience.

Story is the preferred method of relating experiences with one another. A key component to stories of life is an audience. You cannot tell a story if there are no ears to hear. Unfortunately, many stories begging to be told never make it past the lips of the teller. They are destined to fade away, never to be heard or given a chance to affect someone else.

You ask yourself, "Did I do everything I could to make my story heard? Did I share my witness? Did I share the peace of Christ?"

When a story *is* heard, perhaps by a close friend alone, it affects the hearer, who may respond with a new chapter of understanding and comfort. And this may be enough.

But what about the stories that are too big for just the audience of a best friend?

What if a story needs to be heard by a larger audience so action on a bigger scale can take place, creating a new story of justice and reconciliation?

We need storytellers, individuals, and organizations such as World Service Corps, to proclaim the issues of peace and justice. We need to give people a chance to be heard.

This is where the blessings of community are spoken and heard.

Prayer for Peace:

God of peace, we listen, we hear, we learn of you. Show us what you would have us do. Tell us the stories you would have us share.

Spiritual Practice for the Week: Caring for God's Sacred Creation

Each day this week choose a way to notice, give thanks, and care for God's sacred creation. Prayerfully consider one of the following suggested practices or create your own.

Walk in nature with a spirit of gratitude and "holy attention." Write a psalm of praise for the beauty of the Earth or a prayer of healing and blessing for the wounds of the Earth. Learn about and engage in an act of Earth-keeping such as recycling, simple living, fasting from over-consumption of resources. Notice the unique diversity of the planet's creatures and be gentle to plants, animals, trees, and people!

Fall in love with the vast, intricate wonder of God's creation and give thanks.

Peace Covenant:

Today I will share my story, God.

20
Friday
January

World Service Corps (Part II)

By Cory Upson of Independence, Missouri, USA

> *He shall judge between the nations, and shall arbitrate for many peoples; they shall beat their swords into plowshares, and their spears into pruning hooks; nation shall not lift up sword against nation, neither shall they learn war any more.*
>
> —Isaiah 2:4

Outreach Philippines, Incorporated (OPI) gives communities in that nation a chance to be heard.

OPI offers help by training them to organize themselves and to identify needs within their communities. OPI then teaches the villagers how to gain an audience.

It teaches communities to write proposals that tell the story of their basic needs. The newly organized community then sends these proposals to non-governmental organizations (NGO's) and local authorities. They hear the stories and usually respond with new chapters of understanding and, most importantly, with new chapters of action.

Paige Webberley, my World Service Corps partner, and I have been listening to these new chapters in their stories of hope. We have listened to how, through all the difficulties and hardships, they now are finding success because someone took the time to listen and be affected.

I wouldn't trade my summer with World Service Corps for anything. I could see firsthand the results of grace and generosity. I felt blessed by the people and saw action for peace and justice taking place.

Prayer for Peace:

God of hope, we are joyful when we see peace among the nations. We are glad to see acts of justice. We are enlightened when we hear the story of a once-voiceless people.

Spiritual Practice for the Week: Caring for God's Sacred Creation

Each day this week choose a way to notice, give thanks, and care for God's sacred creation. Prayerfully consider one of the following suggested practices or create your own.

Walk in nature with a spirit of gratitude and "holy attention." Write a psalm of praise for the beauty of the Earth or a prayer of healing and blessing for the wounds of the Earth. Learn about and engage in an act of Earth-keeping such as recycling, simple living, fasting from over-consumption of resources. Notice the unique diversity of the planet's creatures and be gentle to plants, animals, trees, and people! Fall in love with the vast, intricate wonder of God's creation and give thanks.

Peace Covenant:

Today, God, I will educate myself on ways to help promote justice.

21
Saturday
January

World Service Corps (Part III)

By Cory Upson of Independence, Missouri, USA

The Lord is a stronghold for the oppressed, a stronghold in times of trouble. And those who know your name put their trust in you, for you, O Lord, have not forsaken those who seek you. Sing praises to the Lord, who dwells in Zion. Declare his deeds among the peoples.
—Psalm 9:9–11

The stories of life are always being rewritten. Problems resolved in one chapter may show up again in another. While serving the World Service Corps in a small village called Sapang Bato in the Philippines, I listened to about 15 villagers talk about the *lean season.*

The people of the Philippines depend on rice for breakfast, lunch, and dinner. The lean season is the four months the villagers have to wait for their newly planted crops to grow so they will have income and food for the other eight months.

After paying high interest rates for years, Outreach Philippines, Incorporated formed its own rice-loan project to meet the problem of the lean season. It made the rice loan more affordable to families and put any profit back into the program.

For three seasons the project was sustainable. However, in 2010 the rice needed was more than the organization could afford. I listened to them try to find ways to cope. The best they can do is try to distribute the rice as evenly as possible while they write a new proposal for help.

I was a captive audience and could not help writing their story into my own. I hope you might help write a new chapter in their story—one of compassion and generosity. Hold them in your prayers so hunger might turn to hope.

Prayer for Peace:

God of the oppressed and Stronghold in times of trouble, we trust in you. We know your justice will prevail, and hunger will be relieved. Thank you for the young people who work with compassion and have an understanding of how to share Christ's peace.

Spiritual Practice:

Jesus discerned hungers of body and spirit, and he fed them through a physical, verbal, spiritual ministry of presence. In a time of listening prayer ask God to help you discern physical or spiritual hungers of people in your congregation, community, and global family. Invite the Spirit to move you to one hospitable act that "feeds" someone's hunger today.

Peace Covenant:

Today, God, I will declare your needs and give hope to someone in trouble.

22
Sunday
January

Respond to God's Call

By Dave Brown, Presiding Bishopric

As Jesus passed along the Sea of Galilee, he saw Simon and his brother Andrew casting a net into the sea—for they were fishermen. And Jesus said to them, "Follow me and I will make you fish for people." And immediately they left their nets and followed him.

—Mark 1:16–18

I was ordained a priest in the Aaronic priesthood as a young adult. Shortly after my ordination, the pastor asked me to go with him to visit a family in our congregation. I had not done this before, so I wasn't sure what to expect. Yet I readily agreed to go.

I trusted the pastor and was willing to help him in any way I could. I thought he probably wanted me to go with him so I could learn to provide family ministry. He was an experienced minister, and it seemed clear he wanted to share with me what he had learned over many years. It seemed obvious to me that I should eagerly accept his willingness to share his experience by receiving it generously.

As we had our visit, I came to understand that he also wanted me with him as a true companion minister, even though I had no experience.

He knew that together we would be able to provide deeper ministry to this family than he could alone. Although I'm not sure I understood it at the time, he was teaching me a lesson about building community.

I think one reason Jesus invited the disciples to follow him was to model how to build community. He needed companions on his journey. We need to learn that ministry by the community is stronger than ministry by any one of us alone.

Prayer for Peace:

God of the universe, God within our hearts, we will follow you. We will cast our nets beyond our voices so all may hear the invitation, so no one will be left uninvited. We will cast long and wide, so all will have opportunity. We will invite with a message of God's grace and gentle love. We will teach peace.

Spiritual Practice for the Week: Encountering Scripture as Continuing Revelation

Each day this week read and pray with the Doctrine and Covenants as continuing revelation of God's vision for the church and creation. Choose a section or focus on recent counsel in Sections 156–164.

Read a few paragraphs slowly three or four times. Pause to pray for deep understanding of meaning after the first reading. Pray for opening of your heart and emotions to the text after the second reading. After the third reading, prayerfully ask to hear the phrase or word that speaks to you or touches your life. Stay with this phrase. What sense of divine presence or invitation comes? What is revealed?

Peace Covenant:

Today, God, I will find a companion minister, so I might serve you better.

23
Monday
January

"Signs" of Faith

By Berneice Clark of Independence, Missouri, USA

> *You who are my disciples must be found continuing in the forefront of those organizations and movements which are recognizing the worth of persons and are committed to bringing the ministry of my Son to bear on their lives.*
>
> —Doctrine and Covenants 151:9

I praise God for the adventures that have blessed my life in my congregation. I have witnessed so many who have responded to the needs of others. More than ever, I have come to believe it's what we do rather than what we say, that becomes our real testimony.

I have found when I am working and serving, I am at my best, and my faith is strongest. Often I felt inadequate to take on new responsibilities. However, I was blessed as I responded. I look back with joy for the times I did respond. Even though I was stretched, I always felt blessed on my journey.

When Brother John Steele came to my congregation and was baptized, a wonderful new challenge was presented. He was hearing-impaired.

My children noticed the offering of a *signing* class and wanted to attend. Our family joined, and this opened new doors of service at church. Our daughter, Emma Sue, signed Handel's *Messiah* when she was 11 years old.

Many others in the community who respond with faith and service show the importance of the enduring principle of the Worth of All Persons.

Prayer for Peace:

Burden-lifting God, help us stretch to meet challenges we face. Bless us with the courage to serve when called. We praise you for the sense of joy when we respond to the needs of others, for this is a step toward peace.

Spiritual Practice for the Week: Encountering Scripture as Continuing Revelation

Each day this week read and pray with the Doctrine and Covenants as continuing revelation of God's vision for the church and creation. Choose a section or focus on recent counsel in Sections 156–164.

Read paragraphs slowly three or four times. Pause to pray for deep understanding. Pray for opening of your heart and emotions to the text after the second reading. After the third reading, prayerfully ask to hear the particular phrase or word that speaks to you or touches your life. Stay with this word or phrase. Listen as fully and openly as you can. What sense of divine presence or invitation comes? What is revealed?

Peace Covenant:

As I become more aware of the worth of all persons, I will respond to their needs.

24
Tuesday
January

Honestly Speaking

By Thomas Nunn of Independence, Missouri, USA

Rejoice always, pray without ceasing, give thanks in all circumstances; for this is the will of God in Christ Jesus for you.

—1 Thessalonians 5:16–18

For years I had not taken seriously the Daily Prayer for Peace.

I participated only a few times. It is not that I trivialized the importance of peace, only that my attitude toward the Daily Prayer for Peace had been that it was a nice church-thing that someone dreamed up with other Temple peace activities.

It meant nothing to me I took it lightly and trivialized it.

Recently, I taught a class on the gospel as interpreted through the Exodus.

As I prepared for the final class, the Holy Spirit began to instruct me, putting together ideas that I never had connected in quite that way. What I received, among other things, was this:

- The tabernacle, and later temple, were set in Israel so people could have a place to regularly and continually communicate with God.
- As Isaiah had prophesied, "This House is to be a House of Prayer for all nations."
- The Temple in Independence, Missouri, is a House of Prayer for the nations today, and the Daily Prayer for Peace is a core ministry central to the purpose of the Temple.

Occasionally the Holy Spirit ministers to me in such a way that I discover something of importance I once had trivialized.

Prayer for Peace:

Listening God, our prayers to you are so important to us. We feel close to you when we pray. We listen and hear how you want us to fill our role as peacemakers.

Spiritual Practice for the Week: Encountering Scripture as Continuing Revelation

Read and pray with the Doctrine and Covenants as continuing revelation of God's vision for the church and creation. Focus on recent counsel in Sections 156–164. Read slowly three or four times. Pray for deep understanding. Pray for opening of your heart and emotions to the text. Prayerfully ask to hear the phrase or word that speaks to you or touches your life. Listen as fully and openly as you can. What sense of divine presence or invitation comes? What is revealed?

Peace Covenant:

I will try to stop what I'm doing and join the Daily Prayer for Peace whenever and wherever I can.

25
Wednesday
January

Gifts for Peace

By Lillian Kirby of Blue Springs, Missouri, USA

> *Sue for peace…to all people; and lift up an ensign of peace, and make a proclamation for peace unto the ends of the earth.*
>
> —Doctrine and Covenants 102:11a–b

A sense of peace and serenity has been a goal for my paintings over the years. I have been challenged to convey to the viewer my personal view of the world through my paintings. My message is that I would like to see the world at peace.

Eventually, the medium of watercolor was my choice. Because of the luminescent quality of watercolor I can use my creativity to express sky, sea, and land. Lighthouses have a special appeal to me as a focal subject. The lighthouse is a metaphor used for guiding us homeward.

Recently I also have tried painting mills and springhouses. The mills symbolize for me the staff of life: grain. We could not live without water and grain.

I progress and learn the most as I attempt to teach others the techniques and joys of watercolor painting. My art library grows as I grow. I refer to those books often in my teaching. I would like to further my art studies to gain more control over my hand, to continue to develop my talent, and to teach others to observe a world full of serenity and beauty.

I would like to apply my God-given gifts to sharing the peace of Jesus Christ.

Prayer for Peace:

God, may we express our creativity in actions that share the peace of Jesus Christ.

Spiritual Practice for the Week: Encountering Scripture as Continuing Revelation

Each day this week read and pray with the Doctrine and Covenants as continuing revelation of God's vision for the church and creation. Choose a section or focus on recent counsel in Sections 156–164.

Read paragraphs slowly three or four times. Pause to pray for deep understanding. Pray for opening of your heart and emotions to the text after the second reading. After the third reading, prayerfully ask to hear the particular phrase or word that speaks to you or touches your life. Stay with this word or phrase. Listen as fully and openly as you can. What sense of divine presence or invitation comes? What is revealed?

Peace Covenant:

Today, God, I will practice to enhance my gifts so I may use them to share Christ's peace.

26
Thursday
January

A New Hospitality

By Susan Skoor, Council of Twelve Apostles

> *When your willingness to live in sacred community as Christ's new creation exceeds your natural fear of spiritual and relational transformation, you will become who you are called to be. The rise of Zion the beautiful, the peaceable reign of Christ, awaits your whole-hearted response to the call to make and steadfastly hold to God's covenant of peace in Jesus Christ.*
>
> —Doctrine and Covenants 164:9b

After World Conference 2010, the people of the island of Huahine in French Polynesia were troubled by the idea of accepting other Christian baptisms as valid. I was with French Polynesia church leaders to share information and answer questions.

For three hours the elderly, youth, and children engaged in understanding the new principles given in Doctrine and Covenants 164. We spoke of God's grace and invitation to all, a grace that we must model ourselves.

Among those present were three people who had been considering joining our church. After a late night and many questions, we retired, hoping we had helped the people to welcome those who received Christian baptism in other denominations.

A key leader on the island visited our breakfast the following morning with news of the results. "Some members came to my house at 5:00 this morning, wanting to talk." My heart sank. An emergency meeting at 5:00 a.m. at the pastor's home couldn't be good.

I was wrong.

"They told me they were so excited about what they heard last night, they couldn't sleep. They had to talk to me about the possibilities. One of the three women who is not a member was with them. She wants to join. She is so happy she can join a church that opens its doors to other Christians in this loving way."

We model God's grace when we open our hearts and our congregations to others who have found Jesus Christ and made heartfelt commitments through baptism. Sometimes people will respond by asking to join our church through confirmation. Sometimes, just knowing the welcome and invitation is there, they will choose to enter the waters of baptism again.

Either way, we rejoice and accept them fully as companions in Community of Christ.

Prayer for Peace:

God of the open doors, open arms, open hearts, may the waters of baptism, as well as the Spirit, part for those who commit to Christ. May the community welcome them.

Spiritual Practice for the Week: Encountering Scripture as Continuing Revelation

Read and pray with the Doctrine and Covenants as continuing revelation of God's vision for the church and creation. Focus on recent counsel in Sections 156–164. Read paragraphs slowly three or four times. Pause to pray for deep understanding. What phrase or word speaks to you or touches your life? Listen as fully and openly as you can. What sense of divine presence or invitation comes? What is revealed?

Peace Covenant:

I will model God's grace and welcome all companion travelers to the community.

27
Friday
January

Perspective

By Paul McCain of Oklahoma City, Oklahoma, USA

The Lord is exalted, he dwells on high; he filled Zion with justice and righteousness; he will be the stability of your times, abundance of salvation, wisdom, and knowledge...
—Isaiah 33:5–6

The view from the front window of an airplane in flight is often awe-inspiring and at times enlightening. This was especially true when flying over the Pacific Ocean and approaching Okinawa. The instruments, of course, locate the island long before you can see it, but when first spotted, it is just a speck far below.

The speck at first looks the size of an insect on the water, but later it becomes recognizable as an island. The airplane I flew is similar in size to some commercial jets today, so I often asked myself, "How are we going to land this big aircraft on that postage stamp?" Of course, intellectually, I knew the military runway was longer than at most commercial airports. But from that perspective, miles from the runway, it seemed an insurmountable feat.

Life is full of similar circumstances—from a distance sometimes the task seems impossible. Not having had the advantage of seeing the problem up close, I sometimes have backed off, lacking the faith to take the next step. The challenge is to figure out which attempts are foolhardy and which just require moving forward in faith.

May we be blessed with discernment to know which endeavors to avoid and which we should face head-on with faith.

Prayer for Peace:

God of wisdom and knowledge, help us to step forward in faith. Help us discern when our choices would be beneficial to the mission of Christ.

Spiritual Practice for the Week: Encountering Scripture as Continuing Revelation

Read and pray with the Doctrine and Covenants as continuing revelation of God's vision for the church and creation. Choose a section or focus on recent counsel in Sections 156–164. Pause to pray for deep understanding. Pray for opening of your heart and emotions to the text. Prayerfully ask to hear the particular phrase or word that speaks to you or touches your life. Stay with this word or phrase. Listen as fully and openly as you can. What sense of divine presence or invitation comes? What is revealed?

Peace Covenant:

Today, God, I will seek and welcome opportunities to exercise my faith.

28
Saturday
January

Discovering Community

By Paige Webberley of Camas, Washington, USA

Shun immature passions and pursue righteousness, faith, love, and peace, along with those who call on the Lord from a pure heart.

—2 Timothy 2:22, adapted

Copious raindrops splashed the sun-scorched ground, sending Filipinos running for cover. I, however, was in no hurry.

With Cory, my World Service Corps partner, I had been playing a game the youth of the village had taught us, and I was thoroughly hot and sweaty.

So I was content to stand in the open, arms outstretched, allowing the downpour to drench me.

Eventually though, I huddled in the shelter of a hut with many members of the village of Sapang Bato: mothers, fathers, kids, teenagers, babies, grandparents, and great-grandparents.

It didn't matter that my skin was a different color than theirs, or that my measly college bank account held more money than any of them would earn in a year.

In that moment, all differences that seemed so obvious melted away, and we were united in a single mission: staying dry.

Sapang Bato was the first of many villages that I visited, and the first in which I experienced the strong sense of community so common in the Philippines. Here I witnessed three, four, and five generations living together, eating together, and caring for one another.

In the fast-paced, consumer-driven society that I left at the beginning of summer, encountering true community is a rarity. But halfway across the world, I had the opportunity to discover such a gem amid unimaginable poverty.

Prayer for Peace:

God of the downpour, God of the mist, wash us clean. Lead us to the realization of the many ways we are blessed. Keep before our mind's eye the impoverished and suffering that need our attention. Prompt us to generosity. Prompt us to peace.

Spiritual Practice:

Sit in your quiet place and center your heart and mind on God's presence. Spend several minutes asking God to bring into your awareness the names and images of children in your life. You may see their faces or hear their voices as you receive these impressions. Listen deeply to the unique gifts and needs of the children who come to mind. Offer a prayer of blessing for each child and the needs you perceive. If you feel led, you also may want to write a note or card and give a message of affirmation and love to each child.

Peace Covenant:

Today I will put away immature and shallow pursuits to find how I can end suffering.

29
Sunday
January

Jesus Amazes and Astounds

By Bunda Chibwe, Council of Twelve Apostles

> *But Jesus rebuked him, saying, "Be silent, and come out of him!" And the unclean spirit... came out of him. They were all amazed, and they kept on asking one another, "What is this? A new teaching—with authority! He commands even the unclean spirits, and they obey him."*
>
> —Mark 1:25–27

I have continually struggled with the reaction of my relatives and friends since my two older children were diagnosed with bipolar disorder—a disease still unknown in my small African community.

The stigma associated with the illness presented added challenges for me to discuss freely and openly among friends about my children's therapy. The fact that two of my children suffer from the same disease raised serious concerns from my relatives.

As I have continued to ponder this, several unanswered questions keep recurring: "Why do people suffer? Why does God allow disease to exist? Why should my children suffer so others might learn lessons?"

Navigating through these questions has blessed me with a deep assurance that as a disciple of Jesus I do not have to understand everything about God or the world. I have discovered that perhaps God's power is not arbitrarily squandered to prevent earthquakes or overrule human freedom.

I have come to realize that perhaps God's power is the power to love and be loved, to call people in all circumstances to work for good. Perhaps, I have concluded, God needs us to help build God's kingdom.

My attitude has changed.

I am more positive about life. My two children continue healing through the support of modern medicine, our family, and the community around them. It is Christ's love and mission that has helped me to understand God is loving and caring.

When we know the way of Christ, we will always be amazed and astounded by his healing and compassionate ministry.

Prayer for Peace:

Amazing and astounding God, healing and compassionate God, help us have the faith to accept your participation in the world, to respond to your love with love.

Spiritual Practice for the Week: Honoring the Worth of All Persons

Each day this week read Psalm 139:13–18. After each reading sit quietly and let the deep meaning of the words sink into your mind, heart, and body. What thoughts and feelings do you have about being "fearfully and wonderfully made" (Psalm 139:14)?

Sense the intimate knowledge God has of you. Ask God for an awareness of the sacred worth of each person on the planet. Weep with God over the soul-wounding forces and events that rob people of dignity and worth. How are you invited to notice, protect, heal, and affirm the spiritual identity of all God's beloved people today?

Peace Covenant:

Today, God, I will set aside my stressful and hounding questions and let your peace flow through me.

30
Monday
January

Unexpected Visitors...a Bonus

By Pam Robison of Independence, Missouri, USA

For you shall go out in joy, and be led back in peace; the mountains and the hills before you shall burst into song, and all the trees of the field shall clap their hands.

—Isaiah 55:12

When I went into the Temple Sanctuary to open the organ for the Daily Prayer for Peace, a small group—a couple of young adults and about six children (ages 7–9)—was looking around.

They asked if I would play something, so I did a couple of verses of "Amazing Grace" and "God of Our Fathers." I invited them into the hall so I could visit more with them because folks were beginning to gather.

They were from a day care in Platte City, Missouri, and had been incorrectly directed by a GPS and ended up here! When they saw the spire they decided they had to find out what this building was, so they came in.

The organ intrigued the kids, so I invited them to the Auditorium, where we could talk more easily and I could show them another organ. So we headed through the tunnel—the kids were excited to know that they were walking underneath the street.

They sat up by the organ. We talked a bit about the church and the organ stops, and I played a couple of pieces for them.

A couple of the kids played piano, so I invited them to try the organ. They were excited but nervous. In the end, I think all the kids had a turn playing some of the keys—and then their leaders took them up by the 32-foot pipes so they could feel the wind when they're played.

One said: "This is the best field trip ever!" Another group from the day care will visit Thursday. We are so blessed to be able to share these instruments of praise.

Prayer for Peace:

It is for you, God, we play our instruments and sing our songs. You inspire our rhythm and poetry, our lyrics and laments. May our hearts and ears be tuned to the harmony of your peace.

Spiritual Practice for the Week: Honoring the Worth of All Persons

Each day this week read Psalm 139:13–18. After each reading sit quietly and let the deep meaning of the words sink into your mind, heart, and body. Imagine God watching you grow in your mother's womb. What thoughts and feelings do you have about being "fearfully and wonderfully made" (Psalm 139:14)?

Ask God for an awareness of the sacred worth of each person on the planet. Weep with God over the soul-wounding forces and events that rob people of dignity and worth. How are you being invited to notice, protect, heal, and affirm the spiritual identity of God's beloved people today? Pray for God's compassion.

Peace Covenant:

God, you will hear nothing but peace and joy come from my mouth.

31
Tuesday
January

Listen!

By Faye Williams of Kennett, Missouri, USA

> *Therefore my people shall know my name; therefore in that day they shall know that it is I who speak; here am I. How beautiful upon the mountains are the feet of the messenger who announces peace, who brings good news, who announces salvation, who says to Zion, "Your God reigns." Listen! Your sentinels lift up their voices, together they sing for joy; for in plain sight they see the return of the Lord to Zion.*
>
> —Isaiah 52:6–8

At our home away from home, we are blessed with a little brook behind the house. When we sit on the back deck, we can hear the bubbling, soothing sound the brook sends our way. We see and hear deer and other wildlife going to drink. They, too, enjoy God's gift.

When we move to the front of the house, we no longer hear the brook's restful sound, its message to us.

It is the same with the Holy Spirit.

When we move away or separate ourselves from God, we fail to listen for the divine voice. We put less-important concerns between us, and soon God's message is not clear. We forget how comforting it is to know God is near and still speaks to us today.

May we stay close so we may always hear the divine voice.

Prayer for Peace:

Keep us near, God, so that we hear your every whisper. Keep our minds open to discern your will. Keep our hearts humble so we may feel your love and accept your grace. Help us break down barriers between us that confuse and impede us. Keep us diligently on the path to peace.

Spiritual Practice for the Week: Honoring the Worth of All Persons

Each day this week read Psalm 139:13–18. After each reading sit quietly and let the deep meaning of the words sink into your mind, heart, and body. Imagine God watching you grow in your mother's womb. What thoughts and feelings do you have about being "fearfully and wonderfully made" (Psalm 139:14)?

Sense the intimate knowledge God has of you and every child ever born. Ask God for an awareness of the sacred worth of each person on the planet. Weep with God over the soul-wounding forces and events that rob people of dignity and worth. How are you being invited to notice, protect, heal, and affirm the spiritual identity of all God's beloved people today? Pray for God's compassion.

Peace Covenant:

Today, God, I will be a focused listener—setting aside trivialities and blocking out worldly noise.

1
Wednesday
February

Choose Gratitude

By Laurie Gordon of Livermore, California, USA

For the mountains may depart and the hills be removed, but my steadfast love shall not depart from you, and my covenant of peace shall not be removed, says the Lord, who has compassion on you.

—Isaiah 54:10

My osteoporotic mom took a windblown tumble a few months ago. Frozen, I watched my worst nightmare unfold in front of me—in slow motion.

My car was packed tight for a camping trip, so we had substituted an old, compact, lightweight walker for her usual bulky, heavy one. I'd planned to drop her off at home before leaving for a few days in Oregon. But no. Here came the wind, and then she was on the ground.

And all that happened to my mom's fragile bones was a tiny fracture in her toe!

Eight hours, four doctors, and two lab visits later, it was clear I would not be making the 10-hour drive any time soon. Mom felt badly because I had canceled my vacation. I felt guilty because I had sacrificed the stability of her usual walker for ease. But, she instinctively had slowed her fall and was not seriously injured. There was only one appropriate response: thankfulness, thankfulness, and more thankfulness.

So we made a pact. We decided to set aside our guilt and "what ifs" in favor of just being grateful. It worked! Genuinely felt, intentionally chosen gratitude dissolved guilt, anxiety, and disappointment.

Spiritual teachers urge gratefulness all the time. From now on I'm taking them seriously. Our lives are like gardens liberally seeded with grace, and they come into full blossom when we choose gratitude.

Prayer for Peace:

Generous God, we offer gratitude for the blessings in our lives—blessings known and unknown. May we always be aware that our response is the most-important part of the blessing. Our response is what causes us to reach out with our blessings and share the peace of Jesus Christ.

Spiritual Practice for the Week: Honoring the Worth of All Persons

Each day this week read Psalm 139:13–18. After each reading sit quietly and let the deep meaning of the words sink into your mind, heart, and body. Imagine God watching you grow in your mother's womb. What thoughts and feelings do you have about being "fearfully and wonderfully made" (Psalm 139:14)?

Sense the intimate knowledge God has of you and every child ever born. Ask God for an awareness of the sacred worth of each person on the planet. Weep with God over the soul-wounding forces and events that rob people of dignity and worth. How are you being invited to notice, protect, heal, and affirm the spiritual identity of all God's beloved people today? Pray for God's compassion.

Peace Covenant:

Today, God, I will start with gratitude for whatever comes my way.

2
Thursday
February

Pickup Sticks

By Carol Scheibner of Independence, Missouri, USA

Therefore, continue to be strong in faith. To you who hear my voice and know my promises I will reveal myself and give my peace, even in the midst of your uncertainties.
—Doctrine and Covenants 158:11a

Whenever a storm blows through my yard, twigs and branches cover my lawn. I have six enormous trees. Usually the day before my trash collector comes, I am outside picking up sticks. This is not fun like the "Pickup Sticks" game.

Many times as I pick up one stick, I see three or four more partly buried or hidden. This reminds me how many people bury themselves, or are buried by others, to the truth and love of Jesus. The wind of adversity shakes them from their foundations, and they become lost.

When one strong person, or a person who has compassion and has "been there," shares the peace of Jesus Christ with others, people come out of hiding. They then can tell others, bringing more "hidden" people into the light.

Let us seek the marginal people who feel excluded from the community, find them, and include them by sharing the peace of Jesus Christ.

Prayer for Peace:

God of the lost, may we not hide from your light. May we not pass by those who need to be picked up and held in your healing arms. May we share peace with one another, so they may in turn share it with others.

Spiritual Practice for the Week: Honoring the Worth of All Persons

Each day this week read Psalm 139:13–18. After each reading sit quietly and let the deep meaning of the words sink into your mind, heart, and body. Imagine God watching you grow in your mother's womb. What thoughts and feelings do you have about being "fearfully and wonderfully made" (Psalm 139:14)?

Sense the intimate knowledge God has of you and every child ever born. Ask God for an awareness of the sacred worth of each person on the planet. Weep with God over the soul-wounding forces and events that rob people of dignity and worth. How are you being invited to notice, protect, heal, and affirm the spiritual identity of all God's beloved people today? Pray for God's compassion.

Peace Covenant:

Today, God, I will watch for and uphold those who seem lost.

3
Friday
February

Keeps on Giving...

By Joann Condit of Phoenix, Arizona, USA

By contrast, the fruit of the Spirit is love, joy, peace, patience, kindness, generosity, faithfulness, gentleness, and self-control. There is no law against such things.

—Galatians 5:22–23

Ron and Kay were in a large retail store, buying a few last-minute items for a vacation drive across the country. They decided to save some time and have a quick hot dog for lunch. Ron went to make the purchase while Kay found a free table.

No one else was in line. As Ron walked to the window, he glanced down. Between his feet was a $20 bill. He picked it up and looked around. There was no way to tell who had dropped it. Over lunch, they decided to give the money to the first person who appeared to have a serious need for it.

Albuquerque, New Mexico, was their destination that first day. They found their hotel and then went to dinner. As they left the restaurant, a young woman with a baby came up to them, asking for help. Imagine her surprise and joy when they handed her not a single dollar, but 20 times that amount.

From that day forward on their trip, Ron and Kay determined to be alert to the needs of people God might put in their way. They found their eyes opened, and they touched several others with their gifts of $20 as they journeyed across the country. It proved to be a most-enriching travel experience. They were blessed to be a blessing.

Prayer for Peace:

Open our eyes, Lord, to those in need. Open our hearts to those searching for peace.

Spiritual Practice for the Week: Honoring the Worth of All Persons

Each day this week read Psalm 139:13–18. After each reading sit quietly and let the deep meaning of the words sink into your mind, heart, and body. Imagine God watching you grow in your mother's womb. What thoughts and feelings do you have about being "fearfully and wonderfully made" (Psalm 139:14)?

Sense the intimate knowledge God has of you and every child ever born. Ask God for an awareness of the sacred worth of each person on the planet. Weep with God over the soul-wounding forces and events that rob people of dignity and worth. How are you being invited to notice, protect, heal, and affirm the spiritual identity of all God's beloved people today? Pray for God's compassion.

Peace Covenant:

Today, God, I will be your messenger of unexpected generosity.

4
Saturday
February

Ocean Waves

By Lu Mountenay of Independence, Missouri, USA

There are many lives waiting to hear the redeeming words of the gospel, or to be lifted from hopelessness by the hands of loving servants. But they will be lost to you without the generous response of disciples who share from their own bounty that others may know the joys of the kingdom.

—Doctrine and Covenants 162:7a

A Psalm of Sharing

When ocean waves…wave back
when wind blows kisses…blush
when willow weeps for you…
bring water, replenish the source of tears
as Earth pirouettes…dance until dizzy.
When sun shines on you, soak up warmth
when tree casts shadows, recline in cool shade
when cloud rains for you,
put out your rain barrel, catch every drop
when hummingbird visits, hold awe-fully still
when sun rises, head east
when sun sets, head west
absorb every moment of Creator's offerings
whatever the master chef prepares, enjoy with smacking lips
Be mindful of how much life offers, make it easier to share.

Prayer for Peace:

Master Chef, may we be mindful and thankful for creation's plenty. May we respond generously to those who have not experienced the bounties and joys of the Earth. May we respond to the hopeless cries of those who have not yet felt your redeeming Spirit and peace.

Spiritual Practice:

Spend time meditating on the act of giving an offering. Begin by asking God for the spirit of generosity. Pray and reflect with these questions: How do I feel when I bring my offering to a worship setting and share it? What deep reasons motivate me to give? What is my best understanding of A Disciple's Generous Response? Considering my financial circumstances, do I feel I am giving to my true capacity? In other words, am I giving the amount I am capable of giving without jeopardizing the needs and well-being of my family? Is God asking me to be more generous? How will I respond?

Peace Covenant:

Giving God, as I look around today at all I have, I will respond to those who have not.

5
Sunday
February

Gather around Jesus!

By Bunda Chibwe, Council of Twelve Apostles

> *As soon as they left the synagogue, they entered the house of Simon and Andrew, with James and John. Now Simon's mother-in-law was in bed with a fever, and they told him about her at once. He came and took her by the hand and lifted her up. Then the fever left her, and she began to serve them. That evening, at sunset, they brought to him all who were sick…*
>
> —Mark 1:29–32

The cholera epidemic in Haiti that followed the devastating 2010 earthquake created panic among people who were slowly recovering from the aftermath of earlier hurricanes. Haiti is full of scenes that are in bitter and striking contrast to the loving intention God expressed in creating the Earth as a sanctuary for life.

I understand and empathize with my Haitian brothers and sisters who feel utterly abandoned, cursed, and isolated from the rest of the world. They navigate crucial challenges experienced by their country while having to deal with their own state of agitation and vulnerability.

Nevertheless, through the grace and power of Jesus Christ and the gospel, most of my Haitian brothers and sisters in Community of Christ have seen their despair turned into joy and renewed faith in God. For them, God continues to be relevant, loving, caring, and compassionate, regardless of the pain and atrocities they experience.

They continue to sing and dance. To them, God's love is not distant or cruel; rather, it is present and capable of restoring them within God's sacred creation. Amid difficulties, my Haitian friends experience the peace of Jesus Christ.

Their example teaches me I have responsibility to share this peace with brave confidence and without fear. We gather around Jesus and learn to serve!

Prayer for Peace:

Healing God, make us strong so we may serve you and the community. Keep us faithful to your purposes so we may share the peace of Christ.

Spiritual Practice for the Week: Examining God's Call to Me and to All

Each day this week reflect on God's call in your life. Begin by prayerfully asking to recall particular moments when you have experienced God's presence and invitation. Write in your journal or just quietly reflect on images and insights that come.

When has God seemed most real in your life? How and when has God called you to use your energies and gifts? When have you felt most deeply connected and responsive to God's movement in your life? When have you felt disconnected or resistant to God's call? How do your gifts and callings connect with the call of God you notice in your family members, friends, congregation, or community?

Peace Covenant:

Today, God, I will put myself in the place of those who have experienced tragedy. I will fast because they hunger. I will respond to their needs with my resources.

6
Monday
February

From Diversity into Community

By Marcia Pugh of Sugar Creek, Missouri, USA

> *May the God of steadfastness and encouragement grant you to live in harmony with one another, in accordance with Christ Jesus, so that together you may with one voice glorify the God and Father of our Lord Jesus Christ. Welcome one another, therefore, just as Christ has welcomed you, for the glory of God.*
>
> —Romans 15:5–7

As I walk my daily meditation in solitude, I often notice a single bird in flight and wonder about its mission. And then I see a line of cars, gathering in number. They all head in the same direction, merging one behind the other like soldiers falling into rhythmic formation. The sound of their engines and the purpose of their joining become exciting with power and energy.

Communion served to a large gathering of those in need of grace; flags from countries around the world displayed in a continuous symbol of unity; flocks of geese, herds of bison, millions of butterflies, their color filling the sky—all give a similar feeling of awe and strength of purpose.

A feeling of reverence comes over me as I watch these progressions toward something greater than ourselves. These progressions have a larger purpose, a cause or force not to be deterred, not to be misdirected by temptations beyond the borders of their calling.

Why can't I move with such initiative and energy toward the purpose God has for me? Why do I yield to the lures of the unimportant and mundane? How I desire to join the awesome companionship of the herd running toward the greatest purpose of life—and not remain the solitary one left behind with a questionable destination.

Or is it possible, as I gaze upon my reflection in the river of life, that I am a lone bird, flying with the strength of wing toward a light of true intent? Celebrate the power of your diversity, which grows into the blessings of community.

Prayer for Peace:

God of harmony and merging lives, shepherd us in your direction. Bring us together to beat out a rhythm of intentional peace.

Spiritual Practice for the Week: Examining God's Call to Me and to All

Each day this week reflect on God's call in your life. Begin by prayerfully asking to recall particular moments when you have experienced God's presence and invitation. Write in your journal or quietly reflect on images and insights that come.

When has God seemed most real in your life? How and when has God called you to use your energies and gifts? When have you felt most deeply connected and responsive to God's movement in your life? When have you felt disconnected or resistant to God's call? How do your gifts and callings connect with the call of God you notice in your family members, friends, congregation, or community?

Peace Covenant:

Today, God, I will search for my unique calling while merging with the community for companionship and strength.

7
Tuesday
February

The Old, Old Path

By Laura Mallett of Cheyenne, Wyoming, USA

> *Jesus Christ, the embodiment of God's shalom, invites all people to come and receive divine peace in the midst of the difficult questions and struggles of life. Follow Christ in the way that leads to God's peace and discover the blessings of all of the dimensions of salvation... The restoring of persons to healthy or righteous relationships with God, others, themselves, and the earth is at the heart of the purpose of your journey as a people of faith.*
>
> —Doctrine and Covenants 163:2a–b

During a dark time when I felt I was alone, I prayed and studied for several months to try to figure out the purpose of my life. Not knowing what to do or where to go in life, I was unsure of everything.

The one assurance I clung to with all my heart and soul was God would never leave my side.

As I was walking one day among trees, I realized I was not alone; someone was walking beside me with their hand extended. I said a quick prayer and extended my hand. I felt a peace I never had felt before. It was the reassurance I needed at that time in my life. I knew all would be well, and God was walking with me in my darkness.

Since that experience many years ago I have had a special place in my heart for the poem, "Footprints," and the traditional Community of Christ hymn, "The Old, Old Path." They both remind me I am never alone. And if I stray off the path, God is there to help me back. If I can't get there by myself, my Savior will carry me.

Prayer for Peace:

God of shalom, in the dark struggles of life, help us accept your grace. Help us be aware of your light and love. Help us on your path to peace.

Spiritual Practice for the Week: Examining God's Call to Me and to All

Each day this week reflect on God's call in your life. Begin by prayerfully asking to recall particular moments when you have experienced God's presence and invitation. Write in your journal or quietly reflect on images and insights that come.

When has God seemed most real in your life? How and when has God called you to use your energies and gifts? When have you felt most deeply connected and responsive to God's movement in your life? When have you felt disconnected or resistant to God's call? How do your gifts and callings connect with the call of God you notice in your family members, friends, congregation, or community?

Peace Covenant:

Holy God, today I will remember it is you who gently guides me on the path. I will be open to your guidance.

8
Wednesday
February

Upon His Shoulders

By Peggy Michael of Cantonment, Florida, USA

For by the grace given to me I say to everyone among you not to think of yourself more highly than you ought to think, but to think with sober judgment, each according to the measure of faith that God has assigned. For as in one body we have many members, and not all the members have the same function, so we, who are many, are one body in Christ, and individually we are members one of another.

—Romans 12:3–5

During the Civil Rights Movement I tried to find my path to help bring reconciliation between the races. Journal-writing helped me on that path. I wrote: "The floodgates of social change have been flung open, never to be closed again. People are delirious with hope that order will subdue the chaos. Then they can finally become citizens of the ultimate kingdom, where the government will be upon his shoulders."

When there were setbacks in this change for equality, in anger I cried out, "I am offended by my enemy." A quiet voice whispered to me, "Do not judge them; love them instead." I then insisted, "I tried to teach the truth, but they refused to listen, so I went away." But my Lord pleaded, "Bring them to me, and I will heal both of you."

I want to be strong enough to stand before the scornful, kind enough to touch those who hurt, pure enough to live among children. I want to be full of grace and generosity. I want to be transformed.

I want the world to know the unity that can be found in diversity.

Prayer for Peace:

We meet you, O God, in many ways. When we are offended, you offer us reconciliation. When we are angry and walk away, you bring us back. We have only to be open and to listen to your quiet voice, and we meet you there. You give us the strength to work for justice. You give us the endurance to march for the peace of Christ.

Spiritual Practice for the Week: Examining God's Call to Me and to All

Each day this week reflect on God's call in your life. Begin by prayerfully asking to recall particular moments when you have experienced God's presence and invitation. Write in your journal or quietly reflect on images and insights that come.

When has God seemed most real in your life? How and when has God called you to use your energies and gifts? When have you felt most deeply connected and responsive to God's movement in your life? When have you felt disconnected or resistant to God's call? How do your gifts and callings connect with the call of God you notice in your family members, friends, congregation, or community?

Peace Covenant:

Creator God, today I will agree to disagree, so I can love the person I otherwise would judge.

9
Thursday
February

Prayer of Love

By Patty Wilson of Cameron, Missouri, USA

We know that we have passed from death to life because we love one another. Whoever does not love abides in death.

—1 John 3:14

"I love you oceans and oceans, forever and ever, always and always. Amen."

For the last 20 years, I have recited this prayer of love to my two daughters at bedtime or when parting. As the years passed grandchildren have been added to the list of those who receive this expression of my loving endearment.

When Preston was born, I started saying it to him. He is now 9, and when I say, "I love you oceans and oceans," he adds, "forever and ever." We finish together with "always and always. Amen."

Zoe is almost 2 years old, and I whisper this prayer of love into her ear as she snuggles close to me. I know one day soon, when I tell her of my love, she, too, will finish the prayer of love that started so many years ago.

What started as an expression of love for two little girls has grown into a prayer of blessing and love for all those I love.

I pray this prayer and sentiments like it will become a prayer of love for all children as they begin their walk of life. I pray they will be cherished, nourished, and assured of God's and our love for them.

Prayer for Peace:

Loving God, we have learned love from you. Let us exemplify it in our speech and in our loving arms. Let us reflect it in our eyes and whispered blessings. May we extend this love to the world's children with abundance.

Spiritual Practice for the Week: Examining God's Call to Me and to All

Each day this week reflect on God's call in your life. Begin by prayerfully asking to recall particular moments when you have experienced God's presence and invitation. Write in your journal or quietly reflect on images and insights that come.

When has God seemed most real in your life? How and when has God called you to use your energies and gifts? When have you felt most deeply connected and responsive to God's movement in your life? When have you felt disconnected or resistant to God's call? How do your gifts and callings connect with the call of God you notice in your family members, friends, congregation, or community?

Peace Covenant:

Today God, I will hold out an offering of myself—not from constraint, but from love.

10
Friday
February

The Seasons of Life

By Norma Cross of Independence, Missouri, USA

For as the earth brings forth its shoots, and as a garden causes what is sown in it to spring up, so the Lord God will cause righteousness and praise to spring up before all the nations.
—Isaiah 61:11

God gives us so much in each season.

Spring has beautiful flowers and birds building nests. Then we have long days of summer for my favorite outdoor fun—barbecues and baseball. Soon the colorful trees of fall are followed by winter and the first snow. It covers the ground, glistens and shines, until the cars and snow boots give it a slushy, gray look. Along comes another fresh snow to make it beautiful again.

Because the seasons are around us continuously, we sometimes forget how beautiful they are. They are signs that let us know God is making a change.

I was at a women's retreat at our tree-filled campground one year, and we took a meditation walk. Somehow I focused on one tree, and I reflected on the leaves. I thought how God's grace allows us to change also.

The leaves come out green and beautiful in the spring. Then as the rain and hot sun hit them day after day they start changing. Bugs and insects crawl on them, twigs hit them. They get nicks, holes, and frayed edges. Some get torn off, though most cling hard. But then when winter comes, they all must go.

Then I realized they have sweetened the earth for a new generation. May each of us live our life that we may sweeten the earth for the next generation.

Prayer for Peace:

God of the generations, as we experience the seasons year after year, generation after generation, may we make responsible choices to ensure the continuation of seasons of peace for our children.

Spiritual Practice for the Week: Examining God's Call to Me and to All

Each day this week reflect on God's call in your life. Begin by prayerfully asking to recall particular moments when you have experienced God's presence and invitation. Write in your journal or quietly reflect on images and insights that come.

When has God seemed most real in your life? How and when has God called you to use your energies and gifts? When have you felt most deeply connected and responsive to God's movement in your life? When have you felt disconnected or resistant to God's call? How do your gifts and callings connect with the call of God you notice in your family members, friends, congregation, or community?

Peace Covenant:

Today, God, I choose peace by my every action.

11
Saturday
February

We Share a Vision

By Sandra Ferguson of Independence, Missouri, USA

Like good stewards of the manifold grace of God, serve one another with whatever gift each of you has received.

—1 Peter 4:10

In his April 5, 2009, address to the church, President Stephen M. Veazey issued a challenge: "Young adults, the church needs you. We need you now. We need you to help us become who we are all yearning to become."

These weren't just words spoken in an address. The First Presidency committed to meet with young adults around the globe to hear their needs, hopes, and vision for Community of Christ.

From California to the British Isles, from Canada to Australia, the three members of the First Presidency traveled, listened, talked, and listened some more. They wanted to hear young adults talk about their vision for the church and where they saw the greatest need for Community of Christ ministry.

Young adults voiced their hopes, dreams, and concerns loud and clear. What a journey. What a vision for the hope of the gospel! Your contributions to World Mission Tithes provide the opportunity for missionary outreach like the Young Adult Vision Project. Thank you for responding with faith.

Prayer for Peace:

God of all we see and cannot see, open us to your vision. Help us feel your presence on our journey to the place you wish us to go. Help us open our minds to the ideas of young people, the future of our community.

Spiritual Practice:

Bring a basket or other container to your place of prayer. Meditate on the link between generosity and discipleship. Write a prayer of commitment, naming specific acts of generosity and sharing to which you feel called. Fold the paper and place the prayer in the offering container you have brought. Close by singing a hymn of gratitude or praise as you offer your gift to God.

Peace Covenant:

Today, God, I will take steps toward the horizon, having faith that your peace lies beyond.

12
Sunday
February

Make Me Clean

By Jim Slauter of Orlando, Florida, USA

A leper came to him begging him, and kneeling he said to him, "If you choose, you can make me clean." Moved with pity, Jesus stretched out his hand and touched him, and said to him, "I do choose. Be made clean!"

—Mark 1:40–41

The Kiev, Ukraine, Friendship Club and Community of Christ congregation are being newly planted in a neighborhood filled with children and young families. My wife, Jan, and I visited the congregation one evening during the summer of 2010 and were introduced by Maria, the pastor and our interpreter.

Kiev was experiencing record-setting heat. Several fans were running in the room where we gathered. Following the opening prayer, a woman ran into the room and whispered to Maria. She told us we needed to go with her to the entryway to pray for a young boy who was experiencing a severe asthma attack. I grabbed the consecrated oil from my backpack, and we were escorted to the boy, who was held in his uncle's arms.

The frantic boy was experiencing extreme respiratory distress, and his skin color was noticeably blue. I remember thinking someone should call an ambulance as we knelt beside him and shared the sacrament of laying on of hands for the sick.

As Jan anointed the boy's head with oil and began to pray, I thought about the language barrier and was reminded the Holy Spirit knows no boundaries. The Spirit was real as we offered our prayers for God's blessing to bring peace and healing to the child.

We experienced the miracle of healing as we prayed. The child's breathing returned to normal, his anxiety calmed, and he fell asleep in his uncle's arms during the confirming prayer of blessing. We opened our eyes and realized the congregation of faithful believers had circled us and joined in faithful petition for the child. The Holy Spirit transcended the barriers of language and culture as our faith united in sacred community, and we were blessed with a testimony of God's grace and generosity.

Prayer for Peace:

Healing God, hear our petitions for healing and increase our faith. Thank you for bridging all barriers, so together we can build peaceable communities.

Spiritual Practice for the Week: Making Responsible Choices

Each day this week prayerfully seek God's guidance in your choices. Discernment invites us to orient our lives toward God and God's vision for us and creation. Begin by reviewing the responsibilities and opportunities in the day before you. Ask God for wisdom and insight about what matters most.

Offer yourself to God with the prayer of Teresa of Avila: "God, what do you want of me today?" Sit prayerfully with this question as you review the day again. Be aware of images, thoughts, names, or actions that come to you. Ask for blessing to live this day compassionately in the spirit of Christ.

Peace Covenant:

Today, healing God, I will accept your grace, and offer my thanks.

13
Monday
February

Go and Do Likewise

By Anonymous of Washington, D.C., USA

> *"You are the light of the world. A city built on a hill cannot be hid. No one after lighting a lamp puts it under the bushel basket, but on the lampstand, and it gives light to all in the house. In the same way, let your light shine before others, so that they may see your good works and give glory to your Father in heaven."*
>
> —Matthew 5:14–16

The small child was so absorbed in building sand castles that water creeping forward with the tide went unnoticed. Suddenly the child was bobbing in the water, trying to grasp onto anything. The pilings nearby were slimy and covered with barnacles—hard to hold onto.

The people sitting on the deck above, laughing and joking on a warm summer day, were unaware of this child floating past them, despite the cries for help. The child grew more desperate as the last piling came near. Then a teenage girl jumped off the deck, held the child, and brought her to safety.

How often are we so preoccupied with our own relationships and day-to-day chores that we do not hear the cries of the person asking for help or do not see the person drifting in life and needing direction? Our attentiveness to the needs of others may save a life, as that teenage girl did.

This is an expression of the mission of Jesus Christ, who asks us to go and do likewise.

Prayer for Peace:

Good Shepherd, make us attentive to your sheep. Help us be aware of those who stray and need to be welcomed home. Let us wrap our arms around those who are flailing and looking for direction. May we be compasses, lifeguards, and peacemakers.

Spiritual Practice for the Week: Making Responsible Choices

Each day this week prayerfully seek God's guidance in your choices. Discernment invites us to orient our lives toward God and God's vision for us and for creation. Begin by reviewing the responsibilities and opportunities in the day before you.

Take these choices into prayer, asking God for wisdom and insight about what matters most. Offer yourself to God with the prayer of Teresa of Avila: "God, what do you want of me today?" Sit prayerfully with this question as you review the day again. Be aware of images, thoughts, names, or actions that come to you. Ask for blessing to live this day responsibly and compassionately in the spirit of Christ.

Peace Covenant:

Today, God, I will quiet my laughing and busyness now and then to listen for need.

14
Tuesday
February

Do Not Be Afraid

By Linda Lyons of Kansas City, Kansas, USA

Peace I leave with you; my peace I give to you. I do not give to you as the world gives. Do not let your hearts be troubled, and do not let them be afraid.

—John 14:27

Ethel and I were to speak at church Sunday morning on "The Spirit Is in Us." I was prepared. But Saturday night my husband phoned to tell me our son had been in a horrible all-terrain vehicle accident in another state. He might have lost an ear. I hung up, paused to pray. Friends helped me pack.

I called the hospital. They would say only that Mike was stable. We quickly gathered a change of clothes, prescriptions, and—oh my!—who would take care of the dogs? I grabbed the extra house key and ran next door. My neighbor drove up just as I was knocking on her door. She quickly accepted the chore of taking care of my dogs. Thank you, God!

Mike was in critical condition with 10 broken ribs, a broken collarbone, and an eight-inch gash on the back of his head. He had both ears. He had been wearing a helmet. Thank you again, God! His friends had called 911, and he was life-flighted to the hospital. He was in the trauma unit when we first saw him, covered with blood and writhing in pain. The hospital would let only two of us stay overnight, and we could see him only 10 minutes.

I stayed near the hospital in Columbia, Missouri, for the next six days. Mike had several surgeries. I drove him home late on the sixth night, and with God's help he continues to get stronger every day.

Ethel handled the sermon. I was prepared to help Sunday, but I guess God prepared me for the accident instead. I never worried. I was never afraid. I knew Mike was in God's hands.

Prayer for Peace:

Eternal Source of comfort, we place our faith in you. We accept your peace, which is not of this world.

Spiritual Practice for the Week: Making Responsible Choices

Each day this week prayerfully seek God's guidance in your choices. Discernment invites us to orient our lives toward God and God's vision for us and for creation. Begin by reviewing the responsibilities and opportunities in the day before you.

Take these choices into prayer, asking God for wisdom and insight about what matters most. Offer yourself to God with the prayer of Teresa of Avila: "God, what do you want of me today?" Sit prayerfully with this question as you review the day again. Be aware of images, thoughts, names, or actions that come to you. Ask for blessing to live this day responsibly and compassionately in the spirit of Christ.

Peace Covenant:

Today God, when I face fearful conditions, I will not be troubled. I will not be afraid.

15
Wednesday
February

Lean on the Community

By Rob Borkowski of Lee's Summit, Missouri, USA

If you truly would be Community of Christ, then embody and live the concerns and passion of Christ. The challenges and opportunities are momentous...will you move forward in the light of your divinely instilled call and vision? The mission of Jesus Christ is what matters most for the journey ahead.

—Doctrine and Covenants 164:9d–f

Have you ever felt overwhelmed, tired, or burned-out? This question was posed at a recent Central USA Mission Center gathering of priesthood members. More than half of the people attending raised their hands. Sometimes ministry is like juggling nine volleyballs all at once.

During the gathering, I demonstrated how overwhelmed we are at times, I tried to keep nine volleyballs in the air at the same time and failed. I invited someone to help me. We failed. No matter how hard we tried, even using different methods of juggling, we just could not keep all the balls in the air.

In ministry we sometimes try to work harder or find different ways of doing things. We often forget to ask for help from our brothers and sisters who serve in the priesthood or other leadership roles. I invited seven more people to help, each from a different priesthood office. With nine of us, each focused on one ball, we could joyfully keep them all in the air.

We smiled and cheered as we sang "Here I am, Lord," keeping time to the music with volleyballs in the air. It was a beautiful example of working together in ministry. We ended the demonstration with all the volleyballs in the air at the same time.

We are engaged in Christ's mission together. We are blessed by community.

Prayer for Peace:

Universal God, we praise you for the blessings of community. We are stronger because of the diversity of our giftedness. Together we continue on Christ's mission.

Spiritual Practice for the Week: Making Responsible Choices

Each day this week prayerfully seek God's guidance in your choices. Discernment invites us to orient our lives toward God and God's vision for us and for creation. Begin by reviewing the responsibilities and opportunities in the day before you.

Take these choices into prayer, asking God for wisdom and insight about what matters most. Offer yourself to God with the prayer of Teresa of Avila: "God, what do you want of me today?" Sit prayerfully with this question as you review the day again. Be aware of images, thoughts, names, or actions that come to you. Ask for blessing to live this day responsibly and compassionately in the spirit of Christ.

Peace Covenant:

Today, God, I will not hesitate to ask for help when I am doing what matters most.

16
Thursday
February

A Trilogy of Spirit Promptings

By Julie Conway-Sword of Gainesville, Florida, USA

> *Hear, O my people of the church, I am Jesus Christ of whom you have sung and testified and in whose name you pray. I am the spirit of love and peace which is in the world and yet not known by the world.*
>
> —Doctrine and Covenants 157:11

The Spirit impressed on me, "You could help him, Julie." As I approached the grocery checkout, I noticed a one-armed man in front of me. He was struggling to extract change from his small coin purse. "May I help you?" I asked.

Looking up, his kind smile showed his gratitude.

Another time I heard, "See if you can assist him, Julie." I wondered *who* I could help. Then rounding the bend in the road I saw a white truck with its right rear wheel in the ditch. Slowly walking from the truck was a man using a cane.

"Is your truck in trouble?" I asked. "Yes, I didn't notice the grass-covered sharp corner as I turned onto this road, and now I need to be towed out of the ditch," he replied. "Stay here, while I get help," I answered. The man climbed back into his truck to wait for a tow.

When I was returning a DVD movie to the library, I passed an elderly man, leaning forward on a bench.

Again, I became aware of the Spirit.

"There's sadness on that man's face, Julie." His head tilted down with a lost look in his eyes. When I was ready to leave, I again passed by. He still sat in a dejected pose.

"Are you all right?" I asked.

"No, I'm depressed, but how did you know?"

"Your head was tilted down."

"I need someone to do something for me," he replied.

"What if I pray for you? Would that help?"

"Oh, yes."

The Spirit is always speaking to us.

Let's watch for the needs so prevalent in our world and listen for what we might do.

Prayer for Peace:

Spirit of love and peace, speak to us—we are listening. You have shown us the way, now guide our steps on the path to peace.

Spiritual Practice for the Week: Making Responsible Choices

Each day this week prayerfully seek God's guidance in your choices. Discernment invites us to orient our lives toward God and God's vision for us and for creation. Begin by reviewing the responsibilities and opportunities in the day before you.

Take these choices into prayer, asking God for wisdom and insight about what matters most. Offer yourself to God with the prayer of Teresa of Avila: "God, what do you want of me today?" Sit prayerfully with this question as you review the day again. Be aware of images, thoughts, names, or actions that come to you. Ask for blessing to live this day responsibly and compassionately in the spirit of Christ.

Peace Covenant:

Today, God, I will keep my eyes open to the needs around me. I will respond as your Spirit leads.

17
Friday
February

Blessings of Community

By Carol Anway of Independence, Missouri, USA

One of the scribes came near and heard them disputing with one another, and seeing that he answered them well, he asked him, "Which commandment is the first of all?" Jesus answered, "The first is, 'Hear, O Israel: the Lord our God, the Lord is one; you shall love the Lord your God with all your heart, and with all your soul, and with all your mind, and with all your strength.' The second is this, 'You shall love your neighbor as yourself.' There is no other commandment greater than these."

—Mark 12:28–31

It was in the winter a few years ago that Joe and I first visited the Stone Church Congregation. It didn't take long to meet people we had known in the past and to make new friends.

We were welcomed warmly and invited to help plan the worship for Easter. We were asked to work in the Stone Church dining room during World Conference. That's where we really got to know many of the community so well.

The year-long preparation for the congregational blessing spiritually enriched us. This preparation culminated in high points for both of us. I offered prayers of thanksgiving that this is the place we worship in our later years; a place where neighborly love is demonstrated.

We are so grateful for the companionship of others who are working to share the peace of Jesus Christ.

Prayer for Peace:

God, you have created within us the heart, the soul, the mind, and the strength to make it possible to love others as we love you and ourselves. If we obey this commandment, we would have your gentle peace on this Earth. Be with us, Creator God, that we might join the companions in our communities and build your peaceable kingdom.

Spiritual Practice for the Week: Making Responsible Choices

Each day this week prayerfully seek God's guidance in your choices. Discernment invites us to orient our lives toward God and God's vision for us and for creation. Begin by reviewing the responsibilities and opportunities in the day before you.

Take these choices into prayer, asking God for wisdom and insight about what matters most. Offer yourself to God with the prayer of Teresa of Avila: "God, what do you want of me today?" Sit prayerfully with this question as you review the day again. Be aware of images, thoughts, names, or actions that come to you. Ask for blessing to live this day responsibly and compassionately in the spirit of Christ.

Peace Covenant:

I will use all my strength this day, God, to focus on loving you and your children.

18
Saturday
February

A Child Shall Lead

By Laura Sutton of Otter Lake, Michigan, USA

> *People should be anxiously engaged in a good cause, and do many things of their own free will, and bring to pass much righteousness; for the power is in them, wherein they are agents unto themselves.*
>
> —Doctrine and Covenants 58:6d, adapted

Recently I learned about a family with two small children (one with special dietary needs) facing difficult circumstances. The house payment and utility shut-off notice amounts exceeded their reduced income.

Because of the wife's job loss, they didn't know what more they could do. I was impressed with their care in handling what they had. The family regularly used coupons to buy groceries, but soon they became desperate.

I stopped one day to leave some information on more resources and talk to them about funds from the Abolish Poverty, End Suffering mission initiative.

Their 6-year-old daughter stepped forward, looked into my eyes, and said, "You almost fooled me, but I know who you are. You're the angel I prayed for."

I tried to tell her I was just a normal person from a church with many people who cared about her and her family. She thought for a minute and said, "That makes sense, too. God's just showing us how to be green. Why would he waste all that angel fuel when there is someone like you around the corner who does just as good a job? So today, you are my angel."

I feel incredibly grateful for all the members of our church who allowed me to be that little girl's angel that day. You are the real angels. Your generous contributions to World Mission Tithes provide hope to families in need. Thank you for responding generously.

Prayer for Peace:

Generous God, may we be generous too. May we respond to your call to be compassionate in our giving for good causes.

Spiritual Practice:

Place your hand on a piece of paper and trace around it to create an outline. Add details of fingernails, wrinkles, or skin color if desired. Look at your hand and meditate on what you do with your hands each day.

Ask God to direct your thoughts to a person in need of blessing, kindness, or healing touch. Pray for wisdom about the specific act needed by this person and discern how and when you will use your hands to complete this ministry.

Peace Covenant:

Today, God, I will plan a sacramental offering to be given tomorrow.

19
Sunday
February

This Is My Son

By Andrew Bolton, Council of Twelve Apostles

> *Six days later, Jesus took with him Peter and James and John, and led them up a high mountain apart, by themselves. And he was transfigured before them, and his clothes became dazzling white, such as no one on earth could bleach them. And there appeared to them Elijah with Moses, who were talking with Jesus…Then a cloud overshadowed them, and from the cloud there came a voice, "This is my Son, the Beloved; listen to him!" Suddenly when they looked around, they saw no one with them any more, but only Jesus. As they were coming down the mountain, he ordered them to tell no one about what they had seen, until after the Son of Man had risen from the dead.*
>
> —Mark 9:2–9

Her name was Rhiannon. I had known her a couple of years as a college student, and we were good friends. One day she invited me to a college play in which she was acting.

I went and was surprised at how well she acted. There was more to humble Rhiannon than I had realized. From that day onward I saw her in a different way. I had badly underestimated her.

This was the experience of Peter, James, and John when they went up the mountain and saw Jesus transfigured before them. They heard a voice say, "This is my Son, the Beloved; listen to him!" Suddenly the rabbi and teacher they were following was more than they had realized. They had badly underestimated him.

"This is my Son, the Beloved; listen to him!" These were the words the founder of Community of Christ heard when he knelt in a grove to pray. Joseph Smith Jr. was a 14-year-old boy who saw a vision of Jesus and heard these words, "This is my beloved son, hear him!" Young Joseph was surprised. He, too, had underestimated Jesus.

There is more to Jesus than we realize, too. We greatly underestimate him. At the heart of Community of Christ's story and testimony is this: Jesus is God's beloved son. We should listen to him above all other voices clamoring for our attention. Listen to Jesus, follow his teachings. Begin with the Sermon on the Mount in Matthew, chapters 5–7.

Prayer for Peace:

Surprise us, mysterious God, with your continuing revelation. Open our minds with new ways to see you, your beloved Son and new ways to peace.

Spiritual Practice for the Week: Embodying God's Shalom

Each day this week find a way to express and embody God's shalom. Begin by prayerfully listening to your longing for peace. Become silent and prayerfully open yourself to God's yearning for peace and the divine vision of shalom. What images, feelings, and words come to you? What prayer for peace comes to you from your time of listening? Speak or write this prayer. What small act of justice, kindness, healing, or peacemaking is God inviting you to consider?

Peace Covenant:

God, I will not underestimate Christ or his teachings.

20
Monday
February

The Faith of a Peacemaker

By Janet Murdock of Annandale, Virginia, USA

Blessed are the peacemakers, for they will be called children of God.

—Matthew 5:9

Shortly after my arrival in Guinea-Bissau in 2008, a series of revenge killings shook the country. They destabilized the nation and led to a sense of insecurity. Communication among leadership broke down. There was no credible national leader to restore stability.

Such events are symptoms of deeper, less-visible problems—lack of trust and effective working relationships. My goal was to organize a workshop to bring together key players in a positive environment to focus on *collaboration*. It took four months and talking to many people to make the workshop happen. It finally did.

You can imagine the stress I felt in the days leading up to the event. I was dealing with people who had no qualms about killing. The affirmation of God's love and presence came to me in the early hours of the first day of the workshop.

I left the office at 2:00 a.m. when I finished my final preparations. As I lay down to rest I heard a noise outside my window. I heard someone walking on broken tiles. The window looked over a narrow passage below a staircase.

I freaked out, grabbed my phone and called Joao, the hotel manager. "Joao there is someone outside my window. Please come…hurry!"

Joao came running, rifle in hand. We climbed the stairs to look down into the pitch-black passage. Joao shined his flashlight.

There in the darkness was a beautiful, blue, iridescent bird with a red head. Something related to a peacock, perhaps.

Having awakened all the hotel's staff and residents, I became the brunt of many jokes, most of which I was happy to laugh at. But, as I finally put my head on my pillow for a few hours of needed sleep, I knew it was a sign, a blessing.

I was enveloped in sense of peace. I felt God's assurance that all would turn out well. Indeed, the event was well-attended. The parties identified key obstacles to collaboration and agreed on a series of measures to help improve their relationships and cooperation. It was a modest, yet good, achievement.

Walk in faith, for there is nothing to fear. Your faith will be richly rewarded.

Prayer for Peace:

God, strengthen our faith as we work for peace.

Spiritual Practice for the Week: Embodying God's Shalom

Each day this week find a way to express and embody God's shalom. Begin by prayerfully listening to your longing for peace. Become silent and imagine you can hear the groaning of the Earth's peoples, nations, and creatures. Prayerfully open yourself to God's yearning for peace and the divine vision of shalom.

What images, feelings, and words come to you? What prayer for peace comes to you from your time of listening? Speak or write this prayer. What small act of justice, kindness, healing, or peacemaking is God inviting you to consider this day, this week?

Peace Covenant:

Today, God, as I look at your birds, I will be reminded I am not alone.

21
Tuesday
February

Child with Wet Hair

By June Russell of Independence, Missouri, USA

> *It is imperative to understand that when you are truly baptized into Christ you become part of a new creation. By taking on the life and mind of Christ, you increasingly view yourselves and others from a changed perspective. Former ways of defining people by economic status, social class, sex, gender, or ethnicity no longer are primary. Through the gospel of Christ a new community of tolerance, reconciliation, unity in diversity, and love is being born as a visible sign of the coming reign of God.*
>
> —Doctrine and Covenants 164:5

I see the child, the child with wet hair, going up the stairs. The child with wet hair was just now reborn of water, soon to be born of the Spirit into an extended loving family as a disciple in Community of Christ.

Child with wet hair, can you even begin to understand? Surrounded by faces, smiling, welcoming, filled with love for you, wanting to be your friends.

Child with wet hair, did you know, are you at all aware, that along your way as you walk and wend, you now will have a special friend? This friend will be with you your whole life. He will be with you to make you strong.

He is committed to you as you are newly committed to him. Trust him, talk to him, listen to him. You are now in his care, child with wet hair.

Prayer for Peace:

God of diverse souls, we offer not only acceptance, but care, compassion, and love for our new sisters and brothers with wet hair. We also gather in those among us who are born of the Spirit, and we extend our love to them. We welcome all other new friends and invite them to join us on our mission for peace.

Spiritual Practice for the Week: Embodying God's Shalom

Each day this week find a way to express and embody God's shalom. Begin by prayerfully listening to your longing for peace. Become silent and imagine you can hear the groaning of the Earth's peoples, nations, and creatures. Prayerfully open yourself to God's yearning for peace and the divine vision of shalom.

What images, feelings, and words come to you? What prayer for peace comes to you from your time of listening? Speak or write this prayer. What small act of justice, kindness, healing, or peacemaking is God inviting you to consider this day, this week?

Peace Covenant:

Today, God, I will take on the mind of Christ and look at others with a new perspective.

22
Wednesday
February

Baptism of Tears

By Jim Hannah of Independence, Missouri, USA

Have mercy on me, O God, according to your steadfast love; according to your abundant mercy blot out my transgressions. Wash me thoroughly from my iniquity, and cleanse me from my sin. … You desire truth in the inward being; therefore teach me wisdom in my secret heart. … Let me hear joy and gladness; let the bones that you have crushed rejoice. … Create in me a clean heart, O God, and put a new and right spirit within me. Do not cast me away from your presence, and do not take your holy spirit from me. Restore to me the joy of your salvation, and sustain in me a willing spirit. … O Lord, open my lips, and my mouth will declare your praise. … Do good to Zion in your good pleasure; rebuild the walls of Jerusalem.

—Psalm 51:1–2, 6, 8, 10–12, 15, 18

The tears that fall when others weep in loss or weep with joy are surely my own—the familiar saltiness, unbidden, overflowing. But the tears are not for *them,* much less for *me.* In those brief moments of union, tears fall for *us,* in all our brokenness and pain. They fall in all our celebrations and joys, in all our inextricable oneness.

It's not that "I *feel* for you" but "I *am* you." And, beneath it all, a mammoth gushing spring feeds those tears, where and when it will. It surfaces from sources so vast, so distant, none can fathom their depths.

But in their release and renewal comes baptism in the blessed union of souls: God's children all around, and within.

Prayer for Peace:

Merciful God, who weeps for the poor, misplaced, and mistreated, we weep for those of us who have been separated from you. We are parched and in need of your refreshing tears. We are in need of each other's tears of joy. Bless us with community. Bless us with peace.

Spiritual Practice for the Week: Embodying God's Shalom

Each day this week find a way to express and embody God's shalom. Begin by prayerfully listening to your longing for peace. Become silent and imagine you can hear the groaning of the Earth's peoples, nations, and creatures. Prayerfully open yourself to God's yearning for peace and the divine vision of shalom.

What images, feelings, and words come to you? What prayer for peace comes to you from your time of listening? Speak or write this prayer. What small act of justice, kindness, healing, or peacemaking is God inviting you to consider this day, this week?

Peace Covenant:

God of grace, today I will accept your forgiveness and continue, with a willing spirit, to share the peace of Jesus Christ.

23
Thursday
February

Being Shepherds of God's Flock

By Myles McCormick of Independence, Missouri, USA

> *...tend the flock of God that is in your charge, exercising the oversight, not under compulsion but willingly, as God would have you do it—not for sordid gain but eagerly. Do not lord it over those in your charge, but be examples to the flock.*
>
> —1 Peter 5:2–3

The life and work of Marina de Merino include a grassroots community-development organization, Association of Community and Environmental Development and Multiple Services of El Salvador.

Instead of taking flight during the unspeakable atrocities of the civil war in the 1980s, Marina stayed to struggle and save the soul of El Salvador. "If we don't set the example, who will?" she explains. A profound statement, as simple as it is true. Having received her philosophy and work methodology directly from her 16-year mentor, Community of Christ missionary Edward Guy, Marina is the embodiment of 1 Peter 5:2–3.

True joy for her community and its successes are evident on her smiling face with every neighborhood meeting, church event, planning session, and worship service. Marina puts in countless hours every week, maintaining friendships with community members.

Marina left her home congregation in Santa Rita to start a new congregation that shares land with her organization's program center. They are not in a fancy building three blocks from a multinational fast-food chain in a glistening metropolis—not even close. They are where the need is greatest, where struggle is not an abstract condition, where the sheep wait.

Those who need and want the love and community that Christ can bring are not lined up outside the churches. They are not counting the minutes until they are told of the grace and divine call God has given each of us. Marina de Merino and her organization are brilliant lights, shining the hope and wholeness offered to all people by recognizing the worth of all persons.

Prayer for Peace:

Tender Shepherd, we are a flock in need of your grace and love. Thank you for your willing shepherds who share the peace of Jesus Christ.

Spiritual Practice for the Week: Embodying God's Shalom

Each day this week find a way to express and embody God's shalom. Begin by prayerfully listening to your longing for peace. Become silent and imagine you can hear the groaning of the Earth's peoples, nations, and creatures. Prayerfully open yourself to God's yearning for peace and the divine vision of shalom.

What images, feelings, and words come to you? What prayer for peace comes to you from your time of listening? Speak or write this prayer. What small act of justice, kindness, healing, or peacemaking is God inviting you to consider this day, this week?

Peace Covenant:

Today, God, I will set aside differences and work in a diverse community for your peace.

24
Friday
February

Melt the Ice with Forgiveness

By Crystal Lichte-Herron of Chadron, Nebraska, USA

> *"You have heard that it was said, 'You shall love your neighbor and hate your enemy.' But I say to you, Love your enemies and pray for those who persecute you, so that you may be children of your Father in heaven; for he makes his sun rise on the evil and on the good, and sends rain on the righteous and on the unrighteous."*
>
> —Matthew 5:43–45

My companion of many years left me for another woman. I was left with more hurt feelings than I thought possible for the human heart to hold.

I am not alone in this circumstance. Neither am I the only person having to fight a dark pathway of bitterness and an inability to forgive.

It has taken 21 years to grow up and away from the state of mind that took me away from my closeness to God. I tried to fix everything myself. What resulted was estrangement from those I loved so dearly. My health and social life suffered.

It wasn't until a visiting evangelist shared with me God's love and the peace of Jesus Christ that I began to wake up. My awakening was slow because I was stubbornly hanging on to my bitterness. I had to learn to let it go.

The only way to do that was to forgive those involved in the breakup of my family. That included forgiving myself.

As I began the process of forgiveness, I felt the dark night of my soul becoming enlightened. It was as if ice were melting away, layer by layer. When the ice was gone, I could feel the warm, loving arms of God wrapped around me.

Whenever I feel the dark feelings coming back, I instantly begin to pray, and God is there, waiting for me.

Prayer for Peace:

I am so grateful, God, for the forgiveness you have shown me. Thank you for showing me the way to peace by forgiving others.

Spiritual Practice for the Week: Embodying God's Shalom

Each day this week find a way to express and embody God's shalom. Begin by prayerfully listening to your longing for peace. Become silent and imagine you can hear the groaning of the Earth's peoples, nations, and creatures. Prayerfully open yourself to God's yearning for peace and the divine vision of shalom.

What images, feelings, and words come to you? What prayer for peace comes to you from your time of listening? Speak or write this prayer. What small act of justice, kindness, healing, or peacemaking is God inviting you to consider this day, this week?

Peace Covenant:

God, I will pray unceasingly so darkness will not enter my soul. I will pray for my enemies so they will be my enemies no longer.

25
Saturday
February

A Taste of SALT

By Barbara Robinson of Flushing, Michigan, USA

> *Let the educational and community development endeavors of the church equip people of all ages to carry the ethics of Christ's peace into all arenas of life. Prepare new generations of disciples to bring fresh vision to bear on the perplexing problems of poverty, disease, war, and environmental deterioration. Their contributions will be multiplied if their hearts are focused on God's will for creation.*
>
> —Doctrine and Covenants 163:4c

The four Michigan mission centers recently created Studies in Advanced Leadership Training (SALT), funded in part by a field missionary grant.

SALT is a three-year training program. Thirty members of the first session received their first taste of SALT in September 2009. This group is meeting three weekends a year for three years, at locations throughout Michigan. Instructors include members of the Community of Christ Seminary for several sessions.

SALT is so popular that plans for a second class are nearly complete. This session will include snowbirds, people who leave Michigan in the winter to live in warmer climates. Using many of the same instructors, this group also will focus studies on scripture, history, and public ministry.

What a fantastic opportunity to learn leadership skills!

Your generous contributions support field ministry through leadership training such as SALT. Thank you for sharing so this important ministry can continue.

Prayer for Peace:

Creator God, may we be the salt of your Earth. May we be lifelong learners, aware that we never can know all there is to know. May we take what we learn and allow ourselves to be formed into disciples who humbly serve you for peace.

Spiritual Practice:

Bring a piece of bread to your worship space and hold it in your hands. Reflect on all the people and processes that made this bread possible. See and remember the farmers growing and harvesting the grain; the millers, bakers, transportation workers, and grocers.

Offer a prayer of gratitude and blessing for all who have worked to create this bread. Feel its texture, look at its color, and smell its fragrance. Take a bite, chew slowly, and let it become part of your body. Ask for compassion and courage to offer bread to all who hunger.

Peace Covenant:

Today, God, I will promote and support programs of lifelong disciple formation.

26
Sunday
February

Remember the Everlasting Covenant

By Blair White of St. Clairsville, Ohio, USA

When the bow is in the clouds, I will see it and remember the everlasting covenant between God and every living creature of all flesh that is on the earth."

—Genesis 9:16

In November of 2005 I found myself in a precarious situation on the Atlantic Ocean. I was helping some friends move their sailboat from Norfolk, Virginia, to the Caribbean. Our 60-foot mast came crashing to the deck, pinning me against the side of the boat. I got free without injury, but we then had to cut the mast and rigging loose to prevent further damage.

With the loss of the mast and rigging, we also lost radio communication. Once we cleared the deck and checked our location and fuel supplies, we discovered we were 200 miles offshore with only 100 miles worth of fuel.

Later that evening we intercepted another boat that gave us one-half of the extra fuel we needed. Its crew contacted another boat ahead of us. Its crew graciously waited to give us the needed remaining fuel.

When we reached the location, I prepared to hang off the side of the boat in 15-foot seas to pick the fuel containers from the water.

At that moment I saw a reassuring rainbow. I knew God would be with me in death or life, as I wasn't sure what this would be. I recalled the promise of the rainbow and in my uncertainty I moved with trust.

Prayer for Peace:

God of the wind and sea, where will you blow our boat? Will we go beyond possibility for a safe return? Will your people, working together, help us to shore? We see your rainbow and have hope and assurance of peace.

Spiritual Practice for the Week: Welcoming Unity in Diversity

Each day this week meditate on unity in diversity. Prayerfully read Doctrine and Covenants 163:8c, which calls "the entire church to become a sanctuary of Christ's peace, where people from all nations, ethnicities, and life circumstances can be gathered into a spiritual home without dividing walls."

Create a large circle with your arms. See and feel the diverse people God invites inside the sanctuary of Christ's peace represented by this circle. Who is easiest to welcome? Whom do you struggle to include? Confess the dividing walls between you and people too different or "dangerous" to invite into your spiritual home. Ask God to forgive and heal barriers that keep you and others from being one in Christ's peace.

Peace Covenant:

Creator God, I will fuel the hopes of another, who will fuel the hopes of another, and so on, and so on.

27
Monday
February

What Matters Most?

By Darrell Belrose of Airdrie, Alberta, Canada

Grace to you and peace from God our Father and the Lord Jesus Christ.
—1 Corinthians 1:3

Greg Goheen was in charge of our staff worship. His theme was "Lent: Its Meaning and Significance." He closed with the statement, "What are you giving up for Lent this year?" I was speechless because I couldn't imagine the Lenten season was upon us again. I had forgotten to take the time to recognize and prepare for it.

Lent for me is not about "giving up something," but evaluating what matters most to me. I ask myself how I can reprioritize my life and better prepare for Easter.

God's ultimate gift to each of us is the sharing of the Son's life so that we may have new life, a transformed life, a resurrected life in our thoughts and actions.

Following our staff meeting, I self-evaluated. I realized relationships were most important to me, and people's lives always reflected the Christ within themselves when they modeled the life of Christ. I decided not to give up anything for Lent but to reflect on a minimum of six people and see how Christ was working in their lives as they celebrated the 40 days leading to Easter.

I soon recognized that to limit myself to six people was impossible. I saw so many friends in the Canada West Mission Centre who lived the meaning of a living God. They were willing to "walk the talk" in their lives.

I am grateful for relationships, for God's touch of tenderness, and for seasons such as Lent that enable us to pause, evaluate, and celebrate the life and ministry of Jesus Christ.

Prayer for Peace:

Creative and nurturing God, help us nurture relationships in which we experience community. Help us begin our preparation for Holy Week and keep Christ at the forefront of our priorities. May we keep peace as our holy pursuit.

Spiritual Practice for the Week: Welcoming Unity in Diversity

Each day this week meditate on unity in diversity. Prayerfully read Doctrine and Covenants 163:8c, which calls "the entire church to become a sanctuary of Christ's peace, where people from all nations, ethnicities, and life circumstances can be gathered into a spiritual home without dividing walls."

Create a large circle with your arms. See and feel the diverse people God invites inside the sanctuary of Christ's peace represented by this circle. Who is easiest to welcome? Whom do you struggle to include? Confess the dividing walls between you and people too different or "dangerous" to invite into your spiritual home. Ask God to forgive and heal barriers that keep you and others from being one in Christ's peace.

Peace Covenant:

God, I will let go of whatever keeps you out of our relationship.

28
Tuesday
February

God's Direction for You

By Lillian Kirby of Blue Springs, Missouri, USA

The path will not always be easy, the choices will not always be clear, but the cause is sure and the Spirit will bear witness to the truth, and those who live the truth will know the hope and the joy of discipleship in the community of Christ. Amen.
—Doctrine and Covenants 161:7

My daughter and her husband invited me to travel to Vietnam. They were taking a once-in-a-lifetime trip to adopt twin baby girls. Their kind pleas for me to join them persisted, and the temptation was strong to go.

I weighed the reasons I should journey with them. I loved to travel. I had never visited Asia. Furthermore, I could be a backup caregiver in case one of the parents became ill.

Yet I hesitated because I felt there was something I would be called to do at home—something urgent. I couldn't pinpoint what it was. So I didn't go.

Two days before the new family returned to the USA, my 89-year-old mother passed away. As her only daughter in town, I had the responsibility of making the funeral arrangements.

God's Spirit was close to strengthen me for this momentous task. A sense of peace engulfed me as I knew for certain God had been faithful and had directed me to listen to divine direction and remain at home.

Prayer for Peace:

Faithful God, we will listen as you guide us. We will stay when you lead us to stay and go when and where you lead us to go. We will work for peace and share it with all we meet.

Spiritual Practice for the Week: Welcoming Unity in Diversity

Each day this week meditate on unity in diversity. Prayerfully read Doctrine and Covenants 163:8c, which calls "the entire church to become a sanctuary of Christ's peace, where people from all nations, ethnicities, and life circumstances can be gathered into a spiritual home without dividing walls."

Create a large circle with your arms. See and feel the diverse people God invites inside the sanctuary of Christ's peace represented by this circle. Who is easiest to welcome? Whom do you struggle to include? Confess the dividing walls between you and people too different or "dangerous" to invite into your spiritual home. Ask God to forgive and heal barriers that keep you and others from being one in Christ's peace.

Peace Covenant:

Today, God, I will listen carefully for your guidance.

29
Wednesday
February

I Have Called You by Name

By Jane Watkins of Lakeland, Florida, USA

But now thus says the Lord, he who created you, O Jacob, he who formed you, O Israel: Do not fear, for I have redeemed you; I have called you by name, you are mine.

—Isaiah 43:1

Months before my first grandchild was due, my daughter asked me a surprising question. What did I want this grandson, already called Jordan, to call me?

In the '50s, this was never a subject for debate—everyone had a grandma and grandpa. There were some derivations such as grandmom and grandpop, meemaw and papaw, granny and gramps. But I found myself in a new cultural milieu where Boomer grandparents were called Pebbles and Peepers, G-Dawg and Unc, Salsa and Rocky!

My daughter printed out a lengthy list of names to review, believing Grandma and Grandpa just didn't fit any more. My grandson already had Puerto Rican paternal grandparents who would be Abuela and Abuelo. The pressure was on. After discussion, the decision was for Gigi and Popi. Gigi! Such French flair; strains of Maurice Chevalier singing "Gigi" floated through my head. Then on January 28, 2008, I officially became Gigi.

I soon became attached to the name. But little did I know the thrill of hearing it spoken by Jordan. On a voicemail I heard his chirpy little voice say, for the first time, "Gigi? Gigi?" My heart nearly burst with joy. Over and over I played this message while recalling the words of our heavenly parent, "I have called you by name, you are mine" (Isaiah 43:1).

May I thrill as well to the knowledge that the Creator knows and loves me dearly enough to call me by name. I am a child of God! I am blessed.

Prayer for Peace:

God of many names—Grandfather, Grandmother—wrap us in your blanket of love. Call to us gently, and we will come running. Tell us your parables and teach us your peace.

Spiritual Practice for the Week: Welcoming Unity in Diversity

Each day this week meditate on unity in diversity. Prayerfully read Doctrine and Covenants 163:8c, which calls "the entire church to become a sanctuary of Christ's peace, where people from all nations, ethnicities, and life circumstances can be gathered into a spiritual home without dividing walls."

Create a large circle with your arms. See and feel the diverse people God invites inside the sanctuary of Christ's peace represented by this circle. Who is easiest to welcome? Whom do you struggle to include? Confess the dividing walls between you and people too different or "dangerous" to invite into your spiritual home. Ask God to forgive and heal barriers that keep you and others from being one in Christ's peace.

Peace Covenant:

I will hear you call my name. I am redeemed, I am blessed.

1
Thursday
March

Reconciliation

By Shirley Remmenga of Fort Collins, Colorado, USA

Mark the blameless, and behold the upright, for there is posterity for the peaceable.
—Psalm 37:37

He was a young man, active in the church and interested in youth work. He came to the youth meetings, had good ideas, helped at camps, and did whatever he could to further the connection between the youth and God.

Unfortunately the atmosphere changed dramatically for him. He was blamed for a problem on a construction project. Without having a chance to tell his side of the story, he was dismissed from the project. He also was denied the privilege of joining in any youth activity.

He withdrew from all church-related activities, pushed his anger, sadness, and rejection to the back of his mind, and tried to move forward in his life. He was partly successful, but his soul was bruised, and the wound remained unhealed.

This happened three years before someone finally asked him to share his side of the story.

A way now has opened for reconciliation and healing. If all the participants will allow God to guide and direct them, this can happen. The wound will heal, an imprisoned life will be freed, and peace will be restored.

Prayer for Peace:

Wounded God, we know you weep when we separate from you and from one another. Open the paths to reconciliation, open the paths to peace.

Spiritual Practice for the Week: Welcoming Unity in Diversity

Each day this week meditate on unity in diversity. Prayerfully read Doctrine and Covenants 163:8c, which calls "the entire church to become a sanctuary of Christ's peace, where people from all nations, ethnicities, and life circumstances can be gathered into a spiritual home without dividing walls."

Create a large circle with your arms. See and feel the diverse people God invites inside the sanctuary of Christ's peace represented by this circle. Who is easiest to welcome? Whom do you struggle to include? Confess the dividing walls between you and people too different or "dangerous" to invite into your spiritual home. Ask God to forgive and heal barriers that keep you and others from being one in Christ's peace.

Peace Covenant:

Today, God, I will make a way for peace, reconciliation, and healing of the spirit.

2
Friday
March

Sundaes on a Sunday

By Roy Schaefer of Independence, Missouri, USA

And you will not have a mind to injure one another, but to live peaceably, and to render to every man according to that which is his due.

—Mosiah 2:24, adapted

The Schaefer family has attended one congregation since 1942. I was 11 years old and was placed in a junior boys' class that met in the sanctuary balcony. After some rowdy behavior by the students, the church school director had difficulty finding a teacher. To his surprise, a young couple, the McCormicks, volunteered.

While most of us don't remember much of what the class studied, we do remember the sense of community. Several of these young men became my closest friends throughout school and college.

The McCormicks took us on several overnight retreats at a park. They regularly invited us to their home, where they made the most-scrumptious sundaes ever.

On reflection, they helped each of us feel they loved us and were happy to share with us as a part of their family.

For years after, several of these young men treasured the friendship and kindness shared by this lovely couple who taught us by who they were rather than by what was in the book. That is our calling in congregations—to build signal communities centered in Christ, who supports everyone equally.

Prayer for Peace:

Compass God, we are thankful for the people who have guided our lives. We are thankful for those who affirm us in our spiritual growth. We thank you for patient peacemakers.

Spiritual Practice for the Week: Welcoming Unity in Diversity

Each day this week meditate on unity in diversity. Prayerfully read Doctrine and Covenants 163:8c, which calls "the entire church to become a sanctuary of Christ's peace, where people from all nations, ethnicities, and life circumstances can be gathered into a spiritual home without dividing walls."

Create a large circle with your arms. See and feel the diverse people God invites inside the sanctuary of Christ's peace represented by this circle. Who is easiest to welcome? Whom do you struggle to include? Confess the dividing walls between you and people too different or "dangerous" to invite into your spiritual home. Ask God to forgive and heal barriers that keep you and others from being one in Christ's peace.

Peace Covenant:

As I have received direction from others, God, I lovingly will guide someone who is wandering from you.

3
Saturday
March

Our Choice: The Earth and the Emptiness or Fullness Thereof

By David Judd of Redcliffe, Queensland, Australia

> *This covenant entails sacramental living that respects and reveals God's presence and reconciling activity in creation. It requires whole-life stewardship dedicated to...protecting the sacredness of creation, and relieving physical and spiritual suffering.*
>
> —Doctrine and Covenants 164:9c

The Koonjewarre family camp was in the mountains of Queensland on Australia's scenic Gold Coast. The camp brought together two ardent and hardworking supporters for the planet, Pat Robinson and Corinne Unger.

Corrine is active in many efforts to sustain ecology, including efforts at Tiona, our church-owned campground on the northern New South Wales coast. Both Corrine and Pat provided information about the environmental resources available through the Community of Christ Earth Stewardship Team—Pat, from her time as a former team member and Corrine as a current team member.

Their energy and enthusiasm about Earth stewardship was obvious as they shared their passion for good stewardship over God's sacred creation. The Earth Stewardship Team, a permanent committee, holds the Earth as its primary concern. Members identify and promote human accountability and responsible behavior toward the Earth. They encourage responsible use of its resources in individual, church, and community life. The enduring principles partnered here are Sacredness of Creation and Responsible Choices.

Your contributions to World Mission Tithes provide missionary outreach through teams such as the Earth Stewardship Team. Thank you for sharing in this worthy cause.

Prayer for Peace:

Covenant God, help us make responsible choices to save this planet you have placed in our care. May we keep it safe as you intended. May we keep it free from war and violence and make it a healthy dwelling for your peace.

Spiritual Practice:

Identify a form of music for meditation. If playing recorded music is not an option, choose a song you can sing or play. Choose music that carries a soulful, spiritual, or healing quality for you. Sit quietly and soak in the melody and resonances. What do you feel or see as you listen? What spiritual message comes? How are you being restored and moved to compassionate response?

Peace Covenant:

Creator God, when I go about my daily tasks, I will make responsible choices about what I use, what I reuse, and how I can recycle. This I'll do with an eye to your sacred creation.

4
Sunday
March

Receive a New Name

By Steve Jones, presiding bishop

> *I will establish my covenant between me and you, and your offspring after you throughout their generations, for an everlasting covenant, to be God to you and to your offspring after you.*
>
> —Genesis 17:7

Following the 2000 World Conference I agreed to co-chair the church name-change process with Apostle Linda Booth. I recalled a profound moment of transformation that I'd nearly forgotten.

I was alone, sitting at the dining room table and preparing a sermon. I recalled an experience I hadn't thought of for more than 35 years. The Holy Spirit was reminding me of my personal connection to the church name-change process.

At a particular moment in my preparation I was no longer in my dining room but was sitting on the ledge of a windowsill in the courthouse of my hometown. The chamber doors opened, and out came my mother and my stepfather from the judge's office.

The bailiff called my name, Steve Hopkins, and I walked slowly and tentatively through the huge wooden doors that would bring me into the judge's chambers. The judge asked me to sit down in front of a large wooden desk across from him.

In what seemed like a loud voice the judge said, "Son, do you know why you're here?" "Yes, my stepfather wants to adopt me." "Yes," the judge said, "that's right. Your father wants to adopt you, and because he loves you so much he wants you to take his name. Do you understand that you will no longer be called by your current name, Steve Hopkins, but that you will be called by his name?" "Yes," I told the judge. I understood that I would be called by a new name, Steve Jones.

Now back in the quiet of my dining room, I marveled at how the Holy Spirit had connected me to a moment in my life the whole church was about to experience. Now I knew why I was co-chairing the church name-change process. My testimony from my life's experience could help others as we experienced God calling us by a new name.

Prayer for Peace:

God, we are yours and desire to be called by your name. Allow the Spirit to connect us to the gift of your Son who brings us an understanding of what it means to be called by your name and to be your peace in the world. Amen.

Spiritual Practice for the Week: Offering Blessings of Community

Each day this week receive and share blessings of community. Begin with a prayer of gratitude for the network of relationships in your life. See and feel connections with family members, spiritual friends, people in your congregation and community, people and creatures in God's sacred web of life. What blessings are flowing to you from these circles?

Reflect, pray, and write in your journal about the call to be "Community of Christ." Go deeper each day as you "discern and embrace" the "divine blessing" of this name that opens you to "become a blessing to the whole creation" (Doctrine and Covenants 163:1). What act of blessing are you invited to complete?

Peace Covenant:

Today, God, I will call myself "Peace," and try to be that peace.

5
Monday
March

Commitment to Worship

By Cindy Korf of North Platte, Nebraska, USA

God is calling for a prophetic community to emerge…that is characterized by uncommon devotion to the compassion and peace of God revealed in Jesus Christ. Through divine grace and wisdom, this faith community has been given abundant gifts, resources, and opportunities to equip it to become such a people.

—Doctrine and Covenants 163:11a

One evening I received a phone call from a woman asking if our church had Wednesday-night prayer and testimony services. I was sorry to say we did not. She responded sadly and asked if we would start having them.

I explained we were a small congregation, and it was difficult just to hold a regular Sunday service during the summer, but she was welcome to come on Sunday. She said she was unable to come on Sunday and needed the worship on Wednesday to keep her going through the week.

I referred her to other churches with Wednesday services. However, she was firm that it be Community of Christ. She told me she was working for a hospital and would be in the area only for the summer.

I was shocked to discover the hospital was over 1½ hours away! She said the three-hour round trip would be worth the companionship and worship. I was flabbergasted!

Who would travel three hours for a one-hour prayer service? If someone was willing to travel three hours, how could those of us who travel only 15 minutes refuse?

I shared this woman's request with the congregation, and we decided to hold Wednesday-night prayer and testimony services. The woman and her daughter came every week and even gave rides to a member.

The summer became richer through the companionship of those services. Not only did I look for and discover new testimonies of God's presence to share at the services, but I heard the prayers and testimonies of others in their walk with God. I thank Charlotte and Christy for showing me true dedication and commitment.

Prayer for Peace:

Universal God, if we are to have an uncommon devotion to your peace, we must use every opportunity to share that peace.

Spiritual Practice for the Week: Offering Blessings of Community

Receive and share blessings of community. Begin with a prayer of gratitude for the network of relationships in your life. See and feel connections with family members, spiritual friends, people in your congregation and community, people and creatures in God's sacred web of life.

What blessings are flowing to you from these circles? Reflect, pray, and write in your journal about the call to be Community of Christ.

Peace Covenant:

Today, God, I will say yes to any opportunity to share the peace of Christ.

6
Tuesday
March

My Life Flows on in Endless Song

By Evelyn Richardson of Nauvoo, Illinois, USA

Therefore my people shall know my name; therefore in that day they shall know that it is I who speak; here am I. How beautiful upon the mountains are the feet of the messenger who announces peace, who brings good news, who announces salvation, who says to Zion, "Your God reigns." Listen! Your sentinels lift up their voices, together they sing for joy; for in plain sight they see the return of the Lord to Zion.

—Isaiah 52:6–8

Some days I find myself humming a hymn, not even realizing I am doing it. It may be that I'm focused on some need or worry in my life. When "light" finally dawns on me, I realize the hymn is the answer to my current concern.

For example, I was worrying about singing for church one Sunday. As I fretfully prepared that morning, I suddenly realized the hymn I was humming was "He Leadeth Me." As I continued preparation to leave for church, I prayed for God's guidance and presence that day. Another hymn, from times past, started running through my mind, "No never alone—he promised never to leave me—never to leave me alone."

If you find your mind wandering into song, stop and listen. It may be the Holy Spirit touching your heart through the words of a hymn.

I hope and pray that I may become more sensitive to the leadings of the Holy Spirit as it comes to my mind in the words of a song. How can I keep from singing?

Prayer for Peace:

God who speaks to us today, open our ears to hear you. Be in our voice that we might sing for joy. Open our eyes that we may see the way to peace.

Spiritual Practice for the Week: Offering Blessings of Community

Each day this week receive and share blessings of community. Begin with a prayer of gratitude for the network of relationships in your life. See and feel connections with family members, spiritual friends, people in your congregation and community, people and creatures in God's sacred web of life.

What blessings are flowing to you from these circles? Reflect, pray, and write in your journal about the call to be "Community of Christ." Go deeper each day as you "discern and embrace" the "divine blessing" of this name that opens you to "become a blessing to the whole creation" (Doctrine and Covenants 163:1). What act of blessing are you invited to complete?

Peace Covenant:

Today, God, I will be the messenger who announces peace.

7
Wednesday
March

The *Right* House, after All

By Linda McDaniel of Independence, Missouri, USA

> *Finally, brothers and sisters, farewell. Put things in order, listen to my appeal, agree with one another, live in peace; and the God of love and peace will be with you.*
> —2 Corinthians 13:11

As the Native American field specialist for Community of Christ, I traveled south to Texas to hopefully start a First People circle in a small town. A dear friend was going with me. Her husband looked up the address on the Internet and printed it for us. We also put the address in the global positioning system to direct us. We were confident we would not get lost.

Finally we came to the town where we were going to stay for the weekend. We looked at the picture of the house from the Internet. The GPS pointed to the same house. We parked and knocked on the door. A gentleman answered and invited us in. We asked if Kaye was there, and he said she had just left. His wife came in and we started visiting.

After about 45 minutes I turned to my friend and said, "I believe we're in the wrong house." It turned out Kaye lived next door. We thanked the family and told them we enjoyed visiting with them and hoped we could share with them again.

We went next door and were warmly greeted at the *right* house.

We asked the neighbors from the *wrong* house to come Sunday to share Communion. They said they would think about it. The next morning there was a knock on the door. We greeted the family from next door with their daughter and her family. We shared Communion, dinner, and companionship.

The GPS, now known to us as "God's pointing system," led us to a hungry family and gave us food to feed them. We started a circle, and we all were fed. We never know where God will lead us. We just need to trust and go.

Prayer for Peace:

Tender Shepherd, lead us to those who need Christ's peace.

Spiritual Practice Spiritual Practice for the Week: Offering Blessings of Community

Each day this week receive and share blessings of community. Begin with a prayer of gratitude for the network of relationships in your life. See and feel connections with family members, spiritual friends, people in your congregation and community, people and creatures in God's sacred web of life.

What blessings flow to you from these circles? Reflect, pray, and write in your journal about the call to be "Community of Christ." Go deeper each day as you "discern and embrace" the "divine blessing" of this name that opens you to "become a blessing to the whole creation" (Doctrine and Covenants 163:1). What act of blessing are you invited to complete?

Peace Covenant:

Today, God, we will share Christ's peace with whoever answers the door.

8
Thursday
March

The Healing Process

By Lillian Kirby of Blue Springs, Missouri, USA

Surely then you will lift up your face without blemish; you will be secure, and will not fear. You will forget your misery; you will remember it as waters that have passed away. And your life will be brighter than the noonday; its darkness will be like the morning. And you will have confidence, because there is hope; you will be protected and take your rest in safety.
—Job 11:15–18

Grief is an emotion and mental condition that can imprison us in cells of self-pity and unhappiness. Recently, a grief-stricken young woman told me she laughs only when her two small sons laugh. She added, "I'll laugh again someday, when I can forgive."

Mourning, despondency, and unforgiving hearts can bury potential feelings of joy resident in all of God's creation.

The joy of health, living, creating, and loving God and one's companions are all possible after the process of grieving.

Even in his trial of infirmity, Job was confident in the power of God to heal. Yes, Job's faith wavered, but it never died. Finally, the Lord turned the captivity of Job to good, when Job prayed for his friends who had wronged him. Further, God gave Job twice as much as he had before.

We can help God in this slow healing process. It is not just the passage of time that heals, but life experiences lived in a prayerful manner. New friends, new avenues of service, new jobs well done—all aid in healing by providing a sense of worth and accomplishment. Let us be forgiving so our lives might again be whole.

Prayer for Peace:

May Christ's healing power move in our lives to make us forgiving and whole for you, God.

Spiritual Practice for the Week: Offering Blessings of Community

Each day this week receive and share blessings of community. Begin with a prayer of gratitude for the network of relationships in your life. See and feel connections with family members, spiritual friends, people in your congregation and community, people and creatures in God's sacred web of life.

What blessings flow to you from these circles? Reflect, pray, and write in your journal about the call to be "Community of Christ." Go deeper each day as you "discern and embrace" the "divine blessing" of this name that opens you to "become a blessing to the whole creation" (Doctrine and Covenants 163:1). What act of blessing are you invited to complete?

Peace Covenant:

God, today I will come out of the dark, lonely night and into the bright, blessed day, knowing I am safe with you always.

9
Friday
March

More Work to Do

By Avis Manchester of Machias, Maine, USA

Out of the depths I cry to you, O Lord. Lord, hear my voice! Let your ears be attentive to the voice of my supplications! If you, O Lord, should mark iniquities, Lord, who could stand? But there is forgiveness with you, so that you may be revered. I wait for the Lord, my soul waits, and in his word I hope…

—Psalm 130:1–5

I was born in 1936 with a serious medical condition. My parents were told my life expectancy was less than 12 years. Later, in the 1960s, I was diagnosed with arthritis, and a doctor told my mother I would be in a wheelchair by the time I was 50. My mother said we would ask God to bless me.

On July 5, 2010, I turned 74 years old. I now walk with a walker but live in my own apartment with my dog. I play the organ for church every Sunday and for other special services. I even drive my own car. God must have more work for me to do, as I have been blessed and healed so often.

Now I face my toughest challenge—the loss of my dear sister, Pauline. It is hard, but I still can hear my mother's counsel to ask God to bless me. God is getting me through, day by day, and I express my love for the Divine throughout the day. I believe we always should tell the Lord how much we love our listening God, who is always with us.

Prayer for Peace:

Listening God, we cry to you for your blessing of peace. We know we have more work to do to bring your light to the path. Forgive us the iniquity of inaction. When we are able, we know your work for peace needs us.

Spiritual Practice for the Week: Offering Blessings of Community

Each day this week receive and share blessings of community. Begin with a prayer of gratitude for the network of relationships in your life. See and feel connections with family members, spiritual friends, people in your congregation and community, people and creatures in God's sacred web of life.

What blessings flow to you from these circles? Reflect, pray, and write in your journal about the call to be "Community of Christ." Go deeper each day as you "discern and embrace" the "divine blessing" of this name that opens you to "become a blessing to the whole creation" (Doctrine and Covenants 163:1). What act of blessing are you invited to complete?

Peace Covenant:

Today God, I will find the work that is left for me to do for peace.

10
Saturday
March

We Share

By Peter Lonsdale of Innaloo, Western Australia, and Greg Short of Canning Vale, Western Australia

> *Faithful disciples respond to an increasing awareness of the abundant generosity of God by sharing according to the desires of their hearts; not by commandment or constraint…Give generously according to your true capacity. Eternal joy and peace await those who grow in the grace of generosity that flows from compassionate hearts without thought of return.*
>
> —Doctrine and Covenants 163:9

After hearing President Stephen M. Veazey's invitation to share a vision and increase World Mission Tithes support, our congregation wanted to do its part to help Community of Christ's efforts.

We recently resolved to give an immediate donation. We encouraged our members to raise the percentage of their contributions for the rest of the year to World Mission Tithes. We will give all loose offerings (except the monthly offering to the Abolish Poverty, End Suffering mission initiative) for the next year to World Mission Tithes.

An exciting spirit of generosity filled our congregation. God has been gracious to us. We are thankful that we have the opportunity to share.

The Perth Congregation encourages every Community of Christ member and congregation to reexamine spending priorities. Let's all do our part to turn the tide of giving and to support the mission of the church!

Your contributions to World Mission Tithes provide the ministry that shares the peace of Jesus Christ throughout the world. Thank you for responding generously.

Prayer for Peace:

Eternal Joy, may we respond to your generosity with our own. May we give out of love as you do, not out of guilt or duty. In this way our generosity can reach its true capacity and will not be constrained.

Spiritual Practice:

Find (or imagine) a globe or map of the world. Look at all the nations and find a country other than your own where you know someone. Notice the geographic distance between your homeland and theirs. Pray for this person. Sense God's love holding you together just as the oceans hold the continents together.

Thank God for the connection you have with this person and with all of God's people around the globe. Ask a blessing on the church as a community sharing Christ's love, drawing all into the family of God.

Peace Covenant:

Today, giving God, I will make offerings—not for inward reward, but for outward compassion.

11
Sunday
March

Tell the Glory of God

By Keith McMillan of Waltham Cross, England

Let the words of my mouth and the meditation of my heart be acceptable to you, O Lord, my rock and my redeemer.

—Psalm 19:14

In the summer of 2010 I traveled with former Apostle Len Young and Apostles Richard James and Jim Slauter to Russia for an American/Russian Friendship Club summer camp. I was hosted by a Russian family I assumed belonged to Community of Christ because of its willingness to host a stranger.

One evening, as we sat in a garden having a wonderful traditional Russian meal, our host asked us why we did what we did. Jim began to share why we believed in a loving and active God who cares about the people of the world—including our new Russian friends. We discussed why Community of Christ would want to involve itself in the lives of people in Borisoglebsk.

Our hosts asked why we would teach young men and women English and hold a summer camp, teaching ideas of peace and the worth of all people. They knew something was different about this church, the concepts, and the love we shared.

They were not members of our church, but we created bonds that night. A tender spirit rested on us all, church member and friend alike. We shared the glory of what God had done in our lives and our church.

God can and does break down walls that humans construct—we saw it that hot summer night. Former Cold War foes had become friends.

As we stood on the train platform later that week, we all shed tears because we hadn't been afraid to share the peace of Jesus Christ.

Prayer for Peace:

Universal God, our rock and redeemer, may we go to the ends of the Earth to share your message of peace. May we break down walls of tension to tell of your glory.

Spiritual Practice for the Week: Connecting with God as Center

Each day this week connect with God through journal writing. Use a notebook, journal, computer, or any available paper. Prayerfully center on your intent to open yourself to God's presence and share what flows from your heart and mind. Your "letter to God" might include thoughts, questions, feelings, needs, artwork, quotes, and scriptures, or it might take the form of a prayer, psalm, or poem.

Try to write at least five minutes each day. What do you experience? Is this an effective way for you to connect with God? What surprises you? What new images or questions from God emerge? What deepens or changes in your relationship with God, Christ, Spirit?

Peace Covenant:

Today, God, I will share your message of peace.

12
Monday
March

Can We Do Less?

By Eleanor St. Clair of Oak Harbor, Ohio, USA

> *"...for I was hungry and you gave me food, I was thirsty and you gave me something to drink, I was a stranger and you welcomed me, I was naked and you gave me clothing, I was sick and you took care of me, I was in prison and you visited me." Then the righteous will answer him, "Lord, when was it that we saw you hungry and gave you food, or thirsty and gave you something to drink? And when was it that we saw you a stranger and welcomed you, or naked and gave you clothing? And when was it that we saw you sick or in prison and visited you?" And the king will answer them, "Truly I tell you, just as you did it to one of the least of these who are members of my family, you did it to me."*
>
> —Matthew 25:35–40

After a back injury, I suffered pain for weeks. I walked bent over for months and required physical therapy. When nearing the end of my insurance coverage, with little improvement, I felt the need to follow the advice of another minister, "If no one is available for laying on of hands for the sick, pray yourself. God will be mindful of the circumstances and honor your prayer."

To my surprise, in three days I was walking upright with less pain and soreness.

As I continued to mend without further physical therapy, God's messengers continued the blessings: I was driven for groceries, invited for weekly meals in a home, and sometimes invited to dine out. There were words of concern and offers of prayer. One called to check on me daily, as did one who kept me informed of congregational needs so I could join in prayer. Another came and salted the snow and ice on my porch and walk. To my delight, I received the gift of *Daily Bread.*

I realized a deeper meaning of how far-reaching the personal ministry in Matthew 25:35–40 can be. It is not always the big events that strengthen our relationships. Mother Teresa said, "I can do the work I do because I regard each one as Jesus." Can we do less?

Prayer for Peace:

Holy Guide, let us not pretend we can't see the hungry and homeless—they are all around. Cause us to look closer until we see you.

Spiritual Practice for the Week: Connecting with God as Center

Each day this week connect with God through journal writing. Use a notebook, journal, computer, or any available paper. Prayerfully center on your intent to open yourself to God's presence and share what flows from your heart and mind.

Your "letter to God" might include thoughts, questions, feelings, needs, artwork, quotes, and scriptures, or it might take the form of a prayer, psalm, or poem. Try to write at least five minutes each day.

What do you experience? Is this an effective way to connect with God? What surprises you? What new images or questions from God emerge? What deepens or changes in your relationship with God, Christ, Spirit?

Peace Covenant:

Today, God, when I look closely, I will see *you*. I will respond to *you*.

13
Tuesday
March

A Testimony about Faith

By Janet Murdock of Annandale, Virginia, USA

Listen to its teachings and discover anew its principles. Do not yearn for times that are past, but recognize that you have been given a foundation of faithful service, even as you build a foundation for what is yet to be.

—Doctrine and Covenants 162:2b

My mother taught me that God does, in fact, speak to us. It is *we,* sometimes, who don't know how to listen. She said God speaks to us through the magnificent creation—through the breath of the wind and messengers in animal or bird form.

Much of the modern world discounts such communication. I prefer to believe two-way communication with the Creator is possible. I will continue to cultivate the ability to listen.

It's not the lack of courage that keeps us from taking leaps of faith but the fear of failure. How sweet it is, then, when we are given a small sign or a quick signal to let us know our courage to step into darkness is known by God.

Such messages can provide us an assurance that God will reward our faith—that God will use us for divine purpose.

The small but distinct messages from God deliver an intense feeling of abiding peace. The messages are precious gifts that instill confidence.

This confidence causes determination to succeed and the belief that transformation is possible, even in the worst places or conditions.

God's habitat includes the darkest depths of turmoil and conflict. The Divine waits for us there. If we have the courage to go to God, God has promised to meet us there and lead us through the chaos into what is yet to be.

Prayer for Peace:

God of revelation, we will listen as you guide us from chaos to peace. May we work side by side with you for justice.

Spiritual Practice for the Week: Connecting with God as Center

Each day this week connect with God through journal writing. Use a notebook, journal, computer, or any available paper. Prayerfully center on your intent to open yourself to God's presence and share what flows from your heart and mind.

Your "letter to God" might include thoughts, questions, feelings, needs, artwork, quotes, and scriptures, or it might take the form of a prayer, psalm, or poem. Try to write at least five minutes each day.

What do you experience? Is this an effective way to connect with God? What surprises you? What new images or questions from God emerge? What deepens or changes in your relationship with God, Christ, Spirit?

Peace Covenant:

Today, God, I will pray and listen closely for your guidance.

14
Wednesday
March

Companions on the Journey

By Geoff Henshaw of Independence, Missouri, USA

> *Open your hearts and feel the yearnings of your brothers and sisters who are lonely, despised, fearful, neglected, unloved. Reach out in understanding, clasp their hands, and invite all to share in the blessings of community created in the name of the One who suffered on behalf of all. Do not be fearful of one another. Respect each life journey, even in its brokenness and uncertainty, for each person has walked alone at times.*
>
> —Doctrine and Covenants 161:3a–b

It was a cold winter morning in Independence as I made my way toward the Temple, where I serve as a volunteer chaplain.

Traveling along a busy road I crossed over a highway and saw a man with a coat over his head. He was carrying several shopping bags. The sidewalks were covered in snow, so the man was forced to walk along the side of the road.

Something tugged at me, and I wrestled with my emotions for several seconds about whether to stop or drive on. I stopped a little farther up the road and waited for the man to catch up.

Normally I am not inclined to offer rides to strangers. However, I asked the man if he needed a ride.

He was Hispanic and spoke no English. I could not speak Spanish, other than being able to greet him in his own language.

The man hesitated momentarily but then got in my car. Through hand motions and street names, I drove him to a place agreed on.

The man offered money, but I declined and said, "adios."

Although I may never cross paths with him again, I have thought about that brief moment. I believe we were companions, both in life's journey and in my car. We had a connection that was spiritual and, I trust, prompted by the Spirit.

Prayer for Peace:

God of our journey, bless us on the path of discipleship. Help us clasp hands and invite all into the community of peace.

Spiritual Practice for the Week: Connecting with God as Center

Each day this week connect with God through journal writing. Use a notebook, journal, computer, or any available paper. Prayerfully center on your intent to open yourself to God's presence and share what flows from your heart and mind.

Your "letter to God" might include thoughts, questions, feelings, needs, artwork, quotes, and scriptures, or it might take the form of a prayer, psalm, or poem. Try to write at least five minutes each day.

What do you experience? Is this an effective way to connect with God? What surprises you? What new images or questions from God emerge? What deepens or changes in your relationship with God, Christ, Spirit?

Peace Covenant:

Today, God, I will remember that I have walked alone at times. I will remember to reach out to those who are alone now.

15
Thursday
March

Casting Off

By Lu Mountenay of Independence, Missouri, USA

Praise the Lord, all you nations! Extol him, all you peoples! For great is his steadfast love toward us, and the faithfulness of the Lord endures forever. Praise the Lord!

—Psalm 117

While knitting last week, I completed the garment, and it was time to *cast off*. I sometimes get frustrated while trying to get the last row of yarn off the needle without dropping a stitch. That would leave a hole. Knitters know what I mean. What I'm trying to say is that it is so much easier to cast *on* than to cast *off*.

In my life, it's the same. It is so easy to cast on, or accumulate things. We tie ourselves down and become burdened with stuff. Sometimes the worst stuff—grudges and hurts. These can add up if we're not careful. When we finally decide to downsize and cast off these burdens, we find it's not as easy as it was to cast them on.

This is when we can turn to the enduring principles. We need to make *Responsible Choices* and discern what is important—our relationships, our faith, our prayer life, our outreach and witness. Then we must choose what needs to go—ill will, resentment, bitterness. Then through *Grace and Generosity* we can forgive and ask for forgiveness. The needle begins to bare itself of the scratchy wool!

We *Pursue Peace (Shalom)* in our new state of freedom from chips that lay heavily on our shoulders. Our next garment will be softened with prayer and love. We encounter the faithfulness of the Lord, which endures forever.

Prayer for Peace:

Divine Garmentmaker, help us be diligent against harboring resentment and complaint. Make us crafters of peace.

Spiritual Practice for the Week: Connecting with God as Center

Each day this week connect with God through journal writing. Use a notebook, journal, computer, or any available paper. Prayerfully center on your intent to open yourself to God's presence and share what flows from your heart and mind.

Your "letter to God" might include thoughts, questions, feelings, needs, artwork, quotes, and scriptures, or it might take the form of a prayer, psalm, or poem. Try to write at least five minutes each day.

What do you experience? Is this an effective way to connect with God? What surprises you? What new images or questions from God emerge? What deepens or changes in your relationship with God, Christ, Spirit?

Peace Covenant:

Today, God, I will not let bitterness crawl into my life. I will cast on your mantle of faithfulness.

16
Friday
March

Make Glad the City of God

By Peggy Michael of Cantonment, Florida, USA

God is our refuge and strength, a very present help in trouble. Therefore we will not fear, though the earth should change, though the mountains shake in the heart of the sea... There is a river whose streams make glad the city of God, the holy habitation of the Most High.
—Psalm 46:1–2, 4

Why do we marvel so at our own handiwork and boast of our small accomplishments? Why should we bask in glory, when we take a portion of the eternal elements—metal, stone, sand—and shape it into empires that alter the skyline? We are pleased as they gleam and glitter in the sunlight.

But in the dark night of our souls we climb into our beds and weep at what we have failed to build within our empty hearts. We don't understand why God loves us. We question if we are worthy. The Creator gave us beauty in our soul, and we crush it; a pure temple, and we defile it.

We are only fractions of the people we could be.

God, you sent your only begotten Son into the world to redeem us. Yet, at times, we turn from his kneeling form as he prays for us. My forgiving Lord, if you still want me, I am yours!

Prayer for Peace:

Forgiving God, we raise our voices in praise and thanksgiving for your blessing. You give us talent, skill, artistry, and imagination. But then we are humbled to see the sacredness of *your* creation.

Our music, no matter how rhythmic, cannot compare to the waves of your seas. Our buildings and sculptures are but imitations of your majestic stone mountains. Our visual arts cannot capture your clouds and rainbows. We cannot put into poetry the love that you are. But we try, because you have put it in us to try for the sake of your glory. May we use these blessings to further your peace.

Spiritual Practice for the Week: Connecting with God as Center

Each day this week connect with God through journal writing. Use a notebook, journal, computer, or any available paper. Prayerfully center on your intent to open yourself to God's presence and share what flows from your heart and mind.

Your "letter to God" might include thoughts, questions, feelings, needs, artwork, quotes, and scriptures, or it might take the form of a prayer, psalm, or poem. Try to write at least five minutes each day.

What do you experience? Is this an effective way to connect with God? What surprises you? What new images or questions from God emerge? What deepens or changes in your relationship with God, Christ, Spirit?

Peace Covenant:

Today I will use the imagination and creativity that you gave me, God, to co-create with you for peace.

17
Saturday
March

An Environment for Proclaiming Christ

By Karin Peter of Adrian, Missouri, USA

Everyone who believes that Jesus is the Christ has been born of God, and everyone who loves the parent loves the child. By this we know that we love the children of God, when we love God and obey his commandments. For the love of God is this, that we obey his commandments. And his commandments are not burdensome…

—1 John 5:1–3

Sometimes when talking about ministries that engage infants, children, youth, and young adults, we use the shortened phrase "children and young adults." But what about the children *of* young adults?

Bob Watkins, Florida USA Mission Center president, asked this question. He strongly encourages mission centers to put their faith in action by making space for young adults—not just to take part in, but to *lead*. This means making space for the children of young adults, as well.

This happened recently when the Southeast USA Mission Center hosted a Vision Project for young adults in the Southern USA Mission Field. During the planning, the mission center staff included a high-quality children's program. Not only did mission center President Craig Lenfestey become involved in the young-adult discussion, he served snacks, supervised play, and did errands for his wife, Brenda.

Brenda, who serves as mission center missionary coordinator, worked with a team to provide the children's ministry.

Their combined efforts allowed many young adults with children to build relationships, take part in discussions, proclaim their commitment to Jesus Christ, and share their vision and hopes for Community of Christ.

Your contributions to World Mission Tithes provide field ministers and ministry that enables young adults with children to share the peace of Jesus Christ. Thank you for making this ministry possible.

Prayer for Peace:

Creator of parents and children, help us promote ministries that demonstrate your love for them. Help us accept *their* leadership. Help us be open to their young and fresh ideas for the journey on the path to peace.

Spiritual Practice:

Sit quietly, close your eyes, and become centered with your breath. Reflect on the statement: "The light of God is in all things." Sense or see a point of light in the distance, coming gradually toward you. With each breath it grows in size and brightness. The light of God reaches you and permeates you with a deep sense of peace. Rest in the light as it surrounds and fills you. Thank God that you live in God's light, and it lives in you.

Peace Covenant:

Today, God, I will set aside my own tired agenda and be open to the brainstorming, mind-warming, plan-forming ideas of the community.

18
Sunday
March

God's Love Endures Forever

By Jane Gardner, High Priest Quorum president

O give thanks to the Lord, for he is good; for his steadfast love endures forever. Let the redeemed of the Lord say so…

—Psalm 107:1–2

The psalmist directs us to voice experiences that convince us God's love endures forever. The children of Israel had been through tough times, but that was not an excuse to withhold praises and thanksgiving for God's presence and deliverance.

In our family, my mother's diagnosis of dementia and the deterioration of her memory have been difficult. Can anything about this situation merit praise to God? Three thoughts immediately come to mind. When in rare, lucid moments Mom can interact and participate with us—Praise God! When Mom gets excited and "plays" with her 2-year-old grandchild, though she doesn't always remember his name—Praise God! When Mom sings the hymns with energy and fervor (sometimes from memory)—Praise God!

It is a matter of perspective. We are thankful for Mom's life as a disciple of Jesus. Even when she can't testify herself anymore—those of us who have been blessed by her life testify that God's love was and continues to be present in her living. With faith we testify it is God's love that sustains us and offers hope for the days ahead.

Prayer for Peace:

Divine Parent, we are humbled when our life roles are reversed, and we become caregivers for our beloved parents. We praise you for being with us on such journeys. We praise you for the memories of times that we feel your enduring love. In those times we are at peace.

Spiritual Practice for the Week: Growing a Gracious, Generous Heart

Each day this week open your heart to God's grace and generosity with a "breath prayer." Let your breath slow and deepen. Be aware of God's breath moving in and out of your heart. Spend several minutes focusing on breathing in God's generosity.

With each breath, silently name one gift for which you are thankful. "God, I breathe in the gift of ______ with thanks." Let your heart expand to contain God's gracious outpouring. With each breath out, name one gift you want to share from the overflow of your heart.

Eternal joy and peace await those who grow in the grace of generosity that flows from compassionate hearts.

—Doctrine and Covenants 163:9

Peace Covenant:

Today, God, I will think back and remember the times I have felt close to you. I will witness of your love to someone who has forgotten.

19
Monday
March

Those Who Sit in Darkness

By Ramona Seeley of Leeton, Missouri, USA

> *"By the tender mercy of our God, the dawn from on high will break upon us, to give light to those who sit in darkness and in the shadow of death, to guide our feet into the way of peace."*
> —Luke 1:78–79

I was making my rounds as a hospital chaplain and went into the intensive-care unit, where there was a young man who had tried to commit suicide.

I entered his room, and we began talking. I tried to tell him how valuable he was in the sight of God. I asked him if he would like a prayer, and he said, "No." He didn't believe in prayer.

I paused and asked him if it was all right if I prayed for him for my own benefit, just so I could feel I had done everything I could for him. He said that would be all right. I took his hand, put my hand on his shoulder, and prayed simply, asking God's Spirit to surround him, fill him with love, and show him how important he was. When I finished, there were tears in his eyes, and I knew he had been touched.

How glad I am that I didn't walk away after the first rejection. I am so glad I followed the leadings of the Spirit and was able to give God's ministry of peace to the young man.

Prayer for Peace:

Merciful God, who draws us out of the dark night of the soul, hold your bright candle so we might see. Shine your star to guide us. Spin your moon to balance us. Lift our spirits so we may journey out of our shells and follow you to peace.

Spiritual Practice for the Week: Growing a Gracious, Generous Heart

Each day this week open your heart to God's grace and generosity with a "breath prayer." Let your breath slow and deepen. Be aware of God's breath moving in and out of your heart. Spend several minutes focusing on breathing in God's generosity. With each breath, silently name one gift for which you are thankful. "God, I breathe in the gift of ______ with thanks." Let your heart expand to contain God's gracious outpouring.

With each breath out, name one gift you want to share from the overflow of your heart.

> *Eternal joy and peace await those who grow in the grace of generosity that flows from compassionate hearts.*
> —Doctrine and Covenants 163:9

Peace Covenant:

Today God, I will not turn my face from your light. I will contemplate my blessings.

20
Tuesday
March

Serenity: A Quiet and Peaceable Life

By Evelyn Spence of Council Bluffs, Iowa, USA

First of all, then, I urge that supplications, prayers, intercessions, and thanksgivings be made for everyone...so that we may lead a quiet and peaceable life in all godliness and dignity.
—1 Timothy 2:1–2, adapted

Ah...serenity! During my career as a teacher, I seldom experienced serenity. But when opportunities were presented, I took advantage of them. In Iowa, when citizens are going to face ice or snow that make road travel perilous...Voila! A snow day! Having a day off from school is as welcome to teachers as to students.

One year, well ahead of an incoming storm, I bought navy beans, ham hocks, and crackers and made sure I had my dessert ingredients. I started my soup and my favorite chocolate cake. As I cooked, I prayed for the safety of those who traveled. I meditated and prayed for those sick or in pain. Later in the day I relaxed and read in the peace and quiet of my home.

Just before noon, my working daughter called. "Do you have power? We are without electricity, and the furnace isn't running." My granddaughters, ages 9 and 11, were at home and were cold. My daughter brought them over in her four-wheel-drive vehicle. Her family, my husband, and I enjoyed the evening meal together. By bedtime their electricity had been restored.

That year serenity encompassed family time, as well as prayerful hours. Now retired, I still seek days when I can feel such serenity...quiet, peaceful, with the assurance of the well-being of my family, and the assurance of the presence of the Lord.

Prayer for Peace:

Thank you, God, for silence—deliberate, yet without tedium. Thank you for serenity—stillness, without feelings of guilt. Thank you for solitude—just enough, without being lonely. Thank you for peace of mind—may we share it with the world.

Spiritual Practice for the Week: Growing a Gracious, Generous Heart

Each day this week open your heart to God's grace and generosity with a "breath prayer." Let your breath slow and deepen. Be aware of God's breath moving in and out of your heart. Spend several minutes focusing on breathing in God's generosity. With each breath, silently name one gift for which you are thankful. "God, I breathe in the gift of ______ with thanks." Let your heart expand to contain God's gracious outpouring.

With each breath out, name one gift you want to share from the overflow of your heart.

Eternal joy and peace await those who grow in the grace of generosity that flows from compassionate hearts.
—Doctrine and Covenants 163:9

Peace Covenant:

Today, God, any moments of serenity, I will share with you.

21
Wednesday
March

Turn Here

By Paul McCain of Oklahoma City, Oklahoma, USA

Finally, brothers and sisters, farewell. Put things in order, listen to my appeal, agree with one another, live in peace; and the God of love and peace will be with you.

—2 Corinthians 13:11

Driving down the highway, I saw at an intersection with a small road a sign that read only, "turn here." Maybe it was put there by a family reunion coordinator, who had let those who would attend know of such a simple clue. Soon, however, my thoughts turned to a possible spiritual message for all who read it.

How many times have I been at a crossroads and wanted some divine signal? Shortly before a job change, I took the matter to the Lord in prayer. I asked, "To what city would you like me to go? What job would you like me to take?" I waited, and an unexpected answer came, "Will you serve me?"

Thinking maybe we had a bad connection, I asked again, "To what city would you like me to go? What job would you like me to take?" Again the answer, although not audible, was, "Will you serve me?"

Then, something like when Peter denied the Lord the third time, I melted with the awareness of the Lord's grace, love, and patience, and I understood clearly. It wasn't where I would be or a particular job that mattered. It mattered only that I serve in my part of the world and serve in peace.

I have thought of that "discussion" many times and have been made aware again of the need to share Christ's peace wherever I am. May we apply that lesson to our choices of where we turn and are found turning to serve God's people.

Prayer for Peace:

God, guide us in our choices. May we choose only the directions that turn us to your peace.

Spiritual Practice for the Week: Growing a Gracious, Generous Heart

Each day this week open your heart to God's grace and generosity with a "breath prayer." Let your breath slow and deepen. Be aware of God's breath moving in and out of your heart. Spend several minutes focusing on breathing in God's generosity. With each breath, silently name one gift for which you are thankful. "God, I breathe in the gift of ______ with thanks." Let your heart expand to contain God's gracious outpouring.

With each breath out, name one gift you want to share from the overflow of your heart.

Eternal joy and peace await those who grow in the grace of generosity that flows from compassionate hearts.

—Doctrine and Covenants 163:9

Peace Covenant:

God, I will not hesitate to make J-turns to get back on the right road to peace.

22
Thursday
March

Home in the Community

By Rozanne Dowell of Independence, Missouri, USA

Sing unto the Lord; for he hath done excellent things: this is known in all the earth. Cry out and shout, thou inhabitant of Zion; for great is the Holy One of Israel in the midst of thee.
—II Nephi 9:136–137

We returned to our "home" congregation after helping get a new congregation off the ground. Fond memories of our good experiences drew us back, and we wanted to renew old acquaintances.

This is the congregation where I studied music and attended women's seminars. I was a friend of the congregation at the time. I since have become a member. Singing in a student recital is also a special memory. What a joy it is to sing for worship services in the beautiful sanctuary. I experienced the Spirit in abundance then and still do today.

Ed and I had two special experiences in our loving congregation. One was when our son, Rob, and his wife, Sarah, were married. The other experience was when our grandson, Joshua, was given the sacrament of blessing of children. Those were happy and special days as our family shared in the blessings of community.

It's great to be back in this accepting, caring, and dedicated congregation. Ed and I are so grateful to be part of it. We look forward to serving God and supporting the goals of the church now and in the future. We will continue in our pursuit of peace.

Prayer for Peace:

Eternal Presence, may we be open to you in our personal and community lives. May we welcome others as we have been welcomed. May we sing your praises of love and peace.

Spiritual Practice for the Week: Growing a Gracious, Generous Heart

Each day this week open your heart to God's grace and generosity with a "breath prayer." Let your breath slow and deepen. Be aware of God's breath moving in and out of your heart. Spend several minutes focusing on breathing in God's generosity. With each breath, silently name one gift for which you are thankful. "God, I breathe in the gift of ______ with thanks." Let your heart expand to contain God's gracious outpouring.

With each breath out, name one gift you want to share from the overflow of your heart.

Eternal joy and peace await those who grow in the grace of generosity that flows from compassionate hearts.

—Doctrine and Covenants 163:9

Peace Covenant:

Today God, I will sing more and talk less.

23
Friday
March

Preparation For Life

By Gary McDonald of Blue Springs, Missouri, USA

> *Humble yourselves, and continue in prayer to him; cry to him when you are in your fields, and over all your flocks; cry to him in your houses, and over all your household, morning, midday, and evening...And when you do not cry to the Lord, let your hearts be full, drawn in prayer to him continually for your welfare, and for the welfare of those who are around you.*
>
> —Alma 16:219, 222, adapted

When I graduated from high school I felt as though I were standing in the junction of a three-pronged path. Which path I took depended on my choices. One was to get a job. Another was to join the army, which I wanted to do. A third was college, but I didn't want to go because I was tired of school. I was having difficulty deciding which path to travel.

That summer I attended reunion at Cloudcroft, New Mexico, high in the mountains. Before this I had not been attending church. At this camp I attended a class taught by Evangelist Glaude Smith, who taught about the evangelist blessing.

After reunion, I decided to join the army, but first I wanted to visit my maternal grandmother, who lived in Independence, Missouri. I believed her to be a spiritual woman, and I wanted to discuss my career choices with her. We spent several weeks together, praying, reading scripture, and visiting. She encouraged me to have my evangelist blessing.

Glaude Smith, who also lived in Independence, set up an appointment for us at church headquarters. He interviewed me to get some idea of what I was seeking. I told him about the paths I could take and my inclination, but I said I wanted God's direction. We set a date and agreed to prepare for the sacrament.

The blessing was a beautiful experience, and I shed tears as the Holy Spirit touched me. Brother Smith gave me counsel to develop my God-given abilities through education to become "a polished shaft" in God's hands. Under the impress of the Holy Spirit I chose to attend college.

I had not made proper preparation, but doors opened as I moved forward in faith. That blessing has guided my life and continues to inspire me.

Prayer for Peace:

Compass God, we need your direction in our lives. May we be faithful and listen when we pray for your guidance to the path of peace.

Spiritual Practice for the Week: Growing a Gracious, Generous Heart

Open your heart to God's grace and generosity with a "breath prayer." Let your breath slow and deepen. Spend several minutes focusing on breathing in God's generosity. With each breath, silently name one gift for which you are thankful. With each breath out, name one gift you want to share from the overflow of your heart.

Peace Covenant:

Today, God, I will pray and discern your direction for my life.

24
Saturday
March

God's Steadfast Love

By Monica and Alex Wharton of New Port Richey, Florida, USA

> *Happy are those...who give food to the hungry...who lift up those who are bowed down...who watch over the strangers; who uphold the orphan and the widow...*
>
> —Psalm 146:5–9, adapted

After selling our home in Buffalo, New York, my 15-year-old son, Alex, and I decided to move. We gave away many of our belongings, packed the rest into a rented moving van, and drove to Tarpon Springs, Florida. With no job prospects, the first six months proved challenging.

On neighborhood walks with our dog I often stopped by a small, white Community of Christ building. I rested on a bench on the church lawn and drew inspiration from the inscribed scripture: "Come to me, all you that labor and are heavy laden, and I will give you rest." One day, after my utilities were disconnected, I prayed for help.

I decided to call the pastor of the Tarpon Springs Congregation. Pastor Lillian met me at the church office. She didn't ask if I attended church—she just met my need. Still overwhelmed that someone cared enough to help us, my son and I received a blessing of aid for car repairs, food, and housing bills.

I was baptized in December 2009. Alex, now 17, recently stated, "The church helped us in spirit, in our finances, in our minds, and especially in our hearts."

Thank you, from our hearts, for your love and care. It is special to be a part of this wonderful family of believers who daily display God's steadfast love! Your contributions to the Abolish Poverty, End Suffering mission initiative help bring hope to those in need.

Prayer for Peace:

Generous God, we would be generous, too. We would give to watch over and uphold strangers. We would invite and welcome them into your fold and cradle them in your peace.

Spiritual Practice:

The chalice prayer is a form of intercession. Create a cup or chalice with your hands in front of your heart. Open your heart to God's concern for the Earth and human family as you hold them in your chalice. See beauty and suffering as you lift the chalice and release the creation (open hands) to be blessed and healed by God.

Form the chalice again and hold people who have particular needs—friends, loved ones, even enemies. Lift them and release them for God's blessing. Place yourself inside the chalice as you confess your deepest needs. Lift and release yourself to God for healing. Say "thank you and amen."

Peace Covenant:

Today God, with hope I will answer the call of someone in need.

25
Sunday
March

Written on Our Hearts

By Andrew Bolton, Council of Twelve Apostles

The days are surely coming, says the Lord, when I will make a new covenant with the house of Israel and the house of Judah. It will not be like the covenant that I made with their ancestors…But this is the covenant that I will make with the house of Israel after those days, says the Lord: I will put my law within them, and I will write it on their hearts; and I will be their God, and they shall be my people…for I will forgive their iniquity, and remember their sin no more.

—Jeremiah 31:31–34

At the heart of today's scripture are these words, "I will put my law within them, and I will write it on their hearts; and I will be their God, and they shall be my people." What does this mean?

I recall the first apostolic sermon I ever heard. It was by Aleah Koury at a church conference in Germany. I was a young adult who had just discovered Community of Christ. Brother Aleah's sermon was simple: "Love releases the power to love." This made sense to me. I could see it working. I knew I was better behaved; more loving when I felt loved. This came from within. When I received love I passed it on without having to think about it. I was just nicer.

I think I behave best of all when I sense God's love for me. My behavior is better not because of fear of punishment or the reward of praise, but because my heart is at peace. The love of God's people opened me up to receive the love of God. I am renewed in God's love through the companionship of the church. That is why I go to church and go to camps and retreats.

Hanging out in the companionship of the sacred community is a way for me to hang out with God.

As I endure in God's love, so my heart is remade to love deeper. God writes on my heart, the words "I love you, and I forgive you. You now have the power to love others."

Prayer for Peace:

Author of the centuries, we open our hearts for a blessing of love from you. We receive and then give what you write on our hearts. Our hearts are at peace and ready to give peace to others.

Spiritual Practice for the Week: Caring for God's Sacred Creation

Each day this week choose a way to notice, give thanks, and care for God's sacred creation. Prayerfully consider one of the following suggested practices or create your own. Walk in nature with a spirit of gratitude and "holy attention." Write a psalm of praise for the beauty of the Earth or a prayer of healing and blessing for the wounds of the Earth. Learn about and engage in an act of Earth-keeping such as recycling, simple living, fasting from over-consumption of resources.

Notice the unique diversity of the planet's creatures and be gentle to plants, animals, trees, and people! Fall in love with the vast, intricate wonder of God's creation and give thanks.

Peace Covenant:

Today God, I will love others because you first loved me.

26
Monday
March

God's Music Flows

By Karen Hutchinson of Loveland, Colorado, USA

> *Let me hear what God the Lord will speak, for he will speak peace to his people, to his faithful, to those who turn to him in their hearts.*
>
> —Psalm 85:8

I've always wondered who else lives with a song running through their head. I always hear some song in my soul. It can be old camp songs, children's songs, classical pieces I've sung, old or new hymns, folk songs. You name it, I hear it. (Right now it's "Old mother Leary left the lantern in the shed.") I can almost tell what my mood is by what I'm hearing. It's something I value and enjoy greatly.

Music has always underwritten my life. I grew up singing and have continued loving to sing, listen, and just enjoy the gift of music. It almost defines who I am. It strengthens and enlivens me daily.

For all of my 70 years it has been a ground for my life. It has become an integral part of who I am. What a joy!

I have accepted music as my personal gift from a Creator who loves me and wants me to enjoy life to the fullest.

The God who encourages me to sing, listen, and participate also has given me the beautiful world we live in. I have a great family that daily blesses me. I have great friends with whom I can share my life. Through music I can connect in astonishing ways to those who need me.

Another personal gift I receive daily, if I listen, is God's divine Spirit. I feel God's presence flowing through me like music. This is when I most feel at peace.

Prayer for Peace:

We turn our hearts to you, O God, and we listen to the peace that you speak. May we always speak this peace to one another.

Spiritual Practice for the Week: Caring for God's Sacred Creation

Each day this week choose a way to notice, give thanks, and care for God's sacred creation. Prayerfully consider one of the following suggested practices or create your own.

Walk in nature with a spirit of gratitude and "holy attention." Write a psalm of praise for the beauty of the Earth or a prayer of healing and blessing for the wounds of the Earth. Learn about and engage in an act of Earth-keeping such as recycling, simple living, fasting from over-consumption of resources. Notice the unique diversity of the planet's creatures and be gentle to plants, animals, trees, and people! Fall in love with the vast, intricate wonder of God's creation and give thanks.

Peace Covenant:

Today, God, I will listen for your voice. I will listen for your music in my soul. I will listen to the music of others.

27
Tuesday
March

Remember the Everlasting Covenant

By Ron Harmon, Council of Twelve Apostles

> *"When the bow is in the clouds, I will see it and remember the everlasting covenant between God and every living creature of all flesh that is on the earth."*
>
> —Genesis 9:16

When I visit places of great historical significance I often wonder about the ordinary people of that time period. What were their hopes and aspirations?

Recently during a gathering of the North East USA Mission Field we had the opportunity to reenter the story of the church in Kirtland, Ohio. We learned about members' hopes for a Christian community based primarily on the experience recorded in Acts, chapter 2. We also learned about their expectation for endowment of the Holy Spirit in their ministry.

As we shared in our weekend together I could almost hear the voices of those early Saints of the Restoration. As a child growing up I experienced the history and sacred space of Kirtland many times.

I sensed in a personal and profound way that I was called to carry on the great and marvelous work these pioneers of faith so courageously pursued.

Our last day together in worship we were blessed with a powerful affirmation that we were endowed in that moment with the power of the Holy Spirit for ministry and mission.

At the heart of this mission is God's covenant of peace that calls us to embrace a radically different vision for our world. This covenant connects me in powerful ways with the early Saints of our movement. It also connects me to the voices of the prophets in Isaiah.

I pray that years from now others will be able to connect with God's covenant of peace as they reenter our story.

Prayer for Peace:

Affirming God, endow us with the power of your Holy Spirit to embrace the ministry and mission to which we are called.

Spiritual Practice for the Week: Caring for God's Sacred Creation

Each day this week choose a way to notice, give thanks, and care for God's sacred creation. Prayerfully consider one of the following suggested practices or create your own.

Walk in nature with a spirit of gratitude and "holy attention." Write a psalm of praise for the beauty of the Earth or a prayer of healing and blessing for the wounds of the Earth. Learn about and engage in an act of Earth-keeping such as recycling, simple living, fasting from over-consumption of resources. Notice the unique diversity of the planet's creatures and be gentle to plants, animals, trees, and people! Fall in love with the vast, intricate wonder of God's creation and give thanks.

Peace Covenant:

I will keep the vision of the covenant rainbow to remind me and inspire me to share the peace of Jesus Christ.

28
Wednesday
March

Invitation to Spiritual Renewal

By Joann Condit of Phoenix, Arizona, USA

Be still, and know that I am God!

—Psalm 46:10

It was late in the afternoon of a retreat in the Arizona mountains, and I was tired—physically, mentally and spiritually. I had no heart for journal writing, meditating, or praying. I sat, chin on my hand, staring at a torrent of rain. Slowly the downpour eased to a drizzle. The trees dripped, stirred by a soft breeze. I brooded.

At a soft pat on the shoulder, I looked up and saw my daughter and grandson, jackets and hair damp with rain, motioning conspiratorially to follow them outside. We walked silently to the road, down a hill, and around a bend, stepping over rivulets in the wet soil. They stopped, pointing with triumph toward the trees.

Tiny streams cascaded over rocks, loud in the silence. Suddenly I saw them…*mushrooms!* Hundreds of mushrooms dotted the hillside. Even as we watched, a giant red-capped one arose visibly, a mat of needles crowning its head like a shaggy wig.

From the miniature to that huge one, they rose in new life. The rain liberated them. We stared, mesmerized.

We returned to the building in silence, under watery sunshine. Fatigue gone, my heart and soul clean and filled with life. I sat down to express my gratitude. I wrote my thanks to God for Laurie and Stephen, their kindness in sharing, for eyes to see miracles, for renewal of body, mind, and soul found in a hillside of mushrooms, and for sunshine after rain.

And, oh yes…thank you for making me know you are God!

Prayer for Peace:

For refreshing of the spirit, for renewal of our bodies, for the sunshine after rain, we praise you, divine Creator.

Spiritual Practice for the Week: Caring for God's Sacred Creation

Each day this week choose a way to notice, give thanks, and care for God's sacred creation. Prayerfully consider one of the following suggested practices or create your own.

Walk in nature with a spirit of gratitude and "holy attention." Write a psalm of praise for the beauty of the Earth or a prayer of healing and blessing for the wounds of the Earth. Learn about and engage in an act of Earth-keeping such as recycling, simple living, fasting from over-consumption of resources. Notice the unique diversity of the planet's creatures and be gentle to plants, animals, trees, and people! Fall in love with the vast, intricate wonder of God's creation and give thanks.

Peace Covenant:

God, I will rise up from my brooding and look for the sacred places of liberation and new growth.

29
Thursday
March

What Matters Most (Part I)

By David Brock, presiding evangelist

> *All this is from God, who reconciled us to himself through Christ, and has given us the ministry of reconciliation; that is, in Christ God was reconciling the world to himself, not counting their trespasses against them, and entrusting the message of reconciliation to us.*
>
> —2 Corinthians 5:18–19

I have this working theory. The power centers where what ultimately matters most in life are not the stock exchanges of London, New York, Beijing, or New Delhi. Nor are they the halls of political power in capital cities such as Brasilia, Canberra, Nairobi, Ottawa, or Moscow.

Yes, I know that decisions made in those places touch billions of Earth's inhabitants and the planet itself. Yes, I know the political party I vote for and the rise and fall of financial markets can change our lives. Yes, I know the latest research in the laboratories of universities can cure or cause disease, stop or start plagues, target and destroy a distant enemy, or develop earthquake-resistant technologies to save millions.

But, my working theory goes something like this: What ultimately matters most may happen in a little chapel built on the side of a pastor's home in an agricultural town in Argentina.

Here people crowd in to sing of the power and presence of the Holy Spirit. They kneel to pray for a parent who is suffering from advanced cancer. They reach out to receive bread and wine and connect to a faith community.

Here are the sinners and saints who span the centuries and solidify forever their identity as children of God.

Prayer for Peace:

Creator God, we would kneel alongside those of our community connected to us in ways that matter most. May we solidify our relationship with them and work together for the peace of Christ.

Spiritual Practice for the Week: Caring for God's Sacred Creation

Each day this week choose a way to notice, give thanks, and care for God's sacred creation. Prayerfully consider one of the following suggested practices or create your own.

Walk in nature with a spirit of gratitude and "holy attention." Write a psalm of praise for the beauty of the Earth or a prayer of healing and blessing for the wounds of the Earth. Learn about and engage in an act of Earth-keeping such as recycling, simple living, fasting from over-consumption of resources. Notice the unique diversity of the planet's creatures and be gentle to plants, animals, trees, and people! Fall in love with the vast, intricate wonder of God's creation and give thanks.

Peace Covenant:

Today, God, I will kneel in prayer to discern, through your Spirit, what matters most.

30
Friday
March

What Matters Most (Part II)

By David Brock, presiding evangelist

> *O let the suffering come to an end all around me, but establish the righteous, you who test the minds and hearts, O righteous God. God is my shield, who saves the upright in heart.*
> —Psalm 7:9–10, adapted

The place that matters most may be the carport in front of a small chapel now transformed into friendship hall. It may be a place where laughter splashes over the conversation and adds a flavor to the meal.

The classiest of restaurants cannot match this meal.

That "hall" is also the place where a sister comes to share the weight of incomprehensible burdens: a grandchild with leukemia and a husband in prison, the scarcity of food in a house without a kitchen, her leg, swollen and festering with a disease doctors cannot cure.

This may be the true hall of power because here the sacrament of laying on of hands for the sick is offered. Here she is renewed by embrace of arms and words of love as she limps away with hope in her heart and a promise to return this evening.

I don't know how well my *what matters most* theory will hold up under tough, objective scrutiny. However, when I have the privilege of placing my hands on the head of a newborn named Melissa in the sacrament of child blessing in another small chapel in Filadelfia, Perú, the theory seems to bear up well.

To say her name aloud in the presence of parents and faith family is all I need. To proclaim her identity as a beloved child of God, to pledge with other sisters and brothers to be her guide and spiritual companion is all I need.

To simply experience the presence of the Holy in and through the child and surrounding us in that small space is all I need.

Prayer for Peace:

God of blessing and burdens, we look to embracing arms for the sacrament of laying on of hands for the sick. We thank you for your holy presence.

Spiritual Practice for the Week: Caring for God's Sacred Creation

Each day this week choose a way to notice, give thanks, and care for God's sacred creation. Prayerfully consider one of the following suggested practices or create your own.

Walk in nature with a spirit of gratitude and "holy attention." Write a psalm of praise for the beauty of the Earth or a prayer of healing and blessing for the wounds of the Earth. Learn about and engage in an act of Earth-keeping such as recycling, simple living, fasting from over-consumption of resources. Notice the unique diversity of the planet's creatures and be gentle to plants, animals, trees, and people! Fall in love with the vast, intricate wonder of God's creation and give thanks.

Peace Covenant:

Today, God, I will kneel in prayer and discern, through your Holy Spirit, what matters most.

31
Saturday
March

What Matters Most (Part III)

By David Brock, presiding evangelist

> *For the mountains shall depart and the hills be removed, but my kindness shall not depart from thee, neither shall the covenant of my peace be removed, saith the Lord that hath mercy on thee.*
>
> —III Nephi 10:18

The hall of power that matters most may be the rough-hewn, semi-permanent Community of Christ structure. It serves as gathering place for the residents of Monte Sión (Mount Zion).

This new, unplanned community of the poor defines the urban sprawl on the brown and treeless hills on the outskirts of Lima, Perú.

It is the place where every Friday and Saturday young adults and the pastor from Callao make the trek from the city.

They climb the steep hillside to teach 40–50 children in a small, dirt-floored room. Here they hang out, play sports, worship, and study with other youth. They pray for jobs, health, food, and schooling for children with parents trying to find a sense of place in the world.

The hall of power that matters most may be the small room where a sister or brother is offered sanctuary. Here they are free to tell of their amazing and heroic journey that merits the writing skills of the best biographers and the money and time of the most-literate readership.

It is the place where after the telling a minister of blessing is privileged to lay hands on the head.

Words of the sacrament of evangelist blessing are shared.

These words can never capture God's presence and promise in a life, yet the Spirit confirms in a way that provides enough…and to spare.

Prayer for Peace:

God of the gathering places, God of two or three, God of the multitudes, hear the prayer for sanctuary from those with heroic stories. We are blessed by these stories. We are blessed to be a blessing.

Spiritual Practice:

Stand or sit with your hands extended in front of you. Prayerfully ponder all the things you hold in your hands that make you feel too full, busy, drained, or tight. Spread your hands up and apart to release these things. Then hold them open and empty them again. Thank God for relationships that fill and feed your spirit. Pray for a generous heart and open hands that reach out to make room for all in the circle of Christ's community.

Peace Covenant:

Today, God, I will kneel in prayer and, again, through your Holy Spirit, discern what matters most.

1
Sunday
April

Blessed Is He Who Comes in the Name of the Lord

By Kris Judd of Kansas City, Missouri, USA

But Jesus said, "Let her alone; why do you trouble her? She has performed a good service for me. For you always have the poor with you, and you can show kindness to them whenever you wish; but you will not always have me... Truly I tell you, wherever the good news is proclaimed in the whole world, what she has done will be told in remembrance of her."
—Mark 14:6–7, 9

Jesus told his followers what eventually would be the result of his bold ministry. They did not want to believe it and even tried to talk him out of it. But he knew the truth and prepared himself for what would not be a desirable event. His life of study, prayer, and ministry required him to release and let go, to remain focused on and connected to his mission, not himself.

I once accepted an assignment to speak in a congregation. While I prepared through study and prayer, and received a good theme to work with, I struggled with my message. I wrote it in notes and then in pages and was ready to offer what I had prepared.

Yet I worried about what *I* would say, how *I* would be received, if *I* would offer what was needed. As I stood to speak, I placed my notes aside and spoke from my heart, going in a different direction but trusting that God was leading my thoughts and words. I let go of *my* needs and focused on what I perceived God wanted to share with God's people.

For Jesus, it was in his ability to see beyond himself and his needs that allowed him to see the needs of God's people. Author Sogyal Rinpoche (*Glimpse after Glimpse*) said, "Although we have been made to believe that if we let go we will end up with nothing, life reveals just the opposite: that letting go is the real path to freedom." Blessed be the One who found that freedom by letting go and who shows us the path, as well.

Prayer for Peace:

God of freedom-giving grace, help us let go of our organized, preplanned, strategized, conformed traditions and open us to receive your spontaneous Spirit and guidance. Help us discern the needs of the people of the moment amid which we find ourselves.

Spiritual Practice for the Holy Week:

Prayerfully ponder the life of Christ. Spread your hands up and apart to release things that prevent you from holding Christ at the center of your life. Thank God for Christ who fills and feeds our spirit. Pray for a generous heart and open hands that reach out to make room for all in the circle of Christ's community.

Peace Covenant:

I will remember the woman who served you, God, and I will serve the poor among us now.

2
Monday
April

"Were You There...?"

By Vera Entwistle of Forster Keys, New South Wales, Australia

The women were terrified and bowed their faces to the ground, but the men said to them, "Why do you look for the living among the dead? He is not here, but has risen.
—Luke 24:5

As we approach Good Friday, I remember a moment that touched me. Members from many of the Mid North Coast, Australia, congregations had gathered at the Johns River Congregation for a special worship service. A soloist was to sing unaccompanied: "Were You There When They Crucified My Lord?" As her clear voice rang out, the congregation became caught up in the words of the hymn.

When she came to the fourth verse, her emotions overcame her. As tears ran down her face we realized she was struggling to continue. After a brief hesitation, members of the congregation gently began to sing with her until she was able to complete her song.

The experience deeply touched those who witnessed it.

As we drove home, I thought how this was a clear example of what we are called to do: When others struggle or are in trouble, we are to gently and lovingly offer support. My prayer is that we always are ready to respond.

Prayer for Peace:

Binder of wounds, thank you for the community that sees our tears and moves to uphold us. Thank you for the community of empathy that hears the unspoken plea. May we join in this community to finish the song that cries out for justice and peace.

Spiritual Practice for the Holy Week:

Prayerfully ponder the life of Christ. Spread your hands up and apart to release things that prevent you from holding Christ at the center of your life. Thank God for Christ who fills and feeds our spirit. Pray for a generous heart and open hands that reach out to make room for all in the circle of Christ's community.

Peace Covenant:

Today I will listen for the silent cries that need to be answered, God.

3
Tuesday
April

Growing Stronger in the Broken Places

By Sharon and Jim Hannah of Independence, Missouri, USA

Reach out in understanding, clasp their hands, and invite all to share in the blessings of community created in the name of the One who suffered on behalf of all.
—Doctrine and Covenants 161:3a

"As long as we are on earth, the love that unites us will bring us suffering by our very contact with one another, because love is the resetting of a body of broken bones" (*New Seeds of Contemplation* by Thomas Merton, New Directions Publishing, 2007).

We, as the body of Christ, are often-broken members of that body. But we don't often talk about our bruises and broken bones—injuries sometimes brought about by the actions or inactions of ourselves, or other members, intentional or not.

Anyone who has been in a deep relationship knows that being close to someone is a risk. Those we love deeply also can hurt us deeply; our guard is down more before them than anyone else.

Love makes us vulnerable, so, ironically, the deepest wounds may be received in the household of faith.

Fight or flight are the two most-common responses. We can injure the one who injured us, or we can distance ourselves from them. But David W. Augsburger tells us there is a third way—*care-fronting*—to care enough about ourselves and about the one who causes us pain to remain in relationship, confronting harmful behavior in the spirit of love (*Caring Enough to Confront* by David W. Augsburger, Gospel Light Publications, 2009).

Confronting in love is a challenging balance of attitudes. It does not mean becoming a doormat, or suffering in silence. It invites a willingness to speak our truth while leaving space for the truth another is experiencing. In all this, we must be taught from within by the One who "leads us into all truth."

When there are injuries or brokenness in the body of Christ—whether we gave that injury, or received it—the way of peace, the way of sacred community, is to acknowledge the pain and move toward healing. The miracle occurs only then: The body grows strongest in its broken places.

Prayer for Peace:

Healing God, reset our broken relationships. Let us hear one another's truth. Let the way of Christ's peace be the way of our community.

Spiritual Practice for the Holy Week:

Prayerfully ponder the life of Christ. Spread your hands up and apart to release things that prevent you from holding Christ at the center of your life. Thank God for Christ who fills and feeds our spirit. Pray for open hands that reach out to make room for all in the circle of Christ's community.

Peace Covenant:

Today God, I will acknowledge pain I have caused or received, and exercise *care-fronting* to heal the relationship.

4
Wednesday
April

Approaching the Resurrection

By Alecia Cripps of Independence, Missouri, USA

> *Support one another in love, confident that my Spirit will be with you even as I have gone before you and shown you the way.*
>
> —Doctrine and Covenants 154:7b

It was a brilliant Sunday morning, and light flooded through the stained-glass windows. I had been on the run since entering the building. Now it was time to slow down, go into the sanctuary, and begin the morning meditation.

As I sat on the rostrum, looking at the congregation, I sensed the presence of the Spirit. I sensed God already had enfolded this congregation in infinite love, light, and caring. I enjoyed those few moments of meditation before beginning the service because I had a chance to stop, look at the faces of those sitting in the sanctuary, and pray for individuals and the community.

As I prayed, I noticed a visitor. It was a friend from long ago. Because of unfortunate events we had become estranged. Through the years I often had prayed for reconciliation, but it was elusive. Finally, I had released my struggles, placing them in God's hands.

As I looked at my friend, the pain was again fresh. But in the comfort of the presence of God I felt a soothing calm. I sensed God's wonderful humor as God said, "You asked for reconciliation. I'm just answering your prayers."

In this Easter season, the power of the resurrected Christ comes alive again. For, you see, it was the resurrected Christ, the Christ who lives and transforms lives today, that met me in the sanctuary that beautiful Sunday morning.

Prayer for Peace:

Reconciling God, we sense your presence among us. We are thankful for the many forms in which you respond to our prayers. Thank you for returning relationships for renewed opportunities to mend. Be with us as we work on interpersonal, as well as international peace.

Spiritual Practice for the Holy Week:

Prayerfully ponder the life of Christ. Spread your hands up and apart to release things that prevent you from holding Christ at the center of your life. Thank God for Christ who fills and feeds our spirit. Pray for a generous heart and open hands that reach out to make room for all in the circle of Christ's community.

Peace Covenant:

Today, God, I will work on mending an estranged relationship.

5
Thursday
April

Journey of Resurrection

By Harriet White of Ogden, Utah, USA

I have been crucified with Christ; and it is no longer I who live, but it is Christ who lives in me. And the life I now live in the flesh, I live by faith in the Son of God, who loved me and gave himself for me.

—Galatians 2:19–20

The first year I decided to purposely prepare for Passion Week, I used Megan McKenna's books to help me in my focus. I was faithful in my daily reading, meditation, and prayer. During Easter break I flew to Kentucky, a yearly pilgrimage to a restored Shaker village, to spend time for spiritual reflection.

While on the flight, in the daily selection for Holy Thursday, McKenna told the story of Jesus washing the disciples' feet. I had read the account often. Still, imagine my surprise when McKenna's telling of the story pierced my soul with new awareness. My thoughts tumbled: "Judas was present at the foot washing. Christ knew Judas would betray him. Christ washed the betrayer's feet."

In startled understanding, the Spirit's words flowed through my mind. "Can you wash the feet of those who betray you?" God was calling me to transformation. It was the beginning of a process of healing past hurts, yet equally important, the beginning of Easter resurrection in my life.

The week before Easter provides us with an opportunity to enter Christ's resurrection in a personal way.

The journey isn't always easy.

What may help in committing to the journey, perhaps, is the sheer expectation, the joy of knowing our old ways will be crucified with Christ, and we will be resurrected as new creations.

Prayer for Peace:

Giver of eternal life, live in me. Open my soul to Christ's sacrificial love. Love through me. Allow me to enter Christ's resurrection and create in me a new person of peace and shalom. As it is with Christ, let it be in me.

Spiritual Practice for the Holy Week:

Prayerfully ponder the life of Christ. Spread your hands up and apart to release things that prevent you from holding Christ at the center of your life. Thank God for Christ who fills and feeds our spirit. Pray for a generous heart and open hands that reach out to make room for all in the circle of Christ's community.

Peace Covenant:

I will wash the feet of past hurts with forgiveness.

6
Friday
April

Reconciling Friday

By Peggy Michael of Cantonment, Florida, USA

Then Jesus said, "Father, forgive them; for they do not know what they are doing."... Then Jesus, crying with a loud voice, said, "Father, into your hands I commend my spirit." Having said this, he breathed his last. When the centurion saw what had taken place, he praised God and said, "Certainly this man was innocent."

—Luke 23:34, 46–47

Had I not looked into the pain-filled eyes of my suffering Lord, perhaps I, too, would have shouted, "Crucify him!" But I did look, and I saw, and I felt.

As the lashes cut into his innocent flesh, I cringed and would have washed his wounds with my salty tears. When his kind voice whispered through swollen lips, "Father, forgive them," I cried out, "Savior, will you also forgive me?"

As I peered into the shadows of my mind, I saw the cross where they nailed his pure form. "How could they do this savage thing?" I demanded. Then a kind voice answered me, "Does not *your* sinfulness also cause my suffering?"

In contrition I responded, "Yes, my Lord, my own rebellion deepened the nail prints. I, too, left you to suffer alone." And repentant tears bathed his righteous feet.

Do we not all deepen his wounds with our separation? But still, we return to his side to receive his grace. It's time to forget our sins, as he does, and continue his work for reconciliation and peace in the world.

Prayer for Peace:

Reconciling God, we return to the wounded side of the Christ and open ourselves to your grace. May we then take our grace-filled lives and use them to share the peace of Christ with others in need of reconciliation.

Spiritual Practice for the Holy Week:

Prayerfully ponder the life of Christ. Spread your hands up and apart to release things that prevent you from holding Christ at the center of your life. Thank God for Christ who fills and feeds our spirit. Pray for a generous heart and open hands that reach out to make room for all in the circle of Christ's community.

Peace Covenant:

God, I will not leave people to suffer alone.

7
Saturday
April

Remembering the Forgotten

By Eileen Turner of Portland, Oregon, USA

> *God, the Eternal Creator, weeps for the poor, displaced, mistreated, and diseased of the world because of their unnecessary suffering. Such conditions are not God's will. Open your ears to hear the pleading of mothers and fathers in all nations who desperately seek a future of hope for their children. Do not turn away from them. For in their welfare resides your welfare.*
> —Doctrine and Covenants 163:4a

Each year during Holy Week I feel privileged to attend a memorial service at the Downtown Chapel in Portland. It always falls on my volunteer day, when I visit people in single-room-occupancy hotels. These are people who have become lost to their families or have become socially marginal.

An interfaith group organized by Operation Nightwatch puts together a memorial service for all those we know have died in the last year. Over time, many names that appear on the list are friends I have visited. Some die homeless on the street, some are victims of violence, and some suffer from poor personal choices and habits.

The service incorporates Catholic, Protestant, Jewish, Muslim, and Native American traditions. There is time for sharing, grieving, weeping, laughing, and memories. I find it appropriate that during this week, as we remember the death and resurrection of Jesus Christ, we can come together to share in the lives of the dead and the living in a meaningful way.

It says to those remaining that "you are not forgotten; you mean something to someone; you are to be honored and respected." Christ often was found among the socially marginal. He lived a radical compassion without thought to how he appeared to the elite and educated.

In a beautiful rendition of an Appalachian gospel song, "I Want Jesus to Walk with Me," the spirit of the message was that I would be safe and protected as long as I was about God's work. The forgotten and socially marginal are all around us and need whatever ministry we can offer.

Prayer for Peace:

Comfort of sufferers, may we seek and find those who need to be comforted. Where it is needed, let us work for justice and share the peace of Christ.

Spiritual Practice:

Sit where you can hear the sound of water—a fountain, stream, or the sea. Pray for God's blessing on all the parched places where there is injustice, oppression, or violence. Pray for God's justice to be released and imagine it flowing over the Earth, restoring righteousness and wholeness. Now, get up and drink a glass of clear, cold water as you pray, "God, let your justice flow through me as a disciple of the Lord Jesus."

Peace Covenant:

I will go to the uncomfortable margins and beyond to relieve suffering.

8
Sunday
April

We Have Seen the Lord

By Scott Murphy, Council of Twelve Apostles

> *Mary Magdalene went and announced to the disciples, "I have seen the Lord"; and she told them that he had said these things to her.*
>
> —John 20:18

When scripture becomes formational in our lives it flows from our capacity to see life and the human condition in the characters of the gospel story.

In John's Gospel witness, we find the story of Mary's encounter with the risen Christ at the empty tomb. In her despair and grief, Mary sees Jesus but does not *actually* see him. That is, until he says her name, "Mary!" That familiar sound opens her heart and life to see Jesus alive.

When I ponder Mary's experience, I realize that too many times I probably see but don't *actually* see the presence of the living Christ in my life. Yet, when the presence of God's Spirit does something in my life, that familiar presence opens my heart and eyes to the awareness that Christ is with me. In those moments of extraordinary surprise and joy, I experience God's gift of grace and hope.

When Mary received this extraordinary news of Jesus' new life, she went and proclaimed to the other disciples, "I have seen the Lord!" Mary's proclamation joined with the disciples' encounter with Jesus. That expanded the proclamation to, "*We* have seen the Lord!" As the Easter story unfolds in our lives, we become part of that expanding witness.

The tomb is empty. Christ is alive. He is present in the world. As disciples, we need to be intentional in seeing where Christ is working among us so we can say with great joy, "We have seen the Lord! Come and let us show you."

Prayer for Peace:

God, you make yourself known to us through your Son. You reveal where Christ is working among us and ask us to join you in sharing his peace. Thank you, God, for the presence of the living Christ.

Spiritual Practice for the Week: Honoring the Worth of All Persons

Each day this week read Psalm 139:13–18. After each reading sit quietly and let the deep meaning of the words sink into your mind, heart, and body. What thoughts and feelings do you have about being "fearfully and wonderfully made" (Psalm 139:14)?

Sense the intimate knowledge God has of you. Ask God for an awareness of the sacred worth of each person. How are you being invited to introduce the hope of Christ into the spiritual identity of all God's beloved people today? Pray for God's compassion.

Peace Covenant:

Today God, I will intentionally see Christ, listen to what he says, and follow where he leads.

9
Monday
April

God Is with Us through Highs and Lows

By Karen Hutchinson of Loveland, Colorado, USA

Finally, brothers and sisters, farewell. Put things in order, listen to my appeal, agree with one another, live in peace; and the God of love and peace will be with you. Greet one another with a holy kiss. All the saints greet you. The grace of the Lord Jesus Christ, the love of God, and the communion of the Holy Spirit be with all of you.

—2 Corinthians 13:11–13

The year 2010 was one of the most-difficult years I have lived. The highs and lows were extreme. I turned 70, and I struggled with that.

I am the oldest of four sisters. Early in the year doctors diagnosed one sister with pancreatic cancer. As she died, another sister was diagnosed with stage four lung cancer.

She is one of the 20 percent of lung-cancer patients who never have smoked, or even been around second-hand smoke. I felt this was unfair.

I never lived with such a feeling of total sorrow and loss as I felt in April and May. But at the time of this deep grief, our granddaughter was preparing for her wedding, and my husband and I were planning a trip for our 50th anniversary. Good friends shared with me in joys and sorrows.

I have never known what will be next in my life. Sometimes I wish I could live only with those high points, but that has never been the truth of life. This year made that point come into sharp focus. If I am honest with myself, I know my life needs to have both those highs and lows. That I can make it through reminds me I am a loved daughter of God.

I still grieve for my sisters, but I remember the good times. I love watching my granddaughter and her new husband as they establish their family. Life becomes enriching and joyous when I find the perspective of being loved. I am blessed!

Prayer for Peace:

God of love and peace, we bless you for your holy communion with us. We would live in your peace and bless one another in peace.

Spiritual Practice for the Week: Honoring the Worth of All Persons

Read Psalm 139:13–18. Sit quietly and let the deep meaning of the words sink into your mind, heart, and body. What thoughts and feelings do you have about being "fearfully and wonderfully made" (Psalm 139:14a)?

Sense the intimate knowledge God has of you and every child ever born. Ask God for an awareness of the sacred worth of each person. Weep with God over the soul-wounding forces and events that rob people of dignity and worth. How are you being invited to notice, protect, heal, and affirm the spiritual identity of all God's beloved people today? Pray for God's compassion.

Peace Covenant:

Today God, I will live through the *lows* in my life, remembering the *highs* will come. I will build up my compassion in this way.

10
Tuesday
April

Trust Restored

By Deb Crowley of Eaton Rapids, Michigan, USA

> *The effect of righteousness will be peace, and the result of righteousness, quietness and trust forever. My people will abide in a peaceful habitation, in secure dwellings, and in quiet resting places.*
>
> —Isaiah 32:17–18

A quiet, unassuming, shy minister was to give the sermon on a Sunday following a week of conflict in the congregation. Nerves were raw, everyone was on edge, trust was broken.

All this was the result of a series of e-mails that hurt individuals. Before long, sides were drawn, and an almost-visible line appeared down the aisle of the church. How could this unpretentious, quiet minister speak to the congregation in a way that might bring healing and reconciliation?

What followed was profound. He said that as he prayed in preparation for Sunday, he sensed the Holy Spirit urging him how to share. He set a telephone and toy car on the podium.

He stated that everyone with a computer ought to have a computer-smashing party! Then they should pick up the phone or get in their car, drive to one another's home, and talk—in person, by phone, face to face, or one on one.

Above all, he counseled that God wept for their pain.

They must not let their differences separate them, and they must remember that with love in action, wounds would heal, and the people would be helped toward wholeness.

There are times God surprises us by using the most-unexpected, untrained, shyest characters to remind us of what matters most. Jesus chose fishermen, tax collectors, those with no college degrees, no standing in political circles or the religious realm. Simple, hard-working men who said, "yes" and followed Jesus.

So watch out! Once the Holy Spirit empowers us, an awesome journey begins!

Prayer for Peace:

Creator God, make us humble servants who listen to your word. Send us companions who heal us on our journey, who face us one on one and teach us the ways of peace and reconciliation.

Spiritual Practice for the Week: Honoring the Worth of All Persons

Read Psalm 139:13–18. After each reading sit quietly and let the deep meaning of the words sink into your mind, heart, and body. Sense the intimate knowledge God has of you and every child. Be aware of the sacred worth of each person. Weep with God over the soul-wounding forces and events that rob people of dignity and worth. How are you invited to protect, heal, and affirm the spiritual identity of others? Pray for God's compassion.

Peace Covenant:

Today, God, I will use my voice, my eyes, my smile, and my touch to heal brokenness.

11
Wednesday
April

Truth and Peace

By Lillian Kirby of Blue Springs, Missouri, USA

These are the things that you shall do: Speak the truth to one another, render in your gates judgments that are true and make for peace…

—Zechariah 8:16

The aroma of incense filled our nostrils. Organ music and bells chimed sacred tunes from lofty spires. A professional soloist's aria swelled melodiously through the sun's rays, which cascaded on us from multihued stained-glass windows.

This was our first family trip to Washington, D.C., and we were visiting the Episcopal Church's National Cathedral.

We were searching for a small statue of Abraham Lincoln, kneeling in prayer in the fields of Gettysburg. I doubted we would find it among all the building projects and magnificent services taking place that Sunday.

But as we were leaving one service, someone spotted the white-marble statue, carefully elevated in a niche in a wall. The sculptor had caught the image of a president who, although not a member of any church, was deeply religious and often kneeled to pray over his weighty decisions.

May we pray, like many leaders around the world, for the strength to make responsible choices.

Prayer for Peace:

God of truth, may we practice truth in love. May we prayerfully discern what you would have us do to share Christ's peace.

Spiritual Practice for the Week: Honoring the Worth of All Persons

Read Psalm 139:13–18. Sit quietly and let the deep meaning of the words sink into your mind, heart, and body. What thoughts and feelings do you have about being "fearfully and wonderfully made" (Psalm 139:14a)?

Sense the intimate knowledge God has of you and every child ever born. Ask God for an awareness of the sacred worth of each person. Weep with God over the soul-wounding forces and events that rob people of dignity and worth. How are you being invited to notice, protect, heal, and affirm the spiritual identity of all God's beloved people today? Pray for God's compassion.

Peace Covenant:

Today, God, I will live the truth in love.

12
Thursday
April

Spice up Your Prayer Life

By Joann Condit of Phoenix, Arizona, USA

> *God is calling for a prophetic community to emerge, drawn from the nations of the world, that is characterized by uncommon devotion to the compassion and peace of God revealed in Jesus Christ. Through divine grace and wisdom, this faith community has been given abundant gifts, resources, and opportunities to equip it to become such a people.*
> —Doctrine and Covenants 163:11a

Mother hated to make sandwiches.

But she made a daily lunch for my father during the long years he spent working in the Pacific Coast shipyards or building airfields. One day she used baloney, and that evening he told her she had made a good sandwich. It was a compliment he soon came to regret.

He got the same sandwich every day for at least six months before he complained. She replied in surprise that he said he *liked* baloney. His reply was direct, "Maysie, no one could like baloney every single day of their lives! It's *boring!*"

I think of that when I find common and repetitive tasks boring. I think of it when my eyes are blind to beauty. I think of it when my prayer life becomes a mere recitation, when I am grateful for the same things day after day, and when each Sunday service varies only by speaker and hymn choice. My spiritual life becomes boring, sad to say.

When I am bored and depressed in spirit, I change my place of daily prayer and the format of the prayer itself. I add new spiritual practices. I look for differences in services of worship and appreciate them. I look up and out at the diversity of this world. I try to make a difference in the lives of those I meet. With these differences, life becomes bright and new again, and the taste is various and good in my mouth.

Prayer for Peace:

God of all nations, may we delve into diverse ways of prayer and worship. May we be led in spiritual practices that deepen our relationship with you and your creation. May we pursue the many ways to share Christ's peace.

Spiritual Practice for the Week: Honoring the Worth of All Persons

Read Psalm 139:13–18. Sit quietly and let the deep meaning of the words sink into your mind, heart, and body. What thoughts and feelings do you have about being "fearfully and wonderfully made" (Psalm 139:14a)?

Sense the intimate knowledge God has of you and every child ever born. Ask God for an awareness of the sacred worth of each person. Weep with God over the soul-wounding forces and events that rob people of dignity and worth. How are you being invited to notice, protect, heal, and affirm the spiritual identity of all God's beloved people today? Pray for God's compassion.

Peace Covenant:

Today, God, I will pray a new prayer in a new place. I will pray deep and long.

13
Friday
April

Plain and Simple

By Flo McDonald of Lee's Summit, Missouri, USA

> *"For my yoke is easy, and my burden is light."*
>
> —Matthew 11:30

My mother liked to read Bible stories to us when we were small. She also read and told other stories that had a message. She laid a foundation for us to be able to understand we could express the love of God in what we do.

Years later I heard someone ask, "Why do the teachings in the Bible have to be so complicated?" I remembered it differently, having been taught the messages of the Bible are plain and simple.

My grandson's favorite Bible story was David and Goliath. He liked the idea that with God's help, little David—with a sling, a stone, and a strong faith in God—could beat the fearful giant of injustice. There is no match for the powerful help God can provide.

Let's take our discipleship seriously and teach our children simple, yet meaningful stories that enable them to understand God's word. They will be better equipped and able to respond to life's challenges. In this way their burden will be lightened.

Prayer for Peace:

Teacher God, we are thankful for your enlightening words. We are thankful for the direction you give. Open our minds so we may learn from our children who understand and are happy to learn of faith.

Spiritual Practice for the Week: Honoring the Worth of All Persons

Read Psalm 139:13–18. Sit quietly and let the deep meaning of the words sink into your mind, heart, and body. What thoughts and feelings do you have about being "fearfully and wonderfully made" (Psalm 139:14a)?

Sense the intimate knowledge God has of you and every child ever born. Ask God for an awareness of the sacred worth of each person. Weep with God over the soul-wounding forces and events that rob people of dignity and worth. How are you being invited to notice, protect, heal, and affirm the spiritual identity of all God's beloved people today? Pray for God's compassion.

Peace Covenant:

I will follow your directions, God, to the path of peace and justice.

14
Saturday
April

Emmanuel, God's Presence

By Brandon Stanley of Thompsonville, Illinois, USA

He went to him and bandaged his wounds, having poured oil and wine on them. Then he put him on his own animal, brought him to an inn, and took care of him. The next day he took out two denarii, gave them to the innkeeper, and said, "Take care of him; and when I come back, I will repay you whatever more you spend."

—Luke 10:34–35

My most-intense experiences as a World Service Corps volunteer took place at the Adela De Leon School in Cartagena, Colombia. I taught English to eager, fifth-grade students. We shared everything: language, games, songs, stories, dances, and poems.

The children saw far more than my skin color.

Though poor, they often expressed generosity and unconditional love by offering me their sandwiches or a bracelet. I felt God's presence every day. At the end of my stay, the students from each class wrote letters.

The messages from these new friends made it clear I had achieved my goals of creating mutual respect and inspiring understanding.

Your generous contributions to World Mission Tithes provide missionary outreach such as World Service Corps' ministry without borders. Thank you for giving generously.

Prayer for Peace:

Universal God, as we learn of the wonderful differences between the Earth's people, may our love grow for one another. May we be as good Samaritans to the stranger. As we discover our common ground, may we use it as a bridge for building peace.

Spiritual Practice:

An important spiritual practice for disciples is praying for members of the body of Christ, particularly those who carry leadership responsibilities. Ask God to guide your awareness to persons who lead the community of faith at congregational, mission center, and World Church levels.

See or sense these persons and ask for insight into any particular physical, emotional, or spiritual needs they may have. Pray for God's outpouring of grace on each servant leader who comes to mind.

Peace Covenant:

Today, God, I will sing songs, read stories, and dance dances of another country.

15
Sunday
April

Believe

By Linda Booth, Council of Twelve Apostles

When it was evening on that day, the first day of the week, and the doors of the house where the disciples had met were locked for fear of the Jews, Jesus came and stood among them and said, "Peace be with you." After he said this, he showed them his hands and his side. Then the disciples rejoiced when they saw the Lord. Jesus said to them again, "Peace be with you. As the Father has sent me, so I send you."

—John 20:19–21

When Thomas heard the other apostles had seen the resurrected Christ he announced that he needed visual and tactile proof to believe what they had seen. A week later Christ again appeared and offered Thomas the opportunity to see and believe.

When Thomas' fingers touched Christ's visible wounds, Thomas confessed, "My Lord and my God!" In that moment Christ blessed future generations that would never see him but would believe in his life, teachings, and resurrection because of the witness of others.

There is a new, growing Community of Christ congregation in Moss Point, Mississippi. It exists because of the witness of one woman named Geraldine, whose life showed the living Christ. When Geraldine started a new job, several co-workers jokingly told her if she stayed with them long enough she'd end up cussing like them.

Geraldine could have ignored them because their lifestyles were different from hers. Instead, she loved them, prayed with them, and showed them new life in Jesus Christ.

Because of her witness, Nedra and her daughters learned about Community of Christ, deepened their discipleship, and were baptized. As faithful disciples, Nedra's family shared its witness, and many more believed and were baptized. The Moss Point Community of Christ now has more than 40 disciples who show others that Christ lives.

As Christ's present-day disciples, we are called to continue to testify of Jesus Christ so that future generations will see, believe, and then witness to others.

Prayer for Peace:

Invisible God, we thank you for the witnesses of the past who have shown you to us. May we witness to others so they may believe.

Spiritual Practice for the Week: Examining God's Call to Me and to All

Reflect on God's call in your life. Begin by recalling experiences of God's presence and invitation. Journal or quietly reflect on images and insights that come. When has God seemed real in your life? When have you felt deeply connected and responsive to God's movement in your life? When have you felt disconnected or resistant to God's call? How do your gifts and callings connect with the call of God you notice in your family members, friends, congregation, or community?

Peace Covenant:

Today, God, I will share my testimony of the peace of Jesus Christ.

16
Monday
April

Pipe Dreams

By Richard Howard of Independence, Missouri, USA

The eyes of the Lord are on the righteous, and his ears are open to their cry. . . . When the righteous cry for help, the Lord hears, and rescues them from all their troubles. The Lord is near to the brokenhearted, and saves the crushed in spirit.

—Psalm 34:15, 17–18

What is a "pipe dream"? It is having hope where there is no hope. In prisons, confined sharp minds and suffering spirits fashion dreams of supplanting injustice.

Such a dream was at the heart of Martin Luther King Jr.'s April 1963 "Letter from Birmingham Jail."

To his colleague ministers, he wrote: "Let us all hope that the dark clouds of racial prejudice will soon pass away and the deep fog of misunderstanding will be lifted from our fear-drenched communities, and in some not too distant tomorrow the radiant stars of love and brotherhood will shine over our great nation with all their scintillating beauty."

During the 49 years since King wrote of that agonizing dream, several daring hints of such a blessed reality have sprung up in various parts of the world. The effect has been to nourish that dream.

We have seen strides made for equality for the women of the world. Work is being done to promote full and equal protection of persons and relationships regardless of sexual orientation under civil laws of many nations. Huge efforts are being made to rescue the world's children from the unspeakable terrors of human trafficking, malnutrition, disease, and poverty.

We see the beginning of freedom for churches, synagogues, and mosques across the world to champion causes of compassionate justice and to work for the rescue of the planet and all beings on it.

Deliberative bodies round the globe spend endless years and resources trying to build a safe path to justice and equity for their diverse constituencies. My pipe dream is that soon we will come to our senses, find courage, and just do it! This should qualify as an authentic pipe dream—hope where there otherwise is no hope.

Prayer for Peace:

God who presides over our reveries, breathe your Spirit into our actions, so that the worthiest of dreams may be fulfilled.

Spiritual Practice for the Week: Examining God's Call to Me and to All

Reflect on God's call for you. Recall particular moments when you have experienced God's presence and invitation. Write in your journal or quietly reflect on images and insights that come. When has God seemed most real in your life? How and when has God called you to use your energy and gifts? When have you felt most deeply connected and responsive to God?

Peace Covenant:

God, today I will just do it!

17
Tuesday
April

Midrash at Hospice with a Dog

By Joy Howard of Boston, Massachusetts, USA

> *Peace I leave with you; my peace I give to you. I do not give to you as the world gives. Do not let your hearts be troubled, and do not let them be afraid.*
>
> —John 14:27

A woman from church and fellow music lover, "E," is in hospice. E is the most-lively hospice patient I've ever known. She told me, "I know I'm terribly ill, I do; yet I'm so at peace. Why is that? Why am I not raging?"

Me: "Well, it's not like any of us gets to opt out of dying."

E: "That's right. Nobody gets out of here alive, do they? But I feel such peace! Maybe if I share my story, other people won't rage when it's their time to die."

Throughout our visit we marveled at Bach's cantatas, at the beautiful view, and the late-afternoon light. Lucy, my golden retriever, settled in for a nap on E's bed while E held her paw.

As the sun sank, E asked, "Do you have time to do me a favor?"

I said, "Sure." She fretted, so I added, "E, as long as I'm breathing, I have time." E sat bolt upright in bed, eyes wide, waved her arms, and said, "Oh! Oh! Yes! Write that down! As long as I'm breathing, I have time. *Yes!* That's it! Write it down!"

At the end of our visit, E wobbled into a standing position with the help of her walker. I leaned in and kissed her on the cheek to say good-bye. She apologized for not being able to hug me because she had to hang onto the walker with both hands. I said I'd be back.

She said, "Within the week! And not without Lucy!"

As Lucy and I walked back to the car, I thought about the space I had just been invited into. It was like a geological seam, this gap between E navigating the mysterious peace she feels at end of her life, and Lucy the dog, who knew what to do as soon as we crossed the threshold of the hospice.

In the Jewish tradition the word for mining this seam is *midrash*—exploring the story between the words.

I spent the whole afternoon in a midrash. There aren't words to describe how it felt. However, I can share some of the story with you.

After all, as long as I am breathing, I have time.

Prayer for Peace:

Comforting God, we are thankful that many times we *receive* a blessing from those we come to bless. We meet you at the place where there is peace.

Spiritual Practice for the Week: Examining God's Call to Me and to All

Reflect on God's call in your life. Recall particular moments when you experienced God's presence and invitation. Write in your journal or quietly reflect on images and insights that come. How can you use your gifts for all?

Peace Covenant:

Today, God, I will measure my time in breaths. I will fill my time with you.

18
Wednesday
April

The Congregation and Beyond

By Fred Clark of Independence, Missouri, USA

> *Who is wise and understanding among you? Show by your good life that your works are done with gentleness born of wisdom. ... But the wisdom from above is first pure, then peaceable, gentle, willing to yield, full of mercy and good fruits, without a trace of partiality or hypocrisy. And a harvest of righteousness is sown in peace for those who make peace.*
>
> —James 3:13, 17–18

My faith journey began more than 50 years ago when I met a young woman who attended Community of Christ. We married and soon were engaged in many activities in our congregation. We became involved in the lives of many children, youth, and adults in the congregation and beyond.

One day I received a call from church leaders, asking if I would be a representative to a not-for-profit corporation operated by another congregation. Before I knew it, I became president of a ministry running 12 buses.

We wanted to start a Sunday school bus service to pick up children. We started with one bus. Shortly it was two, and so on. I think we were picking up as many adults as children.

I will never forget the children. They looked to me as a friend and even invited me to their birthday parties. As they grew up, I performed their weddings and blessed their babies. My ministry has been greatly enriched as I have tried to bring ministry to all of God's children. May we seek God daily as we seek to build Christ's peace in the world.

Prayer for Peace:

God of gentle works and peaceful harvests, we would work with humility and wisdom to share the peace of Christ. Let us plant seeds of ministry that will bloom into crops of mercy, full of good fruits. Bless the work we do in your name.

Spiritual Practice for the Week: Examining God's Call to Me and to All

Reflect on God's call for you. Recall particular moments when you have experienced God's presence and invitation. Write in your journal or quietly reflect on images and insights that come. When has God seemed most real in your life? How and when has God called you to use your energy and gifts? When have you felt most deeply connected and responsive to God?

Peace Covenant:

Today, God, I will plant seeds of hope as I share the peace of Christ.

19
Thursday
April

Peace Begins with Me

By Martha McKain of Lamoni, Iowa, USA

For the mountains may depart and the hills be removed, but my steadfast love shall not depart from you, and my covenant of peace shall not be removed, says the Lord, who has compassion on you.

—Isaiah 54:10

Years ago, while attending a Sunday-night church service, a young family brought the ministry of music. I heard for the first time, "Let There Be Peace on Earth." I thought it was one of the most-beautiful songs I had heard in a long time. What a message it brings.

Today we still are looking for peace that escapes us.

Learning to live peaceably together takes a lot. Not long ago I was visiting with a businessman and told him I was going to spend a couple of weeks in Phoenix, Arizona, where three of my sons live with their families. I smiled and said I wanted to make sure they were living in peace, as I had taught them. He had a twinkle in his eye when he asked, "What if they are not?" My answer was, "I will love them anyway."

"I will love them anyway." Jesus taught and practiced unconditional love as part of his peace. We should keep the covenant of peace and practice it in our own lives by accepting one another where we are in our life's journey.

We may not understand one another's journeys, but all of us are part of God's creation, and we are accepted in that light. May all of our journeys of peace begin with us.

Prayer for Peace:

God of peace, I know that "if it is to be, it is up to me." May I do my part to fulfill the covenant of peace. May I no longer wait for someone else to start but be the next one to act.

Spiritual Practice for the Week: Examining God's Call to Me and to All

Reflect on God's call for you. Recall particular moments when you have experienced God's presence and invitation. Write in your journal or quietly reflect on images and insights that come. When has God seemed most real in your life? How and when has God called you to use your energy and gifts? When have you felt most deeply connected and responsive to God?

Peace Covenant:

God, I will no longer wait, for I know I must act now for your peace.

20
Friday
April

Faith of a Child

By Karin Blythe of Burlington, Iowa, USA

> *"And blessed are all the peacemakers, for they shall be called children of God."*
> —III Nephi 5:56

My entire life I was told that a child's faith is pure and innocent. It was the faith of a child that should be remembered and sought. I was resistant as I learned more about theology and religion.

It seemed that a child's understanding was not enough to fully encompass faithful expression.

But there is a subtle and deep mystery in the faith of a child. It was not the faith that had been inadequate, it was the metaphor I had developed that was incompatible with the intended message.

The mystery spilled over me as I casually took my niece into my arms for the first time. I loved her without reason, without explanation, without hesitation. Holding her changed me. Holding *any* child brings with it a relational experience beyond expression. As the holder, you are making a commitment to protect and care for a being who is absolutely vulnerable in every way.

Children emit a trust beyond compare; a trust that chooses to love without judgment and to completely rely on the arms that envelop them. I cannot imagine a more-beautiful, sensitive, and intimate expression of faith. For so many years I understood the faith of a child as blissful ignorance or willing naiveté. It is neither of those things.

The faith of a child is about love amid vulnerability and trust in the loving embrace of a being much greater than we could ever imagine. It's faith that knows without a doubt we are well cared for and that someone feels responsible for our well-being.

Prayer for Peace:

Creator God, we ask that our prayers for peace not be naive longings, but a condition that—with faith as a child—will come to pass.

Spiritual Practice for the Week: Examining God's Call to Me and to All

Reflect on God's call for you. Recall particular moments when you have experienced God's presence and invitation. Write in your journal or quietly reflect on images and insights that come. When has God seemed most real in your life? How and when has God called you to use your energy and gifts? When have you felt most deeply connected and responsive to God?

Peace Covenant:

Today, God, I will allow your mystery to spill over me and will respond to your call for peacemakers.

21
Saturday
April

"I Tell You This to Break Your Heart"

By Lu Mountenay of Independence, Missouri, USA

> *The earth, lovingly created as an environment for life to flourish, shudders in distress because creation's natural and living systems are becoming exhausted from carrying the burden of human greed and conflict.*
>
> —Doctrine and Covenants 163:4b

On the December 2009 cover of *Sojourners* magazine is a photograph that haunts me. It is the image of an underweight polar bear on a tiny ice floe.

The ice is barely big enough for his four feet, bunched together. His claws hang over the edge. He peers into his reflection in the water as if he is seeing his own ghost. He seems to be wondering, "If I jump in, can I make it to the next unseen ice floe?"

Tomorrow is Earth Day. We in Community of Christ, which claims the Sacredness of Creation as an enduring principle, may want to work toward recognizing *every* day as Earth Day. After we observe the measured disappearance of polar ice, watch with horror the results of oil spills in offshore waters, and hear of the destruction of wildlife because of poison in lakes and waterways, we should be ready to take action.

Listen to part of *Lead*, a Mary Oliver poem about the death of loons caused by lead in the water: "I tell you this to break your heart, by which I mean only that it break *open* and never close again to the rest of the world."

Today I'm thinking of the waters of the Gulf of Mexico and China, but it's happening all over the world. These waters, once teeming with life, shining with hope, *regulating* Earth's course with ebb and flow, have now been *deregulated*. They are compromised by greed.

Lift the coastline inhabitants to God's healing light—the fish, the birds, the mammals. The reptiles, the sand, the grass. The homes, the humans, and their sagging spirits. We have jeopardized the pristine for profit.

Poet Wendell Barry writes, "There are no unsacred places; there are only sacred places and desecrated places." Let us do whatever we can to exercise stewardship of our Earth.

Prayer for Peace:

Creating and sustaining God, we ask your help in working for a healthy, peaceful Earth. Help us look beyond ourselves to find opportunities to bring your balanced ecosystems back to their intended rhythm.

Spiritual Practice:

Place your hands over your face and eyes, pray for insight (pause in silence). Place your hands on your head and ask to be blessed with the mind of Christ (silence). Put your hands over your ears and listen to the needs around you (silence). Put both hands over your heart and ask to share God's compassion and peace (silence). Thank you, God. Amen.

Peace Covenant:

I will try to leave small footprints of large effect for the good of Earth.

22
Sunday
April

You Are My Witnesses

By Jim Slauter of Orlando, Florida, USA

While they were talking about this, Jesus himself stood among them and said to them, "Peace be with you." They were startled and terrified, and thought that they were seeing a ghost. He said to them, "Why are you frightened, and why do doubts arise in your hearts? Look at my hands and my feet; see that it is I myself... Then he said to them, "These are my words that I spoke to you while I was still with you—that everything written about me in the law of Moses, the prophets, and the psalms must be fulfilled." Then he opened their minds to understand the scriptures, and he said to them, "Thus it is written, that the Messiah is to suffer and to rise from the dead on the third day, and that repentance and forgiveness of sins is to be proclaimed in his name to all nations, beginning from Jerusalem. You are witnesses of these things.

—Luke 24:36–39, 44–48

I stood on the seashore of the Black Sea in Odessa, Ukraine, during an early Sunday-morning baptism service. We were a group of 15–20 people surrounded by several hundred beach-goers as the sun rose in the clear blue morning sky.

As we started to sing a song of preparation, I noticed the people around us began to quiet their conversations, play, and laughter. We entered the water and waded out. As we turned to face the small congregation, I was taken by the reverence of the other observers that had spread like a wave along the beach.

I wondered what their reverent respect meant. Were they believers who were excited about this event in complete strangers' lives while being reminded of the importance of their own baptism? Were they indifferent, but silently respectful while questioning the meaning of commitment in a secular world? Perhaps it was both of these.

I will never know what was in the minds of the onlookers; however, I can bear testimony of the power of the Holy Spirit present.

I am thankful to God for the Holy Spirit's power that was at work in the lives of the new disciples, the Odessa Congregation, and hopefully, in the hearts and minds of the reverent observers.

Like the disciples who encountered the living Christ, we, too, met him that morning on the seashore of the Black Sea and were blessed and challenged to willingly witness his peace in our world.

Prayer for Peace:

God on the seashore, God in our hearts, we have heard the risen Christ in your word, we have seen him in the deeds of disciples, we have felt him in spirit.

Spiritual Practice for the Week: Making Responsible Choices

Prayerfully seek God's guidance in your choices. Discernment invites us to orient our lives toward God. Review the responsibilities and opportunities of today. Ask God for wisdom and insight about what matters most. Sit prayerfully with this question. Live this day responsibly and compassionately in the spirit of Christ.

Peace Covenant:

Today, God, I will witness to the curious and turn curiosity into belief.

23
Monday
April

God Is Good

By Merna Short of Melbourne, Victoria, Australia

> *"The Spirit of the Lord is upon me, because he has anointed me to bring good news to the poor. He has sent me to proclaim release to the captives and recovery of sight to the blind, to let the oppressed go free, to proclaim the year of the Lord's favor."*
>
> —Luke 4:18–19

Australia saw many natural disasters over the winter and spring of 2011. Dreadful floods hit Queensland and spread down the east coast, ruining towns, farms, and the landscape. Initial losses totaled billions of dollars. Added to this was the loss of livelihood of thousands of people.

Then cyclones came. The northeast Australia coast and 100 miles inland were affected, and the aftermath also was felt through the center and south of the continent.

Following this were two more cyclones in the northwest and southwest. At this same time a devastating earthquake rocked our New Zealand neighbors. Looking down the months and years it will take to normalize life, I thought of the saying, "How do you climb a mountain? One step at a time."

I have never believed God sends these disasters as punishment. They are part of the cycles of life on this planet. I happened to be reading a study of Jeremiah. It was very uplifting. In it the author says not to get God and life mixed up.

God is not our source of trouble. God is all good. The Divine is our help in times of trouble. I'm sure there will be openings to witness of this over the months ahead. God gives us hope.

Prayer for Peace:

Creator God, we know you weep with us when struggles overwhelm us. We know your comforting Spirit is always with us. Help us look beyond our troubles and recognize your presence, right here, walking beside us and sometimes before us. Wrap us in your arms of peace.

Spiritual Practice for the Week: Making Responsible Choices

Each day this week prayerfully seek God's guidance in your choices. Discernment invites us to orient our lives toward God and God's vision for us and for creation. Begin by reviewing the responsibilities and opportunities in the day before you. Take these choices into prayer, asking God for wisdom and insight about what matters most.

Offer yourself to God with the prayer of Teresa of Avila: "God, what do you want of me today?" Sit prayerfully with this question as you review the day again. Be aware of images, thoughts, names, or actions that come to you. Ask for blessing to live this day responsibly and compassionately in the spirit of Christ.

Peace Covenant:

Today, God, I will look beyond the darkness to see your rainbow of hope.

24
Tuesday
April

Peace Restored

By Shirley Remmenga of Fort Collins, Colorado, USA

But the wisdom from above is first pure, then peaceable, gentle, willing to yield, full of mercy and good fruits, without a trace of partiality or hypocrisy.

—James 3:17

An administrator and an employee at my office were disagreeing on terms of a contract. Both were unhappy and unable to communicate.

I had taken some peacemaking and conflict-resolution classes, so I decided to contact each of them. I invited them to a meeting where they would have a chance to air their complaints, listen to each other, and perhaps develop a plan that would satisfy them both.

Each agreed to try. We met, we listened, and they told their stories. We found a reasonable solution, restoring peace between them.

All three of us were grateful God's peace had been present with us. Good communication, I believe, is essential to the peace process. Good communication doesn't happen until we listen to one another.

Listening is even more impartial and full of mercy if we listen to God.

Prayer for Peace:

Gentle God of wisdom, let your mercy flow among us. Help us express ourselves with gentleness and listen to one another with patience. Form us into beings who can collaborate on the path to peace.

Spiritual Practice for the Week: Making Responsible Choices

Each day this week prayerfully seek God's guidance in your choices. Discernment invites us to orient our lives toward God and God's vision for us and for creation. Begin by reviewing the responsibilities and opportunities in the day before you. Take these choices into prayer, asking God for wisdom and insight about what matters most.

Offer yourself to God with the prayer of Teresa of Avila: "God, what do you want of me today?" Sit prayerfully with this question as you review the day again. Be aware of images, thoughts, names, or actions that come to you. Ask for blessing to live this day responsibly and compassionately in the spirit of Christ.

Peace Covenant:

Today, God, I will listen with an open mind to the ideas of others.

25
Wednesday
April

PAX Reinforces: All Are God's Children

By Anita Wilson of Charlotte, Michigan, USA

> *For in him all the fullness of God was pleased to dwell, and through him God was pleased to reconcile to himself all things, whether on earth or in heaven, by making peace…*
> —Colossians 1:19–20

There are now four Community of Christ members in our PAX (Program of Academic Exchange) organization. Marty received her five-year award last night. I was so pleased because I brought her on board. Sarah, from the Richmond Congregation in Virginia, got her first-year welcome.

I have been with PAX six years, and my sister is in her eighth year. Together we share a strong testimony of the church's call to bring peace to the world through our work in PAX.

It isn't easy work. During the year we deal with problems with host families, students, and government regulations. We often are challenged with the role of peacemaker when plans don't go well, but we use good mediating skills to help us cope.

We are all passionate about what we are doing. We feel blessed to have the opportunity to extend our ministry in this way.

Our work is a powerful testimony that God is at work in the world. God calls each of us to look at those with whom we share this planet, those who may have—at one time—not understood the diverse population with which God has blessed the world.

My weekend with my PAX family and with my Community of Christ sisters who share this work has strengthened my faith. We stand strong in our commitment to be an ensign of peace to a world filled with struggles and cultural misunderstandings. We promote the acceptance of all people regardless of differences. All are God's children.

Prayer for Peace:

God of all nations, where there is misunderstanding, let us bring light. Where there are those who are socially marginal, let us bring the reconciliation of Christ's peace.

Spiritual Practice for the Week: Making Responsible Choices

Each day this week prayerfully seek God's guidance in your choices. Discernment invites us to orient our lives toward God and God's vision for us and for creation. Begin by reviewing the responsibilities and opportunities in the day before you. Take these choices into prayer, asking God for wisdom and insight about what matters most.

Offer yourself to God with the prayer of Teresa of Avila: "God, what do you want of me today?" Sit prayerfully with this question as you review the day again. Be aware of images, thoughts, names, or actions that come to you. Ask for blessing to live this day responsibly and compassionately in the spirit of Christ.

Peace Covenant:

Today, God, with Christ dwelling in my heart, I will continue my peace journey.

26
Thursday
April

Serving the Neighbors We Have

By Cindy Korf of North Platte, Nebraska, USA

All this is from God, who reconciled us to himself through Christ, and has given us the ministry of reconciliation; that is, in Christ God was reconciling the world to himself, not counting their trespasses against them, and entrusting the message of reconciliation to us.

—2 Corinthians 5:18–19

It had snowed again—six inches! Once again the church sidewalks and parking lot needed to be shoveled. This is no easy task with our church campus covering three city blocks.

I went with my husband to remove snow from the sidewalks, parking lot, and stairs. He used a snowblower, while I used a scoop shovel on the stairs.

After an hour of shoveling snow in the cold, I was ready to go home. But, much to my surprise and irritation, my husband pushed the snowblower across the street to a neighbor's house. The people had been standing inside, watching us work for an hour.

Then, he started to blow the snow off their sidewalk! And their driveway! He blew the snow off the sidewalk for the entire block.

I couldn't believe he would help "those" people!

Those were the people who parked in the church parking lot—even in front of the door on Sunday morning. Those were the people who left broken beer bottles in the parking lot and on the lawn that we had to pick up every Sunday morning.

And today they stared at us, never offering to help.

That was when the Spirit tenderly chastised me by bringing the words of the hymn, "Yesu, Yesu" to my mind—"show us how to serve the neighbors we have…"

"Those people" were our neighbors. They were the neighbors we are to serve. And that was exactly what my husband was doing.

Prayer for Peace:

Reconciling God, let us live by Christ's example—not judging, not holding grudges. We simply would love as we are called to do. We would practice peace.

Spiritual Practice for the Week: Making Responsible Choices

Each day this week prayerfully seek God's guidance in your choices. Discernment invites us to orient our lives toward God and God's vision for us and for creation. Begin by reviewing the responsibilities and opportunities in the day before you. Take these choices into prayer, asking God for wisdom and insight about what matters most.

Offer yourself to God with the prayer of Teresa of Avila: "God, what do you want of me today?" Sit prayerfully with this question as you review the day again. Be aware of images, thoughts, names, or actions that come to you. Ask for blessing to live this day responsibly and compassionately in the spirit of Christ.

Peace Covenant:

Today, God, I will practice peace where I have been impatient before.

27
Friday
April

To Be a Disciple

By Norma Cross of Independence, Missouri, USA

> *Do not be discouraged. You have not been promised an easy path, but you have been assured that the Spirit that calls you will also accompany you. That Spirit is even now touching alive the souls of those who feel the passion of discipleship burning deeply within. Many others will respond if you are persistent in your witness and diligent in your mission to the world.*
>
> —Doctrine and Covenants 162:3a–b

I will never forget the anxiety that came over me when I felt a strong call to serve God. I prayed deeply, because I knew I always wanted to serve in that way. I listened, but I said, "Oh, no, I'm not ready to represent you."

With guilt I remembered God calls because of who we are and how we can serve God's people, not for our own comfort.

God called Saul, who had a dedication to what he thought was God's message, but not necessarily to Christ's mission. At first this call was not agreeable to him. Then God saw him change to Paul, a fervent and dedicated disciple.

Peter, as a fisherman, understood the strain of daily toil with heavy nets to earn his bread. He became a devotedly strong fisher of men. John, the beloved, the humble—could it be that Jesus called him because he needed comfort and to feel loved, when it was usually Jesus giving the love.

When we worry about not being ready we must remember God sees each of us as having great worth.

We ask God to lead and direct us to what ministry God has for us to do this day. Be persistent in your witness to the world.

Prayer for Peace:

Broken-hearted God, we confess our need for forgiveness. We often have failed in our discipleship, and yet you love us.

Spiritual Practice for the Week: Making Responsible Choices

Each day this week prayerfully seek God's guidance in your choices. Discernment invites us to orient our lives toward God and God's vision for us and for creation. Begin by reviewing the responsibilities and opportunities in the day before you. Take these choices into prayer, asking God for wisdom and insight about what matters most.

Offer yourself to God with the prayer of Teresa of Avila: "God, what do you want of me today?" Sit prayerfully with this question as you review the day again. Be aware of images, thoughts, names, or actions that come to you. Ask for blessing to live this day responsibly and compassionately in the spirit of Christ.

Peace Covenant:

God, having been forgiven, I covenant anew with you to continue in your service and humbly share the peace of Christ.

28
Saturday
April

Walk Humbly with God

By Karin Peter of Adrian, Missouri, USA

> *"So I say to you, Ask, and it will be given you; search, and you will find; knock, and the door will be opened for you. For everyone who asks receives, and everyone who searches finds, and for everyone who knocks, the door will be opened.*
>
> —Luke 11:9–10

April 19, 2009, is a day LeGenda Ruffins and family will always remember. That was the day of her ordination to the office of deacon at the Moss Point Congregation in Mississippi.

LeGenda is among several emerging leaders responding faithfully to God's call by developing ministry skills through programs such as MEADS (Ministerial Education and Discipleship Studies) offered at International Headquarters.

LeGenda believes the programs opened doors for her and allowed her to develop her ministry skills, helping her become more in tune with the needs of others. She is happy for the opportunity to deepen her commitment to the church and to share the peace of Jesus Christ in ways that will minister to the Moss Point community.

LeGenda greets each day with a smile, peaceful in the knowledge that she walks humbly with God as she provides ministry.

If you visit the Moss Point Congregation, she will be there to offer outstanding ministry, thanks to your contributions to World Mission Tithes, which provide training through the MEADS program. Thank you for responding and sharing generously to enable the continuation of programs like this.

Prayer for Peace:

God of knowledge and wisdom, we thank you for the encouragement to ask for help. We thank you for the guidance to search for ways to serve you. May we learn with humility and share our knowledge with others seeking peace.

Spiritual Practice:

In many languages, God's name contains the sound "ahhh," a sound we make when we are breathing out or sighing. Our prayer will use the ahh names for God with a gentle arm movement that opens us to God's presence. Begin with hands in front of you at chest level and move them up and in a large arc or circle as you breathe out each name for God.

You may speak the name of God or find a single musical note to hold or chant as you sing God's name. Pray or sing each name several times as you call on the God of many names: Yahweh, Adonai, Jehovah, Yeshua, Sophia, Allah, Alpha, Omega. Say or sing "amen" to close.

Peace Covenant:

Today God, I study for peace, being open to your spirit of enlightenment.

29
Sunday
April

Jesus, the Good Shepherd

By Dave Brown, Presiding Bishopric

> *I am the good shepherd. I know my own and my own know me, just as the Father knows me and I know the Father. And I lay down my life for the sheep.*
>
> —John 10:14–15

The Community of Christ congregation where I grew up met in a large room in city hall. We didn't have our own building until I was about 13 years old. We acquired a house to use as our "church."

Even without a traditional church building to meet in I felt like I was part of a community. They asked me to pass out bulletins as people arrived and to help receive the offering. Sometimes I would read a scripture or a story as part of the service. The members of the congregation accepted me as a developing disciple.

As I've thought about my experiences as a child and youth in the church it has become clear to me that what was important was being a part of the community and not so much where we met.

In this passage from John, Jesus tells us that he is the good shepherd, and that he will lay down his life for us.

He also invites us into community by providing the context for his role as the good shepherd.

We cannot truly know Jesus until we know each other. And that is how we create community—by making the effort to know each other in ways that are deeper than just names and greeting one another on Sunday.

When we receive someone else's gifts with joy, as my congregation did with me, we know them better than we did before. The cycle of receiving and sharing with one another helps us all grow in discipleship and create community in Christ.

Prayer for Peace:

Gentle Shepherd, you know us. As we come to know and love our community, we know and love you. As we learn the way of the disciple, we will know the way of peace.

Spiritual Practice for the Week: Embodying God's Shalom

Each day this week find a way to express and embody God's shalom. Begin by prayerfully listening to your longing for peace. Become silent and imagine you can hear the groaning of the Earth's peoples, nations, and creatures.

Prayerfully open yourself to God's yearning for peace and the divine vision of shalom. What images, feelings, and words come to you? What prayer for peace comes to you from your time of listening? Speak or write this prayer. What small act of justice, kindness, healing, or peacemaking is God inviting you to consider this day, this week?

Peace Covenant:

Today, God, I will intentionally get to know the young people around me. I will express my thankfulness for them.

30
Monday
April

It's Never too Late

By Linda Porter of Wiarton, Ontario, Canada

> *"You are the light of the world. A city built on a hill cannot be hid. No one after lighting a lamp puts it under the bushel basket, but on the lampstand, and it gives light to all in the house. In the same way, let your light shine before others, so that they may see your good works and give glory to your Father in heaven."*
>
> —Matthew 5:14–16

On a beautiful spring day, I discovered an old metal pail sitting upside down in a bed of lily of the valley.

When I turned the pail over I discovered underneath some pale, skinny, spindly plants searching for sunshine.

Over the next few days I watched the plants slowly become stronger, greener, and sturdier as they soaked up the much-needed light. Would they ever flower? Would they ever reach their potential, or had the light come too late?

I thought of the pail and how thoughtlessly it had been tossed by the fence last fall, no one aware of its impact on these struggling plants. How thoughtlessly, without realizing the barriers to the light our actions may cause.

Are there barriers you and I can remove to allow someone to come into the light of Christ? Is it too late to start, or can we still be a light of welcome in our community?

Is there someone today with whom you need to share the light of Christ?

Prayer for Peace:

God of light, may we be ever mindful of opportunities to share your radiance, warmth, and love. May we welcome all to your sanctuaries of peace.

Spiritual Practice for the Week: Embodying God's Shalom

Each day this week find a way to express and embody God's shalom. Begin by prayerfully listening to your longing for peace. Become silent and imagine you can hear the groaning of Earth's peoples, nations, and creatures. Prayerfully open yourself to God's yearning for peace and the divine vision of shalom.

What images, feelings, and words come to you? What prayer for peace comes to you from your time of listening? Speak or write this prayer. What small act of justice, kindness, healing, or peacemaking is God inviting you to consider this day, this week?

Peace Covenant:

Today, God, I will look for ways to uncover the good that is hidden so I may share your peace.

1
Tuesday
May

I Can't Wait to Get Back to Camp!

By Tori Simpson of Independence, Missouri, USA

"Blessed are the peacemakers, for they will be called children of God."
—Matthew 5:9

My name is Tori, and I'm 11 years old. Summer camp is my favorite thing. I've gone to camp every year since I was old enough. The first year of junior camp I made a special friend named Amelia. When we left camp, I knew I would miss her a lot.

The next year just before camp, I asked my mom if she thought Amelia would be there, and if she would remember me. My mom asked, "Well, do you remember her?" "Of course," I said. My mom said, "Well, I'm sure she'll remember you." So I felt better, and couldn't wait to get back to camp.

When I saw Amelia, we were a little shy at first, but after about five minutes, we were best friends again. My mom and my grandma both said that some of their best friends were ones they met at camp.

I am thankful for campership money that helps kids like me go to camp. I'm thankful for the counselors. Mostly, I'm thankful to God for good friends like Amelia.

Prayer for Peace:

Loving Parent, we are thankful for the blessings of community. Bless the children who cherish the simple things we often overlook. May we learn peace-sharing from them.

Spiritual Practices for the Week: Embodying God's Shalom

Each day this week find a way to express and embody God's shalom. Begin by prayerfully listening to your longing for peace. Become silent and imagine you can hear the groaning of Earth's peoples, nations, and creatures. Prayerfully open yourself to God's yearning for peace and the divine vision of shalom.

What images, feelings, and words come to you? What prayer for peace comes to you from your time of listening? Speak or write this prayer. What small act of justice, kindness, healing, or peacemaking is God inviting you to consider this day, this week?

Peace Covenant:

Today, God, I will look up an old friend from camp or childhood and make a connection.

2
Wednesday
May

Light up My Life

By Cindy Korf of North Platte, Nebraska, USA

"You are the light of the world. A city built on a hill cannot be hid. No one after lighting a lamp puts it under the bushel basket, but on the lampstand, and it gives light to all in the house. In the same way, let your light shine before others, so that they may see your good works and give glory to your Father in heaven."

—Matthew 5:14–16

I have a box of candles in my cupboard to use if the electricity goes off. However, I have never lit them. Even though I have candles, without a flame they give no light.

At times I am like those candles. I think that I am a "light" to the world, but I have no flame. I go through the motions of being "good" and thinking I am doing what I am supposed to do, but in actuality, I am just an unlit candle sitting in the box.

Without the spirit of Christ sparking my flame, the "light" is hidden, covered under a bushel basket.

To light my candles, I need a flame. To light my life, I need Christ, who causes my light to shine for others.

Prayer for Peace:

God of light, shine through us. Help us to stay luminous with your Spirit brightly glowing in our everyday tasks. May our beam be held high so your glory will be known. May we be filled with Christ-like radiance and illuminate the way to peace.

Spiritual Practice for the Week: Embodying God's Shalom

Each day this week find a way to express and embody God's shalom. Begin by prayerfully listening to your longing for peace. Become silent and imagine you can hear the groaning of Earth's peoples, nations, and creatures. Prayerfully open yourself to God's yearning for peace and the divine vision of shalom.

What images, feelings, and words come to you? What prayer for peace comes to you from your time of listening? Speak or write this prayer. What small act of justice, kindness, healing, or peacemaking is God inviting you to consider this day, this week?

Peace Covenant:

I will not hide your light, God. I will let it shine brightly in my life.

3
Thursday
May

Beyond the Call: Around the Clock

By Deb Crowley of Eaton Rapids, Michigan, USA

> *Keep on doing the things that you have learned and received and heard and seen in me, and the God of peace will be with you.*
>
> —Philippians 4:9

How easy it would have been to ignore the answering machine or not answer the cell phone when the number rang. After all, this was not a new dilemma. Hours spent counseling, lending support, encouraging, supplying food, transporting, and still the caller needed more!

Reluctantly, the pastor responded to the call. This time it was to provide transportation to a mental-health facility. Not the first time. But when one is depressed, it's hard to make yourself do anything, let alone apply for unemployment, seek medical assistance, or even drive to the pharmacy to get your medications. The frustrated pastor wondered if it was all for naught—again!

He took the lost soul to the hospital for evaluation. Sitting in the waiting room, the restless pastor began thinking of all the tasks he could be doing during the few hours he sat there. Precious hours and so much needing attention!

Finally, the hospital would provide transportation for the man to another facility for admission. The pastor thought he was free to go. But, no! The patient requested the pastor stay and travel with him.

Angst and frustration filled the pastor while he begrudgingly rehearsed options in his head.

Suddenly, words floated through his mind as if whispered from above, "I will not leave you nor forsake you." It was a gentle but stern reminder of God's unconditional generosity, to always be available, to never leave, and to be on call around the clock.

The answer was clear. The pastor, humbled and forgiven, accompanied the patient to his home for the next few weeks. Change the world—be unconditionally generous!

Prayer for Peace:

Generous God, so often we ask for your patience and yet refuse to give it to others. Help us open our hearts, God, and never let them close to the call to share the peace of Christ.

Spiritual Practice for the Week: Embodying God's Shalom

Find a way to express and embody God's shalom. Become silent and imagine you can hear the groaning of the Earth's people, nations, and creatures. Open yourself to God's vision of shalom. What images, feelings, and words come to you? What act of justice, kindness, healing, or peacemaking is God inviting you to consider this day, this week?

Peace Covenant:

Today, God, I will go beyond what is expected of me and serve another.

4
Friday
May

My Foundation

By Linda Lyons of Kansas City, Kansas, USA

Mark the blameless, and behold the upright, for there is posterity for the peaceable.
—Psalm 37:37

My daughter called early one morning and said her car was acting up. She wanted to know if I would take her to work. Sure, what are mothers for? When I picked her up in the afternoon, I realized I was low on fuel. I had just had rotator cuff surgery, so I asked her to pump the fuel. Her workplace was in a rough neighborhood.

As she pumped, the store clerk came running out saying we had not paid. Yet, we used a credit card and thought we had already paid. The clerk said he put the wrong pump number in the register, and we got the fuel before the credit card had registered. But we had no way to know that. We were worried we might be charged twice.

We went into the store to work the problem out. One thing led to another, and soon the clerk was shouting at us, claiming we had stolen the fuel. A woman tried to give me the money, saying "Please give him this and get out of here." She feared for our safety.

My daughter and I stayed calm and called the police to help us sort things out. We wanted to make peace with the clerk. The customer-service representative from the credit card company was not helpful.

The next day, as the police suggested, I confirmed that the card had been accessed but not charged. My daughter, my husband, and I went back to the station and paid the clerk the money owed.

Several days later a friend asked if I was scared. I thought about it and, said, "No, I was never afraid because I knew God was with us." My friend said I have the right foundation.

Prayer for Peace:

Foundation of our strength, may we always be aware of your presence. May we be cautious, but not fearful. May we practice peace wherever we find ourselves.

Spiritual Practice for the Week: Embodying God's Shalom

Each day this week find a way to express and embody God's shalom. Begin by prayerfully listening to your longing for peace. Become silent and imagine you can hear the groaning of Earth's peoples, nations, and creatures. Prayerfully open yourself to God's yearning for peace and the divine vision of shalom.

What images, feelings, and words come to you? What prayer for peace comes to you from your time of listening? Speak or write this prayer. What small act of justice, kindness, healing, or peacemaking is God inviting you to consider this day, this week?

Peace Covenant:

God, I will trust in you and look to you for my strength.

5
Saturday
May

Walk among the Wounded

By Peggy Michael of Cantonment, Florida, USA

"You have heard that it was said, 'You shall love your neighbor and hate your enemy.' But I say to you, Love your enemies and pray for those who persecute you, so that you may be children of your Father in heaven; for he makes his sun rise on the evil and on the good, and sends rain on the righteous and on the unrighteous. For if you love those who love you, what reward do you have? Do not even the tax collectors do the same? And if you greet only your brothers and sisters, what more are you doing than others? Do not even the Gentiles do the same? Be perfect, therefore, as your heavenly Father is perfect.

—Matthew 5:43–48

Beloved Creator, I'm thankful for the times you have allowed me to touch the hand of Christ. I yearn to walk among the wounded, gather them in my arms and comfort them.

God, because you reached out to me, I see the need to share the peace of Christ and his redeeming love.

I want to know how to be a friend to the outcast who are lonely and afraid. I want your love to reveal itself through me as I hold their hands and call them by name.

I will share the peace of Christ so we can work together for peace in our world, so there will be no more wounded or outcast.

Prayer for Peace:

God, how awesome you are. I have only to hold out my hand, and there you are, reaching back. I have only to listen, and you speak. I have only to repent, and my heart warms to your grace. I sing, and you accept my praise. God give me strength to use my hands and voice to work for your peace.

Spiritual Practice:

God promises healing for our wounds and losses. Hold (or imagine holding) a pinch of ashes in your hands as you become aware of situations in your life, family, congregation, and world that are broken, lost, or falling apart. Be honest with God about the fear, sadness, or burden you feel. Offer the ashes to God in prayer. Ask God to create beauty, peace, and healing in the places and people who now experience the ashes of despair and grief.

Peace Covenant:

Send others who need a hand, and I will witness of you, God.

6
Sunday
May

Share Boldly

By Jane Gardner, High Priest Quorum president

Then Philip...proclaimed to him the good news about Jesus. As they were going along the road, they came to some water; and the eunuch said, "Look, here is water! What is to prevent me from being baptized?" He commanded the chariot to stop, and both of them, Philip and the eunuch, went down into the water, and Philip baptized him.

—Acts 8:35–38

Twice in the story of Philip and the Ethiopian eunuch, Philip listens to the Holy Spirit and promptly and boldly responds.

First, he changes his route based on the Spirit's direction and comes upon the Ethiopian. Then, at the Spirit's prompting, he shares the good news about Jesus, resulting in the Ethiopian's baptism and "rejoicing."

"Sharing boldly" has been key in the work on the new hymnal for the church.

This collection of poetry and music has a particular goal of expressing Community of Christ's identity, mission, message, and beliefs for our time and into the future. A tall order! One that depends heavily on the Spirit's promptings.

We have been blessed by an outpouring of texts and music to help with this task. At a recent conference of the Hymn Society, we had the privilege of hearing a presentation titled, "A Cry for Justice in Hymnody." One conclusion was a plea for more texts to be written that help us sing about "real-life experiences."

Some lacking areas were real children with real problems, courage and hope for our last days, celebration of abilities rather than disabilities, practicing our faith without degrading other faiths, marginalized people, and women's issues and images.

Based on this session, we could sense the "rightness" of our struggle to find texts to express our denomination's unique and sacred calling. We affirm that this new collection will "share boldly" and help us sing our theology and beliefs, even when these might be perceived as countercultural or radical.

We pray the Spirit's direction and prompting will continue to guide and help us as we strive to be like Philip and boldly state our convictions, in this case, through song.

Prayer for Peace:

Hear our hymns of praise, O God. Our songs are one way we understand you and relate to you; how we thank you and witness of you; how we cry to you for peace and justice in our world.

Spiritual Practice for the Week: Welcoming Unity in Diversity

Each day this week meditate on unity in diversity. Prayerfully read Doctrine and Covenants 163:8c. Create a large circle with your arms. See and feel the diverse people God invites inside the sanctuary of Christ's peace represented by this circle. Who is easiest to welcome? Whom do you struggle to include? Ask God to forgive and heal barriers that keep you and others from being one in Christ's peace.

Peace Covenant:

Today, God, I will sing a new song of peace and justice.

7
Monday
May

A Good Day

By Joe Anway of Independence, Missouri, USA

> *And there came a voice to them, a pleasant voice, as if it were a whisper, saying, "Peace, peace be to you because of your faith in my well beloved, who was from the foundation of the world."*
>
> —Helaman 2:112

In 1956 I was in Independence, Missouri, during World Conference. I had been a member of the church for four years, however, I had experienced deep-seated disappointments. As a result I had decided it would be best to disassociate myself from the church altogether.

I heard that Apostle Donald O. Chesworth was scheduled to preach during the Conference. He was one of my favorite ministers. I decided to attend the service, planning to make it my last act with the church.

I took my place in the Conference Chamber and listened attentively. He was a man of great energy and enthusiasm. But, I was still intent on canceling my church membership.

Not long into the sermon, I became aware something was happening in that sacred space. I could feel a presence I had never experienced. I was aware I was not alone in these feelings. I found myself so filled with what I felt was the Spirit of God that tears flowed freely down my cheeks. I could see others were experiencing the Spirit, too.

At this point Apostle Chesworth departed from his prepared sermon and said he was aware we were *experiencing* the ministry of angels. I don't remember anything else said after that, but I was so full of the Spirit that all thoughts of walking away from the church were forever gone.

I rushed home following the service with a strong impulse to get on my knees and make my life commitment to God's service. Later, I wrote in my scriptures some words that are still there but very faintly now after 56 years: "April 11, 1956—A Good Day."

Prayer for Peace:

Foundation of our faith, whisper to us of your Beloved. He is *our* Beloved, also. We would share his ministry of peace with the world.

Spiritual Practice for the Week: Welcoming Unity in Diversity

Meditate on unity in diversity. Read Doctrine and Covenants 163:8c, which calls us "to become a sanctuary of Christ's peace, where people from all nations, ethnicities, and life circumstances can be gathered into a spiritual home without dividing walls."

Create a large circle with your arms. See and feel the diverse people God invites inside the sanctuary of Christ's peace. Who is easiest to welcome? Whom do you struggle to include? Ask God to forgive and heal barriers.

Peace Covenant:

Today, I will examine the foundation of my faith, God.

8
Tuesday
May

Reconciliation

By Flo McDonald of Lee's Summit, Missouri, USA

If it is possible, so far as it depends on you, live peaceably with all.

—Romans 12:18

I met Sean one day when I took my morning walk in a new neighborhood. He greeted me with a smile and told me his name. He often waited for me to walk by and was a friendly little fellow.

He liked to knock on my door and just stand there. I learned from his mother that he missed his own grandmother, who lived far away in Massachusetts. I invited him to come in and asked what he would like to do. I didn't know what to expect. He usually pointed toward the electric typewriter. He was very careful and typed in his own fashion.

Years went by, and Sean grew up. His mother became ill. I visited her often in her home and later in the nursing home before she passed away. I tried to keep in touch with Sean, but he did not respond.

Some time later I attended a neighborhood block party, and Sean was there. He approached me in a straightforward manner and asked why I was unhappy with him. I was unaware he felt that way. We talked, came to an understanding, and parted friends again.

I was impressed that he made an effort to find out what was amiss. I am convinced the Spirit of God rested on us so we could make our relationship right.

This is the way of Christ so we might be reconciled one to another.

Prayer for Peace:

God of all friendships, guide us with your Spirit to reconciling ministry. Open our hearts to see the perspective of others. May we be at peace with one another.

Spiritual Practice for the Week: Welcoming Unity in Diversity

Each day this week meditate on unity in diversity. Prayerfully read Doctrine and Covenants 163:8c, which calls "the entire church to become a sanctuary of Christ's peace, where people from all nations, ethnicities, and life circumstances can be gathered into a spiritual home without dividing walls."

Create a large circle with your arms. See and feel the diverse people God invites inside the sanctuary of Christ's peace represented by this circle. Who is easiest to welcome? Whom do you struggle to include? Confess the dividing walls between you and people too different or "dangerous" to invite into your spiritual home. Ask God to forgive and heal barriers that keep you and others from being one in Christ's peace.

Peace Covenant:

As much as it is my power, God, I will live peaceably with all.

9
Wednesday
May

Affirmations of Grace

By Tammy Lindle of Independence, Missouri, USA

Let no harmful talk come out of your mouths, but only what is useful for building up, as there is need, so that your words may give grace to those who hear.

—Ephesians 4:29

I recently heard a famous boxer—a former heavyweight champion of the world—hired a guy to follow him around, saying words to build him up and stroke his ego. He'd say, "You're the man!" "There's no one greater than you!" "You're the strongest, fastest, meanest, most-ferocious fighter in the world!" "You are the ultimate fighting champion!"

These words had to be delivered with a style and bravado convincing to the fighter. The words had to be said with passion and be varied enough to be fresh and be *heard* by the fighter.

The one hired to deliver the messages had to believe it himself to make it believable to his boss.

Words have power to shape who we are, how we see ourselves, and what we can become. They have the power to build up and destroy.

I recently discovered how unbelievably helpful words of affirmation are to me. After going through some life-changing events, I am uplifted and blessed by words of love, support, and caring that have come to me from God's people, who share my journey. These words come in cards, through e-mail, text messages, songs sung for my birthday, and long conversations.

These words have come through hugs, smiles, gifts, invitations, food, and shared tears. They have come as one-time-only messages from some and as repeated gestures over many months and in different ways from others.

Each word serves as a testimony of the rich and varied blessings of community connected in Christ. The best part is...we don't have to hire it done.

Prayer for Peace:

Affirming God, thank you for grace in our lives, grace we may share with others. Thank you for the speakers of grace, for they are a blessing to all who hear. They are the instruments who share Christ's peace.

Spiritual Practice for the Week: Welcoming Unity in Diversity

Each day this week meditate on unity in diversity. Prayerfully read Doctrine and Covenants 163:8c, which calls "the entire church to become a sanctuary of Christ's peace, where people from all nations, ethnicities, and life circumstances can be gathered into a spiritual home without dividing walls."

Create a large circle with your arms. See and feel the diverse people God invites inside the sanctuary of Christ's peace represented by this circle. Who is easiest to welcome? Whom do you struggle to include? Confess the dividing walls between you and people too different or "dangerous" to invite into your spiritual home. Ask God to forgive and heal barriers that keep you and others from being one in Christ's peace.

Peace Covenant:

When I find souls in dark shadows, God, I will witness of your love for them and affirm their worth in your sight.

10
Thursday
May

Go to Camp, See the Ramblers, Get a Job

By Jim Holloway of Murfreesboro, Tennessee, USA

The Lord is exalted, he dwells on high; he filled Zion with justice and righteousness; he will be the stability of your times, abundance of salvation, wisdom, and knowledge; trust in the Lord is the key to this treasure.

—Isaiah 33:5-6

In the summer of 1984 I was laid off my job at a construction company in Midland, Michigan. After being off work about a month I went to Iowa to take care of some business that would give us more living money. My wife, Sue, was off to three youth camps. I told her I was going to stop in Chicago and look for a job.

I stayed with friends, Jim and Hazel. After three days and about 20 stops to leave résumés without a single interview, I became discouraged. I returned to Jim and Hazel's in a depressed mood.

Hazel said, "Jim, we were thinking of going to family camp tonight." I replied with little enthusiasm, "Who is preaching?" Hazel said, "No preaching. The Graceland Ramblers, a group of young people from Graceland College in Lamoni, Iowa, are coming to sing."

My Lamoni roots lit up my mood like a Christmas tree as I responded, "Great!"

We got to the campground, had supper, found our seats, and waited for the concert. I felt like my prayers were answered. A man who worked for a telecommunications company came down the row where I was sitting and started talking to me.

Hazel said, "Jim, tell him you are here looking for a job." The next day, I had three interviews, and within six weeks, I was working for his company in Nashville, Tennessee.

Thank you to those members of the 1984 Graceland Ramblers for helping me get a job, simply by going to the family camp. I feel I always can trust in God and God's children, even when things look discouraging. God offers stability.

Prayer for Peace:

God of wisdom, we exalt you for your presence in our lives. We thank you for your disciples who influence and encourage us. May we reach out to others and do the same.

Spiritual Practice for the Week: Welcoming Unity in Diversity

Each day this week meditate on unity in diversity. Prayerfully read Doctrine and Covenants 163:8c, which calls "the entire church to become a sanctuary of Christ's peace, where people from all nations, ethnicities, and life circumstances can be gathered into a spiritual home without dividing walls."

Create a large circle with your arms. See and feel the diverse people God invites inside the sanctuary of Christ's peace represented by this circle. Who is easiest to welcome? Whom do you struggle to include? Confess the dividing walls between you and people too different or "dangerous" to invite into your spiritual home. Ask God to forgive and heal barriers that keep you and others from being one in Christ's peace.

Peace Covenant:

Today, God, I will listen for you, trust in your wisdom, and apply it to my life.

11
Friday
May

Mutual Friends

By Ken Hall of Renton, Washington, USA

Let us then pursue what makes for peace and for mutual upbuilding.

—Romans 14:19

Recently I rediscovered one of my best friends from high school. There had been three of us back then, called by some the "Three Musketeers." We did everything together—hiking, hunting, and fishing. We took the same classes. We daydreamed together.

After high school we went our separate ways. One went to college, and one joined the military. I worked for a year and then joined another branch of the military. We may have seen one another once or twice at first, but we became busy with our own careers.

After I retired from the military, I discovered one of my friends had medical problems. After a few years in and out of hospitals he passed away. I never again heard from my other friend. I went to my 50th high school reunion. I learned that about 20 percent of my graduating class already had passed away. I thought my best friend might have been among them because the graduating committee couldn't locate him.

Five years later my wife went to the graduating class website, and with a few phone calls I found my long-lost best friend, David. We lived only about 20 miles from each other, as we had for about 42 years.

After 55 years we met again. What a glorious day it was! We shook hands and hugged as our wives looked on. Tears came to our eyes.

We are now renewing our friendship, recounting those wonderful days of youth, and looking forward to good days. The reunion was spiritual and social. It was good to be uplifted by and to uphold my friend. I thank God for friends.

Prayer for Peace:

God, thank you for bringing friends into our lives. Thank you for places where we can make lasting friendships. Help us venture to make new friends.

Spiritual Practice for the Week: Welcoming Unity in Diversity

Each day this week meditate on unity in diversity. Prayerfully read Doctrine and Covenants 163:8c, which calls "the entire church to become a sanctuary of Christ's peace, where people from all nations, ethnicities, and life circumstances can be gathered into a spiritual home without dividing walls."

Create a large circle with your arms. See and feel the diverse people God invites inside the sanctuary of Christ's peace represented by this circle. Who is easiest to welcome? Whom do you struggle to include? Confess the dividing walls between you and people too different or "dangerous" to invite into your spiritual home. Ask God to forgive and heal barriers that keep you and others from being one in Christ's peace.

Peace Covenant:

Today, God, I will contact a friend I haven't seen in awhile.

12
Saturday
May

Get up and Go

By Memmory Myers of Decatur, Michigan, USA

> *...so we, who are many, are one body in Christ, and individually we are members one of another. We have gifts that differ according to the grace given to us: prophecy, in proportion to faith; ministry, in ministering; the teacher, in teaching; the exhorter, in exhortation; the giver, in generosity; the leader, in diligence; the compassionate, in cheerfulness.*
>
> —Romans 12:5–8

Since I was a child I've wanted to make a difference. My passion is to experience life and to build cultural acceptance. I am thankful for my time as a World Service Corps volunteer, which helped me grow in many ways.

We climbed mountains, worked with children at vacation Bible school, taught English classes to youth and adults, and attended young-adult gatherings.

What I take home from my experience is rediscovering my faith in God. The church is not just about *preaching* peace; it's also about *living* it.

My time as a World Service Corps volunteer changed my life for the better. Your generous contributions to World Mission Tithes made that change possible. Thank you for giving generously.

Prayer for Peace:

God of the many, God of the individual, may we accept the variety of cultures and gifts with which you have graced us. May we offer them generously for Christ's mission of compassion and peace.

Spiritual Practice:

Hold an imaginary or real bowl of ashes. Let it represent the losses, sufferings, and injustices in the global community. Name things in the bowl that particularly grieve you. Pray a blessing on Community of Christ as it responds to the ashes of God's world with healing words and reconciling actions.

Peace Covenant:

Today, God, I will offer my gifts with generosity and accept the gifts of others with cheerfulness.

13
Sunday
May

Abide in Love

By Scott Murphy, Council of Twelve Apostles

> *As the Father has loved me, so I have loved you; abide in my love…I am giving you these commands so that you may love one another.*
>
> —John 15:9–17

We had just finished lunch and were preparing for the class to begin. Realizing I needed a book from the office. I made my way upstairs. When I came around the corner, a woman named Lisa was outside the office.

I sensed something was wrong. She seemed unsure about being in an unfamiliar space. The look in her eyes and her timid presence expressed her woundedness and sense of unworthiness.

When I asked if I could help her, her soft voice said, "Do you have anything I could eat?" Knowing we had food remaining from lunch, I immediately went to put together a plate of food.

When I came back and placed the plate in her hands, a smile emerged. Tears welled up as she looked at me with the deepest gratitude and said "thank you."

I asked if I could help her with anything else, and she said, "No," and thanked me again as she slowly walked out the door, carrying her food.

I've pondered that experience many times because in that moment with Lisa I felt the presence of God's enduring love as I offered my love for another in need. I did not offer much, but what I had at the time seemed to be enough.

"If you keep my commandments, you will abide in my love…" Choosing to live in the way that Jesus calls us allows us to experience the joy that comes in the sacred love we share with one another. When we abide in love with one another we abide in God's love for us.

Prayer for Peace:

Giving God, in whose love we abide, may our community show that same love to one another. May we practice grace and generosity.

Spiritual Practice for the Week: Offering Blessings of Community

Each day this week receive and share blessings of community. Begin with a prayer of gratitude for the network of relationships in your life. See and feel connections with family members, spiritual friends, people in your congregation and community, people and creatures in God's sacred web of life. What blessings flow to you from these circles?

Reflect, pray, and write in your journal about the call to be "Community of Christ." Go deeper each day as you "discern and embrace" the "divine blessing" of this name that opens you to "become a blessing to the whole creation" (Doctrine and Covenants 163:1). What act of blessing are you invited to complete?

Peace Covenant:

Today, God, I will invite those who are looking from without, to come in and share the love and peace of Christ.

14
Monday
May

The Flood

By Barrie Fox of Kirkby-in-Ashfield, Nottinghamshire, England

> *But seek the welfare of the city where I have sent you into exile, and pray to the Lord on its behalf, for in its welfare you will find your welfare.*
>
> —Jeremiah 29:7

On holiday in the south of England, I had the opportunity to go to the small town of Boscastle, Cornwall, a place I had never visited. It interested me because of what had happened there a few years earlier.

At midday on August 16, 2004, heavy thundershowers developed in the area. Incredible amounts of rain fell in a short time. Boscastle rapidly flooded. Nearly 2 million tons of water were recorded as having swept through the main street and into the harbor. It affected about a thousand residents and visitors.

Fortunately, there were no fatalities. Seven helicopters, which quickly arrived, airlifted more than a hundred people to safety. People helped one another.

The record books in the newly built visitors' center say the flood hit about 60 properties, and some buildings had to be demolished. More than 80 wrecked cars ended up in the harbor. Records called this the largest peacetime rescue in the history of mainland Britain.

My mind could not help but reflect on the Bible story of Noah's flood and the implications of it in the lives of so many people. I am grateful to be able to cling to faith in God and faith in our community. We praise God for companions on our journey who bless us with hope.

Prayer for Peace:

Faithful God, may we remember to call on you when we are overwhelmed. When Earth's powerful elements challenge us, help us see the rainbow.

Spiritual Practice for the Week: Offering Blessings of Community

Each day this week receive and share blessings of community. Begin with a prayer of gratitude for the network of relationships in your life. See and feel connections with family members, spiritual friends, people in your congregation and community, people and creatures in God's sacred web of life.

What blessings flow to you from these circles? Reflect, pray, and write in your journal about the call to be "Community of Christ." Go deeper each day as you "discern and embrace" the "divine blessing" of this name that opens you to "become a blessing to the whole creation" (Doctrine and Covenants 163:1). What act of blessing are you invited to complete?

Peace Covenant:

Today, God, I will be aware of the welfare needs of my community and the world.

15
Tuesday
May

Horseradish and Happy Hearts

By Joann Condit of Phoenix, Arizona, USA

The Spirit of the One you follow is the spirit of love and peace. That Spirit seeks to abide in the hearts of those who would embrace its call and live its message. The path will not always be easy, the choices will not always be clear, but the cause is sure and the Spirit will bear witness to the truth, and those who live the truth will know the hope and the joy of discipleship in the community of Christ. Amen.

—Doctrine and Covenants 161:7

I was in Idaho visiting Mom for the last days of her life. I came from Florida for that precious visit. We talked, we remembered, we laughed, and yes, we cried. Still, it was a time of joy.

One afternoon Dad dug horseradish roots. The next day, Mom and I scrubbed the roots and began to put them through an electric grinder. The roots were tough, pungent. Our eyes streamed with tears. The grinder growled and grew hot from its efforts. We laughed, shouted, shed tears—a memory I cherish still.

I took four small jars of horseradish with me back to Florida. Before we used even the smallest jar, my mother's life had ended. She was 64, and I grieved those lost years that we would never share. Each time I used a dab of horseradish, though, I remembered that beautiful autumn day and our shared laughter and industry.

Two years or more passed, and there remained only one small jar of horseradish. I used it sparingly, fearing that when it was gone, my mother and our joy together would be lost forever. I didn't realize the power of God's blessed gift of memory. A hint of horseradish and I can recall in vivid sound and color that October day 33 years ago. I can see my mother as we built memories.

We never lose those we love when we remember them in joy and gratitude. Pain fades, but joy remains. Thank you, God, for the blessed gift of memory.

Prayer for Peace:

God of laughter, God of tears, we praise you for our happy years.

Spiritual Practice for the Week: Offering Blessings of Community

Each day this week receive and share blessings of community. Begin with a prayer of gratitude for the network of relationships in your life. See and feel connections with family members, spiritual friends, people in your congregation and community, people and creatures in God's sacred web of life.

What blessings flow to you from these circles? Reflect, pray, and write in your journal about the call to be "Community of Christ." Go deeper each day as you "discern and embrace" the "divine blessing" of this name that opens you to "become a blessing to the whole creation" (Doctrine and Covenants 163:1). What act of blessing are you invited to complete?

Peace Covenant:

God, today I will make choices that look ahead to your sure cause.

16
Wednesday
May

Prepare to Witness

By Mary Hathaway of Washington, D.C., USA

> *"And when you do not cry to the Lord, let your hearts be full, drawn out in prayer to him continually for your welfare, and also for the welfare of those who are around you."*
> —Alma 16:222

The night shift at the hospital was quiet, so we nurse's aides had ample time for conversation while we sat at our station. Sometimes talk shifted to church. Joanne belonged to one denomination, and I was seeking spiritual instruction in another faith community. My questions about Joanne's faith were many, and she always had answers. She told me how her church held continuing revelation as a belief.

Though I continued to go to my church for a while, I soon started going to church with Joanne. I was seeking a more-personal relationship with God. I felt I could find it in Joanne's faith community. As I learned more about the sacred story, recorded in scripture and in the life of the church, I made my choice.

The decision to join Community of Christ became the most-significant decision of my life, a decision I have never regretted.

As the decades passed, I often think with gratitude of my friend and co-worker. At an early age she was well prepared for the questions of a seeker. I hope I am as well prepared as Joanne so I, too, can invite others to Christ.

Prayer for Peace:

Revealing God, may we always be your disciples, ready to share our witness. May we share our stories, songs, and prayers. As we gain strength in our identity, may we gain a strong foothold on the path to peace.

Spiritual Practice for the Week: Offering Blessings of Community

Each day this week receive and share blessings of community. Begin with a prayer of gratitude for the network of relationships in your life. See and feel connections with family members, spiritual friends, people in your congregation and community, people and creatures in God's sacred web of life.

What blessings flow to you from these circles? Reflect, pray, and write in your journal about the call to be "Community of Christ." Go deeper each day as you "discern and embrace" the "divine blessing" of this name that opens you to "become a blessing to the whole creation" (Doctrine and Covenants 163:1). What act of blessing are you invited to complete?

Peace Covenant:

Today, God, I will prepare myself to answer the questions of those who are drawn to the community. I will seek them out and share the peace of Christ.

17
Thursday
May

Ugly Hands

By Merna Short of Melbourne, Victoria, Australia

But Jesus said, "Let her alone; why do you trouble her? She has performed a good service for me. For you always have the poor with you, and you can show kindness to them whenever you wish; but you will not always have me. She has done what she could; she has anointed my body beforehand for its burial. Truly I tell you, wherever the good news is proclaimed in the whole world, what she has done will be told in remembrance of her."

—Mark 14:6–9

At a women's retreat we rediscovered the variety of our giftedness. In one exercise we asked ourselves what we liked about our own bodies. Gina thought her hands were ugly, but they were so useful.

She loved cooking, making jam, and knitting. She is also a podiatrist and raises money for the church through all these skills. Through this exercise she realized she had reached out to many people because of her useful hands, which made up for their "ugliness."

Another woman, who always wanted square shoulders on which to drape her clothes, found she had beautiful "Victorian" shoulders. How good is that? When we shared what we saw as beautiful in one another, especially through the inner beauty reflected in our giftedness and our love, we realized how much God has invested in each of us.

Like the woman who bathed Jesus' feet in expensive perfume, we each find our unique way of serving. How much sharing of good news will be remembered because of us? Unexpectedly, we had much to share about our gifts and opportunities to serve with our God-given bodies.

Truly, God's creation is sacred—even ugly hands.

Prayer for Peace:

Creator God, our hands are your hands. Our feet are your feet. We'll do what you want us to do, dear Lord, we'll go where you want us to go.

Spiritual Practice for the Week: Offering Blessings of Community

Each day this week receive and share blessings of community. Begin with a prayer of gratitude for the network of relationships in your life. See and feel connections with family members, spiritual friends, people in your congregation and community, people and creatures in God's sacred web of life.

What blessings flow to you from these circles? Reflect, pray, and write in your journal about the call to be "Community of Christ." Go deeper each day as you "discern and embrace" the "divine blessing" of this name that opens you to "become a blessing to the whole creation" (Doctrine and Covenants 163:1). What act of blessing are you invited to complete?

Peace Covenant:

Today, God, I'll be what you want me to be.

18
Friday
May

Our Family Is Your Family

By Pearl Edwards of Olympia, Washington, USA

> *And above all things, clothe yourselves with the bonds of charity, as with a mantle, which is the bond of perfectness and peace; pray always, that you may not faint until I come; behold, and lo, I will come quickly, and receive you unto myself. Amen*
>
> —Doctrine and Covenants 85:38c

In 1928, my dad and his five grieving children stood at the grave of my mother, who died from injuries suffered in a car accident. My father had been driving us home to Vernon, Texas, from a family celebration. I was 3 years old. My sister was 1½, and the other children were all 12 to 17.

Two months later, my little sister and I found ourselves in the home of my Aunt Pearl, my mother's sister, with her four lively children in Moclips, Washington. One evening on a visit to Aunt Pearl's, a couple, Tom and Louise Armstrong, asked my dad if he would consider having strangers care for his children; they wanted the opportunity.

We went home with the Armstrongs that night. We would live in their home for 12 years. They were Community of Christ members. They became our grandparents, and their family became our family. Because many of them were church members, the folks of the church became our family, too.

As children, we were faithful attendees at Sunday school. When I was 11 I went to a youth camp. During worship in the girls' dormitory, I gave my life to Christ. We sang, "I will go where you want me to go, dear Lord; I will be what you want me to be."

Those words have been the commitment of my life. At age 21 I was baptized and confirmed. My husband and children also were baptized.

The gospel of Jesus Christ has been the basis of my life. I have served in almost all offices of the priesthood and am now an evangelist. I continue to serve in the Olympia Congregation in Washington. How different my life would have been had it not been for the welcoming generosity of my new family.

Prayer for Peace:

Compassionate God, may we reflect your compassion to the lost and lonely. May we think of all children as your children. May we care for them as you care for us.

Spiritual Practice for the Week: Offering Blessings of Community

Each day this week receive and share blessings of community. Begin with a prayer of gratitude for the network of relationships in your life. See and feel connections with family members, spiritual friends, people in your congregation and community, people and creatures in God's sacred web of life.

What blessings flow to you from these circles? Reflect, pray, and write in your journal about the call to be "Community of Christ." Go deeper each day as you "discern and embrace" the "divine blessing" of this name that opens you to "become a blessing to the whole creation" (Doctrine and Covenants 163:1). What act of blessing are you invited to complete?

Peace Covenant:

I will wrap myself in the bonds of charity, God, so I may share your peace.

19
Saturday
May

Offer Gifts

By Carolyn Smith of Greenwood, New York, USA

How does God's love abide in anyone who has the world's goods and sees a brother or sister in need and yet refuses help?

—1 John 3:17

For some time, I sensed our congregation should open a food pantry in our small town. By the summer of 2008, the time to start had arrived. After receiving early funding through the mission center, everything fell into place.

I felt the leading of God's Spirit about offering our gifts through this service more strongly than ever. Volunteers from the church and the community eagerly embraced the ministry—a huge step of faith for our small congregation.

Six months after the pantry opened, we received a grant from the church. Six months after that, amid the economic recession, the largest employer in our area reduced its workforce by 80 percent.

It is clear to me that God was preparing us to provide some relief for the 90 families a month whose food supply we now subsidize. The budget is always a struggle, but whenever there is need, God helps us find a way. Your generous contributions to the Abolish Poverty, End Suffering mission initiative enable Greenwood's pantry to offer ministry to families in need.

Thank you for responding faithfully and generously.

Prayer for Peace:

Loving God, abide in us. Help us to see those in need. Inspire us to help.

Spiritual Practice

The first disciples of Jesus followed to hear his words, to be taught, to learn a new way of living, to practice what they learned in daily life. Prayerfully consider your role as a teacher-learner, disciple-apprentice; a people cultivator in Community of Christ. In your journal write the names of several people you see as teachers or mentors and several you feel called to nurture and encourage in specific ways. Ask God's blessing on you and your congregation as a community of learners. See 1 Corinthians 3:6.

Peace Covenant:

Today, God, I will fast for a meal. I will be mindful of the hungry people of the world as I prepare my offering for tomorrow.

20
Sunday
May

Join in Apostolic Witness

By Linda Booth, Council of Twelve Apostles

> *So one of the men who have accompanied us during all the time that the Lord Jesus went in and out among us, beginning from the baptism of John until the day when he was taken up from us—one of these must become a witness with us to his resurrection.*
>
> —Acts 1:21–22

Without the apostolic witness of those early disciples who proclaimed the living Christ, we would not know of Jesus Christ today. Without our witness, others may never experience the peace of Jesus Christ and the blessings of community.

In December 2007, Tony Tristani Jr.'s doctor told him he had terminal colon cancer. Sitting in the hospital with his wife, Tina, the news was devastating. He couldn't breathe. His eyes wouldn't focus.

Through the whisperings of the Holy Spirit, suddenly his mind became clear. He knew that in life or death he belonged to God. Fear left him—Christ's peace became real.

From that moment on, God's grace was alive in Tony. Each day he would pray, "Jesus, please let this cancer open a door that one person might know of God's goodness." During chemotherapy sessions, talking to colleagues, neighbors, and friends, Tony's apostolic witness was bold, inspiring, and transformational.

His message to companion disciples was: "You don't have to have cancer to live your life and witness of Jesus. All a person has to do is accept God's love and share that love with others."

In January 2011, Tony died. While many of us cried over the loss of an exceptional friend, we remembered him saying, "Don't weep for me…I shared my faith along the way with hundreds of people who wanted to talk about God."

May Tony's life inspire us to be bold in our witness, recognizing that each day is a precious opportunity to share Christ with others.

Prayer for Peace:

Comforting God, bring your grace to life in us, so we may share it with those who are in fear and pain. In life and death, we belong to you.

Spiritual Practice for the Week: Connecting with God as Center

Each day this week connect with God through journal writing. Use a notebook, journal, computer, or any available paper. Prayerfully center on your intent to open yourself to God's presence and share what flows from your heart and mind. Your "letter to God" might include thoughts, questions, feelings, needs, artwork, quotes, scriptures, or it may take the form of a prayer, psalm, or poem.

Try to write at least five minutes each day. What do you experience? Is this an effective way to connect with God? What surprises you? What new images or questions from God emerge? What deepens or changes in your relationship with God, Christ, Spirit?

Peace Covenant:

Today, God, I will bear my witness and boldly share your love.

21
Monday
May

Friendly Football

By Geoff Henshaw of Independence, Missouri, USA

> *He shall judge between the nations, and shall arbitrate for many peoples; they shall beat their swords into plowshares, and their spears into pruning hooks; nation shall not lift up sword against nation, neither shall they learn war any more.*
>
> —Isaiah 2:4

I was born in Australia and now live in the USA with my wife. While I have adapted to the differences in culture, I also have kept some affection for the unique cultural identities of Australia. One difference between America and Australia is football. In America the rule of football is Gridiron, while in Australia we use Australian Rules.

But this story is not about football. However, it is about a friendship that I treasure from my years growing up in the church in Australia. I followed a particular football team, which Jack and Mitta Gunning also followed. Jack was a World Church appointee and served in an administrative role in Victoria. Because of our common interest, Jack, Mitta and their son, Barry, invited me to join them when they watched our team play.

Mitta would pack a basketful of sandwiches, cakes, biscuits, and hot drinks. Together we cheered our team. Mitta brought enough food for all during the day-long outing. Whether rainy or sunny, whether our team won or lost, it was always a wonderful day.

Reflecting on those times, it was not about the football. Such days were about a relationship between friends and love that was offered by Jack and Mitta to me, an impressionable young person growing up in the church.

My roots in the church and my relationship with Christ were strengthened with the love shown by two of my spiritual mentors.

Prayer for Peace:

God of all nations, if we must have borders, we pray that all countries might have friendly borders. We would embrace the differences between cultures and unite in the diversity. We thank you for the friends who have influenced our lives for peace.

Spiritual Practices for the Week: Connecting with God as Center

Each day this week connect with God through journal writing. Use a notebook, journal, computer, or any available paper. Prayerfully center on your intent to open yourself to God's presence and share what flows from your heart and mind.

Your "letter to God" might include thoughts, questions, feelings, needs, artwork, quotes, and scriptures, or it might take the form of a prayer, psalm, or poem. Try to write at least five minutes each day.

What do you experience? Is this an effective way to connect with God? What surprises you? What new images or questions from God emerge? What deepens or changes in your relationship with God, Christ, Spirit?

Peace Covenant:

With all my senses, God, I will appreciate the cultures of all people of the Earth.

22
Tuesday
May

What Matters Most

By Karin Blythe of Burlington, Iowa, USA

> *The mission of Jesus Christ is what matters most for the journey ahead.*
> —Doctrine and Covenants 164:9f

Inner-city schools ring with a different tone than any other place I have been. Maybe the bells are louder, or the sound lasts longer, or it rings deeper within the soul. Those bells brought me Johnny, a student I will never forget.

I had to make a disciplined effort to love and care for Johnny because he was a challenge and often an obstacle to learning in my classroom.

When the morning bell rang, I knew Johnny was at school, but I was never sure where. Sometimes he hid between lockers, or made a space for himself in my closet. Sometimes he roamed the halls and disrupted other classrooms.

Early in the school year I had to decide what mattered most as I considered Johnny and his life. His smile could always melt my anger and frustration, and we both knew his actions were not his identity; they were not his *being*. Johnny was too young for the decisions of his life, and he was screaming for intervention, attention, and compassion.

So Johnny and I made a silent pact to value only what matters most—compassionate acceptance.

Johnny needed to be valued just because he existed, without any expectation or judgment. Johnny needed love that was unconditional, the kind of love that Jesus spent a lifetime expressing, explaining, and advocating. Johnny is a constant reminder to me that we all are called to find "what matters most" and to move forward with that objective and mission as a constant guide.

Prayer for Peace:

Wisdom, guide us in our search for what matters most. Help us find our part in the mission of Jesus Christ. Help us share his love and peace.

Spiritual Practice for the Week: Connecting with God as Center

Each day this week connect with God through journal writing. Use a notebook, journal, computer, or any available paper. Prayerfully center on your intent to open yourself to God's presence and share what flows from your heart and mind.

Your "letter to God" might include thoughts, questions, feelings, needs, artwork, quotes, and scriptures, or it might take the form of a prayer, psalm, or poem. Try to write at least five minutes each day.

What do you experience? Is this an effective way to connect with God? What surprises you? What new images or questions from God emerge? What deepens or changes in your relationship with God, Christ, Spirit?

Peace Covenant:

I will not judge others. I will love and accept those who challenge me most.

23
Wednesday
May

Patio Prayer

By Elizabeth Else of St. Thomas, Ontario, Canada

And the peace of God, which surpasses all understanding, will guard your hearts and your minds in Christ Jesus.

—Philippians 4:7

Advertisements constantly bombard us: Buy this, achieve that, travel here, or do this and you will find happiness. We aspire for, focus on, and become addicted to the pursuit of happiness.

There are times of achievement, gain, or experience that do produce a measure of happiness, but then the moments, like the objects, pass.

I, too, wish to be happy. I remember those fleeting moments when "all's right with the world." However it was during illness, professional uncertainty, and great personal pain that I understood deep joy.

In the summer of 2002, I was at a crossroads. I experienced painful betrayal and devastating losses. I had just recovered from an illness. My career was uncertain. Although moving was a certainty, the destination was unknown.

Late one Sunday evening after my English students had left our tea party, I went out to the patio. I was drawn into the beauty of the night—the sound of crickets, the smell of flowers, and the sight of a full moon shining on the garden.

I began to pray. As I praised God in my usual way, I entered a state of praise as never before. I thanked God for the opportunity to meet new friends and to serve overseas. Joy bubbled up from somewhere deep inside. An hour later, I said, "Amen."

Life continues with its ups and downs—momentary happiness and challenges. I live, as many do, in the valleys of each day rather than on the mountaintops of exquisite experiences. However, the joy of that summer night's prayer remains to sustain me in trials, support me in my serving, and to pull me back to the center when caught in the pursuit of something less.

Prayer for Peace:

Guard our hearts, God, against shallow desires. Challenge us to want what you want for us—that which provides deep, lasting joy for our soul. With this deep joy to carry us, we are able to be at peace with the ebb and flow of pleasure and pain.

Spiritual Practice for the Week: Connecting with God as Center

Each day this week connect with God through journal writing. Use a notebook, journal, computer, or any available paper. Prayerfully center on your intent to open yourself to God's presence and share what flows from your heart and mind.

Your "letter to God" might include thoughts, questions, feelings, needs, artwork, quotes, and scriptures, or it might take the form of a prayer, psalm, or poem. Try to write at least five minutes each day.

What do you experience? Is this an effective way to connect with God? What surprises you? What new images or questions from God emerge? What deepens or changes in your relationship with God, Christ, Spirit?

Peace Covenant:

I will forget my temporal aspirations, God, and drink deeply of your living and everlasting waters.

24
Thursday
May

How Would You Prepare?

By Vera Entwistle, Forster Keys, New South Wales, Australia

> *...who executes justice for the oppressed; who gives food to the hungry. The Lord sets the prisoners free...*
>
> —Psalm 146:7

A cartoon is called "Calvin and Hobbes." Calvin marches into the living room early one morning. His mother is in her favorite chair, drinking coffee. She is amazed at how young Calvin is dressed.

A large space helmet encases Calvin's head. He wears a long cape. In one hand he holds a flashlight and in the other a baseball bat. What's wrong, his mother asks. "Nothing, so far," says Calvin. "But you never know. Something could happen, and if anything does, I am going to be ready for it."

As he leaves the room his mother says, "I think *I* need a suit like that."

During the last few weeks our congregation has focused on personal meditation. I remembered Calvin, and I realized some days I feel I need an outfit like Calvin had.

Then today comes the news of some dear friends, church leaders in Nepal, who have gone into hiding. Their lives were threatened because of their faith. How would any of us prepare for a threat like that?

In times like these I am thankful for God's love and assurance. I feel I need to sing a hymn by Frances Ridley Havergal: "I am trusting thee, to guide me, Thou alone shalt lead; every day and hour supplying all I may need."

Prayer for Peace:

Comforting God, set free those who suffer for your cause. Assure us that your peaceable kingdom will prevail.

Spiritual Practice for the Week: Connecting with God as Center

Each day this week connect with God through journal writing. Use a notebook, journal, computer, or any available paper. Prayerfully center on your intent to open yourself to God's presence and share what flows from your heart and mind.

Your "letter to God" might include thoughts, questions, feelings, needs, artwork, quotes, and scriptures, or it might take the form of a prayer, psalm, or poem. Try to write at least five minutes each day.

What do you experience? Is this an effective way to connect with God? What surprises you? What new images or questions from God emerge? What deepens or changes in your relationship with God, Christ, Spirit?

Peace Covenant:

Today, God, I will trust in you to set the prisoner free. I will do what I can to work for justice.

25
Friday
May

It Happened at a Celebration

By Shirley Remmenga of Fort Collins, Colorado, USA

> *May the God of steadfastness and encouragement grant you to live in harmony with one another, in accordance with Christ Jesus, so that together you may with one voice glorify the God and Father of our Lord Jesus Christ.*
>
> —Romans 15:5–6

The wedding ceremony ended, and all the wedding party and most of the guests gathered for the reception meal. My grandniece had asked me to give the prayer of blessing for the newlyweds and the meal.

I happened to sit next to the husband of another grandniece, someone I hardly knew. I offered the prayer, and as I sat down, he said, "Where did you find that prayer?" I answered, "I wrote it." He responded, "It was so right, I think you ought to publish it as a wedding blessing!"

His simple remark somehow connected us—not because of the prayer itself, but because of the presence of the Holy Spirit in that place at that moment.

Our relationship will forever be one of connectedness, and neither of us will forget it. I am so grateful God is present in our celebrations, as well as in our life struggles.

I have decided to apply this blessing to all my relationships:

"Creator God, may we keep the communication lines between us and our loved ones open and kind, so we can tell one another our joys, concerns, and deep feelings. For when we share these, we will be able to meet the challenges that every relationship faces and be able to continue to journey together in love.

"Help us, God, remember that it is important that we all continue to develop our own individuality so our togetherness does not become a chain that binds us, but wings that help us soar. Strong, secure individuals enhance exciting relationships—ones that definitely include you, God. Bless us to this beginning. Amen."

Prayer for Peace:

God of blessing, we feel your presence in life's celebrations as well as in our struggles. May we magnify our relationships as we recognize your presence in them. May your presence guide us on the road to peace.

Spiritual Practice for the Week: Connecting with God as Center

Each day this week connect with God through journal writing. Use a notebook, journal, computer, or any available paper. Prayerfully center on your intent to open yourself to God's presence and share what flows from your heart and mind.

Your "letter to God" might include thoughts, questions, feelings, needs, artwork, quotes, and scriptures, or it might take the form of a prayer, psalm, or poem. Try to write at least five minutes each day.

What do you experience? Is this an effective way to connect with God? What surprises you? What new images or questions from God emerge? What deepens or changes in your relationship with God, Christ, Spirit?

Peace Covenant:

Creator God, I will encourage freedom in relationships—freedom to seek you as individuals.

26
Saturday
May

Pay Attention

By Jeff Anderson and Larry McGuire of Baltimore, Maryland, USA

> *You who are my disciples must be found continuing in the forefront of those organizations and movements which are recognizing the worth of persons and are committed to bringing the ministry of my Son to bear on their lives.*
>
> —Doctrine and Covenants 151:9

The Power House ministry in inner-city Baltimore is a blessing to countless children, youth, and adults. It is also a place for dreams of peace.

The recent addition of a Young Peacemakers trailer—complete with displays—means people can pay attention to those dreams as they become real.

Principals of two schools agreed to support Young Peacemakers as part of their educational experience. Now children of broken dreams and broken neighborhoods can experience what it means to have a place of safety and peace.

Thanks to generous gifts, including a missionary grant from World Mission Tithes, building peace in the Power House is a reality that touches countless children. Thank you for responding generously.

Prayer for Peace:

Divine Architect, help us, as disciples, to design ministries that will witness of your Son. May we provide sanctuary for those who feel unsafe. May we each recognize the worth of all persons as they are and in their potential to be peacemakers.

Spiritual Practice:

What is the voice of God saying to us? Do we hear the whispers of God's longing for shalom, God's dream of beauty and wholeness for all creation? Do we hear the voice of God calling to us in faces and eyes, in the sounds of suffering and joy, in scripture and sacred word, in tears and laughter, in silence and noise?

Spend a few moments reflecting on when and how God's voice has spoken to you. When did you first feel called to join God in the pursuit of peace and justice? How does that call to shalom continue to come to you through the many voices of God?

Peace Covenant:

Today, God, I will pay attention to ways I can make dreams of peace come true.

27
Sunday
May

Speak of God's Power

By Richard James, Council of Twelve Apostles

> *"In the last days it will be, God declares, that I will pour out my Spirit upon all flesh, and your sons and your daughters shall prophesy, and your young men shall see visions, and your old men shall dream dreams. Even upon my slaves, both men and women, in those days I will pour out my Spirit; and they shall prophesy."*
>
> —Acts 2:17–18

I was attending a leaders meeting in Germany four years ago. I could not speak German, so the discussions were translated for me. It was a long day, and much was discussed. On some issues there was not a clear way forward.

At the end of the day we gathered in a circle for worship, which again was translated for me. It started with a scripture from Johannes (John), which I recognized.

Then a time was available for people to share their thoughts on the day and their hopes for the church.

I suddenly had a remarkable experience.

As I looked around the circle a person would come to my mind, and then words came into my head. Then that person stood up. As the words were translated, they were the same words I had heard in my mind. This happened five times consecutively.

This was a powerful expression of the Holy Spirit. Perhaps it was similar to the experience of the early disciples at Pentecost. As I reflected on my experience I heard the words again in my mind that "we need to listen to one another, as we are all speaking words from God. If we only listen to a few voices we do not get the whole message."

As we engage in discernment it is important that we listen to everyone, so God's voice can be heard. I am humbled by the powerful way God moved that day and that I was reminded "all are of worth." I also was reminded the Holy Spirit works in wonderful ways to help us in Christ's mission.

Prayer for Peace:

Revealing God, open our ears to one another so we may hear your whole message. We all are called—may we all call for the peace of Christ.

Spiritual Practice for the Week: Growing a Gracious, Generous Heart

Each day this week open your heart to God's grace and generosity with a "breath prayer." Let your breath slow and deepen. Be aware of God's breath moving in and out of your heart. Spend several minutes focusing on breathing in God's generosity.

With each breath, silently name one gift for which you are thankful. "God, I breathe in the gift of ______ with thanks." Let your heart expand to contain God's gracious outpouring. With each breath out, name one gift you want to share from the overflow of your heart.

> *Eternal joy and peace await those who grow in the grace of generosity that flows from compassionate hearts.*
>
> —Doctrine and Covenants 163:9

Peace Covenant:

Today, God, I will listen for your call and then join my voice with other peacemakers around the world.

28
Monday
May

Pray It Back

By Lu Mountenay of Independence, Missouri, USA

> *I lift up my eyes to the hills—from where will my help come? My help comes from the Lord, who made heaven and earth.*
>
> —Psalm 121:1–2

Dear God,

In your grace and forgiving nature, won't you let me take back my prayer? You must know I didn't mean it as soon as it spilled from my mouth. You must know it wasn't truth that was escaping from my broken heart. At least, then, if you release it back to me, I won't feel so dishonest. After all, I was just trying to be brave.

Do you remember my pathetic prayer? It was right after my son lost his fight with leukemia. It was at his memorial service and went something like this…

"Gentle Shepherd, from a mother's loving arms
I release my son into *your* loving arms.
From a mother's care and concern,
I release him into your salvation.
Thank you, Creator God, for allowing us the blessing
of being co-creators with you of this being we called Isaac Samuel.
Thank you for the 25 years,
the laughter…the tears.
From his infancy to his parenthood—in the seeming blink of an eye.
Thank you for Community of Christ, which was with him
constantly during his long, hard fight for life.
And now, thank you for releasing him
from his final struggle
into your peace. Amen"

Do you remember?

When the first anniversary of his death approached, and time wasn't doing its expected healing job, I realized how much I really didn't mean that prayer. So, to make up for my misplaced "acceptable" behavior, I went into the woods and I screamed as loudly as I could. I know you were there to hear me, God…like you were there to hear my prayer.

Yours truthfully, Isaac's mom (on his birthday)

Prayer for Peace:

Understanding God, when we lift our eyes to the hills to find you, sometimes they are full of tears. Bless us with your comfort, God, and strengthen us to be your disciples of peace.

Spiritual Practice for the Week: Growing a Gracious, Generous Heart

Open your heart to God's grace and generosity with a "breath prayer." Let your breath slow and deepen. Spend time focusing on breathing in God's generosity. With each breath, silently name one gift for which you are thankful. "God, I breathe in the gift of ______ with thanks." With each breath out, name one gift you want to share from the overflow of your heart.

Peace Covenant:

Today God, I will be strong and remember the blessings of comfort the community brings.

29
Tuesday
May

God's Faithfulness

By Dorene Kilburn of Stratford, Ontario, Canada

Righteousness shall be the belt around his waist, and faithfulness the belt around his loins.
—Isaiah 11:5

This morning, when I looked on our backyard, I got a wonderful surprise. A three-inch-tall clump of daffodils had pushed up through the earth!

A couple of days before, a foot of snow had hidden the promise. The snow, except for huge mounds on the front lawn, disappeared with yesterday's rain. Winter has not yet left, but God is providing signs of rebirth—a glimpse of blessings to come.

I pondered the broader message this might have for me. Do I live in expectation of blessing that is as much a part of God's love for us as the changing seasons God created?

My life took an unexpected turn this past year, and the journey now includes me being caregiver because my husband has a debilitating disease. Still, there are wonderful surprises, moments that tell me God blesses us on the journey. I know I must live in expectation of that blessing.

As Dietrich Bonhoeffer said, "God is with us in the evening and the morning, and very definitely on every new day."

Prayer for Peace:

God of dusk, dawn, and every new day, send us your innermost spring. Awaken us with your hidden, unfolding seasons. In the cold winter, assure us the warmth of spring will come. Help us know the promise of fall when we endure the stifling heat of summer. We have faith in your comfort when we face struggles.

Spiritual Practices for the Week: A Gracious, Generous Heart

Open your heart to God's grace and generosity with a "breath prayer." Let your breath slow and deepen. Spend several minutes focusing on breathing in God's generosity. With each breath, silently name one gift for which you are thankful. "God, I breathe in the gift of ______ with thanks." With each breath out, name one gift you want to share from the overflow of your heart.

Peace Covenant:

I will wait on your promises, God, knowing they will complete their sacred circle.

30
Wednesday
May

Love Your Neighbor in Prison

By Lillian Kirby of Blue Springs, Missouri, USA

One of the scribes came near and heard them disputing with one another, and seeing that he answered them well, he asked him, "Which commandment is the first of all?" Jesus answered, "The first is, 'Hear, O Israel: the Lord our God, the Lord is one; you shall love the Lord your God with all your heart, and with all your soul, and with all your mind, and with all your strength.' The second is this, 'You shall love your neighbor as yourself.' There is no other commandment greater than these."

—Mark 12:28–31

The telephone rang in the chaplain's office at the Temple, and I answered it, receiving a most-unusual request. The call was from a prison inmate. He could make only outgoing calls, and I couldn't call him back because of prison regulations.

His first question was, "Does your church believe in a heaven and a hell?"

Section 76 of Doctrine and Covenants came into the conversation as I steered it toward Community of Christ's belief in God's grace and forgiveness.

Apparently this is what he needed to hear. Next, he confessed he could not forgive his mother, who would not come to see him in prison. She was ashamed her son had committed a crime for which he was incarcerated.

I carefully steered our talk to God's forgiveness of the sincerely repentant. I looked down on my desk, and my Bible was open to the Psalms. The psalmist had repented and prayed for God to forgive him. I read several chapters to this upset, needy man.

With help from the Holy Spirit, I persuaded him to forgive his mother and to call her on Mother's Day to tell her he loved her. With a contrite heart and a voice filled with emotion, he thanked me and agreed not only to call his mother, but to start on his own path of repentance.

Prayer for Peace:

Thank you, God, for our neighbors, who are poor, needy, socially marginal, and imprisoned. May we extend to them our love, which is your love. May we extend to them also our radical hospitality. In accepting this mission, we come closer to peace.

Spiritual Practice for the Week: Growing a Gracious, Generous Heart

Open your heart to God's grace and generosity with a "breath prayer." Be aware of God's breath moving in and out of your heart. Focus on breathing in God's generosity. Silently name one gift for which you are thankful. Let your heart expand to contain God's gracious outpouring. With each breath out, name one gift you want to share.

Eternal joy and peace await those who grow in the grace of generosity that flows from compassionate hearts.

—Doctrine and Covenants 163:9

Peace Covenant:

Today God, I offer you love from my heart, soul, mind, and strength.

31
Thursday
May

Sing at the Top of Your Lungs

By Mary Humphrey of Independence, Missouri, USA

Make a joyful noise to the Lord, all the earth; break forth into joyous song and sing praises. Sing praises to the Lord with the lyre, with the lyre and the sound of melody. With trumpets and the sound of the horn make a joyful noise before the King, the Lord.

—Psalm 98:4–6

Last summer I went to Middle School Camp at Lake Doniphan. I remember I felt close to God many times. Two of my fondest memories of that closeness were on walks where we could reflect, pray, and just have some time with God.

The first walk was called the walk of faith. On the walk of faith, we were led outside and blindfolded. We then walked over and around many obstacles as if in the dark of night. The only thing guiding us was a rope. I found God in this activity because we realized God is always there—even when we couldn't see the barriers and obstacles. God kept us safe that entire journey, and for that, I grew in God.

The second walk did not have a name, but it was just as memorable. We had our campfire, starting with the usual silly, fun songs and skits. Then it got serious. Everyone sang at the top of their lungs, praising God. Then, as a cabin group, we were led to talk to one of the pastors for a prayer before we were sent to the woods with only a candle in our hands.

As I walked, I thought about whom I was living my life for.

Was it for me? If not, who? Then I realized it was God. God is the one I want to live my life for. God gave me my life, my breath, and the place I live. I walked off that trail, crying, and I was greeted by people who love me, people who God put there for me.

So, thank you, God.

Prayer for Peace:

Can you hear our joyful noise, Lord? We want you to hear how loved we feel; how much we love you. Thank you for your guidance on the path to peace.

Spiritual Practice for the Week: Growing a Gracious, Generous Heart

Each day this week open your heart to God's grace and generosity with a "breath prayer." Let your breath slow and deepen. Be aware of God's breath moving in and out of your heart. Spend several minutes focusing on breathing in God's generosity.

With each breath, silently name one gift for which you are thankful. "God, I breathe in the gift of ______ with thanks." Let your heart expand to contain God's gracious outpouring. With each breath out, name one gift you want to share out of the overflow of your heart.

Eternal joy and peace await those who grow in the grace of generosity that flows from compassionate hearts.

—Doctrine and Covenants 163:9

Peace Covenant:

Even though I go through some dark times, God, I will trust you are there.

1

Friday
June

One Person at a Time

By Peggy Michael of Cantonment, Florida, USA

Open your hearts and feel the yearnings of your brothers and sisters who are lonely, despised, fearful, neglected, unloved. Reach out in understanding, clasp their hands, and invite all to share in the blessings of community created in the name of the One who suffered for all. Do not be fearful of one another. Respect each life journey, even in its brokenness and uncertainty, for each person has walked alone at times. Be ready to listen and slow to criticize, lest judgments be unrighteous and unredemptive. Be patient with one another, for creating sacred community is arduous and even painful. But it is to loving community such as this that each is called. Be courageous and visionary, believing in the power of just a few vibrant witnesses to transform the world. Be assured that love will overcome the voices of fear, division, and deceit.

—Doctrine and Covenants 161:3a–c

I like to talk to God. I tell God I'm frustrated because I hear the cries of many people, and I cannot answer them all. I can only imagine God's frustration!

I have a friend who is angry. A stranger just walked by with his head bowed low. A young woman came to me, trembling in fear, for she is caught in a net of poor choices. I care for all of them, but I run around, scarcely touching the lives of anyone because I'm trying to help them all.

Back to you, God: Did I hear you say, "Be still, and I will direct you; look into one pair of yearning eyes, hug one person, call one name in prayer"? I will give up my frustration to God and I will be led to one person at a time.

Prayer for Peace:

God of children of every race and tongue, hear our lament. Heal our angry hearts, raise our bowed heads to the joyful sky. Wipe away our fears as you end the falling of our tears. Send Earthly angels from Christ's community to hold each one of us to your healing light. May each one respond so the burden will be light, so his yoke will be easy, and so his peace will prevail.

Spiritual Practice for the Week: Growing a Gracious, Generous Heart

Each day this week open your heart to God's grace and generosity with a "breath prayer." Let your breath slow and deepen. Be aware of God's breath moving in and out of your heart. Spend several minutes focusing on breathing in God's generosity.

With each breath, silently name one gift for which you are thankful. "God, I breathe in the gift of ______ with thanks." Let your heart expand to contain God's gracious outpouring. With each breath out, name one gift you want to share from the overflow of your heart.

Eternal joy and peace await those who grow in the grace of generosity that flows from compassionate hearts.

—Doctrine and Covenants 163:9

Peace Covenant:

God, lead me to one person who needs me, and I will respond today.

2
Saturday
June

World's Worst Conditions

By Lu Mountenay of Independence, Missouri, USA

> *God, the Eternal Creator, weeps for the poor, displaced, mistreated, and diseased of the world because of their unnecessary suffering. Such conditions are not God's will. Open your ears to hear the pleading of mothers and fathers in all nations who desperately seek a future of hope for their children. Do not turn away from them. For in their welfare resides your welfare.*
> —Doctrine and Covenants 163:4a

I am looking at a map of the world. It is published and distributed by Doctors Without Borders. Across the top, in bold, red letters, is written, "We find out where conditions are the worst—the places where others are not going—and that's where we want to be."

Imagine *wanting* to be among the worst conditions in the world.

If anyone can say that and mean it, they are a better person than I. I have much admiration for the people of this program. I have heard the stories of how they help those who otherwise would have been doomed to malnutrition, disfiguration, pain, a crippled body, or even death.

On the spiritual side, the ministrations of the health professionals show people that someone cares. This benefits the self-esteem of those who suffer. They may come to realize there is hope, after all; there is a God, after all. They have worth in the sight and heart of this God.

As the scripture says, those conditions are not the will of God. Clearly those conditions are not the will of these health ministers, either.

Programs like Outreach International and the mission initiative of Abolish Poverty, End Suffering also have opened ears to hear the pleadings of the suffering in all nations. Let's all open our ears. Shalom.

Prayer for Peace:

God of the beautiful gardens, God of the worst conditions in the world, we yearn to be your disciples everywhere you are. Give us the desire and strength to overcome our self-centeredness to make this journey. Lead us on the path to the suffering and let us take your peace.

Spiritual Practice:

Offer a silent prayer for the gift of God's compassion. Cup your hands and ask God to make you aware of the suffering that causes the Earth and its inhabitants to groan and weep. Be open to faces or places, sounds or voices, feelings of connection with those who suffer. Imagine catching the tears of those you see and holding them in your hands. Prayerfully discern active responses of ministry or healing God invites you to complete for those who weep.

Peace Covenant:

Today God, I will lay out a map on the table before me. I will pray for a corner of the world in need. I will open my ears to them and be led to respond.

3
Sunday
June

Worship the Lord

By Barbara Borkowski of Lee's Summit, Missouri, USA

And one called to another and said: "Holy, holy, holy is the Lord of hosts; the whole earth is full of God's glory."

—Isaiah 6:3, adapted

Communion Sunday has always been significant in my life. As a child I was encouraged to fast on those "first" Sunday mornings in preparation for our Communion experience. Later in life, as an Aaronic priest, I had the privilege of serving Communion. I have always understood the Lord's Supper as an expression of holy sacredness and grace.

While I often have served Communion and presided over many Communion services, I typically am not the one who prepares the bread and grape juice. But, at a pastor and leaders meeting a few years ago, I had that opportunity.

I was alone as I prepared for the sacrament, and my thoughts and prayers were on both the meeting and the people I knew would be present.

As I broke the bread into pieces and then poured grape juice into tiny cups, I became aware of the many people who had prepared Communion throughout my life. It was a holy moment as I honored their commitment to God and the community of believers they served.

Holy moments are sacred and full of grace. They remind us that God is so much more than we know or understand. May our praise join the generations and the ages by declaring, "Holy, holy, holy is God!"

Prayer for Peace:

Holy God of grace, we kneel at your table, full of forgiveness and aware of being forgiven. With this new beginning may we direct our efforts to sharing the peace of Jesus Christ.

Spiritual Practice for the Week: Caring for God's Sacred Creation

Each day this week choose a way to notice, give thanks, and care for God's sacred creation. Prayerfully consider one of the following suggested practices or create your own.

Walk in nature with a spirit of gratitude and "holy attention." Write a psalm of praise for the beauty of the Earth or a prayer of healing and blessing for the wounds of the Earth. Learn about and engage in an act of Earth-keeping, such as recycling, simple living, fasting from over-consumption of resources. Notice the unique diversity of the planet's creatures and be gentle to plants, animals, trees, and people! Fall in love with the vast, intricate wonder of God's creation and give thanks.

Peace Covenant:

I will declare your holiness, God, in word and deed.

4
Monday
June

Respect the Planet

By Karen Hutchinson of Loveland, Colorado, USA

How beautiful upon the mountains are the feet of the messenger who announces peace, who brings good news, who announces salvation, who says to Zion, "Your God reigns."
—Isaiah 52:7

I love the mountains.

We have lived in Colorado almost 50 years and never have tired of the beauty that surrounds us. We're close to the mountains, but we also have the prairies right outside our windows.

The contrast is perfect—this panorama completes my soul's need for nature's wonder. I know beauty and wonder are everywhere in the world. This just happens to be the spot for me to savor.

Our natural world feeds me. It shows me our Creator also enjoys the beauty all around us. Because of the contrast we see from our windows, I can begin to glimpse the glory God has given us.

I also can look out that same window and see the results of our disrespect for this world. We have not taken responsibility for protecting our part of the world.

I know this neglect and misuse of our land has happened all over the world. We have not valued and protected this gift of life we have been given.

Greed, selfishness, and ignorance can be the way people live—even surrounded by the great beauty we have. I believe the Creator weeps for the neglect that our selfish ways have caused in leaving the world less than it ought to be.

It's hard to make great changes in conditions that are far off, but I can make every effort to protect the part of the world I live in. I can try to make this small part of creation a better place, in gratitude and respect for God.

Prayer for Peace:

Source of all being, we have caused you to weep. In many places we have trashed your creation. We pray, Creator, that we have not done irreparable damage, and that we will get on the right path soon. Teach us stewardship of the Earth and teach us of your peace.

Spiritual Practice for the Week: Caring for God's Sacred Creation

Choose a way to notice, give thanks, and care for God's sacred creation. Prayerfully consider one of the following suggested practices or create your own.

Walk in nature with a spirit of gratitude and "holy attention." Write a psalm of praise for the Earth or a prayer of healing and blessing for the wounds of the Earth. Learn about and engage in an act of Earth-keeping, such as recycling, simple living, fasting from over-consumption of resources. Notice the unique diversity of the planet's creatures and be gentle to plants, animals, trees, and people! Fall in love with the vast, intricate creation and give thanks.

Peace Covenant:

Today, God, I will strengthen my recycling efforts and my efforts to use less of the Earth's resources.

5
Tuesday
June

Unconditional Blessings

By Steven L. Shields, Lee's Summit, Missouri, USA

> *You have put gladness in my heart more than when their grain and wine abound. I will both lie down and sleep in peace; for you alone, O Lord, make me lie down in safety.*
>
> —Psalm 4:7–8

Not long ago I discussed with a friend what makes up a "blessing." He believed signs that God had blessed a person included a middle-class salary, a decent house, and good health. I disagreed.

Like my friend, I grew up in a middle-class household in a wealthy and powerful nation. I thought that "blessing" meant possessions like the three-bedroom, two-bathroom, house we lived in, the family cars, the camping trailer, three square meals a day, and television.

Those who had less were not as blessed. We mistakenly thought those with physical ills were often not as faithful. Praying meant that we must first thank God for all the *things* we thought God had given us; then ask God for the *things* we still wanted.

Much of my adult life and ministry has taken place far from my homeland. I worked with people who did not enjoy wealth and plenty of material goods. These are people who barely had enough food to survive from one day to the next; people who could not access preventive health care.

Yet, the people were happy. They went about their tasks with joy. They held a pure, simple faith that God actively engages in their existence. Their lively worship reflected their reliance on God. Surely, they were blessed.

Psalm 4 expresses a state of blessedness for disciples to seek. Isn't having "gladness in my heart" more important than an abundance of "grain and wine"? Isn't it a greater blessing to be able to "lie down in safety" and "sleep in peace"?

As we recount our blessings, let us not focus on physical things, but on the spiritual blessedness that God gives us generously and unconditionally.

Prayer for Peace:

God of blessing, we would seek that which brings us close to you. Bless us with the desire to share the peace of Jesus Christ with the world.

Spiritual Practice for the Week: Caring for God's Sacred Creation

Prayerfully consider the following practices or create your own. Walk in nature with a spirit of gratitude and "holy attention." Write a psalm of praise for the beauty of the Earth or a prayer of healing and blessing for the Earth. Learn about and engage in an act of Earth-keeping such as recycling, simple living, fasting from overconsumption of resources. Notice the unique diversity of the planet's creatures. Fall in love with the vast, intricate woncer of God's creation.

Peace Covenant:

Today, God, I will recount my spiritual blessings.

6
Wednesday
June

Dare to Look at Pain

By Ron Yager Sr. of Independence, Missouri, USA

Collectively and individually, you are loved with an everlasting love that delights in each faithful step taken. God yearns to draw you close so that wounds may be healed, emptiness filled, and hope strengthened… Come before your Eternal Creator with open minds and hearts and discover the blessings of the gospel anew. Be vulnerable to divine grace.

—Doctrine and Covenants 163:10a–b

A few years ago I served as camp pastor at a senior high camp. A need for ministry presented itself. The first-year camper was a high-school senior. She arrived at camp with visible emotional pain. Early in the week she felt the love of Christ coming to her through the love of her companion campers. They were willing to carry her pain.

The change in her expression was visible. Midweek, after mail call, her world came crashing down. She ran off toward the waterfront with her heart being torn to pieces. One could feel the hurt as the camp listened to her deep sobs. I headed to where she sat at the end of the dock.

We sat in silence for a while. When she was ready she told me her mother had filed for a divorce, and her father would not be home when she returned from camp. This young woman loved both her parents and was torn with the news of loss.

As she talked it through, we pulled together some thoughts that might help. When we finished she was ready to face the situation, being strengthened by the newly found love she had in Christ and her camp friends. The blessings of community are often what get us through tough times.

As followers of the Christ we must be ready to answer the call of the brokenhearted, supporting them until all are strong enough to stand on their own.

Prayer for Peace:

Teacher of ministry, help us to see the pain of others. Help us to bring them to a place of peace.

Spiritual Practice for the Week: Caring for God's Sacred Creation

Choose a way to notice, give thanks, and care for God's sacred creation. Prayerfully consider one of the following suggested practices or create your own. Walk in nature with a spirit of gratitude and "holy attention." Write a psalm of praise for the Earth or a prayer of healing and blessing for the wounds of the Earth. Learn about and engage in an act of Earth-keeping such as recycling, simple living, fasting from over-consumption of resources.

Notice the unique diversity of the planet's creatures and be gentle to plants, animals, trees, and people. Fall in love with the vast, intricate creation and give thanks.

Peace Covenant:

Today God, I will not turn away from wounds that I may tend with your help.

7
Thursday
June

Bring Forth the Kingdom

By Cindy Korf of North Platte, Nebraska, USA

> *Posterity will serve him; future generations will be told about the Lord, and proclaim his deliverance to a people yet unborn, saying that he has done it.*
>
> —Psalm 22:30–31

One Sunday morning while visiting a congregation, I sat in the back pew next to a mentally challenged man. After an inspiring church service, the congregation rose to conclude by singing "Bring Forth the Kingdom."

My neighbor's energy and enthusiasm was truly Spirit-filled. He stood and rocked to the music.

At each refrain his joyful voice rang, "Bring forth the kingdom." Each time he shouted he would turn and look at a person—asking the person to share the call, "Bring forth the kingdom."

When we reached the last refrain he shouted with conviction, "Bring forth the kingdom! Bring forth the kingdom! Bring forth the kingdom!" Then, he turned, gazed into my eyes, and said, "Bring forth the kingdom of God."

He was getting it. I was touched and humbled. I prayed, "Lord, through you we can be the salt of the Earth, the salt to bring forth the kingdom of God."

Prayer for Peace:

God of past, present, and future generations, your name will be proclaimed by this generation and those to follow. Your deliverance will be a joy to the people of all nations. We pray we will be part of the building of your kingdom; your eternal, peaceable kingdom.

Spiritual Practice for the Week: Caring for God's Sacred Creation

Choose a way to notice, give thanks, and care for God's sacred creation. Prayerfully consider one of the following suggested practices or create your own.

Walk in nature with a spirit of gratitude and "holy attention." Write a psalm of praise for the Earth or a prayer of healing and blessing for the wounds of the Earth. Learn about and engage in an act of Earth-keeping, such as recycling, simple living, fasting from over-consumption of resources. Notice the unique diversity of the planet's creatures and be gentle to plants, animals, trees, and people! Fall in love with the vast, intricate creation and give thanks.

Peace Covenant:

I will learn how to be salt of the Earth, God, and bring forth signal communities in your name.

8
Friday
June

It's about Hope

By Deb Crowley of Eaton Rapids, Michigan, USA

Lift up your eyes and fix them on the place beyond the horizon to which you are sent. Journey in trust, assured that the great and marvelous work is for this time and for all time.
—Doctrine and Covenants 161:1a

As our congregation prepared for a service of healing and hope, praying and imagining the power of God's Spirit that would attend us, there was no disappointment.

Songs, prayer, testimony, and Communion together set the stage for powerful blessing during the sacrament of laying on of hands for the sick.

Everyone agreed that God's light literally shone upon the congregation.

As the first person sat in the chair for a prayer of blessing, surrounded by the members of the priesthood and others in support, the day's first ray of sunshine shone through the skylight. It landed on the person in the chair and those praying for her.

The ministers who prayed all could testify of the increased intensity of sunshine at the moment they laid hands on the head of the person in the chair.

God blessed us with healing and filled souls with hope. Hope that there is a bright future for each one, for the church, for humanity. As we continue to live adventurously with a vision of hope in God, what surprises and blessings await us!

Prayer for Peace:

God of the horizon, draw our eyes to you. We praise you as our source of shining hope. We trust in your vision of peace.

Spiritual Practice for the Week: Caring for God's Sacred Creation

Choose a way to notice, give thanks, and care for God's sacred creation. Prayerfully consider one of the following suggested practices or create your own.

Walk in nature with a spirit of gratitude and "holy attention." Write a psalm of praise for the Earth or a prayer of healing and blessing for the wounds of the Earth. Learn about and engage in an act of Earth-keeping, such as recycling, simple living, fasting from over-consumption of resources. Notice the unique diversity of the planet's creatures and be gentle to plants, animals, trees, and people! Fall in love with the vast, intricate creation and give thanks.

Peace Covenant:

God of peace, I will venture to embody and share the peace of Christ.

9
Saturday
June

Cast Your Nets

By Lynn Brady of Brainerd, Illinois, USA

> *And the king will answer them, "Truly I tell you, just as you did it to one of the least of these who are members of my family, you did it to me."*
>
> —Matthew 25:40

The Brainerd Congregation in Chicago decided to involve itself in the surrounding neighborhood. We recently began an after-school tutoring program.

Our goal is to cast our nets and help connect the children and families of three grammar schools and one high school within five miles of our congregation.

Our tutoring program meets two days a week.

Volunteers include retired educators, high-school students, young adults, service professionals, neighbors, and church members. Students receive help with homework and added studies in specific areas.

High-school students who volunteer receive community-service learning hours, needed for their graduation.

We are excited about providing this outreach ministry that directly supports families and shows our investment in the education of the children in our community. Your generous contributions to World Mission Tithes provide full-time field ministers who help envision ministry such as Brainerd's program.

Thank you for giving generously.

Prayer for Peace:

God of our deep inner soul that we struggle so hard to find, God of our outward reach that is our calling, stay with us on our journey. Inspire us to service. Bridge us to community so we may share the peace of Jesus Christ.

Spiritual Practice:

Community of Christ is called to ministries of peace, reconciliation, and healing of the spirit. PeacePathways is a website that shares peace and justice ministries, resources, and opportunities.

Visit *www.peace-pathways.org* and prayerfully discern one ministry that speaks to you or captures your attention. Offer a prayer of blessing on the peace organization you select. Listen quietly to see if God is calling you to additional responses to this ministry or another ministry of peace, reconciliation, or healing. If you cannot visit the website, offer a prayer of blessing on all peace ministries.

Peace Covenant:

With love as my purpose, God, I will find the "least of these" and serve them as I would serve you.

10
Sunday
June

God's Love Is Steadfast

By Susan Skoog, Council of Twelve Apostles

> *Beloved, let us love one another, because love is from God; everyone who loves is born of God and knows God.*
>
> —1 John 4:7

Kathy was a victim of cerebral palsy from birth. Confined to a wheelchair and speech-impaired, she overcame many barriers to attend university.

Her goal was to become a counselor to other cerebral palsy victims. After many years of study and trial, she succeeded.

For two years, I served as her aide in the university dormitory. I dressed and fed her, helped with homework, and tutored her in algebra and statistics. Kathy was brilliant, computing algebra problems in her head and then dictating to me what to write. She was a friend, a sister, and a mentor as she shared her indomitable spirit and determination to live a full, giving life.

Throughout the church, countless people serve as caregivers for others Year after year they give unstintingly to help family or friends suffering from Alzheimer's, cancer, or other debilitating illnesses. Their lives revolve around their loved one, a relationship founded on steadfast love and generous sharing of time, energy, and understanding.

My experience with Kathy tells me they also receive steadfast love unconditionally. The mutuality of sharing brings joy to a difficult task, and promotes patience when energy wanes at the end of a hard day.

God's love is steadfast. 1 John 4:7 says, "love is from God; everyone who loves is born of God and knows God." Community is based on mutual caregiving in large and small ways. Each of us expresses the steadfast love of God when we give of ourselves to others.

Prayer for Peace

Loving God, thank you for your steadfast love. Thank you for your presence in our days, providing peace and serenity as we serve others. May they sense your peace in us.

Spiritual Practice for the Week: Encountering Scripture as Continuing Revelation

Each day this week read and pray with the Doctrine and Covenants as continuing revelation of God's vision for the church and creation. Choose a favorite section or focus on recent counsel in Sections 156–164.

Read a few selected paragraphs slowly three or four times. Pause to pray for deep understanding of meaning after the first reading. Pray for opening of your heart and emotions to the text after the second reading. After the third reading, prayerfully ask to hear the particular phrase or word that speaks to you or touches your life. Stay with this word or phrase. Listen as fully and openly as you can. What sense of divine presence or invitation comes? What is revealed?

Peace Covenant

When called to care, I will give unconditionally in a spirit of peace and joy.

11
Monday
June

Heritage of Hope

By Karin Blythe of Burlington, Iowa, USA

Out of the depths I cry to you, O Lord. Lord, hear my voice! Let your ears be attentive to the voice of my supplications! . . . I wait for the Lord, my soul waits, and in his word I hope.
—Psalm 130:1–2, 5

My greatest fear is insignificance. I dread that my life will mean nothing; that I will amount to little more than a blip on the radar screens of human existence.

I was shattered by the news that my uncle was slowly dying from the effects of Agent Orange. He had faithfully served in a war early in his life. His experiences forever affected him.

I grew up hearing stories of his childhood and the person he used to be. But the stories never included his life after the war. He went through hell and came out on the other side. It took him years to get to the other side, but he made it. Shortly after that, he found the cancer.

I couldn't help but be angry, frustrated, and confused. He gave every ounce of himself for an unkind and ungrateful world. It didn't seem fair.

As I was embracing frustration and confusion, my uncle chose a higher path. He chose beauty and forgiveness. He chose to embrace life and to give even more generously. He chose hope—hope that came amid the darkest of nights. And then I realized his significance rests in me. I am his heritage, and his life will continue through my life. My life will continue through the lives of those who love me.

There is no option for insignificance in the grand design of community and compassion. Just as Jesus is remembered in the hearts of so many, we will be remembered by each person who has felt God's presence through us.

Prayer for Peace:

God of hope, we wait on you for our hope. Grant us strength and discipline to work for peace.

Spiritual Practice for the Week: Encountering Scripture as Continuing Revelation

Each day this week read and pray with the Doctrine and Covenants as continuing revelation of God's vision for the church and creation. Choose a favorite section or focus on recent counsel in Sections 156–164.

Read a few selected paragraphs slowly three or four times. Pause to pray for deep understanding of meaning after the first reading. Pray for your heart and emotions to open to the text after the second reading. After the third reading, prayerfully ask to hear the particular phrase or word that speaks to you or touches your life. Stay with this word or phrase. Listen as fully and openly as you can. What sense of divine presence or invitation comes? What is revealed?

Peace Covenant:

I will remember the peacemakers who have gone before me and left their heritage of peace.

12
Tuesday
June

Grace and Peace for the Journey

By Dorene Kilburn of Stratford, Ontario, Canada

Grace to you and peace from God our Father and the Lord Jesus Christ.
—1 Corinthians 1:3

Having lived well beyond the proverbial "four score and 10," I find myself viewing life from a different perspective at this time in my journey. I remember what we, as teenagers, thought of someone in their 50s. Definitely ancient and over-the-hill! But God has a purpose for us at every stage in our lives.

Reflecting on my journey, I recognize God has been with me every step. God has saved me from poor choices, even gotten me through life-threatening situations. God has allowed me to live in my faith community in a nation other than my homeland and has provided me with mountain-top experiences.

Yes, we face detours and rough spots in the road. However, God's guidance has been evident in my life. I am grateful I still can undertake major responsibilities in my home congregation. Supporting others on their spiritual journey brings me joy. It is often someone who doesn't yet realize *we are not human beings on a spiritual journey; we are spiritual beings on a human journey.*

Even with all the world's woes, we are living in exciting times. The president of Community of Christ, Stephen M. Veazey, recently has called us to join together on a challenging new journey. He affirmed that "it's the mission of Jesus Christ that matters most for the journey ahead."

I'm looking with great expectation to a future that will bring healing to our hurting world, and I'm excited to be able to join in this journey, sharing the peace of Jesus Christ.

Prayer for Peace:

God of peace and grace, help us be faithful to what matters most on life's journey. May we support one another in spirit and mission as we share the peace of Jesus Christ.

Spiritual Practice for the Week: Encountering Scripture as Continuing Revelation

Each day this week read and pray with the Doctrine and Covenants as continuing revelation of God's vision for the church and creation. Choose a favorite section or focus on recent counsel in Sections 156–164.

Read a few selected paragraphs slowly three or four times. Pause to pray for deep understanding of meaning after the first reading. Pray for your heart and emotions to open to the text after the second reading. After the third reading, prayerfully ask to hear the particular phrase or word that speaks to you or touches your life. Stay with this word or phrase. Listen as fully and openly as you can. What sense of divine presence or invitation comes? What is revealed?

Peace Covenant:

Today, God, I will find a spiritual companion for the journey.

13
Wednesday
June

Stirring Sounds

By Greg Clark of Independence, Missouri, USA

Let the assembly of the peoples be gathered around you, and over it take your seat on high.
—Psalm 7:7

The conductor stood, baton poised. Every member of the Kansas City Symphony focused on him, waiting for his command.

The event was a free public concert at the Community of Christ Auditorium in Independence, Missouri. It was more than an afternoon of superb music; it was a theological metaphor.

I marveled as the sound of strings, rumble of timpani, and caress of woodwinds washed over me. I watched and listened, admiring the musical creation of the conductor and the instrumentalists as they worked together, striving for musical perfection.

Of course, earlier, the performers sounded anything but harmonious. That was when the musicians were tuning up. They went their own ways without regard for one another, and they paid no attention to any leader. The result, predictably, was a cacophony, clashing sounds that hurt the ear.

Then the conductor entered. Clearly, the musicians trusted his leadership as his baton passionately slashed, stabbed, and swooshed through the air. Between numbers, he talked with the audience, showing his humor, joy, and love for music.

As wonderful as it was, it was just a concert. The conductor was merely a man. How much greater must God be—how much more wonderful the blessings of creation if we but follow God's lead.

Prayer for Peace:

Divine Conductor, direct us as instruments of harmony and peace.

Spiritual Practice for the Week: Encountering Scripture as Continuing Revelation

Each day this week read and pray with the Doctrine and Covenants as continuing revelation of God's vision for the church and creation. Choose a favorite section or focus on recent counsel in Sections 156–164.

Read a few selected paragraphs slowly three or four times. Pause to pray for deep understanding of meaning after the first reading. Pray for your heart and emotions to open to the text after the second reading. After the third reading, prayerfully ask to hear the particular phrase or word that speaks to you or touches your life. Stay with this word or phrase. Listen as fully and openly as you can. What sense of divine presence or invitation comes? What is revealed?

Peace Covenant:

Today, God, I will come to you finely tuned and ready to play my part in your vision.

14
Thursday
June

Well-used Faith

By Vera Entwistle of Forster Keys, New South Wales, Australia

...the fruit of the Spirit is love, joy, peace, patience, kindness, generosity, faithfulness, gentleness, and self-control. There is no law against such things.

—Galatians 5:22–23

The "Antiques Road Show" is one of my favorite television programs. I tune in, hoping to discover one of my possessions is worth a lot of money.

The show's drama comes from people not recognizing the value of what they have. To them it may just be a dust collector; maybe they received it as a gift. They don't realize its value.

I wonder if the same can be said about me and my faith? Does it gather dust until some crisis comes along and I need something to cling to?

Our son had a medical crisis and was rushed into emergency surgery. His dad and I jumped in the car to dash to his bedside when a call came from the hospital that surgery was imminent. We asked that our son be given a phone so we could talk to him. His first words were, "Mom and Dad, I am so scared, and there's no one here to pray for me."

Today, as I look at my now-healthy son, the memory of that experience reminds me to dust off my faith and hold onto my testimony of a God who cares for us all, even when we are not in crisis.

Prayer for Peace:

God of love, joy, faith, and peace, let us remember to practice these fruitful gifts when we are secure, as well as when we are afraid. Let our hearts be at peace, knowing we have our well-used faith in you to rely on.

Spiritual Practice for the Week: Encountering Scripture as Continuing Revelation

Each day this week read and pray with the Doctrine and Covenants as continuing revelation of God's vision for the church and creation. Choose a favorite section or focus on recent counsel in Sections 156–164.

Read a few selected paragraphs slowly three or four times. Pause to pray for deep understanding of meaning after the first reading. Pray for your heart and emotions to open to the text after the second reading. After the third reading, prayerfully ask to hear the particular phrase or word that speaks to you or touches your life. Stay with this word or phrase. Listen as fully and openly as you can. What sense of divine presence or invitation comes? What is revealed?

Peace Covenant:

God, I will keep my faith ready to go.

15
Friday
June

"Try Tears!"

By Barrie Fox of Kirkby-in-Ashfield, Nottinghamshire, England

> *Peace I leave with you; my peace I give to you. I do not give to you as the world gives. Do not let your hearts be troubled, and do not let them be afraid.*
>
> —John 14:27

I live near Nottingham in England. Nottingham is where William Booth, founder of the Salvation Army, was born in 1829. He was, for a few years, a Methodist minister and then became an evangelistic preacher. In the east end of London he founded what he called the Christian Mission. This became the Salvation Army in 1878.

Members of the Salvation Army have told me that one of Booth's followers approached him and said he found his required tasks, as an active member of the Salvation Army, were starting to prove too difficult. He asked Booth what he could do about it.

Booth told him to "try tears."

Christ calls all would-be disciples to confide in him, cry with him, and at any opportunity, work for and with him.

When we let God and Jesus come into our lives, we can set in motion changes in our daily living. This change helps us to subdue disappointments, fears, and worries that so often confront us. Most people experience failures and worries, big or small, at some time.

When this happens in my life, it helps me to continue to be grateful for my blessings and not be afraid of asking God's help.

Prayer for Peace:

God of living waters, you have invited us to drink freely and without fear. We give thanks that you leave us your peace and ease our troubled hearts.

Spiritual Practice for the Week: Encountering Scripture as Continuing Revelation

Each day this week read and pray with the Doctrine and Covenants as continuing revelation of God's vision for the church and creation. Choose a favorite section or focus on recent counsel in Sections 156–164.

Read a few selected paragraphs slowly three or four times. Pause to pray for deep understanding of meaning after the first reading. Pray for your heart and emotions to open to the text after the second reading. After the third reading, prayerfully ask to hear the particular phrase or word that speaks to you or touches your life. Stay with this word or phrase. Listen as fully and openly as you can. What sense of divine presence or invitation comes? What is revealed?

Peace Covenant:

God, I will not be afraid to ask for your help and peace.

16
Saturday
June

The Presence of the Community

By Betty Snapp of Independence, Missouri, USA

When your willingness to live in sacred community as Christ's new creation exceeds your natural fear of spiritual and relational transformation, you will become who you are called to be. The rise of Zion the beautiful, the peaceful reign of Christ, awaits your wholehearted response to the call to make and steadfastly hold to God's covenant of peace in Jesus Christ.
—Doctrine and Covenants 164:9b

Not long ago I realized we are all connected. This occurred to me when memories flooded my mind of friends and community companions who have accompanied me on my faith journey.

Reflections of my Community of Christ congregation flashed through my mind, like a movie playing before my eyes. It slowly rolled back and revealed the faces and personalities of so many who played key roles in my journey.

Those faces, many of whom have passed away but are not forgotten, strengthened and supported my faith over the years. They are bits of memories that will last a lifetime—a woven tapestry, a strong rope that keeps me securely, faithfully, and spiritually connected.

I see the beautiful smiles and love of the nursery and children's Sunday school classes (including hugs). I hear kind words of enthusiasm offered to everyone. I feel acceptance given that gets us through another difficult week. I hear inspirational sounds offered by those who are gifted with music.

I am changed by the spoken word. I am filled with God's presence joining the presence of the community.

My faith journey thrives on these powerful connections from the past and the present. Because of the blessings of community in my congregation, I can keep my connection with God and do my part to share the peace of Jesus Christ.

Prayer for Peace:

God of connections, we thank you for all who have gone before us and helped shape our journey. We thank you for your presence, which graces us with companionship. We thank you for the future filled with hope and faith to follow your path to peace.

Spiritual Practice:

Sit quietly as you enter intercessory reflection and prayer. Ask God to bring people to your heart who need prayer. Be open to images of the people or spiritual insight into their needs. Listen for signals from their lives and let the depth of God's love become powerful and real to you. Ask a prayer of blessing and healing for them.

Peace Covenant:

Mystery God, as it is made known to me, I will be ready to do what I am called to do.

17
Sunday
June

Chosen to Serve

By Greg Savage of Lee's Summit, Missouri, USA

> *...And Samuel said to Jesse, "Send and bring him; for we will not sit down until he comes here." He sent and brought him in. ...The Lord said, "Rise and anoint him; for this is the one." Then Samuel took the horn of oil, and anointed him in the presence of his brothers; and the spirit of the Lord came mightily upon David from that day forward.*
>
> —1 Samuel 16:11–13

God commanded the prophet Samuel to search out Jesse, for the Lord would anoint one of his sons eventually to be king. As each son came forward, Samuel thought this would be the one, but the Lord said, "no" to each one.

Finally, Samuel asked Jesse, "Are all of your sons here?" Jesse confirmed the youngest son was tending sheep. Samuel called Jesse's son, David, to appear before him. As he did, the Lord told Samuel to "Rise and anoint him, for this is the one."

Early in the ministry of Jesus, he called for several to become his disciples. The chosen 12 were each unique, and Jesus brought unity to their diversity. In John 15:16, Jesus told his disciples "You did not choose me but I chose you. And I appoint you to go and bear fruit, fruit that will last..."

My evangelist blessing counsels me to bring my life to the table as an offering. I have experienced "the blessedness that is happiness, has its foundation in him, in his purpose, in his power, in his...love."

When my wife, Becky, became director of Leadership Development for Community of Christ, I was reassigned. Never in my dreams did I imagine I would I be chosen to serve as pastor of the Stone Church Congregation. I received this assignment with mixed emotions—shock and awe!

However, as I began to learn about the congregation's history, I met many members, and the Spirit gently reminded me this was God's work and not mine. It was a rewarding experience to work beside those committed to the mission of Jesus Christ. My evangelist blessing told me that my greatest satisfaction and joy in life would be when I was promoting oneness with God. The Spirit of the Lord has richly blessed me in my chosen ministry.

Prayer for Peace:

God of grace, we would be your ministers and servants. We pray that all will find their calling. Bless us with faith and strength to promote peace for you.

Spiritual Practice for the Week: Honoring the Worth of All Persons

Each day this week read Psalm 139:13–18. After each reading sit quietly and let the deep meaning sink into your mind, heart, and body. What thoughts and feelings do you have about being "fearfully and wonderfully made" (Psalm 139:14a)?

Sense the intimate knowledge God has of you and every child ever born. Ask God for an awareness of the sacred worth of each person. Weep with God over the soul-wounding forces and events that rob people of dignity and worth. How are you invited to notice, protect, heal, and affirm the spiritual identity of all God's people?

Peace Covenant:

I will remember, God, that you chose me. In response, I will go and bear the fruit that lasts.

18
Monday
June

Beauty in the Desert

By Paul McCain of Oklahoma City, Oklahoma, USA

> *...let them seek peace and pursue it. For the eyes of the Lord are on the righteous, and his ears are open to their prayer.*
>
> —1 Peter 3:11–12

It was a hot, dry, windy spring day in Oklahoma, and two of my granddaughters and I made the 45-minute trip to Norman for the Medieval Fair. We had to walk a long way from where we parked to the fair entrance. We then walked around for hours in the blowing dust, detouring through shady spots when we could.

At the fair we saw something that, for me, made it all worthwhile. There is an organization that rescues birds of prey. It helps the birds get ready to reenter the world they are born for. The trainers explained many interesting facts, but the best part was when they let the birds demonstrate their flying abilities.

It's not often one gets to see a hawk, falcon, or owl fly just inches above your head, going from one trainer to another.

My mind went to all the people in world who need rescuing—people who are injured, or in some way struggling. Like the trainer-spokesman at the fair, who dreamed as a youth of being able to experience nature more fully, I, too, want to be more involved in the rescue process.

I want to share the story of how vulnerable we are and often need to be rescued. I want to share the One who authors rescue plans. God's ears are open to the prayers of those in need.

May we all be open to the needs of those around us and be willing to join in the rescue of souls, whatever circumstances they are in.

Prayer for Peace:

See our tears, merciful God, hear us when we cry. We need your divine guidance for our lives. Be with us as we seek your peace.

Spiritual Practice for the Week: Honoring the Worth of All Persons

Each day this week read Psalm 139:13–18. After each reading sit quietly and let the deep meaning of the words sink into your mind, heart, and body. Imagine God watching you grow in your mother's womb. What thoughts and feelings do you have about being "fearfully and wonderfully made" (Psalm 139:14a)?

Sense the intimate knowledge God has of you and every child ever born. Ask God for an awareness of the sacred worth of each person on the planet. Weep with God over the soul-wounding forces and events that rob people of dignity and worth. How are you being invited to notice, protect, heal, and affirm the spiritual identity of all God's beloved people today? Pray for God's compassion.

Peace Covenant:

As you have rescued me through Christ, God, I will open myself to the needs of another.

19
Tuesday
June

Place

By David Brock, presiding evangelist

> *Fulfill the purposes of the Temple by making its ministries manifest in your hearts... Let it stand as a towering symbol of a people...who now seek the peace of Jesus Christ throughout the world.*
>
> —Doctrine and Covenants 161:2b

I am surprised with joy in the oddest places, impelled to take off my shoes or kneel in the most unlikely of spaces.

Like you, I've learned the holy One is not bound by geography or architecture. Harsh deserts work, as do forested mountains. God may well meet us as we step across black water running through a narrow walkway between plastic and cardboard hovels in a sprawling city slum.

Sacrament can happen while washing clothes along a crowded river. Divinity may overwhelm us as we watch a slant of late-afternoon light make its way across the floor in a hospital room where our loved one is slowly dying. There's no predicting where God might break through the ordinary in our lives.

Yet, we have a need to create spaces of beauty, to use our own hands to build structures that evoke a sense of wonder. Maybe "the highest calling of the architect," says Alain Botton, "is to render vivid to us who we might ideally be.... Early Christianity and Islam...proposed that beautiful buildings had the power to improve us morally and spiritually. They believed that rather than corrupting us...exquisite surroundings could edge us toward perfection... could reinforce our resolve to be good" (Velma Ruch, *Summoned to Pilgrimage*).

At times, we might learn more about humility by walking through the shadow of the cross in the Worshiper's Path of the Temple and more about the nature of kindness in a stained-glass window than in a holy book.

So, we have responded to the call to build the Temple; a place that breathes to life those intuitions that affirm there is above all a Divinity "in whom we live, and move, and have our being" (E.A. Sovik). The shape of this building becomes a representation of the pilgrim's journey.

This is a road by which the human soul searches for the center and proceeds along the way from chaos to cosmos, from brokenness and confusion to that still point where true life is to be found (Ruch).

Prayer for Peace:

Holy One, may the emerging ministries of the Temple be manifest in us.

Spiritual Practice for the Week: Honoring the Worth of All Persons

Read Psalm 139:13–18. Let the deep meaning of the words sink into you. Be aware of the sacred worth of all persons. How does God invite you to notice, protect, heal, and affirm the spiritual identity of all God's people today?

Peace Covenant:

I will hear the call of the sacred places and find you there, holy One.

20
Wednesday
June

Our Youth: Growing in God

By Sarah and Becky Humphrey of Independence, Missouri, USA

Draw near to God, and he will draw near to you.

—James 4:8

Sarah writes:

Where I feel God the most is at Planet Rock. This is a youth group sponsored by the Walnut Gardens Congregation of Community of Christ.

Planet Rock has helped me to meet new people and connect with God.

Whenever I am there we pray, and I can feel God. It helps me get to know God better. The prayers that people share are inspiring to me because I can feel God's Spirit even closer. We all feel God in different ways, and Planet Rock is where I can feel God near.

Becky writes:

Last summer I had the opportunity to go on the church history caravan. When we were closest to one another and God was when we were on the bus, sharing our beliefs and becoming friends. It was during the long and exhausting hours of driving that we all grew in God. In work and play, God is there for us to know.

Prayer for Peace:

Close and loving God, we would grow even closer to you. Thank you for all the experiences that make it possible. Thank you for the activities of our community, which values us and engages us in ways that bring us together. Thank you for providing avenues of peace.

Spiritual Practice for the Week: Honoring the Worth of All Persons

Each day this week read Psalm 139:13–18. After each reading sit quietly and let the deep meaning of the words sink into your mind, heart, and body. Imagine God watching you grow in your mother's womb. What thoughts and feelings do you have about being "fearfully and wonderfully made" (Psalm 139:14a)?

Sense the intimate knowledge God has of you and every child ever born. Ask God for an awareness of the sacred worth of each person on the planet. Weep with God over the soul-wounding forces and events that rob people of dignity and worth. How are you being invited to notice, protect, heal, and affirm the spiritual identity of all God's beloved people today? Pray for God's compassion.

Peace Covenant:

God, I will support the programs of the community that engage our youth in positive ways.

21
Thursday
June

The Comeback

By Crystal Lichte-Herron of Chadron, Nebraska, USA

> *For the mountains may depart and the hills be removed, but my steadfast love shall not depart from you, and my covenant of peace shall not be removed, says the Lord, who has compassion on you.*
>
> —Isaiah 54:10

We came back from our vacation to a home and garden that had been devastated by a sudden summer hailstorm. After scraping mud from the sides of the house, we repainted. However, we couldn't save the vegetable garden.

The flower garden looked forlorn until new green shoots appeared on the morning glory plants. We were so happy to see them! The most amazing fact was how the plants hit the hardest made a comeback. They were not as lush as before the storm, but they brought a few beautiful blue flowers that lifted our hearts and gave us hope for the future of the perennials.

Storms in life hit all of us. At those times, it is vitally important to open ourselves to God's grace and love, just as the flowers open to the sun and the rain. God is always present for us. As we survive our storms and share our testimonies of God's love and help, we can share the peace of Jesus Christ.

Prayer for Peace:

Ever-present God, we praise you for the return of the perennials every year. We praise you for your steadfast love and your unfaltering covenant of peace. We feel your compassion during our storms. Help us share that compassion through the peace of Jesus Christ.

Spiritual Practice for the Week: Honoring the Worth of All Persons

Each day this week read Psalm 139:13–18. After each reading sit quietly and let the deep meaning of the words sink into your mind, heart, and body. Imagine God watching you grow in your mother's womb. What thoughts and feelings do you have about being "fearfully and wonderfully made" (Psalm 139:14a)?

Sense the intimate knowledge God has of you and every child ever born. Ask God for an awareness of the sacred worth of each person on the planet. Weep with God over the soul-wounding forces and events that rob people of dignity and worth. How are you being invited to notice, protect, heal, and affirm the spiritual identity of all God's beloved people today? Pray for God's compassion.

Peace Covenant:

Today, God, I will make a mental list of the hidden perennials in my life and watch with joy for their return.

22
Friday
June

Surely God Blessed Him

By Gary McDonald of Blue Springs, Missouri, USA

> *I will both lie down and sleep in peace; for you alone, O Lord, make me lie down in safety.*
> —Psalm 4:8

Kyle is a family friend of many years. On a recent visit we discovered he was in terrible health. Kyle suffered from congestive heart failure, diabetes, and breathing complications. He was legally blind. Kyle was seriously overweight and didn't have one day of the week when he honestly could say he felt good.

One afternoon he asked us to take him to the doctor. We said we would, but first we wanted to tell him about the sacrament of laying on of hands for the sick. He listened with patience, respect, and interest. Afterward he asked for that sacrament. After praying we took him to the doctor.

The doctor admitted him to the hospital. The doctor said Kyle needed about 50 pounds of fluid drained from his chest. During the procedure his heart stopped beating. The staff revived him but could not complete the drainage. While he was in intensive care I prayed for him again.

At one point the hospital staff thought Kyle was going to die. I tried to prepare his friend. Together we prayed once more for Kyle and his precarious condition. Two days later he was released from the hospital.

Kyle began walking and swimming. His need for extra oxygen disappeared. The doctor put him on a strict diet, and he lost weight. Today Kyle is a healthy, whole man who spends his time helping others in need. Surely God has blessed him.

Prayer for Peace:

Healing God, we thank you for the sacraments. We thank you for the possibility of wholeness in our lives. We thank you for our safety and our peace.

Spiritual Practice for the Week: Honoring the Worth of All Persons

Each day this week read Psalm 139:13–18. After each reading sit quietly and let the deep meaning of the words sink into your mind, heart, and body. Imagine God watching you grow in your mother's womb. What thoughts and feelings do you have about being "fearfully and wonderfully made" (Psalm 139:14a)?

Sense the intimate knowledge God has of you and every child ever born. Ask God for an awareness of the sacred worth of each person on the planet. Weep with God over the soul-wounding forces and events that rob people of dignity and worth. How are you being invited to notice, protect, heal, and affirm the spiritual identity of all God's beloved people today? Pray for God's compassion.

Peace Covenant:

God, I will remember to come to you in prayer when I am in need.

23
Saturday
June

Two Copper Coins

By Mary Hathaway of Washington, D.C., USA

> *A poor widow came and put in two small copper coins, which are worth a penny. Then he called his disciples and said to them, "Truly I tell you, this poor widow has put in more than all those who are contributing to the treasury. For all of them have contributed out of their abundance; but she out of her poverty has put in everything she had, all she had to live on."*
>
> —Mark 12:42–44

Because I have finances to meet my needs, I decided whatever coins I found in my travels I would donate to the World Hunger Fund. Once, this brought an unexpected return.

A woman ahead of me in line had finished her grocery checkout. I noticed she and the cashier were fumbling in their purses, looking for coins. Fishing out my coin purse, I handed her two pennies. I told her I knew I had the pennies because I had planned on putting them in the World Hunger "can" at church. She accepted the pennies and completed her purchase.

Then to my astonishment she turned back to me and handed me a dollar bill, "for the World Hunger can" she said. The giving of those two coins had returned 200 fold. Praise God for generous people who help us by contributing to the mission initiative of Abolish Poverty, End Suffering, which fights hunger.

Prayer for Peace:

Generous God, may we be generous too. May we give all we can to Abolish Poverty, End Suffering. May we encourage the redirection of funds spent on war to spend them on feeding people, helping those who hurt, and sharing Christ's peace.

Spiritual Practice:

Watch the trees outside your window for a few moments. Close your eyes and meditate on Alma's words about seeds and trees. If you were to plant and grow the Word of God in your heart, what kind of tree might symbolically represent this process? Envision the word-seed as it grows into a tree of life and blessing. Ask God to show you how to begin. (See Alma 16:152–173 Book of Mormon RAV.)

Peace Covenant:

Today, God, I will set up my personal World Hunger "can." I will empty my pockets each day as I empty my soul in prayer—that the money will be used to great effect.

24
Sunday
June

Stand for God

By Susan Skoor, Council of Twelve Apostles

...all the earth may know that there is a God in Israel, and that all this assembly may know that the Lord does not save by sword and spear; for the battle is the Lord's and he will give you into our hand.

—1 Samuel 17:46–47

David was a youth without training in warfare when he confronted Goliath. Saul agreed to let David fight Goliath, but he tried to clothe David in armor that impeded his agility and motion. No one expected David to succeed.

Armed with trust in God and the youthful skills honed in tending sheep, David proved himself and stood strong in faith for God.

When I attended university the young adults took the initiative to plan creative worship services and travel to congregations around Columbia, Missouri. Although some of our ideas were strange and perhaps less than worshipful, we were warmly welcomed wherever we went. No one dismissed us as too young to plan worship services, nor did they weigh us down with tradition and precautions.

Consequently, we had the opportunity to learn by doing. We grew in our ability to plan and carry out meaningful worship services. As we interacted with older adults and began to know them as friends, we began thinking of their needs as we did our planning.

We moved in faith, offering skills still new and untried, standing strong for God. We were secure in the loving embrace of older, wiser people who accepted us as we were, with raw energy and commitment to God. I am who I am today in part because of the generosity of the adults in Columbia, Missouri, who nurtured and loved me in years of exploration.

Now it's time for my generation to empower the youth and young adults as they step up to lead in new ways. I want to give them my armor and encourage them to follow my methods and perspective. However, I will trust them to stand strong for God and slay their own giants in their own way.

Prayer for Peace:

God of all generations, we offer thanks for young adults and youth. Thank you for their vitality, creativity, and joy. Help us build bridges of peace and empowerment between their lives and the lives of older adults.

Spiritual Practice for the Week: Examining God's Call to Me and to All

Each day this week reflect on God's call in your life. Begin by prayerfully asking to recall particular moments when you have experienced God's presence and invitation. Write in your journal or quietly reflect on images and insights that come.

When has God seemed most real in your life? How and when has God called you to use your energies and gifts? When have you felt most deeply connected and responsive to God's movement in your life? When have you felt disconnected or resistant to God's call? How do your gifts and callings connect with the call of God you notice in your family members, friends, congregation, or community?

Peace Covenant:

I will seek wholeness among the generations in the spirit of shalom.

25
Monday
June

The Wind in Our Sails

By Marian Hassell of Richmond, Virginia, USA

Love is patient; love is kind; love is not envious or boastful or arrogant or rude. It does not insist on its own way; it is not irritable or resentful; it does not rejoice in wrongdoing, but rejoices in the truth. It bears all things, believes all things, hopes all things, endures all things.
—1 Corinthians 13:4–7

"It took the wind right out of my sails." I never gave it much thought before, but suddenly this phrase had new meaning. For a sailboat, it would be a time of no movement. The force of the wind enabling forward motion would be temporarily gone.

For a person, it might be an event with an emotional impact that makes response temporarily impossible.

I felt that way as I heard the news of the young freshman violinist. I was stunned. He had jumped from a bridge after being mortified by his roommate and a friend. A life of promise was gone.

Shaming a friend was a cruel act. I might dismiss these two students as people who have nothing in common with me. I would never do anything like that. But what if, in my still moments, I examine not the behavior of those students, but my own actions or inactions.

How do I reach the model of love lived out by Jesus? Am I fulfilling my commitment as a disciple to be a loving servant in my family, at work, at school, at the shopping center? Jesus tells us his disciples are to be known by their love. What would loving people look like? How would they behave? The scripture reading for today gives a concrete list of attributes: patient, kind, not envious, or boastful, or arrogant, or rude, rejoices in truth, bears all things, believes all things, hopes all things, endures all things.

If I am honest, when the wind has gone out of my sails I remember times I have fallen short. That's in the past. Today brings opportunities to move in love—serving as the disciple I feel called to be.

Prayer for Peace:

God of grace, forgive me for all the times I have not been patient or kind. Forgive me for not rejoicing in the truth, for not promoting hope and peace. Help me be mindful of my call to discipleship wherever and whenever there is need.

Spiritual Practice for the Week: Examining God's Call to Me and to All

Each day this week reflect on God's call in your life. Begin by prayerfully asking to recall particular moments when you have experienced God's presence and invitation. Write in your journal or quietly reflect on images and insights that come.

When has God seemed most real in your life? How and when has God called you to use your energies and gifts? When have you felt most deeply connected and responsive to God's movement in your life? When have you felt disconnected or resistant to God's call? How do your gifts and callings connect with the call of God you notice in your family members, friends, congregation, or community?

Peace Covenant:

Today, God, I will look to the model of Jesus and practice *his* love.

26
Tuesday
June

Learn Faith and Love from a Child

By Flo McDonald of Lee's Summit, Missouri, USA

Shun wasteful passions and pursue righteousness, faith, love, and peace, along with those who call on the Lord from a pure heart.

—2 Timothy 2:22, adapted

A deep moment of awakening may come at any time. All are called to be humble and teachable. I received words of encouragement and was blessed by a simple act of kindness.

One day I was trying to paint the high ceilings in my dining room. I stood on the stepladder with the paint and a roller, reaching for the ceiling. I had been working for some time and was getting tired. I began to complain about what a hard job it was.

My first grandson, a toddler, was watching me. He walked to the ladder, hugged it as best he could, looked up at me and said in a loving and compassionate little voice, "My grandma—I'll fix it for you."

I immediately was humbled and ashamed. I stopped painting and took time to give my grandson a big hug and assured him I was all right. This child loved me so much he was willing to help, even though he couldn't.

I have never forgotten that moment. I have come to appreciate the lesson I learned through the words and love of a small child.

There have been times in my life when I have made a great effort to respond to some need only to find I wasn't needed after all. Although I sometimes have thought my time was wasted, I believe that when making the effort willingly, prepared, and with love, our intentions are affirmed in the sight of God.

Prayer for Peace:

We call on you, God, with a desire for a pure heart. May we not wait for comfortable tasks that we are sure we can do. We would not be waiters, but doers. May we be brave enough to share the peace of Jesus Christ.

Spiritual Practice for the Week: Examining God's Call to Me and to All

Each day this week reflect on God's call in your life. Begin by prayerfully asking to recall particular moments when you have experienced God's presence and invitation. Write in your journal or quietly reflect on images and insights that come.

When has God seemed most real in your life? How and when has God called you to use your energies and gifts? When have you felt most deeply connected and responsive to God's movement in your life? When have you felt disconnected or resistant to God's call? How do your gifts and callings connect with the call of God you notice in your family members, friends, congregation, or community?

Peace Covenant:

Today, God, I will accept the challenge and risk myself for peace.

27
Wednesday
June

The Lost Puppy

By Elizabeth Booth of Fort Gratiot, Michigan, USA

> *The effect of righteousness will be peace, and the result of righteousness, quietness and trust forever. My people will abide in a peaceful habitation, in secure dwellings, and in quiet resting places.*
>
> —Isaiah 32:17–18

One brilliant summer day, Bridget my shih tzu puppy, lay in the window, longing to go outside.

She turned and looked at me, her big, black eyes saying, "Please let me go out and enjoy the yard."

I opened the door, and she tore into the backyard.

Little did she know she was about to get more than she bargained for. She found a small hole in the wooden fence, and suddenly Bridget's world got much bigger.

Minutes later I realized she was gone. In desperation I called and called. Suddenly I realized what had happened. I tried and tried to coax her back through the same hole. But in the excitement of exploring and discovering a different world in the neighbor's yard, she wouldn't come.

Soon, though, she found her new surroundings unfriendly and became frightened. But she just wouldn't answer my call. In desperation I called my grandsons, Dylan and Ethan. They went around the fence and into the neighbor's yard, picked up Bridget, and helped her back into her yard.

For many people Bridget's story becomes real as they are enticed by the lure of the world. They wander away from their families and church. They become lost. Unable to find their way home, they begin praying for Jesus to search for them. Finding them, he'll lead them back, where once again they can dwell in Christ's peace.

Prayer for Peace:

Tender Shepherd, who never forgets any sheep, find us when we get lost. Bring us back to the path leading home. Bring us back to the path leading to peace.

Spiritual Practice for the Week: Examining God's Call to Me and to All

Each day this week reflect on God's call in your life. Begin by prayerfully asking to recall particular moments when you have experienced God's presence and invitation. Write in your journal or quietly reflect on images and insights that come.

When has God seemed most real in your life? How and when has God called you to use your energies and gifts? When have you felt most deeply connected and responsive to God's movement in your life? When have you felt disconnected or resistant to God's call? How do your gifts and callings connect with the call of God you notice in your family members, friends, congregation, or community?

Peace Covenant:

When I am lost, God, I will turn to you for guidance.

28
Thursday
June

Fully Immersed in the Spirit

By Elizabeth Else of St. Thomas, Ontario, Canada

Then the eyes of the blind shall be opened, and the ears of the deaf unstopped... For waters shall break forth in the wilderness, and streams in the desert; the burning sand shall become a pool, and the thirsty ground springs of water...the grass shall become reeds and rushes.
—Isaiah 35:5, 7

Several years ago, I was sailing the Aegean Sea. I love being "on" the water and enjoy boating. However, I'm not a strong swimmer and have always been a little hesitant to be "in" the water.

We dropped anchor to explore an area with a sunken city. While others were snorkeling, I stood, unmoving, with my head well out of the water and looked down. I could see the outlines of old house walls, partial doors, windows, and many fish. I thought I was seeing the site well enough.

Another traveler, who knows me well, noticed my reticence to fully immerse myself. Although gently encouraging in the past, and respectful of my right to make decisions, on this occasion she insisted, "You need to try snorkeling."

She took off her goggles and snorkel and put them on me before I could make an excuse. I hesitantly took the plunge.

Suddenly, I saw spectacular sights. The fish had vibrant colors. I saw each stone of the ruins in minute detail. I swam through the doors and examined old walls. Even hearing was different as I listened through the medium of water rather than air. Because I was immersed, I was able to experience a new world of color, creatures, ancient civilization, and sound.

Just as immersing ourselves in water can bring a new world of understanding, so immersing ourselves in the spiritual world can bring new ways of relating to the divine presence around us.

May we be open to a new awareness of God's love and call. Take the plunge. Experience the joy and possibilities of a new way. Be fully immersed in the Spirit.

Prayer for Peace:

Mysterious God, may our eyes be open to learn new ways of seeing and our ears to new ways of hearing. May we discover anew your creation and new ways to quench our thirst with your living water.

Spiritual Practice for the Week: Examining God's Call to Me and to All

Reflect on God's call in your life. Recall particular moments when you have experienced God's presence and invitation. Write in your journal or quietly reflect on images and insights that come. When has God seemed most real in your life? How and when has God called you to use your energy and gifts? How do your gifts and callings connect with God in your family members, friends, congregation, or community?

Peace Covenant:

With the living water of Christ, I will thirst no more for the temporal. I will be one with the Spirit.

29
Friday
June

Put Yourself in Your Pastor's Shoes

By Gary Piper of Fort Gratiot, Michigan, USA

> *Be merciful, just as your Father is merciful.*
>
> —Luke 6:36

Community of Christ pastors have a great deal of responsibility. Like an iceberg, many roles of the pastor are below the surface, where they cannot be seen, only experienced. From time to time we need to remember some important vulnerabilities of a pastor.

Pastors are not superhumans. They have families, which are important to them. *Your* family is important to the pastor, as well. Many Community of Christ pastors also have full-time jobs outside the church. Pastors do not have all the answers. Believe it or not, they even make mistakes!

It may amaze you to learn that pastors are not all things to all people. They can get frustrated. I've even known pastors to get sick, now and then. Pastors have feelings and need to get away for a healthy rest. Unless it's urgent, don't call them while they're on one of their rare vacations.

Here's where *you* come in: Pastors need to be encouraged and loved. They need to be forgiven. Never forget them and other church leaders in your prayers. Your pastor needs you as much as you need your pastor!

One of the greatest struggles of a pastor is how to make the best use of time. Of all the members of the congregation the pastor has perhaps the most potential for being fragmented, pulled this way and that. The pastor also is the person in greatest need of help. So now you know your job.

Prayer for Peace:

Merciful God, we would be merciful, too. Let us put ourselves in the shoes of our leaders. Let us follow them on the road to peace.

Spiritual Practice for the Week: Examining God's Call to Me and to All

Each day this week reflect on God's call in your life. Begin by prayerfully asking to recall particular moments when you have experienced God's presence and invitation. Write in your journal or quietly reflect on images and insights that come.

When has God seemed most real in your life? How and when has God called you to use your energies and gifts? When have you felt most deeply connected and responsive to God's movement in your life? When have you felt disconnected or resistant to God's call? How do your gifts and callings connect with the call of God you notice in your family members, friends, congregation, or community?

Peace Covenant:

Today, God, I will work side by side with my congregational leaders and show them support.

30
Saturday
June

Take Bread from My Repentant Hand

By Peggy Michael of Cantonment, Florida, USA

And again, I say unto you, Sue for peace, not only the people that have smitten you, but also to all people; and lift up an ensign of peace, and make a proclamation for peace unto the ends of the earth.

—Doctrine and Covenants 102:11a–b

How can I ask forgiveness of the Lord, while I am yet sinful? I meditate about tomorrow's Communion service. How can I take the bread, the wine—blessed to the souls of those who partake? The line is thin, and I stumble easily. Would I be taking the symbols of Christ's love and grace in vain? Should I refrain from eating, though I need wholeness so desperately?

I wonder. Do those on their knees beside me fight these silent battles as I do? I strive so hard for lofty goals that seem so unattainable. Yet, I will eat, and drink, and believe that God's love will overcome my sinfulness. Tomorrow, as I leave the table, I will feel forgiveness, my soul restored.

I have made my inward journey to peace. Now my outward journey challenges my proud heart; a pride that may flaunt silken garments in the face of beggars and hollow-cheeked children. No. I will lower my eyes to see their tattered forms. I will hear their hungry whimpers and hasten to their side. Then, perhaps, *they* will forgive me and take a piece of bread from my repentant hand. Grace and generosity endure.

Prayer for Peace:

God of the table of peace, we thank you for our place at the table. We are happy to serve all who will come to your table. Let us go out and invite others to come to the table of peace.

Spiritual Practice:

Compassion is a fruit of the spiritual life. When we open a space for God, we become vessels and channels for the flow of God's justice and healing. Enter into quiet prayer and ask God to open your heart to those who are hungry.

What spiritual and physical hungers do you become aware of? What people or groups come into your mind and heart? What responses are you invited to make?

Pray about and write down the response or action you choose to complete. Is it a phone call; a pantry donation; a check for Abolish Poverty, End Suffering or Outreach International; a visit? Move into completing this action as you leave your prayer space.

Peace Covenant:

Today, God, I will proclaim peace to all who will hear.

1
Sunday
July

Do Not Fear

By Paul Davis, Kansas City, Missouri, USA

> *"...If I but touch his clothes, I will be made well." Immediately her hemorrhage stopped; and she felt in her body that she was healed of her disease. Immediately aware that power had gone forth from him, Jesus turned about in the crowd and said, "Who touched my clothes?"... But the woman, knowing what had happened to her, came in fear and trembling, fell down before him, and told him the whole truth. He said to her, "Daughter, your faith has made you well; go in peace, and be healed of your disease."*
>
> —Mark 5:28–34

It used to be that I wasn't crazy about the story of the woman with the hemorrhages. I think it's that word "hemorrhages"—an ugly word. Her unsightly illness defines her. She has no name. She's not "my lovely friend, Dierdre," say, but the "woman who had suffered from hemorrhages for 12 years." Is that what everyone called her?

I'm learning how to read poems. Now I'm aware that poetry can appear out of nowhere, uninvited, out of ugliness and long-suffering, an interruption not expected. As a poem, the scripture might read something like this:

She had endured much under many
physicians,
had spent all she had;
she was no better, but rather grew worse;
she had heard about him, came up
behind him in the crowd,
touched his cloak,

I have a simple reason for wanting to follow Jesus. He discovered the secret of seeing beauty where I couldn't see at all. I want to see that beauty in the poem:

knowing what had happened to her,
she came in fear and trembling,
fell down before him,
told him the whole truth. He
said to her, "Daughter."

Prayer for Peace:

God, we follow your Son, reaching for his healing garment, clinging to the holy hem with faith that we will become whole, faith that we will see beauty and hope in our lives where we once may have seen despair, faith that we will see peace where we once saw war.

Spiritual Practice for the Week: Making Responsible Choices

Each day this week prayerfully seek God's guidance in your choices. We are invited to orient our lives toward God and creation. Review the responsibilities and opportunities in the day before you. Pray, asking God for wisdom and insight about what matters most. Sit prayerfully with this question as you review the day. Ask for blessing to live this day responsibly and compassionately in the spirit of Christ.

Peace Covenant:

God, I will look at the hemorrhages of this Earth and see the beauty that Jesus sees.

2
Monday
July

Rethinking Priorities

By Dorene Kilburn of Stratford, Ontario, Canada

Out of the depths I cry to you, O Lord. Lord, hear my voice! Let your ears be attentive to the voice of my supplications!...I wait for the Lord, my soul waits, and in his word I hope.
—Psalm 130:1–2, 5

How easy it is to neglect time with God when we have no particular need for Divine help! I recently was reminded of that. I was in a mild frenzy, not eager to face a written test to renew my driver's license. In my province, at a certain age, seniors must take tests every two years.

Because I have a long history of exam anxiety, I spent more early morning time in prayer and meditation in preparation for the test. Failing the test was not an option for me because my husband isn't driving now. I do all the shopping and get us where we need to go.

When I looked at my watch on the morning of the test, I could hardly believe the thought that went through my head: "*Oh, it's later than I thought. Maybe I'll just skip the centering prayer that I've included in my quiet time these past few weeks.*"

Listening more intently to God through the centering prayer has been such a blessing to me, and I was rationalizing I could do without it. God doesn't find excuses to ignore me, and I shouldn't be pushing God into the background.

I now can report that I passed the test, no doubt because of the extra time I spent with God and with the prayers of some dear friends. A lesson learned. I wait for God...and in God's word I find hope!

Prayer for Peace:

Hear my voice, Lord and I will wait to hear your voice. I have hope in the peace of Jesus Christ.

Spiritual Practice for the Week: Making Responsible Choices

Prayerfully seek God's guidance in your choices. Discernment invites us to orient our lives toward God's vision for creation. Begin by reviewing the responsibilities and opportunities in the day before you. Take these choices into prayer, asking God for wisdom and insight about what matters most. Ask for blessing to live this day responsibly and compassionately in the spirit of Christ.

Peace Covenant:

Today, God, I will bring you to the center of my life and spend time with you.

3
Tuesday
July

Joy Shining in Her Face

By Louita Clothier of Lamoni, Iowa, USA

> *For in him all the fullness of God was pleased to dwell, and through him God was pleased to reconcile to himself all things, whether on earth or in heaven, by making peace…*
> —Colossians 1:19–20

During the years my mother struggled with Alzheimer's disease, I increasingly turned to my friend, Margaret, for deep talks. After Mom's death, Margaret became my surrogate mother. Her infectious energy and constant sunny disposition brought joy to my heart. She personified the words in her favorite hymn, "My life flows on in endless song…How can I keep from singing?"

Eventually Margaret entered a nursing home, and I continued to spend time with her. One day as she slept, I studied the face of my dear friend. The crinkles in her face formed a permanent sunny smile, even while she slept. It was as if nature ran a beauty spa. Time gradually had sculpted Margaret's face into an enduring expression of inner beauty. Those happy lines and wrinkles were her reward for eight decades of radiating inner joy to those around her.

I realized that in our later years our faces do not allow us to hide our lifelong outlook. Frowning produces permanent frown marks; smiling produces smile wrinkles. Margaret always showed interest in other people, and she communicated it with her face. Even as she grew increasingly weak, her entire face lit up when she was in a conversation.

Thich Nhat Hanh, a Vietnamese Buddhist monk, once said, "Sometimes your joy is the source of your smile, but sometimes your smile can be the source of your joy." Many people enter a room and say, "Here I am." Margaret entered, and her face said, "Ah, there you are!"

I'm sure Margaret had reasons to be gloomy many times, but her smiling, enthusiastic habit energized herself and those around her. She had a face in which God would be pleased to dwell. Smile, your spirit is showing!

Prayer for Peace:

Smiling God, may we smile and reflect your peaceful Spirit.

Spiritual Practice for the Week: Making Responsible Choices

Each day this week prayerfully seek God's guidance in your choices. Discernment invites us to orient our lives toward God and God's vision for us and for creation. Begin by reviewing the responsibilities and opportunities in the day before you. Take these choices into prayer, asking God for wisdom and insight about what matters most. Offer yourself to God with the prayer of Teresa of Avila: "God, what do you want of me today?" Sit prayerfully with this question as you review the day again. Be aware of images, thoughts, names, or actions that come to you. Ask for blessing to live this day responsibly and compassionately in the spirit of Christ.

Peace Covenant:

Today, God, I will reconcile all concerns in my life and make peace.

4
Wednesday
July

Steadfast Community

By Lynn Brady of Chicago, Illinois, USA

For the mountains shall depart and the hills be removed, but my kindness shall not depart from thee, neither shall the covenant of my peace be removed, saith the Lord that hath mercy on thee.

—III Nephi 10:18

The announcement was made months ahead in the weekly bulletin of our congregation. We invited all to come hear and watch our church president, Stephen M. Veazey, give his annual address to the church. We made plans to watch the big screen in the sanctuary. We ordered lunch. We made child-care provisions.

Our morning worship ended at 1:00 p.m., leaving five hours before the president's address. The people gathered in companionship and expectancy. Suddenly the lights flickered, and the church was without electricity. We tried to restore the power by resetting the fuses. No success. We called the electric company, and it told us the problem already had been reported. The agent said service should resume by 5:30 p.m.

My heart raced, fearing we wouldn't be able to watch the event. People began to express concern, and some said we should leave. But I was prayerful God would restore the electricity in time.

Praise God—at 5:15 p.m. there was light! We began to set up for viewing the address but couldn't connect to the Internet. People began to share more concerns, and a few left. I am grateful for the steadfast group that remained. The people gathered around a nine-inch laptop computer screen in a church office to watch and listen about "What Matters Most."

That day I happily witnessed a determined group of people seeking our enduring principle of Continuing Revelation. In humility, individually and as a community, they prayerfully listened to understand God's will for our lives, the church, and creation.

Prayer for Peace:

God of kindness and mercy, we wait on your words for us. We are expectant of your sharing direction for our lives, focusing on what matters most.

Spiritual Practice for the Week: Making Responsible Choices

Prayerfully seek God's guidance in your choices. Discernment invites us to orient our lives toward God's vision for creation. Begin by reviewing the responsibilities and opportunities in the day before you. Take these choices into prayer, asking God for wisdom and insight about what matters most. Sit prayerfully with this question as you review the day again. Be aware of images, thoughts, names, or actions that come to you. Ask for blessing to live this day responsibly and compassionately in the spirit of Christ.

Peace Covenant:

Today, God, I will listen closely to what you instill in the leaders of our community.

5
Thursday
July

Wind Chimes

By Lu Mountenay of Independence, Missouri, USA

For just as the body is one and has many members, and all the members of the body, though many, are one body, so it is with Christ. For in the one Spirit we were all baptized into one body—Jews or Greeks, slaves or free—and we were all made to drink of one Spirit. Indeed, the body does not consist of one member but of many.

—1 Corinthians 12:12–14

I was sitting on my patio watching for hummingbirds and listening to the wind chimes. No hummers showed up for their free breakfast, so I decided to *watch* the wind chimes, as well as listen to them.

First, I noticed that when the breeze stopped, the melody stopped—obviously. The chimes had to touch one another to make sound. It was a team effort. One chime alone could not make the music, and they needed the outside force, wind, to move.

I think this is like community. We must touch each other's lives to create compositions of blessing, praising God for the spirit that blows us into action, the outside force moving into us and allowing us to move and touch others.

Second, I focused on the different length of each chime. Short for the high notes and long for the deep notes.

We need them all—working together to make the melody complete. Each is important for a full range of notes.

Again, this reminds me of life. I would not like to think of what our communities would be like without the contribution of each member—the long and the short (me).

Our differences are what add to the variety of our worship, companionship, and outreach. Through our diversity, we have a unity that has blessed our community and created harmony to move forward in mission, sharing the peace of Jesus Christ.

Prayer for Peace:

God of diversity, bless us in our callings. May we foster companionship and the Blessings of Community by reaching out to one another. May we build lasting peace based on our enduring principles and our wish to share the peace of Christ.

Spiritual Practice for the Week: Making Responsible Choices

Prayerfully seek God's guidance in your choices. Discernment invites us to orient our lives toward God's vision for creation. Begin by reviewing the responsibilities and opportunities in the day before you. Take these choices into prayer, asking God for wisdom and insight about what matters most. Ask for blessing to live this day responsibly and compassionately in the spirit of Christ.

Peace Covenant:

Today God, I will not withhold myself from your diverse choir. I will encourage various voices to join the call to peace.

6
Friday
July

Energy and Passion for Music

By Hannah Snyder of Ashland, Ohio, USA

> *. . . and with gratitude in your hearts sing psalms, hymns, and spiritual songs to God. And whatever you do, in word or deed, do everything in the name of the Lord Jesus, giving thanks to God the Father through him.*
>
> —Colossians 3:16–17

The following is a letter written to Hal McKain of Lamoni, Iowa, after a band camp at Graceland University:

I am among the many kids who were part of the Glassmen Drum and Bugle Corps in the summer of 2010. We were part of an event that often gets brushed off by sports athletes and their coaches. That's why it was significant you noticed our rehearsal behind your house that Sunday. Music can be emotional, but even so, it's easy to forget why we got into music in the first place—to touch people.

As I sit in my apartment in Ohio, sipping water out of my Graceland University water bottle, I am reminded of that night's ensemble. The sunset was beautiful, everyone was full of energy and passion, and the run-through was successful. You helped us remember why we love drum corps when we needed reminding most.

On the previous night we were in Minneapolis, Minnesota. Because of a huge storm, we stood in an ice hockey rink for hours, cold, hungry, and tired. In the morning one of our buses broke down for what seemed like the millionth time, and we had to leave it behind for repairs. We had little sleep and even less patience.

I want you know how much your kind words and your gift touched each member of the drum corps. My friends and I slipped our lucky dollar coins in the front pocket of our uniforms for every show of the tour. It reminds me of our day at Graceland. It reminds me that every day we have the opportunity to touch others without even realizing how much it could mean to them.

Prayer for Peace:

God of music and the rhythms of the Earth, we thank you for those who touch our lives with kindness and share with us the peace of Christ.

Spiritual Practice for the Week: Making Responsible Choices

Prayerfully seek God's guidance in your choices. Discernment invites us to orient our lives toward God's vision for creation. Begin by reviewing the responsibilities and opportunities in the day before you. Take these choices into prayer, asking God for wisdom and insight about what matters most. Ask for blessing to live this day responsibly and compassionately in the spirit of Christ.

Peace Covenant:

Today God, I will not brush off or pass by those who are making an effort to touch others. I will recognize their efforts and show my appreciation for them.

7
Saturday
July

Into the Future

By Sandra Ferguson of Independence, Missouri, USA

> *. . . You received without payment; give without payment.*
>
> —Matthew 10:8

During the final morning of the 2010 International Leaders Meeting, President Stephen M. Veazey spoke about the future of the church. A young man had written to him about his struggles over the years, resulting in several attempts to commit suicide.

Through contact with a church member the young man received a copy of Doctrine and Covenants 164. Deeply touched by what he read, he described it as "simple, pure, revealed truth (that) washed my soul in hope and life."

The letter so moved President Veazey that he and his wife, Cathi, decided to increase their contributions to World Mission Tithes so all may experience the hope of the gospel.

He then invited those in the assembly to increase their contributions to World Mission Tithes, as well.

The next week, the Presiding Bishopric received this note from Human Resource Director Steve Graffeo: "Requests from the international field for automatic monthly salary deductions for World Mission Tithes continue. Moved during the morning session last week, several came into the office personally with their requests. Requests continued as they traveled home."

Contributions to World Mission Tithes—from all members and friends of the church—are critical in sharing the hope of the gospel and saving lives physically, relationally, and spiritually. Thank you for responding by giving generously.

Prayer for Peace:

Creator God, you have blessed us so generously. May we respond by being generous so physical and spiritual needs of others are met. May we share the hope and peace of Jesus Christ.

Spiritual Practice:

Gather a small mound of stones. Meditate on the stones as symbols of differences and destructive acts that continue to separate and wound the human family. Name and anoint each "stone wound" with a drop of water or scented oil. Offer them to God in a prayer for healing and reconciliation.

Peace Covenant:

Today, God, I will try to be aware of those in emotional stress. I will share the hope of Christ with them.

8
Sunday
July

Proclaim the Good News

By John Wight, senior president of seventy

"And (Jesus) could do no deed of power there, except that he laid his hands on a few sick people and cured them. And he was amazed at their unbelief.... "So (the 12) went out and proclaimed that all should repent. They cast out many demons, and anointed with oil many who were sick and cured them."

—Mark 6:5–6, 12–13

As I walked into the mission center conference, the pastor of a congregation I had visited a few months earlier approached and excitedly began sharing some news.

"We started praying for a family to come to the congregation, and we now have that family," he said with a smile. "The parents and three children!"

This story illustrates well the principles expressed in today's scripture reading. When we are willing to exercise our faith and proclaim the good news, good things happen.

This congregation's "proclamation" began by simply opening the front doors of the church to the neighborhood. The mother who began bringing her family members explained they had noticed the open doors and decided they should go into the church.

The next "proclamation" came in the welcoming ministry expressed by the congregation members. They shared the love and peace of Jesus Christ in ways that allowed this family to feel at home; to feel part of the community.

The final "proclamation" was in sharing God's word and the identity, mission, message, and beliefs of Community of Christ.

Unlike the people of Nazareth in the reading whose unbelief amazed Jesus, the congregation members chose to put their faith to work like the 12 who Jesus chose. As a result, they have been blessed with five new participants in their "family."

Prayer for Peace:

Faithful God, douse our burning unbelief with your living water. Clear the doubt from our hearts that we may proclaim your love and peace.

Spiritual Practice for the Week: Embodying God's Shalom

Each day this week find a way to express and embody God's shalom. Begin by prayerfully listening to your longing for peace. Become silent and imagine you can hear the groaning of the Earth's peoples, nations, and creatures. Prayerfully open yourself to God's yearning for peace and the divine vision of shalom.

What images, feelings, and words come to you? What prayer for peace comes to you from your time of listening? Speak or write this prayer. What small act of justice, kindness, healing, or peacemaking is God inviting you to consider this day, this week?

Peace Covenant:

Today, God, I will find a listener to hear of my own repentance and forgiveness.

9
Monday
July

Growing in God

By Steve Bradford of Lee's Summit, Missouri, USA

We know that all things work together for good for those who love God, who are called according to his purpose.

—Romans 8:28

The summer after my senior year at Graceland University I served as a Graceland representative. My main assignment was to attend Community of Christ youth and family camps all over the USA. I promoted Graceland and supported the events and ministries at the camps.

I confess I would have done it without pay. I loved it…I loved being around the youth and young adults of the church. I loved their energy, and I loved that I didn't have to grow up right away and get a *real* job.

At camp I felt safe to be the person I wanted to be. I connected to the Divine, and nothing could get in my way.

My soul was on fire, and it sustained me through the summer.

I came to understand my job wasn't recruiting. It was about ministry and creating communities where youth and young adults could feel safe—safe to be the people *they* wanted to be and feel connected to the Divine so nothing could get in *their* way.

I am convinced fire burns within each of us. It burns hot and bright, and it's not our own. It comes from God, and we have a responsibility to feed it and reflect it to our families *and* strangers alike.

That summer changed me. It solidified my connection to God and the church and helped me understand my gifts. I had to stretch and express myself in ways that were uncomfortable. It made me want to be a better person, and I go back every year. Some people shudder at the thought of spending a week with a cabin full of six to eight teenagers, but I love it. I see the impact camp has on their lives.

I'm thankful for Community of Christ, which continues to challenge me. My theological understanding has been nudged to greater understanding. But just like that summer, I feel safe here. This is my sanctuary.

Prayer for Peace:

Creator God, we thank you for sanctuaries where we feel close to you and can gather strength to share the peace of Jesus Christ.

Spiritual Practice for the Week: Embodying God's Shalom

Find a way to express and embody God's shalom. Prayerfully listen to your longing for peace. Become silent and imagine you can hear the groaning of the Earth's people, nations, and creatures. What images, feelings, and words come to you? Speak or write a prayer. What small act of justice, kindness, healing, or peacemaking is God inviting you to consider this day, this week?

Peace Covenant:

With strength from you, God, I will share the good news.

10
Tuesday
July

Reconciliation: Worth the Effort

By Hal McKain of Lamoni, Iowa, USA

> *But the wisdom from above is first pure, then peaceable, gentle, willing to yield, full of mercy and good fruits, without a trace of partiality or hypocrisy.*
>
> —James 3:17

There's a reason it's called SPECTACULAR (or more commonly, SPEC). It's an annual, week-long camp for high school students sponsored by Community of Christ and Graceland University. And, true to its name, it is spectacular!

A university campus is the perfect place for the myriad of activities. Exhibited each year are good sportsmanship, talent, and equal opportunity in sports, arts, crafts, music, drama, and worship opportunities.

Many leaders volunteer for the week and pay their own registration fee. I have enjoyed attending all of these camps since they started. I have been privileged to run the swim meet.

We realize when humans are involved there usually will be a few uncomfortable times. I had one at the swimming pool during a meet. A spectator was behaving inappropriately. I asked him to stop. He continued to argue, and finally I let him have the last word.

On the last day of camp, I saw him heading out the door, so I quickly went to him, gave him a shiny, new US dollar coin and told him it might bring him luck.

The belligerent look on his face changed immediately to a big smile. I don't know if we'll ever meet again, but I believe we will joyously remember that moment—a brief effort at reconciliation.

Prayer for Peace:

Patient God, give us understanding for the person who may be hurting. Let us set aside differences and reach out with smiles.

Spiritual Practice for the Week: Embodying God's Shalom

Each day this week find a way to express and embody God's shalom. Begin by prayerfully listening to your longing for peace. Become silent and imagine you can hear the groaning of the Earth's people, nations, and creatures. Prayerfully open yourself to God's yearning for peace and the divine vision of shalom.

What images, feelings, and words come to you? What prayer for peace comes to you from your time of listening? Speak or write this prayer. What small act of justice, kindness, healing, or peacemaking is God inviting you to consider this day, this week?

Peace Covenant:

Today God, I will understand another's pain.

11
Wednesday
July

What's the Difference?

By Barrie Fox of Kirkby-in-Ashfield, Nottinghamshire, England

You are a good and faithful people, but sometimes you fail to see the power that is resident in your own story and fellowship. Look carefully, listen attentively, and sense the Spirit among you.

—Doctrine and Covenants 162:8a

Many details surround us in our daily lives. Yet we somehow are not aware of them until a particular incident draws them to our attention.

We then find ourselves quietly mouthing the words, "Well, I never noticed that."

I am thinking of some wonders of nature. We don't notice them at the time, but perhaps remember them later and are thankful for their blessing.

Acts of kindness done for us but not realized or fully appreciated at the time later are grasped for their significance.

Recently, in a short homily I gave in my home congregation, I used the four kings from an ordinary deck of cards to illustrate this point.

I simply held up the cards and asked the congregation to tell me the major differences between them (other than their color and suit). In the few seconds I allowed, nobody could offer the answers I was seeking.

The king of spades is the only one of the four looking to his left. The king of hearts is the only one that doesn't have a moustache. The king of diamonds is the only one showing just one eye and not carrying a sword; he carries an ax.

The playing cards are not important, but this simple illustration makes the point that we don't always notice little differences that might be important.

My homily also discussed relationships and focused on wanting to be more aware of the needs, worries, and concerns of others. We talked about gifts not used to their full potential. Relationships and positive awareness can be valuable in our efforts to serve God and to offer ministry where needed.

Prayer for Peace:

Open my eyes, O Lord, that I may see. Let me listen attentively. Let me sense your Spirit of peace among us.

Spiritual Practice for the Week: Embodying God's Shalom

Find a way to express and embody God's shalom. Begin by prayerfully listening to your longing for peace. Become silent and imagine you can hear the groaning of the Earth's peoples, nations, and creatures. Prayerfully open yourself to God's yearning for peace and the divine vision of shalom.

What images, feelings, and words come to you? What prayer for peace comes to you from your time of listening? Speak or write this prayer. What small act of justice, kindness, healing, or peacemaking is God inviting you to consider this day, this week?

Peace Covenant:

Today, God, I will not take for granted the blessings around me.

12
Thursday
July

Nearly Crushed in Spirit

By Deb Crowley of Eaton Rapids, Michigan, USA

The Lord is near to the brokenhearted, and saves the crushed in spirit.
—Psalm 34:18

She found herself in a second failing marriage. With seven children under age 14 to care for, she was distraught and did not know what to do.

The first marriage ended when the father opted to spend the week's paycheck at the bar rather than buy food for the family. Her next husband was abusive to her and the children. They lived in a broken-down, drafty hovel, which she struggled to turn into a comfortable home. How had life taken such a wrong turn?

She lived miles from her family support system. She had grown up in a healthy home, her mom making sure she went to church regularly. Her folks had always supported her, but now they lived far away and were at an age when travel was hard. Long-distance phone calls were expensive, and she had long separated herself from church and friends.

She knew without God's help, there was no hope. She dusted off the family Bible, gathered the children, and read from the book with unpracticed cadence. She knelt and prayed.

Her action spoke volumes. It made an impression that would be remembered 50 years later. Were her prayers answered as her faith expected? Not knowing the exact substance of her petition, it's hard to know. But God responded to this mother's need and the long-term needs of the children.

This experience taught me that God is ever-present. A mother's hope and love caused her to fall to her knees for guidance when her own efforts were not enough. Life is no less complicated, but we never have to go it alone. God is ever faithful.

My mother's legacy was a desperate act that resulted in bountiful blessing. Seven children, in their own way, accept and follow Christ—not just in times of trouble, but in their daily walks. Their Bibles are not dusty. Prayer is not awkward. God is real. An awesome answer to a mother's prayer!

Prayer for Peace:

Be near us, God. Hear our prayers. We have faith in your mercy. Lead us to peace for the sake of the children of the world.

Spiritual Practice for the Week: Embodying God's Shalom

Find a way to express and embody God's shalom. Imagine you can hear the groaning of the Earth's people, nations, and creatures. Open yourself to God's divine vision of shalom. What images, feelings, and words come to you? Speak or write a prayer. What small act of justice, kindness, healing, or peacemaking is God inviting you to consider this day, this week?

Peace Covenant:

Today, God, on my knees I will pray for all that is not right in my life.

13
Friday
July

Janey and Dorcas

By Cindy Korf of North Platte, Nebraska, USA

But seek the welfare of the city where I have sent you into exile, and pray to the Lord on its behalf, for in its welfare you will find your welfare.

—Jeremiah 29:7

The story of Dorcas is told in the New Testament in Acts. Her kindness and generosity are praised.

In the Yuma Congregation in Colorado is a woman who might display the generosity and kindness of Dorcas. Her name is Janey.

One evening when I returned home from work, I was surprised to see her car parked in front of my house. She had brought supper, knowing I had been ill. Not finding me home, she had taken the supper into the house, put it in the oven, set the table, and washed the dishes piled in the sink.

Another time, I complimented her on a beautiful brooch. She took it off and pinned it to my blouse, saying, "It's yours. It looks better on you than me."

During a visit to Yuma for church, she asked me to come into a private room. She handed me a beautiful beaded dress. She said, "I heard that you've been unable to find a dress for your son's wedding. You can have mine."

We are blessed by the presence of people like Dorcas and Janey, who are examples of the gospel, generous and caring for the welfare of others.

Prayer for Peace:

We pray for cities, God, and on behalf of all people whose welfare is in danger. May we be generous and kind wherever we go on our journey to peace.

Spiritual Practice for the Week: Embodying God's Shalom

Each day this week find a way to express and embody God's shalom. Begin by prayerfully listening to your longing for peace. Become silent and imagine you can hear the groaning of the Earth's peoples, nations, and creatures. Prayerfully open yourself to God's yearning for peace and the divine vision of shalom.

What images, feelings, and words come to you? What prayer for peace comes to you from your time of listening? Speak or write this prayer. What small act of justice, kindness, healing, or peacemaking is God inviting you to consider this day, this week?

Peace Covenant:

Today, God, I will consider another's welfare before my own.

14
Saturday
July

Christ is Our Foundation

By Nelda Kerr of Claremont, California, USA

> *...for during a severe ordeal of affliction, their abundant joy and their extreme poverty have overflowed in a wealth of generosity on their part. For, as I can testify, they voluntarily gave according to their means, and even beyond their means, begging us earnestly for the privilege of sharing in this ministry to the saints—and this, not merely as we expected; they gave themselves first to the Lord and, by the will of God, to us.*
>
> —2 Corinthians 8:2–5

I spent one year as a World Service Corps volunteer in Peru. Monte Sion is a poor community. Several women each have five or more small children. At first it seemed their lives had little in common with mine. I am a young woman who travels the world without worry or duty of working for my family. But during the time I was there, we learned our basic human needs are the same.

We all can identify with yearning for a strong family and the hope for a bright future.

I came to call these women my "mommas." When I missed the comfort of my own mother their touch, laughter, and kind eyes offered me comfort. On my last day in the village we wept at the joy we found in one another, promising we always would carry one another in the deepest place of our hearts, with Christ as our foundation.

Your contributions to World Mission Tithes provide missionary outreach through programs such as World Service Corps, a ministry without borders. Thank you for responding faithfully by giving generously.

Prayer for Peace:

Universal God, help us tear down our walls and borders. Help us join hands and hearts in our outreach ministry. Send us, either in person or by our tithes, to places in need. Help us share hope and the peace of Christ worldwide.

Spiritual Practice:

Today's intercessory prayer is adapted from the Quaker tradition. Become still and turn your attention to God. Prayerfully identify a person in need of healing, blessing, or guidance. Close your eyes and imagine God's presence surrounding the person. See or sense the person being held in God's light. Continue holding the person in the light and release the person into whatever blessing God knows is needed.

Words are not necessary. Trust the spirit to see and penetrate more deeply than human awareness. Thank God and close with amen.

Peace Covenant:

Today, God, I will give myself *first* to you.

15
Sunday
July

Set Your Hope on Christ

By Becky Savage, First Presidency

He destined us for adoption as his children through Jesus Christ, according to the good pleasure of his will, to the praise of his glorious grace that he freely bestowed on us in the Beloved.
—Ephesians 1:5–6

In this text, the Apostle Paul is assuring the Jews and Gentiles of the early Christian church at Ephesus that they are all God's children. Paul's message also tells each of us that we, too, are adopted into God's family. The blessing is secured through the sacrifice of Jesus Christ. It is difficult to imagine the magnitude of this gift.

My husband and I spent many years, through multiple medical procedures, medications, and therapies, trying to have children. Modern science, while helpful for many, could not resolve our physical conditions. After much prayer and discussion we decided to apply for adoption. We were blessed with the gift of two beautiful daughters.

Some tell us how wonderful we are for adopting. I do not feel we have done anything special. In fact, we are the ones who have been adopted. Our daughters make us a family. They continue to bless us. Through them, we are learning to receive, accept, and give love.

God's promise, given so many years ago in Ephesus, is still happening today. Jesus came as our brother. He adopted those he met into this amazing family. He has adopted each of us into God's loving family. No wonder we set our hope on Christ.

Prayer for Peace:

God of family, we open our arms to all you put in our reach. We accept and embrace them. We have hope in the peace we can share.

Spiritual Practice for the Week: Welcoming Unity in Diversity

Each day this week meditate on unity in diversity. Prayerfully read Doctrine and Covenants 163:8c, which calls "the entire church to become a sanctuary of Christ's peace, where people from all nations, ethnicities, and life circumstances can be gathered into a spiritual home without dividing walls."

Create a large circle with your arms. See and feel the diverse people God invites inside the sanctuary of Christ's peace represented by this circle. Who is easiest to welcome? Whom do you struggle to include? Confess the dividing walls between you and people too different or "dangerous" to invite into your spiritual home. Ask God to forgive and heal barriers that keep you and others from being one in Christ's peace.

Peace Covenant:

Today, God, I will reach further to expand my family and community. I will share the peace of Christ with them.

16
Monday
July

Listening to the Spirit

By Geoff Henshaw of Independence, Missouri, USA

> *Let me hear what God the Lord will speak, for he will speak peace to his people, to his faithful, to those who turn to him in their hearts.*
>
> —Psalm 85:8

In 2002 my wife and I boarded the train in Melbourne, Australia, to travel to Sydney. We had spent the last month visiting with Dad. That morning, he had decided to come to the railway station to see us off. My nephew also was traveling with us to Albury. The public-address system asked people who were not traveling to disembark because the train was getting ready to leave.

Dad got off the train and walked from the station. I told my wife and nephew I was going to watch him leave. Dad did not realize I was watching him. I reboarded the train, and my nephew asked, "Why did you do that?" I replied, "You never know. I may not see him again."

On September 13, 2002, my father passed away from a massive heart attack. I have thought about that moment at the train station many times. It may be argued that it was a mere coincidence that I got off the train to watch Dad. However, I choose to believe a "prompting of the Spirit" caused me to watch my Dad for the last time.

I will always be grateful for that experience. It was a reassurance to me of the presence and blessing of the Holy Spirit in the sadness and joys of life.

Prayer for Peace:

God whose Spirit speaks to us, may we always be listening. May we always turn our hearts to you, for you are our guide to peace.

Spiritual Practice for the Week: Welcoming Unity in Diversity

Each day this week meditate on unity in diversity. Prayerfully read Doctrine and Covenants 163:8c, which calls "the entire church to become a sanctuary of Christ's peace, where people from all nations, ethnicities, and life circumstances can be gathered into a spiritual home without dividing walls."

Create a large circle with your arms. See and feel the diverse people God invites inside the sanctuary of Christ's peace represented by this circle. Who is easiest to welcome? Whom do you struggle to include? Confess the dividing walls between you and people too different or "dangerous" to invite into your spiritual home. Ask God to forgive and heal barriers that keep you and others from being one in Christ's peace.

Peace Covenant:

Today, God, I will listen to you with all my heart.

17
Tuesday
July

To Pursue the Holy

By Coralie Rose of Puyallup, Washington, USA

The temple shall be dedicated to the pursuit of peace. It shall be for reconciliation and for healing of the spirit.

—Doctrine and Covenants 156:5a

A year before the June 1997 Leadership Conference in Independence, Missouri, a need to personally experience the Temple began to take hold of my mind. My chance for this to become a reality seemed so remote that I thought it more likely I would visit the beautiful and sacred building in spirit only.

As I turned this idea over in my mind, the passage from the Doctrine and Covenants describing the purpose of the Temple rose before me. Dedicated to the pursuit of peace, reconciliation and healing of the spirit—the Temple has a worthy purpose indeed.

A special gathering of Community of Christ members would surely raise the probability of some manifestation of the Holy Spirit ministering among those present, I thought. Perhaps I could discern the Spirit at a gathering such as the Leadership Conference.

My friend, Lynn, invited me to attend with her, and a way to visit the Temple began to open. The smaller leadership gathering would give me space to see and feel the Temple. I volunteered to usher and greet attendees. Surely I would be able to discern any movement of the Holy Spirit among the congregation assembled there.

The Worshiper's Path was nearly deserted as I hurried in. I slowed as I approached the shadow of the cross. I immediately was aware of the Holy Spirit, characterized by a blend of peacefulness and power filling the entire pathway.

My soul rejoiced, and I gladly would have stayed forever in that moment, basking in the Spirit's healing presence. I also understood my task was to continue on my way. Reluctantly, but full of hope, I moved up the pathway, awed and assured of God's love.

Prayer for Peace:

God of all sacred places, which is to say, God of all creation, go before us. Touch us with your healing spirit. Lead us in our pursuit of peace.

Spiritual Practice for the Week: Welcoming Unity in Diversity

Each day this week meditate on unity in diversity. Prayerfully read Doctrine and Covenants 163:8c, which calls "the entire church to become a sanctuary of Christ's peace, where people from all nations, ethnicities, and life circumstances can be gathered into a spiritual home without dividing walls."

Create a large circle with your arms. See and feel the diverse people God invites inside the sanctuary of Christ's peace represented by this circle. Who is easiest to welcome? Whom do you struggle to include? Confess the dividing walls between you and people too different or "dangerous" to invite into your spiritual home. Ask God to forgive and heal barriers that keep you and others from being one in Christ's peace.

Peace Covenant:

Today, God, I will cherish the sacredness of the space around me. I am open to your Spirit.

18
Wednesday
July

For the Glory of God

By Katie McClaran of Independence, Missouri, USA

> *You are the light of the world. A city built on a hill cannot be hid. No one after lighting a lamp puts it under the bushel basket, but on the lampstand, and it gives light to all in the house. In the same way, let your light shine before others, so that they may see your good works and give glory to your Father in heaven.*
>
> —Matthew 5:14–16

Because of my wish to be modest as I do good deeds, I always have been conflicted by the message of one of my favorite scriptures, "Let your light shine…that they may see your good works" (Matthew 5:16).

I want to live not for personal recognition but, as the passage states, to glorify "your Father in heaven," which explains the purpose of letting my light shine.

I want my actions always to reflect Christ and my faith community, the place I have found my greatest fulfillment, joy, and peace. Whatever influence I might have, I always hope it represents the influence our faith community had on my discipleship and invites others to Christ.

Companionship with disciples in Community of Christ and God has provided my strongest source of strength, especially during struggles of my youth. My church community continues to be meaningful in the lives of my children and grandchildren.

Prayer for Peace:

You have called us the light of the world, O God. You are the source of our light. We are enlightened by your flame. We are warmed by your Spirit. What we do before others is for your glory. When we practice shalom, it is to share the peace of Christ.

Spiritual Practice for the Week: Welcoming Unity in Diversity

Each day this week meditate on unity in diversity. Prayerfully read Doctrine and Covenants 163:8c, which calls "the entire church to become a sanctuary of Christ's peace, where people from all nations, ethnicities, and life circumstances can be gathered into a spiritual home without dividing walls."

Create a large circle with your arms. See and feel the diverse people God invites inside the sanctuary of Christ's peace represented by this circle. Who is easiest to welcome? Whom do you struggle to include? Confess the dividing walls between you and people too different or "dangerous" to invite into your spiritual home. Ask God to forgive and heal barriers that keep you and others from being one in Christ's peace.

Peace Covenant:

God, the light and talents you have given me are precious. I will not hide them.

19
Thursday
July

Vessels

By Norma Cross of Independence, Missouri, USA

> *For as in one body we have many members, and not all the members have the same function, so we, who are many, are one body in Christ, and individually we are members one of another.*
>
> —Romans 12:4–5

In getting ready to ask for a blessing for my great-granddaughter, I realized that when babies come into the world they share many similarities. They each have a spark of God in them, and they need food, dry diapers, and comfort. We start filling that little "treasure in an earthen vessel."

A vessel is a container with a purpose, whether a vase for flowers or a human being for a soul.

Parents have a big input. Teachers have input. Extended family members have input.

What do we fill that sweet little child vessel with? Grumbling? Or a cheery "hello" and exclamation of how glad we are to see them? Do we show them we are a joyful people?

At church a 3-year-old told my husband he was his best friend. Sunday school teachers may not be remembered for everything they teach, but the love emanating from them will last a lifetime. Children need security and to feel the church community is a good place to be.

God created us like vessels. God made each one different. We each have our own purpose. My task is to be the best vessel I can and to serve the purpose for which I was created. Realizing this, we need each one to help build the kingdom. I cannot do it on my own.

Prayer for Peace:

Universal God, we are many different people longing to be one in your Spirit. Thank you for the different gifts offered by each one to share Christ's peace.

Spiritual Practice for the Week: Welcoming Unity in Diversity

Meditate on unity in diversity. Prayerfully read Doctrine and Covenants 163:8c, which calls "the entire church to become a sanctuary of Christ's peace, where people from all nations, ethnicities, and life circumstances can be gathered into a spiritual home without dividing walls."

Create a large circle with your arms. See and feel the diverse people God invites inside the sanctuary of Christ's peace represented by this circle. Who is easiest to welcome? Whom do you struggle to include? Ask God to forgive and heal barriers that keep you and others from being one in Christ's peace.

Peace Covenant:

God, I will consider my tools and vessels to discern what is needed for your work.

20
Friday
July

Extended Family

By Gary McDonald of Blue Springs, Missouri, USA

If it is possible, so far as it depends on you, live peaceably with all.

—Romans 12:18

Several years ago a major corporation laid me off. The company's out-placement services introduced me to another large employer, which found a position for me in Ohio. Our family went there as—complete strangers.

We looked up the closest Community of Christ congregation and began attending. The people were kind and generous, and they quickly welcomed Claire and me into their church family.

We found ourselves in a culture that valued families and family life. Family ties were close.

It was common after services for people to group into their family units and go to lunch. Occasionally we would be unintentionally left out. The feeling was awkward.

The enduring principle of Blessings of Community suggests that as disciples we extend and expand our idea of family. We ought to grow to the point where every human being is part of our own family.

When a child half a world away is starving, it is "our" child who is suffering. Or when the elderly have no place to go, it's "our" grandparents who are left out and lonely.

I believe this is one direction God is leading Community of Christ today.

We can drop the idea of human division and develop a unity that knows no boundaries. We are all creations of our heavenly Parent. Through Christ we are one, meant to live peaceably with and inclusive of all.

Prayer for Peace:

Universal God, may we embrace the world as our own village. Unite us in our diversity and expand our range of concern to include sharing Christ's peace with all.

Spiritual Practice for the Week: Welcoming Unity in Diversity

Meditate on unity in diversity. Prayerfully read Doctrine and Covenants 163:8c, which calls "the entire church to become a sanctuary of Christ's peace, where people from all nations, ethnicities, and life circumstances can be gathered into a spiritual home without dividing walls."

Create a large circle with your arms. See and feel the diverse people God invites inside the sanctuary of Christ's peace represented by this circle. Who is easiest to welcome? Whom do you struggle to include? Ask God to forgive and heal barriers that keep you and others from being one in Christ's peace.

Peace Covenant:

Today, God, I will work for peace in my global village.

21
Saturday
July

Let Your Light Shine

By David Nii of Centennial, Colorado, USA

> *Yet it is incumbent upon the Saints...to be in the world but not of it, living and acting honestly and honorably before God and in the sight of all people, using the things of this world in the manner designed of God, that the places where they occupy may shine as Zion...*
> —Doctrine and Covenants 128:8b–c, adapted

The Arizona USA Mission Center deeply felt the recent worldwide economic challenge. A state known for the Grand Canyon, sunshine, and prickly cacti had more than its share of people experiencing the humbling and uplifting testimony of Christ's love through Oblation support.

A young family needing help with rent, food, and clothing for their children found comfort from a congregation and pastor. A mother going through divorce received aid that provided her family a new start. Several families found temporary relief with rent and bills while looking for jobs and healing from long-term unemployment. A member who reconnected with the church in the face of serious illness and bankruptcy received aid to return home to heal among family.

Struggle, injury, and challenges—these are all temporary conditions when compared to the constancy and depth of God's love and grace. Meeting people amid need is never an easy ministry, yet even the cacti bloom when given enough water and nourishment. And as the cactus reaches toward the sky, donations to the Abolish Poverty, End Suffering mission initiative lift people to God and let our light shine.

The Arizona USA Mission Center says, "Thank you for responding faithfully by giving generously!"

Prayer for Peace:

Giver of light, may we be honest and honorable; may we be generous so your light may shine within us. May we be disciples who build signal communities that shine with peace.

Spiritual Practice:

Light a candle and sit quietly, reflecting on the fire and light of God. Pay attention to your breathing and let it become calmer and deeper as you focus on God's presence. Ask God to breathe in you. Imagine each breath carrying the light of God into your lungs, bloodstream, and every cell in your body until you are filled with God's Spirit.

Now envision breathing out God's compassion and grace each time you exhale. Pray to have the spirit of Christ radiate from your life like the gentle flame of a candle.

Peace Covenant:

Today, God, I will appraise my life to discover what is *of the world*.

22
Sunday
July

We Are One

By Richard James, Council of Twelve Apostles

So he came and proclaimed peace to you who were far off and peace to those who were near; for through him both of us have access in one Spirit to the Father. So then you are no longer strangers and aliens, but you are citizens with the saints and also members of the household of God, built upon the foundation of the apostles and prophets, with Christ Jesus himself as the cornerstone.

—Ephesians 2:17–20

Sometimes we can be uncaring and call people by hurtful names. Two of my friends in school carried such unkind names—they were *Penguin* and *Brick*. People thought it was good fun to use these names. However, it made my friends feel sad and angry.

In Ephesus this is exactly what was happening. People were calling one another cruel names (Jews and Gentiles, circumcised and uncircumcised) and Paul was telling them to stop. It must not be this way, he said.

Christ made us all one, for he has torn down the separation between God and us and with one another. In Christ we find peace, for he is our peace. We are all of equal worth to God and so do not build up walls that can separate one person from another. Using unkind names can cause sadness, resentment, and anger. People can become isolated and vulnerable. As disciples we stand with the vulnerable and help build bridges of understanding between people.

Let us therefore see every person as sisters and brothers in Christ, regardless of what label society may want to give them. Can we challenge our cultures that build walls of separation between people, that label people with hurtful names? Can we build sacred communities that are sanctuaries of Christ's peace?

Our congregations are such places. In such places we affirm we are one in Christ Jesus.

Prayer for Peace:

God of many names, we have many names too. May we always use welcoming, positive, inclusive names when we speak with one another. May we break down the walls that divide. May we unite in Christ's peace.

Spiritual Practice for the Week: Offering Blessings of Community

Each day this week receive and share blessings of community. Begin with a prayer of gratitude for the network of relationships in your life. See and feel connections with family members, spiritual friends, people in your congregation and community, people and creatures in God's sacred web of life. What blessings are flowing to you from these circles?

Reflect, pray, and write in your journal about the call to be Community of Christ. Go deeper each day as you "discern and embrace" the "divine blessing" of this name that opens you to "become a blessing to the whole creation" (Doctrine and Covenants 163:1). What act of blessing are you invited to complete?

Peace Covenant:

Today, God, there will be no strangers in my life—I will make them friends.

23
Monday
July

God's Love Embodied in Christ

By Deb Crowley of Eaton Rapids, Michigan, USA

Jesus Christ, the embodiment of God's shalom, invites all people to come and receive divine peace in the midst of the difficult questions and struggles of life. Follow Christ in the way that leads to God's peace and discover the blessings of all of the dimensions of salvation.
—Doctrine and Covenants 163:2a

"I love you more than all the macaroni and cheese in the world!"

It was a game I began with my granddaughter when she was 3. When saying good-bye, good night, I would try to convey my unconditional love for her though we often are hundreds of miles apart. When the game started, she would look at me, giggle, and respond, "Silly Grammie!" Then she would say "I wuv you, too!"

Now she is a grown up 5-year-old, and her world has expanded. She responds to my "I love you more than all the little friends in the world" with her own imaginative, "I love you more than all the houses and stars in the world!" And she still giggles!

It is more than a game. It is a fun way to assure Cadence of how precious she is to me, how I will love her forever no matter what, and that I will always be there for her.

Traveling through the magnificent mountains of Tennessee, sailing atop the mind-boggling expanse of the Atlantic Ocean, the indescribable beauty of Lake Huron and Lake Michigan, I hear God say, "I love you more than all of this!"

God's love for you and me, for each person on Earth, is beyond comprehension.

Humanity is often cruel, disrespectful of the Earth, and rebellious. It often denies God's existence. Yet God's love never wavers.

God speaks love through the beauty of creation. God speaks unconditional and unfathomable love through human relationships. Reminders are everywhere. Assurance of God's love was part of God's game plan. God said, "I love you more than life itself." For God so loved the world, he sent his only Son, Jesus Christ, into the world so we might have everlasting life.

Christ is the embodiment of God's shalom—love and peace.

It's our turn. "God, I love you more than…"

Prayer for Peace:

God, it's hard to express how much we love you. We praise you for the ultimate expression of your love—Jesus Christ, the Prince of Peace.

Spiritual Practice for the Week: Offering Blessings of Community

Receive and share blessings of community. Be aware of and feel connections with people and creatures in God's sacred web of life. Write in your journal about the call to be "Community of Christ." Go deeper each day as you discern what act of blessing you are invited to complete.

Peace Covenant:

Today, God, I will look at the world in another way—seeing your love in all that I behold.

24
Tuesday
July

Your Son Loves You

By Paul McCain of Oklahoma City, Oklahoma, USA

> *...and live in love, as Christ loved us and gave himself up for us, a fragrant offering and sacrifice to God.*
>
> —Ephesians 5:2

I received an e-mail from my son with "Your Son Loves You" in the subject line, and I found myself reflecting on that statement. I thought, "Perhaps my Creator would like to hear me voice my love more often."

I pondered whether I remembered to tell my Earthly father often enough that I loved him before he passed. He and I did not have a tradition of often sharing emotions. I know he loved his children but just didn't say it out loud.

He also struggled with understanding God's love and the grace available to him. He lived with me his last few years. I sometimes would overhear him praying, pouring out his soul to God. I feel it was a relief for him to pass into the presence of the One he trusted.

I wondered if I try hard enough to be the father to my son that makes it easier for him to love. With his busy life, I appreciate his decision to be intentional with staying in touch and sharing with me. He sends me special cards for Father's Day, reminding me of the important part I have played in his life. He says he knows his success stems, at least in part, from principles taught him as he grew up.

When we talk on the phone we close the conversation with "I love you," a tradition valued beyond measure.

I hope my grandson, even at his young age of 6, tells his father he loves him and faithfully continues to do so throughout his life. May we often feel the nudge to share with those close to us how we feel. May we also share our feelings of love with God.

Prayer for Peace:

Loving God, may we never forget to express our love for you. May all we do for one another be love in action. May we share Christ's peace as part of that love.

Spiritual Practice for the Week: Offering Blessings of Community

Receive and share blessings of community. Pray gratitude for your network of relationships. See and feel connections with family members, spiritual friends, people in your congregation and community, and creatures in God's sacred web of life. What blessings flow to you from these circles? Reflect, pray, and write in your journal about the call to be Community of Christ. Discern what act of blessing you are invited to complete.

Peace Covenant:

Today, God, I will let you know, in some tangible way, how much I love you.

25
Wednesday
July

The Grackle's Kingdom

By E.J. Chappelle of Rosharon, Texas, USA

Let us then pursue what makes for peace and for mutual upbuilding.
—Romans 14:19

A common scene outside my window includes a big, male grackle in all his iridescent glory. He lands quickly beside a piece of bread thrown for him. Rather than starting his easy meal, he turns to a few smaller grackles nearby. He stomps his feet at them with his beak skyward, scattering his rivals for the bread.

However, the other grackles do not leave. More arrive, and sparrows, too. As the big guy chases away *this* bird, then *that* bird, all have a turn at a few bites of the bread, which was left untended by its guardian. Still, this alpha grackle persists until he has his victory, and all the other birds are gone…with the bread.

The grackle's secondary priority of defending the meal left him without a single bite.

I have a lot in common with that grackle. I often lose my priorities to momentary distractions. I ask myself if I am careful enough to seek first what matters most and avoid senseless distractions—to seek first the peaceable kingdom of God.

Prayer for Peace:

God of peace, teach us what matters most. Help us to avoid distractions on our journey to peace. May we keep an eye single to Christ's mission and your glory.

Spiritual Practice for the Week: Offering Blessings of Community

Each day this week receive and share blessings of community. Begin with a prayer of gratitude for the network of relationships in your life. See and feel connections with family members, spiritual friends, people in your congregation and community, people and creatures in God's sacred web of life.

What blessings flow to you from these circles? Reflect, pray, and write in your journal about the call to be "Community of Christ." Go deeper each day as you "discern and embrace" the "divine blessing" of this name that opens you to "become a blessing to the whole creation" (Doctrine and Covenants 163:1). What act of blessing are you invited to complete?

Peace Covenant:

Today, God, I will build up others as I share Christ's peace.

26
Thursday
July

Communities of Joy, Hope, Love, and Peace

By Elizabeth Else of St. Thomas, Ontario, Canada

> *May the God of hope fill you with all joy and peace in believing, so that you may abound in hope by the power of the Holy Spirit.*
>
> —Romans 15:13

The mission statement of Community of Christ is "We proclaim Jesus Christ and promote communities of joy, hope, love, and peace." I have experienced the gift of this mission.

Although I am an only child, I prefer to live in community. My family teasingly compared me to a puppy that loves to be around people. I am fortunate to have traveled the world and to have found community in so many places. What a blessing!

When I was finishing my first missionary term in Korea, I was looking at teaching in Asia, but nothing had been finalized. A month before I was to leave and a few days before I needed to make a commitment to seek a specific position, I discovered I had cancer. Suddenly my life turned upside down.

I had to return to North America. I had no home, no job, and I faced financial and medical crises. And yet, because of the love of communities around the world, I felt I was cradled in love.

My Korean community flew into action. It made flight reservations, helped me pack, said prayers, and cooked my favorite Korean food. I discovered not only family and friends, but communities throughout the worldwide church had put me on their prayer lists.

In Seattle I was welcomed into a home where I was lovingly cared for. I was able to work out the financial and medical challenges. Often the treatments were unpleasant and tiring. It took a year and a half to recover and feel fit again.

Communities of joy, hope, love, and peace carried me through. Groups of people called "communities" shared God's love.

Prayer for Peace:

God of hope, I am so blessed to be part of Christ's community. May all that I do be an invitation to others to come into this community so they may experience joy, hope, love, and peace.

Spiritual Practice for the Week: Offering Blessings of Community

Each day this week receive and share blessings of community. Begin with a prayer of gratitude for the network of relationships in your life. See and feel connections with family members, spiritual friends, people in your congregation and community, people and creatures in God's sacred web of life.

What blessings flow to you from these circles? Reflect, pray, and write in your journal about the call to be "Community of Christ." Go deeper each day as you "discern and embrace" the "divine blessing" of this name that opens you to "become a blessing to the whole creation" (Doctrine and Covenants 163:1). What act of blessing are you invited to complete?

Peace Covenant:

Today, God, I will welcome and care for the stranger among us.

27
Friday
July

Paying Attention

By Norma Mercurio of Columbus, Ohio, USA

These are portentous times. The lives of many are being sacrificed unnecessarily to the gods of war, greed, and avarice. The land is being desecrated by the thoughtless waste of vital resources. You must obey my commandments and be in the forefront of those who would mediate this needless destruction while there is yet day.

—Doctrine and Covenants 150:7

It was a beautiful holiday weekend. The sun was shining, and the temperature was perfect, but I was too focused on myself to notice. It was a lonely weekend, so I did what would cheer me up. I hopped in the car with a lawn chair and book, bought some candy, and drove to a park. It's a beautiful park, built around a lake that has become a place of peace for me.

As I arrived, one of the many ducks that call the park home greeted me. However, he wasn't interested in me; he wanted my candy! I set my chair by the water and delved into my treat. The duck got aggressive in trying to get me to share. Finally, I became irritated and chased that candy-loving duck away. (Everyone knows candy isn't good for ducks!)

I settled back in my chair and began to read the words of Richard Foster on the discipline of study. "We now come to the least-recognized but perhaps the most important field of study: the observation of reality in events and actions. The easiest place to begin is with nature. …We begin the study of nature by paying attention. We see flowers or birds. We observe them carefully and prayerfully" (*Celebration of Discipline*, Harper: San Francisco, 1988, p. 73).

As I read and thought about those words, I suddenly had the feeling I wasn't alone. I looked beside my chair, and there was the duck, just lying by my side. He didn't come back to ask for candy, only to be a companion in my loneliness. I felt he and all God's creatures were asking me for their protection by my living simply.

I knew in that moment God had come to me through one of God's creatures. I need never be alone. I need only pay attention.

Prayer for Peace:

Creator God, we would cherish the Earth for which we are stewards. Help us pay close attention to your creatures. Help us live simply and, as far as possible, not intrude on their habitat. Help us share Christ's peace with our neighbors in nature.

Spiritual Practice for the Week: Offering Blessings of Community

Each day this week receive and share blessings of community. Begin with a prayer of gratitude for the network of relationships in your life. See and feel connections with family members, spiritual friends, people in your congregation and community, people and creatures in God's sacred web of life.

What blessings flow to you from these circles? Reflect, pray, and write in your journal about the call to be "Community of Christ." Go deeper each day as you "discern and embrace" the "divine blessing" of this name that opens you to "become a blessing to the whole creation" (Doctrine and Covenants 163:1). What act of blessing are you invited to complete?

Peace Covenant:

Today, God, I will downsize my resource consumption.

28
Saturday
July

Active Service

By Evelyn Sperce of Council Bluffs, Iowa, USA

> *. . . when you are in the service of your fellow beings you are only in the service of your God.*
> —Mosiah 1:49

I volunteer as a cashier at the Community of Christ Thrift Store in Council Bluffs, Iowa. The sale of donated goods helps provide food, clothing, and household goods for those in need.

Even though I work just one morning a week, I am blessed to interact with a wide range of people. I meet customers of all descriptions from many faith communities. It is good to get to know them and feel I am helping them.

Co-workers come from several Community of Christ congregations. Other co-workers are friends from other denominations. Our jobs include working the cash register, sorting items, pricing, and setting up displays.

Most volunteers are retirees, some older than 90. One of my favorite quotes from a woman who worked until she was 95 was, "If I stop moving, I might as well be dead." I know what she means. If I just sit in my chair and am not physically working, I lose muscle tone or gain weight. I guess you could say this job benefits my health. It also helps me keep alive my interaction with others.

The best part of this job is that I can serve God by serving others.

Prayer for Peace:

God of both poor and rich, help us give according to our true capacity. Accept our service to our companions as service to you. May we serve those in need of justice and in need of peace.

Spiritual Practice:

Meditate on a time when you learned about community from someone who took you in, fed you, taught you, shared stories and wisdom with you. What did you learn? Prayerfully create a list of qualities you need to learn from spiritual mentors and friends. Then write the names of people who serve as teachers, models, coaches, or encouragers in your life as a disciple. Offer a prayer of gratitude and blessing for these spiritual "relatives" and friends.

Peace Covenant:

Today, God, I will consider what I have and what I can give with generosity.

29
Sunday
July

Come and Be Fed

By Becky Savage, First Presidency

"There is a boy here who has five barley loaves and two fish. But what are they among so many people?" Jesus said, "Make the people sit down." Now there was a great deal of grass in the place; so they sat down, about five thousand in all. Then Jesus took the loaves, and when he had given thanks, he distributed them to those who were seated; so also the fish, as much as they wanted.

—John 6:9–11

During the winter months a congregation in Florida offers a free soup-and-pie dinner for the neighborhood.

The population nearly doubles at that time of year as people journey away from the cold and snow of the North. Local and winter-resident church members collectively prepare delicious soups and scrumptious pies to share.

It is difficult to anticipate the number of neighbors coming to be fed. Each year we offer prayers of thanksgiving and celebration in anticipation of the feast. While the members offer gifts of time, food, and hospitality, they know it is God who generously provides the blessings.

During one of these meals the congregation experienced a miracle of abundance. As the dinner crowd moved in and out of the friendship hall, the number waiting in line continued to grow.

It was apparent more people than expected were coming.

Each time the ladle was dipped left little doubt the soup was nearly gone. Miraculously, as the people came, each received a full bowl of soup and a slice of pie. After the last neighbor was served, the soup was completely gone.

The neighbors came to be fed, and the congregation rejoiced, knowing it, too, was fed.

Prayer for Peace:

God of abundance, we have faith in the full pot of soup. May we welcome the stranger and share our food. May we share the peace of Christ.

Spiritual Practice for the Week: Connecting with God as Center

Each day this week connect with God through journal writing. Use a notebook, journal, computer, or any available paper. Prayerfully center on your intent to open yourself to God's presence and share what flows from your heart and mind. Your "letter to God" might include thoughts, questions, feelings, needs, artwork, quotes, and scriptures, or it may take the form of a prayer, psalm, or poem.

Try to write at least five minutes each day. What do you experience? Is this an effective way for you to connect with God? What surprises you? What new images or questions from God emerge? What deepens or changes in your relationship with God, Christ, Spirit?

Peace Covenant:

Today I will make soup with the best herbs and vegetables. I will find someone with whom to share your goodness and peace.

30
Monday
July

Companionship in England

By Donald Kirby of Blue Springs, Missouri, USA

> *Let contentions and quarreling among you cease. Sustain each other in peace, and ye shall be blessed with my Spirit, in comforting and strengthening you for my work.*
> —Doctrine and Covenants 117:13

While stationed in the Air Force near Enfield, England, I attended a church family camp. One day the campers went on a tour north of London. The countryside and the remains of some Roman ruins were on the agenda. We chartered a 45-passenger bus and looked forward to this exciting day.

We boarded the bus and started north (or so we thought). The driver made a wrong turn, and we ended up going south. Most of us were dozing and had faith the driver knew what he was doing. After almost two hours, he turned around and started in the right direction. But he had forgotten where to turn, adding two more hours to what, at first, was a three-hour tour. Each passenger had a different idea of which way we should head.

We were indeed lost.

We were getting hungry, and no restaurants were in sight. Apostle Arthur Oakman started to calm the angry riders. He then led us in singing a hymn, "The Lord's My Shepherd." Soon we were on the right road, going back to the Enfield church building. We missed seeing the Roman ruins but enjoyed the day together.

We once were lost, but found community.

Prayer for Peace:

Tender Shepherd, help us find our way home. Lead us to community and hospitality. Help us realize the company we keep is more valuable than the destination. We pray for your Spirit on the path to peace.

Spiritual Practice for the Week: Connecting with God as Center

Each day this week connect with God through journal writing. Use a notebook, journal, computer, or any available paper. Prayerfully center on your intent to open yourself to God's presence and share what flows from your heart and mind. Your "letter to God" might include thoughts, questions, feelings, needs, artwork, quotes, and scriptures, or it may take the form of a prayer, psalm, or poem.

Try to write at least five minutes each day. What do you experience? Is this an effective way for you to connect with God? What surprises you? What new images or questions from God emerge? What deepens or changes in your relationship with God, Christ, Spirit?

Peace Covenant:

On today's journey, God, I will praise the pilgrimage from moment to moment, as well as mile to mile.

31
Tuesday
July

The Steadfast Compassion of the Lord

By Linda Porter of Maryland Heights, Missouri, USA

For the mountains may depart and the hills be removed, but my steadfast love shall not depart from you, and my covenant of peace shall not be removed, says the Lord, who has compassion on you.

—Isaiah 54:10

When my son was 2, we took a vacation to Tucson, Arizona. It wasn't summer, but it already was hot. James and his sister, Jeni, wanted to play at the park.

Soon James was screaming, and Jeni came running to tell us he was hurt! We ran to the slide. It was so hot, he had burned his leg on the guard rail.

The bone was showing through his red and raw skin. The burn had taken off a chunk of skin. We rushed to the emergency room. The doctors on call came running to look at James' leg. They called a specialist, and he said the wound could not heal without skin grafts.

The doctor wrapped James' leg in gauze, put a patch over it, and told us to see our own doctor as soon as possible. That was Monday. We couldn't get an appointment until Thursday. By Wednesday afternoon, the wound was weeping and infected. We knew something terrible was happening.

We located the Tucson Central Congregation of Community of Christ and took James to prayer service. After the sacrament of laying on of hands for the sick I had a great sense of relief.

The next day the doctor looked at the wound and said the emergency doctors were alarmed for no reason. The wound already had started to heal. He predicted James would have an ugly scar on which no hair would grow.

Today we have to tell James which leg was wounded because it not only healed—it healed perfectly. We learned faith is not only a journey—it is a growing vine with events along the way that allow it to bloom.

Prayer for Peace:

Compassionate God, we believe in your healing light. We know your tears attend our own. We know your covenant of peace will not fail.

Spiritual Practice for the Week: Connecting with God as Center

Each day this week connect with God through journal writing. Use a notebook, journal, computer, or any available paper. Prayerfully center on your intent to open yourself to God's presence and share what flows from your heart and mind. Your "letter to God" might include thoughts, questions, feelings, needs, artwork, quotes, and scriptures, or it may take the form of a prayer, psalm, or poem.

Try to write at least five minutes each day. What do you experience? Is this an effective way for you to connect with God? What surprises you? What new images or questions from God emerge? What deepens or changes in your relationship with God, Christ, Spirit?

Peace Covenant:

Today, God, I will not hesitate to call on you with my concerns.

1
Wednesday
August

Endurance

By Gary Piper of Fort Gratiot, Michigan, USA

By your endurance you will gain your souls.

—Luke 21:19

Don't you just love it when you rediscover something Jesus said but you knew all along? It's like a burst of energy when your strength is gone. It's like a gust of wind causing your kite to soar higher. I found "something Jesus said" in Luke: "By your endurance you will gain your souls."

Years ago I was walking to an appointment with an orthopedic surgeon. We were to set the date for the first of several surgeries on my hips. The decision I made to have the surgery did not come easily.

The question I wrestled with was whether I would *quit* walking in pain or face my fear of the future.

Walking out that morning I remember thinking my time of enduring pain and fear was ending. At the same time, deep in my heart I felt Jesus smiling at me.

After surgery I faced another period of endurance—artificial hips are not as good as something God made. Since that first life-changing surgery there have been many times when I've prayed, "I am tired of enduring, I want to quit." Yet just before quitting, deep inside I hear one word, "Don't!"

If you are on the verge of quitting, I have one word for you—don't! If you need a reason to endure to the end, I have one more word for you. The word will give you the strength to take one more step and begin a new life of endurance. The word is "Jesus."

Prayer for Peace:

Enduring God, thank you for sending Jesus into our lives to give us strength. Thank you for helping us walk toward his peace, step by faithful step.

Spiritual Practice for the Week: Connecting with God as Center

Each day this week connect with God through journal writing. Use a notebook, journal, computer, or any available paper. Prayerfully center on your intent to open yourself to God's presence and share what flows from your heart and mind. Your "letter to God" might include thoughts, questions, feelings, needs, artwork, quotes, and scriptures, or it may take the form of a prayer, psalm, or poem.

Try to write at least five minutes each day. What do you experience? Is this an effective way for you to connect with God? What surprises you? What new images or questions from God emerge? What deepens or changes in your relationship with God, Christ, Spirit?

Peace Covenant:

Today, God, I will take one more step toward peace.

2
Thursday
August

Sharing the Peace

By Steven L. Shields of Lee's Summit, Missouri, USA

> *You who are my disciples must be found continuing in the forefront of those organizations and movements which are recognizing the worth of persons and are committed to bringing the ministry of my Son to bear on their lives.*
>
> —Doctrine and Covenants 151:9

My congregation did the good deeds expected from a group of disciples. We found a nearby pantry program and began collecting canned goods for a monthly donation. The pantry appreciated our efforts, and we provided many meals for families in need.

But we were not involved in the lives of the people being served. The pantry was several miles away in another part of the city. We simply would drop our donations and return home.

We had a strong sense of mission that our call was to serve people in the part of town where we gathered in sacred community. The congregation believed the church should be a center of ministry. However, our numbers were few. We simply could not staff a community-based program on our own.

But we knew people in our neighborhood needed help because, as pastor, I often would get telephone calls. I shared my concerns with other pastors at the monthly ministerial association meeting. I found they felt the same; their congregations sensed what mine sensed.

Several of us shared our concerns and hopes with our congregations and other community organizations. One church offered a spare classroom to house a small office, a pantry, and clothing distribution. Boy Scout and Girl Scout troops conducted food drives, supermarkets gave shopping bags. Service clubs and businesses donated money, services, and food.

Together we combined several small forces into one larger force. Together we served the needs of our neighbors. Together we shared the peace of Jesus Christ.

Prayer for Peace:

God of this deep and wide planet, whether we serve faraway or near our homes, we know your Spirit will be with us. Make me a servant...make me a servant today.

Spiritual Practice for the Week: Connecting with God as Center

Each day this week connect with God through journal writing. Use a notebook, journal, computer, or any available paper. Prayerfully center on your intent to open yourself to God's presence and share what flows from your heart and mind. Your "letter to God" might include thoughts, questions, feelings, needs, artwork, quotes, and scriptures, or it may take the form of a prayer, psalm, or poem.

Try to write at least five minutes each day. What do you experience? Is this an effective way for you to connect with God? What surprises you? What new images or questions from God emerge? What deepens or changes in your relationship with God, Christ, Spirit?

Peace Covenant:

Today, God, I will work with the community to be your willing servant.

3
Friday
August

Don't Say or Do...Just Be

By Lillian Kirby of Blue Springs, Missouri, USA

> *"Be still, and know that I am God! I am exalted among the nations, I am exalted in the earth." The Lord of hosts is with us; the God of Jacob is our refuge. Selah.*
>
> —Psalm 46:10–11

What do you say when you don't know what words to use? We used to think saying and doing were more important than *being*. I believe differently now. Sometimes our best response to people in need is to *be* a silent presence. Being there sometimes is more important than talking or taking action.

The last Sunday I attended my home congregation, I experienced a blessing of being. I had been through a difficult divorce and was about to move my family 1,500 miles to the Midwest. I already was feeling homesick, dejected, and desperate as I played the organ for the morning worship. I knew it would be the last time in a congregation where I had many sacred worship memories.

After the postlude, I quickly left the organ and retreated to the first pew, where I sat in silence as tears flowed down my cheeks. I turned my head and saw a sweet, elderly aunt, Bertie, had come to sit beside me and share my grief.

She didn't have to say a word. Her kind presence brought peace to my soul. I will always remember her sacred ministry in that moment of my need. She was my refuge on behalf of God, whose presence we shared.

Prayer for Peace:

Ever-present God, may we be still with you. May we be present for one another. May we be your instruments of sanctuary and peace.

Spiritual Practice for the Week: Connecting with God as Center

Connect with God through journal writing. Prayerfully center on your intent to open yourself to God's presence and share what flows from your heart and mind. Your "letter to God" might include thoughts, questions, feelings, needs, artwork, quotes, and scriptures, or it might take the form of a prayer, psalm, or poem.

Try to write at least five minutes each day. What do you experience? Is this an effective way to connect with God? What surprises you? What new images or questions from God emerge? What deepens or changes in your relationship with God, Christ, Spirit?

Peace Covenant:

Today, God, I will be present for another's need.

4
Saturday
August

A Grateful Heart

By Rick Maupin, Council of Twelve Apostles

> *Do not withhold good from those to whom it is due, when it is in your power to do it. Do not say to your neighbor, "Go, and come again, tomorrow I will give it"—when you have it with you.*
>
> —Proverbs 3:27–28

As we walked through the village of Los Mulos in the Dominican Republic, poverty was everywhere. As we entered the homes of our church members and friends, it was even more obvious that these good people had little worldly wealth.

One young man lived in a one-room house that measured about 8 by 10 feet. The room served as bedroom, kitchen, living room, and storage closet. His bed consumed about half the floor space of the entire house.

He greeted us with a smile and shook our hands, but it was clear he was seriously ill. He spoke of the pain from a leg wound that made it almost impossible for him to walk. His wound was seriously infected.

Our brother was unemployed and had no money to buy food or get medical help. Our local church financial officer provided help to meet his needs through Oblation. A few months later, the wound had nearly healed.

Our brother has a grateful heart for the prayers and financial aid that helped him through a difficult time. Your contributions to World Mission Tithes made a significant difference in this young man's life.

Thank you for responding by giving generously.

Prayer for Peace:

Healing God, may we take part in your healing ways. May we not hold back anything we might do to help others when there is so much need *now*. Bless us in our efforts to pursue peace and justice.

Spiritual Practice:

Take a walk and find a tree where you can sit (or imagine walking and sitting beneath a tree). Lean against the tree and feel the texture of the bark. Listen to the wind move through the leaves. Sit quietly and sense God's presence flowing through the tree and all creation. Offer a prayer of gratitude for your connection to all living things. Ask for grace to discern and carry out one small act of justice or healing that creates greater wholeness for the plants, animals, trees, waters, air, and land that are part of the community of creation.

Peace Covenant:

Now, God, I will assess the needs of World Mission Tithes and respond to my true capacity. I will prepare my offering for tomorrow.

5
Sunday
August

Remembering the Body of Christ

By Stassi Cramm, Council of Twelve Apostles

But speaking the truth in love, we must grow up in every way into him who is the head, into Christ, from whom the whole body, joined and knit together by every ligament with which it is equipped, as each part is working properly, promotes the body's growth in building itself up in love.

—Ephesians 4:15–16

I love Apostle Paul's image that we are all part of the body of Christ. This image took deeper meaning for me when I shared in a Communion service with a dear friend.

We gathered with global leaders at the Temple in Independence, Missouri. We each were invited to the table to receive bread and grape juice.

I sensed God's Spirit was weaving us together to embody Christ in the world. We were instructed to take the bread and juice back to our seats and wait until everyone was served so we could eat together.

As I sat, I realized my friend would not be able to eat her bread. You see, she has a medical condition that restricts her ability to eat certain foods, including bread made from wheat. No gluten-free bread was available, so she had taken the regular bread to avoid creating confusion with the servers.

As the instruction came to eat and drink, she reached toward her purse so she could drop the bread in there. I reached out and caught the bread as she dropped it. She looked at me and smiled. As I ate her bread with mine, I knew we were "joined and knit together."

It was a simple exchange, but it brought to life the sense of each part of the body "working properly." I did what she couldn't do, and she joyfully let me. In that moment, I had a profound sense of remembering the body of Christ and building ourselves up in love.

Prayer for Peace:

Bread of life, we share in remembrance of the body of your son. We share to unify the community. We become catchers of the dropped bread and act in one another's stead. Where there is anything lacking, we will fill it with love and peace.

Spiritual Practice for the Week: Growing a Gracious, Generous Heart

Each day this week open your heart to God's grace and generosity with a "breath prayer." Let your breath slow and deepen. Be aware of God's breath moving in and out of your heart. Spend several minutes focusing on breathing in God's generosity.

With each breath, silently name one gift for which you are thankful. "God, I breathe in the gift of ______ with thanks." Let your heart expand to contain God's gracious outpouring. With each breath out, name one gift you want to share from the overflow of your heart.

Eternal joy and peace await those who grow in the grace of generosity that flows from compassionate hearts.

—Doctrine and Covenants 163:9

Peace Covenant:

Today, God, as in your scripture, where any ligament is not equipped, I will build it up in love.

6
Monday
August

Skimming the Surface or Going Deep

By Cindy Korf of North Platte, Nebraska, USA

Learn of me, and listen to my words; walk in the meekness of my Spirit and you shall have peace in me.

—Doctrine and Covenants 18:2n

As a child I loved to visit my grandparents in southwestern Colorado. I'd walk along the hilltops with my grandmother, who showed me how to find ancient pottery shards. With the flat of her foot she would scuff the top of the loose soil, skimming the surface of the ground and revealing a small gray shard of an ancient clay pot.

When I walked along the irrigation ditches with my granddad, often he would use his shovel to dig a trench for water to flow to a parched field. As he dug deep into the ground, going far below the surface, he sometimes found bigger pieces of pottery or even stone grinding tools.

I often find my spiritual life the same way. I go along, skimming just the surface, learning only about remnants. If I dig deeper, I will find a treasure far more valuable. God, help me go beyond skimming the surface, and go deeper to learn of your peace.

Prayer for Peace:

God of wisdom, help us to learn of you. Help us express what we learn. May we go deep into the rich soil of your Spirit and find the treasure of Christ's peace.

Spiritual Practice for the Week: Growing a Gracious, Generous Heart

Each day this week open your heart to God's grace and generosity with a "breath prayer." Let your breathing slow and deepen. Be aware of God's breath moving in and out of your heart. Spend several minutes focusing on breathing in God's generosity. With each breath, silently name one gift for which you are thankful. "God, I breathe in the gift of ______ with thanks." Let your heart expand to contain God's gracious outpouring.

With each breath out, name one gift you want to share from the overflow of your heart.

Eternal joy and peace await those who grow in the grace of generosity that flows from compassionate hearts.

—Doctrine and Covenants 163:9

Peace Covenant:

Today, God, I will not wait for your Spirit. I will dig for your Spirit, which waits for me.

7
Tuesday
August

The Faith of a Child

By Paul McCain of Oklahoma City, Oklahoma, USA

And blessed are the peacemakers, for they shall be called children of God.
—III Nephi 5:56

Our church building in Stillwater, Oklahoma, was falling down. After many years of planning, many hours of meetings and discussions, we finally were ready to break ground for a new building.

Hopefully, by the time you read this, we will be in the new building.

At the groundbreaking ceremony I took many photos. I wanted those present to remember the event and those not present to be able to join the celebration. The most-precious photos were of small children jumping up and down on the heels of shovels. They were trying to do what the big folks were doing—breaking ground.

One child in particular took my interest. She was shorter than the shovel and tried to figure out how to use it. She tried to stand it straight up, and she tried to push the blade into the ground from an almost-horizontal position.

She was celebrating with the others. She was setting an example of effort and faith, all she could do from her position so low to the ground. I hope her grandchildren see the pictures of her. They will see what determination is all about. Her enthusiasm didn't let anything stop her.

May we see and follow the examples set by our children as we work for the peaceable kingdom.

Prayer for Peace:

God of peace, may we look to our children as examples of faithfulness and enthusiasm. May we apply these tools to sharing Christ's peace.

Spiritual Practice for the Week: Growing a Gracious, Generous Heart

Each day this week open your heart to God's grace and generosity with a "breath prayer." Let your breathing slow and deepen. Be aware of God's breath moving in and out of your heart. Spend several minutes focusing on breathing in God's generosity. With each breath, silently name one gift for which you are thankful. "God, I breathe in the gift of ____ with thanks." Let your heart expand to contain God's gracious outpouring.

With each breath out, name one gift you want to share from the overflow of your heart.

Eternal joy and peace await those who grow in the grace of generosity that flows from compassionate hearts.
—Doctrine and Covenants 163:9

Peace Covenant:

Today, God, I will learn fresh skills for peace from a child.

8
Wednesday
August

When the Spirit Calls...

By Gary McDonald of Blue Springs, Missouri, USA

> *The temple shall be dedicated to the pursuit of peace. It shall be for reconciliation and for healing of the Spirit.*
>
> —Doctrine and Covenants 156:5a

I received a call from a member of our congregation who asked me to visit her father in the hospital. I agreed to meet her there. My wife, Claire, went with me. We went in, sat down, and waited.

While waiting, a woman came through the emergency-room doors, pushing a wheelchair. In the chair sat a woman in perhaps her late teens or early 20s who was doubled up and crying loudly.

She was seriously upset and wracked with pain.

Something inside me said, "You're an elder. Go over and offer the sacrament of laying on of hands for the sick." I told myself, "No." I really didn't want to do that for a complete stranger in such a public place.

Then I began to feel guilty.

Shortly after, our friend came in with her father. She checked him in quickly because they thought he was suffering a heart attack. We followed them into a ward and waited. When the doctor finished I offered the sacrament of laying on of hands for the sick. The prayer comforted this man of faith.

As we were leaving we passed the young woman in the wheelchair. She was still crying loudly and in great pain. Again the voice inside urged me to offer the sacrament to her. Again I denied the voice and kept walking. We went through the doors and were almost across the parking lot when I heard a voice ring out. "Gary. Come back. There's someone here who needs prayer."

I knew who that someone was, and we returned.

I introduced myself to a person who might have been her mother. I explained I was a minister and asked if she wanted me to pray for her daughter. She immediately said, "Yes."

She was grateful. During the prayer she kept saying, "Thank you Jesus." After the prayer we visited a while and then left. Later we learned the young woman had quieted down after the prayer and seemed comforted. The lesson for me was, when the Spirit calls...answer.

Prayer for Peace:

Holy Spirit, we are listening for you. Call us to reconciliation and healing of the spirit. Call us to peace. We will answer your call.

Spiritual Practice for the Week: Growing a Gracious, Generous Heart

Open your heart to God's grace and generosity with a "breath prayer." Let your breathing slow and deepen. Spend several minutes focusing on breathing in God's generosity. With each breath, silently name one gift for which you are thankful. "God, I breathe in the gift of ______ with thanks." With each breath out, name one gift you want to share from the overflow of your heart.

Peace Covenant:

Today, God, I will answer your call and do what you call me to do.

9
Thursday
August

At His Feet

By Michelle Booth of Grain Valley, Missouri, USA

Protect me, O God, for in you I take refuge.

—Psalm 16:1

I'm a wife, mother of three, stepmother of two, full-time worker, daughter, sister, and friend. I have serious health issues. Life can be overwhelming, and 2010 was full of distress.

I became ill and had to take time off work. Two of my children endured hospital stays and months of medical treatment. All five of my children are teenagers and busy with school and extracurricular events. They bring much joy to my life but keep me busy! Thankfully I have an encouraging husband who brings joy and carries the loads of life beside me.

I wish I could say I handle all these roles well. I don't.

I try to control everything around me. I don't try to control the people, just all that happens in our busy lives. That's difficult to admit! My family and friends remind me, "Leave it at the feet of Jesus." It's something I know, but often forget.

One evening life became unbearable. I went to my bedroom, slammed the door behind me, fell to the floor and wept. I cried a cleansing cry.

As my crying settled, I realized I was kneeling in front of a chair with my forehead on the floor. However it didn't feel like my head was touching the floor. My head was on Jesus' feet as he sat in the chair in front of me, bent over with his loving Spirit wrapped around me like a blanket. I knelt there a few more minutes cherishing Christ's love for me.

Protect me, O God, for in you I take refuge. This is part of my daily reflection. I didn't learn to give up control and give it to Christ in just one evening. I am still learning to let go, but I'm getting better at it.

Prayer for Peace:

You are our sanctuary, O God. We call on you for strength when we are weak. You send your light when we are in dark places. You lift us when we are low. Send us the peace of your Son, O God, that we may share it with the world.

Spiritual Practice for the Week: Growing a Gracious, Generous Heart

Each day this week open your heart to God's grace and generosity with a "breath prayer." Let your breathing slow and deepen. Be aware of God's breath moving in and out of your heart. Spend several minutes focusing on breathing in God's generosity. With each breath, silently name one gift for which you are thankful. "God, I breathe in the gift of ______ with thanks." Let your heart expand to contain God's gracious outpouring.

With each breath out, name one gift you want to share from the overflow of your heart.

Eternal joy and peace await those who grow in the grace of generosity that flows from compassionate hearts.

—Doctrine and Covenants 163:9

Peace Covenant:

Today, God, I will give up control of my concerns to you.

10
Friday
August

Those Who Make a Difference with Love

By Flo McDonald of Lee's Summit, Missouri, USA

Collectively and individually, you are loved with an everlasting love that delights in each faithful step taken. God yearns to draw you close so that wounds may be healed, emptiness filled, and hope strengthened.

—Doctrine and Covenants 163:10

A friend asked me to help identify people from old photos for a record kept by the historian of our congregation. Many of the pictures dated to my childhood. As I looked at them, I found I was looking through the eyes of a child. From my childhood perspective I was unsure about some of the people. Others I recognized immediately. Sometimes I knew names but not faces.

Looking through the eyes of an adult, using memory as a guide, it was helpful to note the characteristics of the person as well as the date. The ones I remembered best were those who had made a difference in my life, who had shown me love.

As I thought about those special people, I remembered an old movie, "It's a Wonderful Life."

It was about an unhappy and desperate man who wished he never had been born. He had the unusual experience of being shown that along the way he had touched many lives and made a wonderful difference. His life had been worth living, after all. When he came to that realization, he was the happiest man alive.

I am thankful for those who helped me on life's journey.

They expressed God's love for me through their love. As they served and gave of themselves, we grew and came closer to God.

Prayer for Peace:

How do we know of your love for us, God? We know by the love shown through your disciples, by the care given, and the peace we are taught.

Spiritual Practice for the Week: Growing a Gracious, Generous Heart

Each day this week open your heart to God's grace and generosity with a "breath prayer." Let your breathing slow and deepen. Be aware of God's breath moving in and out of your heart. Spend several minutes focusing on breathing in God's generosity. With each breath, silently name one gift for which you are thankful. "God, I breathe in the gift of ______ with thanks." Let your heart expand to contain God's gracious outpouring.

With each breath out, name one gift you want to share from the overflow of your heart.

Eternal joy and peace await those who grow in the grace of generosity that flows from compassionate hearts.

—Doctrine and Covenants 163:9

Peace Covenant:

Today, God, I will let someone know how deeply they touched my life.

11
Saturday
August

Tangible Love for Peace

By Cathy Sheppard of Paducah, Kentucky, USA

...when you are in the service of your fellow beings you are only in the service of your God.
—Mosiah 1:49

The Tri City Community of Christ Peace Club draws children from the entire county. Established several years ago the program now focuses on broader family ministry.

Peace Club families attend services, seek baptism and confirmation, and receive family and home ministry. Peace Club ministries touch the lives of hundreds of children and families. The ministry includes securing housing, medical care, food, clothing, utilities, employment, and other services.

Partners include schools, community pantries, law enforcement, children's services, the domestic-violence office, and court advocacy agencies. Peace Club ministries share the peace of Jesus Christ by bringing restoration and healing into the lives of children and adults.

The generosity of Community of Christ helps to support the Tri City Peace Club through Tangible Love grants, now funded through the Abolish Poverty, End Suffering mission initiative. Congregational leaders carefully plan and prioritize these services to provide ministry.

Your contributions to World Mission Tithes share Christ's peace in ways that bring hope and healing to families, congregations, and the greater community. Thank you for giving generously.

Prayer for Peace:

God, we feel your presence in our lives. We feel your Spirit engaging us to action in the community. Bless us as we journey to the forefront to recognize the worth of persons and share the love and peace of Christ.

Spiritual Practice:

Hold (or imagine holding) a glass cup, bowl, or vase. Explore its shape, texture, and color. Let the container symbolize your life as it is being formed. Write on strips of paper (or in your journal) the things that are not yet just and whole in your life. Place the strips in the glass container and hold it in your hands. Pray a prayer of confession and petition, asking God to continue to breathe in and on you, shaping you into a just and compassionate person.

Peace Covenant:

Today, God, I will recognize the worth of all persons.

12
Sunday
August

Speak the Truth

By Kris Judd of Kansas City, Missouri, USA

Put away from you all bitterness and wrath and anger and wrangling and slander, together with all malice... and live in love, as Christ loved us and gave himself up for us, a fragrant offering and sacrifice to God.

—Ephesians 4:31, 5:2

Living in Christian community doesn't make us immune from falsehoods, but more accountable for truth-telling. It is how we handle the lack of truth that speaks to our nature as disciples of Jesus.

A situation occurred several years ago in a small congregation that prided itself on being "a family" that protected and affirmed one another. One member accused another of an offense that was frightening and surprising.

Because the accuser had been victimized in the past by others, the reaction of members was to move to her defense and confront the accused. The accused, who had been victimized in his own right throughout life, felt hurt, furious, and powerless in his defense. He left church that day, determined not to return.

Later, he contacted a member he trusted and told his side of the story. After a brief investigation, it became apparent the accusation held no truth.

Neither the accuser nor the accused attended church for awhile, and it would have been easy for this small group of disciples to let the issue slide by and be forgotten. But then two members who were especially close to the accuser confronted her gently but firmly with the truth.

She tearfully admitted her story was not true.

A community that is family will bear with one another through the difficulties to search out and affirm the truth. May we all live as such family in our own congregations.

Prayer for Peace:

Affirming God, help us seek truth. May we be slow to judge. May we drop the stones we want to throw and walk away, knowing we, ourselves, are sinners. May we build bridges and work to share the peace of Jesus Christ.

Spiritual Practice for the Week: Caring for God's Sacred Creation

Each day this week choose a way to notice, give thanks, and care for God's sacred creation. Prayerfully consider one of the following suggested practices or create your own.

Walk in nature with a spirit of gratitude and "holy attention." Write a psalm of praise for the beauty of the Earth or a prayer of healing and blessing for the wounds of the Earth. Learn about and engage in an act of Earth-keeping such as recycling, simple living, fasting from over-consumption of resources. Notice the unique diversity of the planet's creatures and be gentle to plants, animals, trees, and people! Fall in love with the vast, intricate wonder of God's creation and give thanks.

Peace Covenant:

Today, God, I will look for and speak the truth.

13
Monday
August

Jesus: Our Word and Hope for the World

By Mnqobi Ngwenya, of Bulawayo, Zimbabwe

> *But there is forgiveness with you, so that you may be revered. I wait for the Lord, my soul waits, and in his word I hope…*
>
> —Psalm 130:4–5

Among all the earthquakes, tsunamis, nuclear-waste dangers, political uprisings, floods, tornadoes, wars, and poverty, I hunger and thirst for the word of God.

Those conditions prompt me to think about the meaning of the times in which we live.

I am reminded each time I read the newspaper or watch the news on television not to ignore what is happening around the world. I seek the word of Jesus. We need to seek the words of wisdom and hope from Jesus to help us live in these times.

I have asked myself whether the church is aligned with its mission and vision, considering the times in which we find ourselves. It is. Reading *Daily Bread* not only prepares us but assures me of this. *Daily Bread* keeps refreshing us in our journey of faith and discipleship.

To stay faithful to Jesus' work, we need to embrace the teachings of Christ. If we can focus on the hope of Christ, it will help us through difficult times. Let us spend time immersed in his word so we can remain hopeful and not be overwhelmed by current events.

When there seems to be no reason for trust, just trust the Divine. God will not let you down.

Prayer for Peace:

Living God, please give us strength to endure the difficult times we sometimes face, and may the love and peace of Jesus Christ be with us to share.

Spiritual Practice for the Week: Caring for God's Sacred Creation

Each day this week choose a way to notice, give thanks, and care for God's sacred creation. Prayerfully consider one of the following suggested practices or create your own.

Walk in nature with a spirit of gratitude and "holy attention." Write a psalm of praise for the beauty of the Earth or a prayer of healing and blessing for the wounds of the Earth. Learn about and engage in an act of Earth-keeping such as recycling, simple living, fasting from over-consumption of resources. Notice the unique diversity of the planet's creatures and be gentle to plants, animals, trees, and people! Fall in love with the vast, intricate wonder of God's creation and give thanks.

Peace Covenant:

Today, God, I will immerse myself in the word of Christ.

14
Tuesday
August

Shadow Boxing

By Greg Clark of Independence, Missouri, USA

> *...Prepare yourselves through much study and earnest prayer. Then, as you go forth to witness of my love and my concern for all persons, you will know the joy which comes from devoting yourselves completely to the work of the kingdom. To this end will my Spirit be with you. Amen.*
>
> —Doctrine and Covenants 156:11

The shadow boxer, taking short quick steps, drifts across the green field. He throws jabs and uppercuts, connecting with nothing more than air. He holds his hands in a protective position, shoulders hunched forward, elbows close at his sides. A hooded gray sweatshirt masks his identity, but not his intensity.

He throws combination after combination. Left-right. Left-right. Left-right-left. Uppercut. He's training. Working out. Trying to get stronger.

Each short step, each jab brings him closer to his goal. Closer to a time when his punches will connect.

The shadow boxer reminds me of my prayer life. He tries different tactics: jabs, uppercuts, even roundhouses. I try different prayer forms: *lectio divina*, intercessory, gratitude. Just as the boxer throws punch after punch without connecting, I sometimes feel like I throw prayer after prayer at God, without response.

Of course, I know God always hears me. It's just that I don't always listen well. Perhaps it's because I'm in a defensive stance, not leaving myself vulnerable to God's presence.

Finally, I realize what's happening. Just as the shadow boxer's repeated punches lead to better physical conditioning, my repeated prayers lead to better spiritual conditioning. So I'll keep praying.

The more I work out spiritually, the better I'll be prepared in my relationship with God.

Prayer for Peace:

Listening God, may we be still and connect with you. May our prayers be earnest, two-way communication so we can hear your call for peace.

Spiritual Practice for the Week: Caring for God's Sacred Creation

Each day this week choose a way to notice, give thanks, and care for God's sacred creation. Prayerfully consider one of the following suggested practices or create your own.

Walk in nature with a spirit of gratitude and "holy attention." Write a psalm of praise for the beauty of the Earth or a prayer of healing and blessing for the wounds of the Earth. Learn about and engage in an act of Earth-keeping such as recycling, simple living, fasting from over-consumption of resources. Notice the unique diversity of the planet's creatures and be gentle to plants, animals, trees, and people! Fall in love with the vast, intricate wonder of God's creation and give thanks.

Peace Covenant:

God, I will try to let go of my prayer agenda, and attend to yours.

15
Wednesday
August

Community Machinery

By E.J. Chappelle of Rosharon, Texas, USA

For whoever keeps the whole law but fails in one point has become accountable for all of it.
—James 2:10

The forklift brakes failed. I quickly found and replaced worn seals in a wheel cylinder, refilled the fluid, and bled the lines. The brakes were good as new for a few days.

Then another wheel cylinder blew. I repeated the repairs, and a week later the master cylinder went out. Not long after replacing this part, a fluid line ruptured.

This was frustrating, because it would have been easier to replace the whole system at one time rather than one piece at a time. I should have seen something worse coming. An old truck did this same thing to me years ago. When one part of a brake system fails, all of it needs repair.

I am not a brake system. But I feel I have an important role to fill as part of the community machinery. When I'm ill or distracted and can't perform a chore properly, most everything else I try suffers, as well.

It's good we are not machines that must wait on mechanics to repair us when we break down. Rather, we have a loving Savior to call on for grace and guidance. Jesus loves us even with our flaws, and he leads us on our path of discipleship.

Prayer for Peace:

God whose love is law, we are not flawless in our discipleship. Bear us up in your grace to become whole and to fulfill your covenant of peace.

Spiritual Practice for the Week: Caring for God's Sacred Creation

Each day this week choose a way to notice, give thanks, and care for God's sacred creation. Prayerfully consider one of the following suggested practices or create your own.

Walk in nature with a spirit of gratitude and "holy attention." Write a psalm of praise for the beauty of the Earth or a prayer of healing and blessing for the wounds of the Earth. Learn about and engage in an act of Earth-keeping such as recycling, simple living, fasting from over-consumption of resources. Notice the unique diversity of the planet's creatures and be gentle to plants, animals, trees, and people! Fall in love with the vast, intricate wonder of God's creation and give thanks.

Peace Covenant:

Today, God, I will try to be aware of ways I fall short of being a lifelong disciple. I will pray for your help to become whole.

16
Thursday
August

Play, Little Pilgrim, Play

By June Russell of Independence, Missouri, USA

> *...I have heard your prayers when you have cried out to me, and I have been with you in the places where you occupy. I am aware of your desires to serve me and my assurance is that as you go forth, your offerings of faith and service are acceptable to me.*
>
> —Doctrine and Covenants 157:16b

For some time I was concerned and frustrated because I no longer could be as active in church and social gatherings as I was when younger. I felt I could not be much help to others. One morning I woke early with new and unusual thoughts drifting through my mind. That day I wrote this poem:

In my listening time today, I seemed to hear the Good Lord say,
"I have given you this day. Play, little pilgrim, play!
"Those who need your help today, I will bring along your way
"That you may brighten up their day. Play, little pilgrim, play!
"Rest, little pilgrim, rest, I know you're doing your very best.
"Leave cares with me and you will see, you'll be blest, little pilgrim, blest."

Since then, I have been writing poetry, something I had not done since my high school days. I laugh aloud as I write nursery rhymes for my two granddaughters. I have found freedom from old expectations, new challenges, and returning joy in living. I thank you, God, for your goodness and grace.

Prayer for Peace:

As we listen for you, God, we find new ways to serve. Our lives open to new opportunities, and we are pleased to offer our gifts that we might share the peace of Christ.

Spiritual Practice for the Week: Caring for God's Sacred Creation

Each day this week choose a way to notice, give thanks, and care for God's sacred creation. Prayerfully consider one of the following suggested practices or create your own.

Walk in nature with a spirit of gratitude and "holy attention." Write a psalm of praise for the beauty of the Earth or a prayer of healing and blessing for the wounds of the Earth. Learn about and engage in an act of Earth-keeping such as recycling, simple living, fasting from over-consumption of resources. Notice the unique diversity of the planet's creatures and be gentle to plants, animals, trees, and people! Fall in love with the vast, intricate wonder of God's creation and give thanks.

Peace Covenant:

Today, God, I will look for new ways to serve your people.

17
Friday
August

Hiding From God?

By Merna Short of Melbourne, Victoria, Australia

But this is the covenant that I will make with the house of Israel after those days, says the Lord: I will put my law within them, and I will write it on their hearts; and I will be their God, and they shall be my people. No longer shall they teach one another, or say to each other, "Know the Lord," for they shall all know me, from the least of them to the greatest, says the Lord; for I will forgive their iniquity, and remember their sin no more.

—Jeremiah 31:33–34

Bobby's parents were blind. They rejoiced when he was born a sighted child.

When Bobby was about 2, he became aware when he displeased his mother. He would run and try to hide. He soon realized he couldn't hide. His mother always knew where he was. But if he held his breath she couldn't find him immediately.

How long can you hold your breath? Have you ever made a poor choice? Has an unwise decision had you holding your breath, awaiting the results, hoping it would come out all right? Have you undermined your credibility with a thoughtless act? At these times have you wanted to hide your face?

I have good news for you. No matter how we mess up, we don't need to hide from God. We are written on God's heart. God not only knows where we are, but he gives us redeeming grace. God is not blind to our failures but accepts us as we are.

We are God's people.

Prayer for Peace:

Covenant God, we have your laws of love and grace written on our hearts. Forgive us if we ever try to hide from you. Find us and draw us close. Find us so we may find peace.

Spiritual Practice for the Week: Caring for God's Sacred Creation

Each day this week choose a way to notice, give thanks, and care for God's sacred creation. Prayerfully consider one of the following suggested practices or create your own.

Walk in nature with a spirit of gratitude and "holy attention." Write a psalm of praise for the beauty of the Earth or a prayer of healing and blessing for the wounds of the Earth. Learn about and engage in an act of Earth-keeping such as recycling, simple living, fasting from over-consumption of resources. Notice the unique diversity of the planet's creatures and be gentle to plants, animals, trees, and people! Fall in love with the vast, intricate wonder of God's creation and give thanks.

Peace Covenant:

Today, God, my heart is open to receive your message.

18
Saturday
August

Seize the Day

By Karin Peter of Adrian, Missouri, USA

There are many lives waiting to hear the redeeming words of the gospel, or to be lifted from hopelessness by the hands of loving servants. But they will be lost to you without the generous response of disciples who share from their own bounty that others may know the joys of the kingdom... The call to respond is urgent. Look to the needs of your own congregations, but look also beyond your walls to the far-flung places where the church must go. Each disciple needs a spiritual home. You are called to build that home and care for it, but also to share equally in the outreaching ministries of the church. In that way the gospel may be sent to other souls also yearning for a spiritual resting place.

—Doctrine and Covenants 162:7a, d

Young adults and their friends from diverse ethnic and social backgrounds attended the Florida USA Mission Center's "Seize the Day" retreat. Imari Dantzler, a young adult from Jacksonville, Florida, invited several friends to join him at the weekend event.

Many of his friends are from urban, low-income, and high-risk areas. Accepting the invitation was a first step to experiencing the acceptance associated with discipleship in Community of Christ.

Imari is an inviter, just like his dad, Seventy Leonard Dantzler.

Your contributions to World Mission Tithes provide ministry and ministers such as Imari, Leonard, and others throughout the Florida USA Mission Center.

The invitational ministry of young adults in Jacksonville and in the mission center leads the way to becoming a people who share the peace of Jesus Christ in new and exciting ways. Thank you for responding so generously.

Prayer for Peace:

Inviting God, lead us to those who yearn for a spiritual resting place. May we welcome them as you would welcome them.

Spiritual Practice:

The Daily Prayer for Peace is a spiritual practice that takes place year-round in the Independence and Kirtland temples and many congregations in Community of Christ. Each day we pray for a different country. Go to the front of this book and identify the country for today.

Read the information provided about the country or do your own research. Listen and ask God for images and insights about the people, environment, and needs of this country. Speak or write a prayer of blessing and peace for this part of God's world.

Peace Covenant:

Today, God, I open myself to be led beyond my congregational walls and to respond to the needs I find there.

19
Sunday
August

Make Melody to the Lord

By Dale Luffman, Council of Twelve Apostles

> *...but be filled with the Spirit, as you sing psalms and hymns and spiritual songs among yourselves, singing and making melody to the Lord in your hearts, giving thanks to God the Father at all times and for everything in the name of our Lord Jesus Christ.*
> —Ephesians 5:18–20

Faithfulness and perseverance are given power when the Saints gather together frequently for worship as a body. They are filled with the Spirit, singing psalms, hymns, and spiritual songs. They are to do this so they might be conformed to Christ by the Spirit, infused with its nurturing, empowering presence. They are to be transformed into the likeness of Christ.

It has been said that time is redeemed in and through worship. Worship orients. Worship begins in the heart and in the ear and enters into one's being—the core of the disciple's life. That is why God calls the community to "make melody to the Lord in your hearts." It is always timely to worship!

I've observed that worship, for the most part, is not a solitary exercise. Worship depends on the connections that one has with all the body of Christ. We experience the body of Christ [Christ with us!] when we worship as a body.

In a real sense there is no solitary disciple. We are because we are a part of a larger community of witness, both interdependent and communal. We connect with Christ and are made to be the body of Christ with our brothers and sisters.

Thanksgiving is the natural response of the worshiper. As the triune God is acknowledged by members of the community of faith gathered in Christ, life is given a certain perspective, orientation, and celebration. This leads to thanksgiving—making a melody to the Lord.

Prayer for Peace:

God with us, we long to connect with you, Christ, and the community.

Spiritual Practice for the Week: Encountering Scripture as Continuing Revelation

Each day this week read and pray with the Doctrine and Covenants as continuing revelation of God's vision for the church and creation. Choose a favorite section or focus on recent counsel in sections 156–164. Read a few selected paragraphs slowly three or four times. Pause to pray for deep understanding of meaning after the first reading.

Pray to open your heart and emotions to the text after the second reading. After the third reading, prayerfully ask to hear the particular phrase or word that speaks to you or touches your life. Stay with this word or phrase. Listen as fully and openly as you can. What sense of divine presence or invitation comes? What is revealed?

Peace Covenant:

Today, God, I will sing to you in my heart. Thank you for hearing my prayer-song.

20
Monday
August

Just a Conduit

By Shirley Remmenga of Fort Collins, Colorado, USA

> *...do good; seek peace, and pursue it.*
>
> —Psalm 34:14

"Call Cara!" said the voice within my mind. I thought, *yes, I need to call her soon*, but I continued to go about my business. The voice flashed across my consciousness again. "Call Cara!"

This time I called. When Cara answered she was crying and wanted me to go to her house. When she opened the door, she put back her head and made a desperate sobbing noise from deep in her soul. I opened my arms, and we held each other.

When she could talk she said she was in a dark state of depression. She was able to share only between her soul-searing sobs. Finally, she calmed down.

We decided she was on overload and needed to release some responsibilities. Cara needed to take some time off. She needed about two weeks of medical leave.

She already knew of a place, offered by a friend, where she could rest, meditate, and recoup. She called her friend before I left and made her plans. She thanked me for holding her, listening to her, and weeping with her.

She asked how I knew she needed help. I couldn't ignore the urgency of the voice from within and went to her on a mission urged by God. Help came from God, and Cara then could make a positive decision to take time off and heal. She opened herself to God's grace and peace.

The Spirit of God helped her walk through her "woundedness," and she became whole again.

Prayer for Peace:

Loving God, help us listen for your compassionate voice and go where you lead us. Send us to those who seek peace.

Spiritual Practice for the Week: Encountering Scripture as Continuing Revelation

Each day this week read and pray with the Doctrine and Covenants as continuing revelation of God's vision for the church and creation. Choose a favorite section or focus on recent counsel in Sections 156–164. Read a few selected paragraphs slowly three or four times.

Pause to pray for deep understanding of meaning after the first reading. Pray to open your heart and emotions to the text after the second reading. After the third reading, prayerfully ask to hear the particular phrase or word that speaks to you or touches your life. Stay with this word or phrase. Listen as fully and openly as you can. What sense of divine presence or invitation comes? What is revealed?

Peace Covenant:

Today God, I will not hesitate to follow your lead.

21
Tuesday
August

Blessings of Community

By Lu Mounteray of Independence, Missouri, USA

First of all, then, I urge that supplications, prayers, intercessions, and thanksgivings be made for everyone...so that we may lead a quiet and peaceable life in all godliness and dignity.
—1 Timothy 2:1–2

In our office suite, a colleague and friend makes morning rounds as faithfully as a doctor. She stops at everyone's office or cubicle to say hello and ask how they're doing. She then stays to listen!

She is a leadership specialist, but her actions go beyond what is required of her. She even brings doughnuts to share every other Friday!

When she was away from the office for a few weeks, we made lighthearted complaints about not having our doughnuts. We soon came to realize, however, that it was her presence we missed, not the doughnuts (well, maybe a little). Anyone could bring doughnuts, but not everyone could fill the void and match her humble and generous nature.

When my sister died, my friend sent thoughtful cards almost every day for several weeks. Someone had done the same for her when her sister died, and she paid it forward in a beautiful way. I was glad when she came back to bless us with her listening skills, warm smile, and presence. She is surely one of the blessings of our workplace community.

Prayer for Peace:

We pray to you, God, for our families, our friends, our work mates, and the strangers we have not yet met. We thank you for friends and future friends. As they become part of our community may they be blessed as we have been blessed. May we treat them with dignity and acceptance. May we meet them with your shalom.

Spiritual Practice for the Week: Encountering Scripture as Continuing Revelation

Each day this week read and pray with the Doctrine and Covenants as continuing revelation of God's vision for the church and creation. Choose a favorite section or focus on recent counsel in Sections 156–164. Read a few selected paragraphs slowly three or four times.

Pause to pray for deep understanding of meaning after the first reading. Pray to open your heart and emotions to the text after the second reading. After the third reading, prayerfully ask to hear the particular phrase or word that speaks to you or touches your life. Stay with this word or phrase. Listen as fully and openly as you can. What sense of divine presence or invitation comes? What is revealed?

Peace Covenant:

Today, God, I will remember to be thankful for the giver, as well as the gift.

22
Wednesday
August

Mutual Ministers

By Evelyn Spence of Council Bluffs, Iowa, USA

> *. . . but with righteousness he shall judge the poor, and decide with equity for the meek of the earth. . .*
>
> —Isaiah 11:4

I accompanied my husband to a retirement home to serve the sacrament of the Lord's Supper to three residents. We arrived just after they finished their noon meal and gathered in one of their apartments. After we completed the sacrament, we visited for a while. It was such a joy!

We shared news of common acquaintances. We remembered events from the past. We went to minister to *them*. They, being full of humility and meekness, ministered to *us*. We parted with joyful hearts. This is my humble and simple testimony: We were blessed to be a blessing.

Prayer for Peace:

Ministering God, we would bring ministry, too. We would bring blessing as we are blessed. We are humbled by the gifts you give us to share. May we also share the peace of Jesus Christ.

Spiritual Practice for the Week: Encountering Scripture as Continuing Revelation

Each day this week read and pray with the Doctrine and Covenants as continuing revelation of God's vision for the church and creation. Choose a favorite section or focus on recent counsel in Sections 156–164. Read a few selected paragraphs slowly three or four times.

Pause to pray for deep understanding of meaning after the first reading. Pray to open your heart and emotions to the text after the second reading. After the third reading, prayerfully ask to hear the particular phrase or word that speaks to you or touches your life. Stay with this word or phrase. Listen as fully and openly as you can. What sense of divine presence or invitation comes? What is revealed?

Peace Covenant:

Today, God, I will open my heart to receive the blessings offered by others.

23
Thursday
August

Love Your Neighbor

By Eleanor St. Clair of Oak Harbor, Ohio, USA

One of the scribes came near and heard them disputing with one another, and seeing that he answered them well, he asked him, "Which commandment is the first of all?" Jesus answered, "The first is, 'Hear, O Israel: the Lord our God, the Lord is one; you shall love the Lord your God with all your heart, and with all your soul, and with all your mind, and with all your strength.' The second is this, 'You shall love your neighbor as yourself.' There is no other commandment greater than these."

—Mark 12:28–31

I was blessed beyond measure by the workers, Shawn and Jason, who installed a weatherization package in my house. I bonded quickly with them.

On other jobs they normally ate lunch in their truck. By invitation, they sat at the table with me on the first day. The second day, Jason ate a plate of pasta with great appetite. The third day I served a homemade peach pie. They loved the homemade, whole-wheat bread, which we broke together daily for two weeks.

Of course, breaking bread included testimonies of Christ, the *Bread of Life*, which made their eyes light up.

They went beyond what was required in repairing houses and said, "We like to make sure our customers are happy when our team leaves a job." I assured them they were serving God by serving their neighbors.

When they finished, we shared good-byes and hugs.

Jason remarked, "You said that you once cooked for millionaires. I felt like a millionaire when I sat at your table and ate what you so lovingly prepared."

Shawn said, "I want you to know you have made me want change in my life."

Christ was among us. We were deeply touched. They assured me that if they were assigned near my area again, they would be back for a visit. "And food," I said. "Yes, spiritual food," was their response.

I miss them.

Feasting together was a joy, but sharing God's love was the greatest. We are told many will respond if we share our testimony of God's love and the peace of Jesus Christ. I thank God for their response.

Prayer for Peace:

Loving God, we respond to you with love. We know we are blessed when we share your love with our neighbors. Help us extend our love to the stranger with hospitality and generosity. May we show our love for you by sharing the peace of Jesus Christ.

Spiritual Practice for the Week: Encountering Scripture as Continuing Revelation

Read and pray with the Doctrine and Covenants as continuing revelation of God's vision for the church and creation. Choose a favorite section or focus on recent counsel in Sections 156–164. Pause to pray for deep understanding. Pray for opening of your heart.

Peace Covenant:

God, today I will extend the hand of peace to a stranger.

24
Friday
August

Attend to that which Is Their Due

By Dawn Squires of Melbourne, Victoria, Australia

> *And you will not have a mind to injure one another, but to live peaceably, and to render to all persons according to that which is their due.*
>
> —Mosiah 2:24, adapted

Six-year-old Susie went to visit her grandparents. She wanted to talk with her granddad, but he was working in the garden. He was busy planning a whole new outlay for his plot of earth and was not in the mood for his little magpie's constant chatter.

He didn't want to give her the attention she felt she was due. Eventually he said, "Not now Susie. You run inside and talk to Grandma, and I'll talk to you later."

Susie answered, "You know Grandpa, if you were a little girl and I was the granddad, I wouldn't tell you to go inside. I would listen to what you had to say."

Sometimes our best advice comes from little children.

I wonder how often we are immersed in our own priorities when God wants to talk to us. May we focus on what God has to say and give attention when it is due.

Prayer for Peace:

Listening God, may we be listeners too. May we set aside trivial activities and pay attention to what matters most. May we seek the lonely and befriend them. May we find the lost and share with them the peace of Christ.

Spiritual Practice for the Week: Encountering Scripture as Continuing Revelation

Each day this week read and pray with the Doctrine and Covenants as continuing revelation of God's vision for the church and creation. Choose a favorite section or focus on recent counsel in Sections 156–164. Read a few selected paragraphs slowly three or four times.

Pause to pray for deep understanding of meaning after the first reading. Pray to open your heart and emotions to the text after the second reading. After the third reading, prayerfully ask to hear the particular phrase or word that speaks to you or touches your life. Stay with this word or phrase. Listen as fully and openly as you can. What sense of divine presence or invitation comes? What is revealed?

Peace Covenant:

Today, God, I will lay aside whatever distracts me from listening to you.

25
Saturday
August

Seek First the Kingdom

By David Nii of Centennial, Colorado, USA

> *But strive first for the kingdom of God and his righteousness, and all these things will be given to you as well.*
>
> —Matthew 6:33

The Coeur d'Alene Congregation in Idaho is three blocks from an alternative high school. Many discussions centered on how to seek first the kingdom. The opportunity came when conversations with school officials brought a tangible need to the awareness of the congregation.

Dozens of homeless students did not have access to basic hygiene products. It was an easy decision for the congregation, in partnership with the school, to provide personal hygiene kits that included items such as soap, shampoo, dental care, and deodorant.

Coeur d'Alene received grant funds through World Mission Tithes to assemble the kits. The kits also included church contact information that invited students to connect with Community of Christ ministries.

As a continuing outreach, the church is open as a weekly meeting space for the youth to discuss their many challenges, including addiction issues.

Your contributions to World Mission Tithes are touching the lives of youth. Thank you for responding faithfully and giving generously.

Prayer for Peace:

Caregiver God, inspire us to serve you by caring for our companions in need. We hold our youth and all their struggles up to you for healing. May we join in that healing by sharing from our first fruits. May we do our part by sharing the peace of Jesus Christ.

Spiritual Practice:

Imagine what it would be like to gather with members of your congregation under a tree and be taught by Jesus. What would the tree look like? What would you most like to learn? What changes would happen in your congregation as it became a community of disciples? Write or speak a prayer, asking God to bless you and your congregation in learning to become disciples of Christ.

Peace Covenant:

Today, God, I will first seek ways I can help build your signal community.

26
Sunday
August

Stand Firm

By Dale Luffman, Council of Twelve Apostles

> *Finally, be strong in the Lord and in the strength of his power. Put on the whole armor of God...and having done everything, to stand firm...As shoes for your feet put on whatever will make you ready to proclaim the gospel of peace. With all of these, take the shield of faith...Take the helmet of salvation, and the sword of the Spirit, which is the word of God.*
> —Ephesians 6:10–13, 15–17, adapted

This is a wonderful passage of scripture! It aims to provide the Christian community with advice on how to live the Christian life in a hostile culture and climate. The writer has described "the old life" (Ephesians 4:17—6:9) and now in this passage gives the disciple advice about Christian discipline.

The suggestion of spiritual warfare reflects Christian pacifism. Christians in the early centuries refused to take up weapons of war and violence. The battle in which Christians understood themselves to be engaged was a spiritual battle.

Unfortunately, the Christian notion of warfare against spiritual forces has been glibly shifted to the justification of violence and war—justifying armed conflict. The early Christian community would have been horrified, and would have seen contemporary justification of violence and war by Christians as heretical. Christians understood spiritual forces to be fallen. The call was for Christians to resist those powers.

Early Christians were pacifists, something we too often forget. They understood themselves to be called by Christ to avoid bearing arms against or on behalf of human agents. Why? Because the battle was a spiritual one. Christians were admonished: "be strong in the Lord and in the strength of his power."

No early Christian took up weapons against persecutors. Many died as martyrs. They were good peacekeepers! Christians, according to Ephesians, bring a witness to the gospel of peace, with only "the whole armor of God" as their protection. The word of God would act on their behalf, destroying the powers of darkness and evil, even death itself.

As extremists of hope they were bold in their proclamation and in their living, bringing peace into the presence of dark days. They stood firm!

Prayer for Peace:

Spiritual Fortress, thank you for the strength you give us to proclaim your peace.

Spiritual Practice for the Week: Honoring the Worth of All Persons

Read Psalm 139:13–18. Sit quietly and let the deep meaning of the words sink into your mind, heart, and body. What thoughts and feelings do you have about being "fearfully and wonderfully made" (Psalm 139:14a)? Sense the intimate knowledge God has of you. Ask God for an awareness of the sacred worth of each person on the planet. How are you being invited to notice, protect, heal, and affirm the spiritual identity of all?

Peace Covenant:

Today, God, I will put on your armor, slough off the need to justify violence, and stand firm in your peace.

27
Monday
August

Remembering Chuck

By Louita Clothier of Lamoni, Iowa, USA

Open your hearts and feel the yearnings of your brothers and sisters who are lonely, despised, fearful, neglected, unloved. Reach out in understanding, clasp their hands, and invite all to share in the blessings of community created in the name of the One who suffered for all… Respect each life journey, even in its brokenness and uncertainty, for each person has walked alone at times.

—Doctrine and Covenants 161:3a–b

Anyone who knew Chuck Church was drawn to him by his big smile, cheerful personality, and optimistic outlook despite his lifelong physical struggle with the abnormal condition of his legs. He did not allow his circumstances to make him angry at life.

His parents treated him like other children. His strong faith; love of music; and steadfast wife, Eldeen, were all building blocks in his strength to overcome the condition that sentenced him to crutches and eventually a wheelchair.

Chuck had a glorious baritone voice. When our choir performed an Easter cantata, Chuck was the obvious choice to sing the part of Jesus Christ.

His voice still sings in my mind when I read the Holy Week scriptures. Chuck's favorite solo was a rendition of the psalm "I will sing unto the Lord for as long as I live. I will praise the Lord while I have my being."

Sometimes I felt that just struggling on his crutch-canes to his place to perform, he already had acted out those words.

In the end our friend, in his weakened condition, could not defeat cancer. The last time I saw Chuck, our congregation choir had gathered around the hospital bed Eldeen had set up in their living room. No one remembers what we sang, only that we did. But I clearly remember the words Chuck spoke at that time: "I'll be just fine."

In his heart Chuck was always "just fine." He taught us that it's not one's circumstances that determine happiness, but attitude toward those circumstances.

Prayer for Peace:

Loving God, we bring our attitudes to you for your blessing. May we remember, those who are challenged may not always have a community of support and often walk alone. May we learn from those whose spiritual strength brings peace to the world.

Spiritual Practice for the Week: Honoring the Worth of All Persons

Read Psalm 139:13–18. After each reading sit quietly and let the deep meaning of the words sink into your mind, heart, and body. Sense the intimate knowledge God has of you and every child ever born. Ask God for an awareness of the sacred worth of each person on the planet. Weep with God over the soul-wounding forces and events that rob people of dignity and worth. How are you being invited to notice, protect, heal, and affirm the spiritual identity of all God's beloved people today? Pray for God's compassion.

Peace Covenant:

I will open my heart to the lonely, loving God, and share your peace with them.

28
Tuesday
August

Thirst for Wisdom

By Jan Stoneking of Plano, Illinois, USA

But the wisdom from above is first pure, then peaceable, gentle, willing to yield, full of mercy and good fruits, without a trace of partiality or hypocrisy. And a harvest of righteousness is sown in peace for those who make peace.

James 3:17–18

God has given me so much. I appreciate this chance to testify of the power of the Holy Spirit for the peaceable kingdom of God!

Several years ago, after prayer and thoughtful consideration, I asked God to take away my addiction to romance novels and replace it with a thirst for good books. Until that prayer, I rarely had been aware of my prayers being answered so quickly and definitively. From that time until now, I have had no wish to read shallow fiction all the time. Although some fiction is worthwhile, today my library is full of good, spiritual, life-enhancing books.

This new discipline led to reading the Bible from cover to cover with an intense thirst for God's word and direction. Today I still find myself amazed at the awesome nature of the Holy Spirit and its transforming power in my life.

Prayer for Peace:

God of wisdom, may we be peaceable, gentle, and full of mercy. Fill us with knowledge of what you would have us learn. Sow in us a thirst for your word. May we harvest the will to share the peace of Jesus Christ.

Spiritual Practice for the Week: Honoring the Worth of All Persons

Each day this week read Psalm 139:13–18. After each reading sit quietly and let the deep meaning of the words sink into your mind, heart, and body. Imagine God watching you grow in your mother's womb. What thoughts and feelings do you have about being "fearfully and wonderfully made" (Psalm 139:14a)? Sense the intimate knowledge God has of you and every child ever born.

Ask God for an awareness of the sacred worth of each person on the planet. Weep with God over the soul-wounding forces and events that rob people of dignity and worth. How are you being invited to notice, protect, heal, and affirm the spiritual identity of all God's beloved people today? Pray for God's compassion.

Peace Covenant:

Today, God, I will take time to learn more of you and your vision.

29
Wednesday
August

A Plan for Hope

By Gary Piper of Fort Gratiot, Michigan, USA

But seek the welfare of the city where I have sent you into exile, and pray to the Lord on its behalf, for in its welfare you will find your welfare. ...For surely I know the plans I have for you, says the Lord, plans for your welfare and not for harm, to give you a future with hope.
—Jeremiah 29:7, 11

Since retiring from my 42-year employment in 2009, the plans and dreams my wife and I shared have been on hold because of circumstances beyond our control. Since then I have struggled with occasional periods of mild depression. Even so, I have not changed what matters most to me, but I have gone deeper into my relationship with Christ.

After thinking deeply on the underlying cause of my depression, I found it comes when my own feelings of self-worth are at their lowest. Recently I revisited what matters most to me, not to change my answer, but to examine what my relationship with Christ means and on what it is based.

One of my first thoughts centered on how much I must matter to Jesus Christ because of his life and ministry. And if I matter to him, then for me to honor that relationship I must matter to me as well.

I feel that to honor God's gift of life I ought to honor the lives of others also.

Their welfare is important in the eyes of God and me.

Prayer for Peace:

God of hope, we honor the future you hope for us by being aware of our calling. May we attend to the welfare of those to whom you send us. May our lives be sanctuaries of your peace for them and the world.

Spiritual Practice for the Week: Honoring the Worth of All Persons

Each day this week read Psalm 139:13–18. After each reading sit quietly and let the deep meaning of the words sink into your mind, heart, and body. Imagine God watching you grow in your mother's womb. What thoughts and feelings do you have about being "fearfully and wonderfully made" (Psalm 139:14a)? Sense the intimate knowledge God has of you and every child ever born.

Ask God for an awareness of the sacred worth of each person on the planet. Weep with God over the soul-wounding forces and events that rob people of dignity and worth. How are you being invited to notice, protect, heal, and affirm the spiritual identity of all God's beloved people today? Pray for God's compassion.

Peace Covenant:

Today, God, I will pray and act on what matters most in the cities and the world around me.

30
Thursday
August

Foundation of Forgiveness

By Candy Brayton of Independence, Missouri, USA

Listen to its teachings and discover anew its principles. Do not yearn for times that are past, but recognize that you have been given a foundation of faithful service, even as you build a foundation for what is yet to be.

—Doctrine and Covenants 162:2b

"Forgive us our trespasses, as we forgive those who trespass against us." For many years I have struggled with this prayer phrase. The trespass against me was at the profoundly life-altering far end of the spectrum. It took my innocence, sense of safety, and well-being.

I've struggled with shame, anger, helplessness, and hopelessness. The trespasser never took responsibility for the actions, never admitted the suffering caused.

My church family's response has been to pray *with* me and *for* me—always encouraging me to find peace and strength through forgiveness. Some of those helping me have described forgiveness as "wiping the slate clean, and starting anew." Another answer was "to forget."

I asked, "How do I do this?" Well-intentioned people have given flowery phrases about love and the healing of the Holy Spirit. Or, "If you have faith, you just do it."

However, phrases like "not enough faith" and "not a good enough Christian" added to my previous self-criticism. I felt even more miserable.

I continued to pray—desperate for insight that would help me understand.

I found the book, *Five Stages of Grief* (Kubler-Ross, 1969), which included denial, anger, bargaining, depression, and acceptance. It was one of those "eureka" moments.

I saw myself shifting through each of those stages. I let myself grieve what I had lost. The shift of view has helped me move forward to the "acceptance" stage.

I no longer need to hear remorse from the trespasser. I'm no longer angry when I think of that person.

It may not be how some might define "forgiveness," but with the help of the sacred community, I find myself more at peace.

Prayer for Peace:

Reconciling God, we know you weep with us when we are in our dark places. Stay with us when we hurt. We know forgiving helps us find peace.

Spiritual Practice for the Week: Honoring the Worth of All Persons

Read Psalm 139:13–18. After each reading sit quietly and let the deep meaning of the words sink into your mind, heart, and body. Sense the intimate knowledge God has of you and every child ever born. Ask God for an awareness of the sacred worth of each person on the planet. Weep with God over the soul-wounding forces and events that rob people of dignity and worth.

Peace Covenant:

God, I will call on you and Christ's community when my ability to forgive is challenged.

31
Friday
August

Friends Wait Close By

By Peggy Michael of Cantonment, Florida, USA

> *He said also to the one who had invited him, "When you give a luncheon or a dinner, do not invite your friends or your brothers or your relatives or rich neighbors, in case they may invite you in return, and you would be repaid. But when you give a banquet, invite the poor, the crippled, the lame, and the blind. And you will be blessed, because they cannot repay you, for you will be repaid at the resurrection of the righteous."*
>
> —Luke 14:12–14

It would be limiting to choose only the friends who give us pleasure. We would become dull, lazy, and self-content. We might even lapse into a mutual-admiration society. We need people close to us who touch raw nerves and spur us into thoughtful action. People who make us ask questions. Yes, we need diverse friends.

We may need to break down walls to find these friends. People build barriers that shut out love. They sometimes hide deep within lonely prisons that echo their anguish. Don't they know that friends wait close by who yearn to hold them and speak peace to them? Why must people perish in their webs of pain when help is near? When friends are near?

Everywhere I see people haunted by lost dreams and troubled minds. They mourn, for no one touches their hands and tells them of sweet justice. Let me be the one who touches them, Lord.

Prayer for Peace:

God of the lonely, God of those who mourn, may we, in our work for peace and justice, include them in our work. May we invite them to our banquet. May we invite them into our community of love.

Spiritual Practice for the Week: Honoring the Worth of All Persons

Each day this week read Psalm 139:13–18. After each reading sit quietly and let the deep meaning of the words sink into your mind, heart, and body. Imagine God watching you grow in your mother's womb. What thoughts and feelings do you have about being "fearfully and wonderfully made" (Psalm 139:14a)? Sense the intimate knowledge God has of you and every child ever born.

Ask God for an awareness of the sacred worth of each person on the planet. Weep with God over the soul-wounding forces and events that rob people of dignity and worth. How are you being invited to notice, protect, heal, and affirm the spiritual identity of all God's beloved people today? Pray for God's compassion.

Peace Covenant:

I will take the hands of marginalized persons and lead them to a place where prayers are answered.

1
Saturday
September

Discipleship NOW!

By David Nii of Centennial, Colorado, USA

> *The expectation for disciples to continually magnify their callings through spiritual growth, study, exemplary generosity, ethical choices, and fully accountable ministry is always present. How can the Spirit fill vessels that are unwilling to expand their capacity to receive and give according to a full measure of God's grace and truth?*
>
> —Doctrine and Covenants 163:6c, adapted

A field initiative called Discipleship NOW! began in the Western USA Mission Field to help equip disciples for mission This initiative provides a strengthened environment for disciple formation that includes learning, practical application, and spiritual formation to magnify ministry and witness in the life of the church.

Discipleship NOW! is a three-year experience that requires significant commitment from participants and mission center leaders: six weekend classes over two years followed by a one-year practicum in mission. Four locations across the field serve as centers of learning and living out faithful mission-focused discipleship.

World Church ministers provide the instruction and spiritual formation sections of Discipleship NOW! Grants from World Mission Tithes provide funding. More than 90 people currently take part. This initiative widens the foundation for disciples to invite others to experience the peace of Christ and witness of God's generous and unconditional grace.

Your contributions to World Mission Tithes provide field ministry such as Discipleship NOW! Thank you for giving so generously.

Prayer for Peace:

Guiding Shepherd, help us magnify our callings. Help us grow spiritually. Help us study and learn to make ethical choices. Make us vessels ready to be filled.

Spiritual Practice:

Spend some time meditating on leaves. Take a walk and look at leaves on trees. Watch leaves bud, sway in the wind, fall to the ground. Hear them crunch under your feet. Gather a small supply to place in a basket or vase. Use sight, smell, touch, and hearing to explore the qualities of leaves. Consider how leaves bring healing, life, and beauty to our lives. Close with prayer about your desire to offer healing as generously as a leaf on a tree (Revelation 22:2).

Peace Covenant:

NOW, God, no more excuses. I will make myself fully accountable.

2
Sunday
September

Give Us Clean Hearts

By Art Smith of Independence, Missouri, USA

Then he called the crowd again and said to them, "Listen to me, all of you, and understand: there is nothing outside a person that by going in can defile, but the things that come out are what defile."

—Mark 7:14–15

We often use any excuse to judge others. As I travel to other countries, and make new friends, people confide in me. Often conversation finds its way to judging others.

Jesus bumped into the same problem. If people weren't keeping themselves busy judging Jesus or his followers, then his own disciples were busy judging someone else. Often we use our own cultural rules and assumptions as a measuring stick to keep ourselves feeling comfortably superior.

Various cultural traditions are beautiful. I love the languages, the dances, and the festivals. I especially love the food! There are many traditions and related rules. Weddings and funerals are rich in regiment. However, if you're a foreigner it's not so bad to show up dressed the wrong way, or to sit or stand at the wrong moment, or to mess up and not offer the fitting gift. Locals, however, can be criticized for making the same mistake.

Once someone tried to prove to me what a terrible person *another* church member was. The person in question had a different ethnic origin than the speaker. When his mother died, they brought her to the church and laid her body out for the wake. After awhile the family went home to sleep, leaving the deceased mother's body in the deserted sanctuary.

To my friend, whose culture dictated the family stay with the body until burial, this was a travesty and proved to him the person in question lacked moral character.

While culture can be beautiful, we would be well-served to avoid using our own culture to judge others. The cultural differences or slip-ups may not harm, but our judgments of others might.

Prayer for Peace:

God of grace and understanding, put your nonjudgmental nature on us. Help us remember that we don't know the reasons and motives of others. Help us accept other cultural practices so we may unite in our diversity, unite for the sake of peace.

Spiritual Practice for the Week: Examining God's Call to Me and to All

Reflect on God's call for you. Prayerfully recall particular moments when you have experienced God's presence and invitation. Write in your journal or quietly reflect on images and insights that come. How do your gifts and callings connect with the call of God you notice in your family members, friends, congregation, or community?

Peace Covenant:

Today, God, I will be mindful of what I might say about another and mindful about thoughts that may cause me to speak negatively.

3
Monday
September

We Give from Our Abundance

By Barrie Fox of Kirkby-in-Ashfield, Nottinghamshire, England

> *How does God's love abide in anyone who has the world's goods and sees a brother or sister in need and yet refuses help?*
>
> —1 John 3:17

As I take just a moment to reflect on my life, I become most aware of how blessed I am. Of course events don't always work out the way I hope, but I am conscious of how much I have for which I am grateful.

I am sure many of us, in our better moments, would admit this. I am thrilled when I reflect on the blessings and opportunities I have had.

I am a little shaken when I admit to myself how I have let some of my advantages just slip by almost unnoticed.

Worship, song, scripture, and prayer constantly remind us who and whose we are and of our worth to God. Despite all the issues with which we struggle, we have much to be grateful for.

Those who express their gratitude do so by their contributions to humanity. From this wealth of giftedness we try to help others—the world's goods, health, self-esteem, and an awareness of the love of God. It is ours to share.

The church has always depended on people like Barnabas of the scriptures—people who seem always ready to seek and bring out the best in others by sharing Christ's peace and justice. The name Barnabas means "Son of Encouragement." I am grateful that I have known such people in my life. People need us. How can we refuse to help?

Prayer for Peace:

Abiding Love, we would be your instruments. Invest in us that we may share the love and peace of Jesus Christ.

Spiritual Practice for the Week: Examining God's Call to Me and to All

Each day this week reflect on God's call in your life. Begin by prayerfully asking to recall particular moments when you have experienced God's presence and invitation. Write in your journal or just quietly reflect on images and insights that come.

When has God seemed most real in your life? How and when has God called you to use your energies and gifts? When have you felt most deeply connected and responsive to God's movement in your life? When have you felt disconnected or resistant to God's call? How do your gifts and callings connect with the call of God you notice in your family members, friends, congregation, or community?

Peace Covenant:

Today, God, I will express my gratitude by sharing with others.

4
Tuesday
September

Learning: A Prelude to Teaching (Part I)

By Barbara Howard of Independence, Missouri, USA

...he will be the stability of your times, abundance of salvation, wisdom, and knowledge...
—Isaiah 33:6

Emily, a child with Down syndrome, saw some visitors sit in the congregation. She immediately ran over and gave a huge hug to every person in the row. The spirit of love abounded.

During the service I kept going back to the scene. There were many visitors in the sanctuary, so I decided I would be a learner. In that moment I vowed to welcome each guest rather than going to beloved old friends and having my usual Sunday chat.

The more I ponder that moment I realize how easy it is when we are older to think of ourselves as teachers. Learning may be a more-significant calling.

Learning can be difficult. Comfort sometimes keeps us from risking new ways of thinking, of wrestling with new ideas. Learning is an act of change. In recent years we've been asked to learn how to be more open, vulnerable, more accepting, and more loving. Such actions need practice and commitment.

Or do they? Does Emily deliberately commit herself to embracing visitors at church, or does she just follow her open, Spirit-led heart? She seems so open to the Spirit, so eager to embrace others.

Our calling as disciples is an opportunity as teacher-learners to spend time with those who are younger. They will teach us to delight in new technology, to move our bodies to music in church, to laugh, and to embrace. It makes me want to enroll in *Childhood 101*.

Prayer for Peace:

God of wisdom, teach us to be learners. Open our hearts to what the children would teach us. Let us be young-at-heart peacemakers.

Spiritual Practice for the Week: Examining God's Call to Me and to All

Each day this week reflect on God's call in your life. Begin by prayerfully asking to recall particular moments when you have experienced God's presence and invitation. Write in your journal or just quietly reflect on images and insights that come.

When has God seemed most real in your life? How and when has God called you to use your energies and gifts? When have you felt most deeply connected and responsive to God's movement in your life? When have you felt disconnected or resistant to God's call? How do your gifts and callings connect with the call of God you notice in your family members, friends, congregation, or community?

Peace Covenant:

Today, God, I will listen with my heart and learn to be a teacher.

5
Wednesday
September

Learning: A Prelude to Teaching (Part II)

By Barbara Howard of Independence, Missouri, USA

The wolf shall live with the lamb, the leopard shall lie down with the kid, the calf and the lion and the fatling together, and a little child shall lead them.

—Isaiah 11:6

One of the most-difficult learning experiences for me has been to listen to people whose ideas seem completely different from my own. However, when I truly listen I realize their commitment and enthusiasm for their own point of view is much like my own.

So, rather than argue or turn off my listening, I am trying to learn to listen with my heart. If I do this, even though we still see the world differently, I can love and accept them in ways that were not possible before. Learning about them changes the way I look at them.

Learning can precede our teaching. Spending time with those different from ourselves in settings other than church can open doors for ministry. Spending time with those in other age groups can give us new insights about community. Learning and practicing the spiritual disciplines can teach us to recognize the leading of God's Spirit more readily.

Every experience offers a chance to learn. In recent weeks we've had the blessing of many houseguests. (My neighbor suggested we were "overwhelmed with company," but we assured her we were blessed with friends.) During these special times, while being grateful for this faith community that created such a web of associations, I realize how much our guests taught me about scripture, prayer, and the value of laughter and joy. They were my teachers and I the learner. I want to use these lessons in my ministry.

Look around. Who's been teaching you?

Prayer for Peace:

Tender Shepherd, lead us as your lambs. May we realize the uncorrupted wisdom of children and humbly follow them to your peaceable kingdom.

Spiritual Practice for the Week: Examining God's Call to Me and to All

Each day this week reflect on God's call in your life. Begin by prayerfully asking to recall particular moments when you have experienced God's presence and invitation. Write in your journal or just quietly reflect on images and insights that come.

When has God seemed most real in your life? How and when has God called you to use your energies and gifts? When have you felt most deeply connected and responsive to God's movement in your life? When have you felt disconnected or resistant to God's call? How do your gifts and callings connect with the call of God you notice in your family members, friends, congregation, or community?

Peace Covenant:

Today, God, I will open myself to the ideas of others and humbly learn what I thought I already knew.

6
Thursday
September

The Soccer Net

By Lillian Kirby of Blue Springs, Missouri, USA

Sustain each other in peace, and ye shall be blessed with my Spirit, in comforting and strengthening you for my work.

—Doctrine and Covenants 117:13

My 12-year-old grandson came to my house one hot, muggy Sunday afternoon. Everyone else in his family was napping, and he was bored and looking for an exciting activity. He asked me if he could build a soccer goal net from some old wood and nails.

This monumental project seemed unattainable to me, but I gave him permission to try. The novice carpenter began work in my driveway, having a vision in his mind. He made many trips to the basement for the old scrap wood and some nails. Occasionally, I went outside to encourage him in the 6- by 12-foot lumber puzzle being nailed, hammered, and fashioned into the wanted shape.

Several hours later his father viewed the project. He lent support and encouragement, but eventually he convinced Jordan the wood wasn't sturdy enough. It soon collapsed. Yet, surprisingly, my grandson went away happy.

Some of life's goals are like this project. We start with enthusiasm and vision but sometimes are frustrated before completing the task.

What we learn during the building of our lives is worth the laborious steps and mistakes made on the journey. Although disappointments come our way, may we continue our journeys, with Christ-like goals and values. With the help of God and the sacred community we can reach our goals.

Prayer for Peace:

Master Carpenter, sometimes our best-laid plans go wrong. Thank you for the sacred community that supports and strengthens us to reach our goals. May our goals be your goals. May we be builders of ways to share Christ's peace.

Spiritual Practice for the Week: Examining God's Call to Me and to All

Each day this week reflect on God's call in your life. Begin by prayerfully asking to recall particular moments when you have experienced God's presence and invitation. Write in your journal or just quietly reflect on images and insights that come.

When has God seemed most real in your life? How and when has God called you to use your energies and gifts? When have you felt most deeply connected and responsive to God's movement in your life? When have you felt disconnected or resistant to God's call? How do your gifts and callings connect with the call of God you notice in your family members, friends, congregation, or community?

Peace Covenant:

Today, God, I will lend encouragement to the work of another.

7
Friday
September

With a Song in My Heart

By Flo McDonald of Lee's Summit, Missouri, USA

The poor shall eat and be satisfied; those who seek him shall praise the Lord. May your hearts live forever! All the ends of the earth shall remember and turn to the Lord; and all the families of the nations shall worship before him.

—Psalm 22:26–27

The first time I went on vacation alone, many changes had taken place in my life. I decided to go to my home state of Washington. I stayed with my brother and his wife and was free to come and go. Because most of the time I was without a companion, I decided to visit people I knew who would welcome company.

My sister was in poor health because of an inoperable brain tumor. I decided to spend much of my time visiting with her. I remembered others I knew who also were confined or unable to freely move. I planned each day, and for three weeks I made daily visits, taking time out for lunch and a swim now and then.

One dear friend loved the outdoors. She was most often in a wheelchair, yet I managed to take her out with a walker for the day. She enjoyed riding in the car, eating breakfast in a restaurant, and spending the rest of the day at the lake.

I was blessed to be able to share time with those who needed companionship. The words of a hymn kept coming to my mind. "Take time to be holy, speak oft with thy Lord. Abide in him always and feed on his word. Make friends of God's children, bless those who are weak, forgetting in nothing his blessing to seek" (William D. Longstaff).

My vacation was fulfilling. I am glad I took the time to care, show love, and give cheer. We freely receive God's Spirit. Freely share it with others.

Prayer for Peace:

We worship you, God, and enjoy your good Spirit. May we share songs of peace with those who are lonely. May we praise you together as one community.

Spiritual Practice for the Week: Examining God's Call to Me and to All

Each day this week reflect on God's call in your life. Begin by prayerfully asking to recall particular moments when you have experienced God's presence and invitation. Write in your journal or just quietly reflect on images and insights that come.

When has God seemed most real in your life? How and when has God called you to use your energies and gifts? When have you felt most deeply connected and responsive to God's movement in your life? When have you felt disconnected or resistant to God's call? How do your gifts and callings connect with the call of God you notice in your family members, friends, congregation, or community?

Peace Covenant:

Today, God, I will bless as I have been blessed.

8
Saturday
September

Prepare the Way

By Rick Maupin, Council of Twelve Apostles

> *Generously share the invitation, ministries, and sacraments through which people can encounter the Living Christ who heals and reconciles through redemptive relationships in sacred community. The restoring of persons to healthy or righteous relationships with God, others, themselves, and the earth is at the heart of the purpose of your journey as a people of faith.*
> —Doctrine and Covenants 163:2b

What would it be like to live in an area that did not have someone serving in the priesthood office of evangelist? Community of Christ members and friends in the Dominican Republic have known what it is like.

However, through the commitment and dedication of Fred Cole, an evangelist from Harlingen, Texas, and Presiding Evangelist David Brock, members and friends in this tiny Caribbean nation now also know the "ministry of blessing."

Recently Fred and David traveled there to teach classes about the ministry of the evangelist and the sacrament of the evangelist blessing. David gave evangelist blessings to several members during his recent visit.

This marked the first sharing of this sacrament with Dominican Republic members of the church in their home country. Your contributions to World Mission Tithes prepared the way to make this possible. Thank you for responding faithfully and giving generously.

Prayer for Peace:

God who blesses us, may we also bless one another. May we be instruments to restore relationships with you and one another. May we remain a people of faith, on the path to peace in our world.

Spiritual Practice:

For this body prayer, we will use simple postures with phrases from Doctrine and Covenants Section 163. Create a bowl with your hands, close your eyes, and meditate with the phrase, "*God the Eternal Creator weeps.*" Imagine your bowl catching God's tears. End this posture by emptying the container over your head and being anointed by God's tears.

Create a large circle with your arms as if hugging someone and meditate with the phrase: "*God yearns to draw you close so that wounds may be healed.*" End by placing your hands over your heart.

Now create your own body posture of openness to God and meditate on the phrase: "*Be vulnerable to Divine Grace.*" Say amen by bowing to God with palms together.

Peace Covenant:

Today God, I will bless as I have been blessed.

9
Sunday
September

All Are Worthy

By Wim van Klinken, director of International Headquarters

> *Now the woman was a Gentile, of Syrophoenician origin. She begged him to cast the demon out of her daughter. He said to her, "Let the children be fed first, for it is not fair to take the children's food and throw it to the dogs." But she answered him, "Sir even the dogs under the table eat the children's crumbs." Then he said to her, "For saying that, you may go—the demon has left your daughter."*
>
> —Mark 7:26–29

Jesus' encounter with the Syrophoenician woman is a vital story in Mark's Gospel. This Gentile woman points out to Jesus, and thus to us, the blessings and the promise of the kingdom, symbolized by bread, are not just for the *faithful few*, but for all.

She challenges a tendency in those days, and still prevalent today, that we share and associate only with those who are our friends or family. We associate with those who share the same beliefs or moral standards. We share with those of our own tribe or nation, or those who do not threaten our existence.

When bread is perceived a scarcity, we protect it. We share it only with those in our circle. Therefore we protect our borders, raise import duties, and in our church hear voices to limit our Oblation and our job opportunities to members.

The gospel message shows us that all are worthy to be part of and should receive the blessings of life. Not on Caesar's terms to protect the powerful, not on our worldly terms to protect our wealth, but on God's terms of love and generosity for all, particularly the powerless, poor, and marginalized.

Jesus' vision of the peace of God made him reach out and include those not considered worthy, those perceived as sinners, outcasts, and foreigners. Shalom, Zion, is established fully only when all are able to partake of the bread, not on our limiting conditions, but on God's condition of love and the enduring principle of the Worth of All Persons.

Prayer for Peace:

God of shalom, may we observe by your wide, wide arms that you exclude no one from *your* love. May we learn from your deep, deep Spirit that no one should be excluded from *our* love. Encourage us to make peaceful encounters with all.

Spiritual Practice for the Week: Making Responsible Choices

Each day this week prayerfully seek God's guidance in your choices. Discernment invites us to orient our lives toward God and God's vision for us and for creation. Begin by reviewing the responsibilities and opportunities in the day before you. Take these choices into prayer, asking God for wisdom and insight about what matters most.

Offer yourself to God with the prayer of Teresa of Avila: "God, what do you want of me today?" Sit prayerfully with this question as you review the day again. Be aware of images, thoughts, names, or actions that come to you. Ask for blessing to live this day responsibly and compassionately in the spirit of Christ.

Peace Covenant:

Today, God, I will reach outside my circle of friends to show companionship with those who are marginalized.

10
Monday
September

Approachable God

By Peggy Michael of Cantonment, Florida, USA

> *...who made heaven and earth, the sea, and all that is in them; who keeps faith forever; who executes justice for the oppressed; who gives food to the hungry. The Lord sets the prisoners free; the Lord opens the eyes of the blind. The Lord lifts up those who are bowed down; the Lord loves the righteous. The Lord watches over the strangers; he upholds the orphan and the widow...*
>
> —Psalm 146:6–9

God is our all, beyond all, yet is so approachable. God is involved in every breath we take.

God's Spirit coaxes noble feelings from our hearts and forms words of praise in our minds.

God touches and fills each one to overflowing, but we cannot express even a tiny portion of what our Creator means to us. However, I will try...

God of glory, God of wonder, every fiber of my being yearns to know you, to do your bidding, to dwell in your holy presence. Forgive me for the times I wasted my strength on lesser concerns, and tried to shape my life with my own hands.

Still, you call to me and urge me onward. O God of the ages, could you possibly reflect your glory in this fragment of flesh?

Prayer for Peace:

Liberating God, protector of orphans, we bow down, and you lift us up. We praise you as the source of all creation and blessing. Shine your healing light on us. Open our blind eyes to the obstacles to peace and we will overcome.

Spiritual Practice for the Week: Making Responsible Choices

Each day this week prayerfully seek God's guidance in your choices. Discernment invites us to orient our lives toward God and God's vision for us and for creation.

Begin by reviewing the responsibilities and opportunities in the day before you. Take these choices into prayer, asking God for wisdom and insight about what matters most. Offer yourself to God with the prayer of Teresa of Avila: "God, what do you want of me today?"

Sit prayerfully with this question as you review the day again. Be aware of images, thoughts, names, or actions that come to you. Ask for blessing to live this day responsibly and compassionately in the spirit of Christ.

Peace Covenant:

God, today I will try to express to you how much you mean to me as my Creator and Comforter.

11
Tuesday
September

Hear God's Voice above the Din

By Cindy Korf of North Platte, Nebraska, USA

> *Therefore, continue to be strong in faith. To you who hear my voice and know my promises I will reveal myself and give my peace, even in the midst of your uncertainties.*
>
> —Doctrine and Covenants 158:11a

With the solitude of the trees, I like to walk along a path to a small clearing that overlooks the South Platte River. From this vantage point, if I listen carefully, I can hear the soft murmur of the river.

Unless I go to this spot, it is difficult to hear the river because of noise from the highway that runs next to it. Tractor-trailers, cars, motorcycles, and trucks constantly zoom along. There is no stopping their noise.

My life is much the same. The world constantly clangs and bangs around me. Even when I search for quiet time to be alone with God, the world barges in—whether it's a phone ringing or my own thoughts, consumed with daily events.

It is hard to hear God's voice above the noise of the world. Yet, like the water that always quietly flows in the river, I know God is present. I just have to shut out the noise of the world and listen for God's voice. I center myself and am immersed in the *living* water.

Prayer for Peace:

Ever-present God, we hear you in the quiet waters and in the breeze of the swaying trees. Help us hear you above the din of traffic and busyness. Help us listen for your words of peace that we may share them with the world.

Spiritual Practice for the Week: Making Responsible Choices

Each day this week prayerfully seek God's guidance in your choices. Discernment invites us to orient our lives toward God and God's vision for us and for creation.

Begin by reviewing the responsibilities and opportunities in the day before you. Take these choices into prayer, asking God for wisdom and insight about what matters most. Offer yourself to God with the prayer of Teresa of Avila: "God, what do you want of me today?"

Sit prayerfully with this question as you review the day again. Be aware of images, thoughts, names, or actions that come to you. Ask for blessing to live this day responsibly and compassionately in the spirit of Christ.

Peace Covenant:

Today, God, I will set aside busyness and listen for you.

12
Wednesday
September

God Isn't Done with Me Yet

By Willa Frey of Fairbanks, Alaska, USA

Even children make themselves known by their acts, by whether what they do is pure and right.

—Proverbs 20:11

The students of my classroom were finishing their work, collecting homework assignments, and in other ways preparing for the end of another school day. A beautiful day called eagerly to the children to come out and play.

Susan was finishing a drawing she had been working on for some time—she had a few minutes to spare. She walked up to my desk slowly and, a little anxiously, offered the drawing to me with these words, "This is for you."

She had carefully traced a picture from the front of her binder. It was a happy, pig-tailed girl with a missing front tooth (much like herself). It said, "Just be patient. Remember, God isn't done with me yet." I accepted the picture with a smile, commenting on her careful work.

I thanked her and reminded her to remember God wasn't done with *me* yet either, and I asked her to please be patient with me. We were *both* "works in progress" as was everyone else in the room.

A quick hug and a smile assured her we were companions on life's journey.

Prayer for Peace:

Divine Parent, may our children know you understand their "growing pains." May they know your creative Spirit will guide them to be all they are capable of being; that they have companions on the journey who are still growing, too. May we grow together as we share the peace of Jesus Christ.

Spiritual Practice for the Week: Making Responsible Choices

Each day this week prayerfully seek God's guidance in your choices. Discernment invites us to orient our lives toward God and God's vision for us and for creation.

Begin by reviewing the responsibilities and opportunities in the day before you. Take these choices into prayer, asking God for wisdom and insight about what matters most. Offer yourself to God with the prayer of Teresa of Avila: "God, what do you want of me today?"

Sit prayerfully with this question as you review the day again. Be aware of images, thoughts, names, or actions that come to you. Ask for blessing to live this day responsibly and compassionately in the spirit of Christ.

Peace Covenant:

Today, God, I will be open to the ways I need to change and grow to help bring about the peaceable kingdom.

13
Thursday
September

Congregational Blessing

By Terry Snapp of Independence, Missouri, USA

> *Let the church be admonished that the times are portentous and demand faithful adherence to the faith and work of the church, that mankind may be blessed...*
>
> —Doctrine and Covenants 137:6a

During the more than 30 years Betty and I have attended our congregation many moments and people have made our experience a wonderful faith adventure.

Recently, the reality of God's love for the community became real to me through the experience of a congregational blessing—an opportunity for an evangelist to bless the congregation in its work to share the peace of Jesus Christ.

I have no doubt that God inspired the words shared. For me, the beautiful spirit that was present and the loving invitation of those words reinforced the wonderful message of the blessing itself. At the same time, it added to all that had preceded it during the worship service.

The blessing stood out as a beautiful experience of realizing God was among us at that moment in a way that touched me deeply. For me, it was and will always be a moment of truth and inspiration.

It served as a vivid reminder for me that God is real and loves us intensely. God is with us, not just in the sanctuary, but wherever we are and as we share the peace of Jesus Christ.

Prayer for Peace:

God of blessing, we praise you for the sacraments that strengthen our connection to you and one another. We thank you for your servants, who pray for us in community and individually. We are comforted and strengthened by those acts. May we use that strength to share Christ's peace in the world.

Spiritual Practice for the Week: Making Responsible Choices

Each day this week prayerfully seek God's guidance in your choices. Discernment invites us to orient our lives toward God and God's vision for us and for creation.

Begin by reviewing the responsibilities and opportunities in the day before you. Take these choices into prayer, asking God for wisdom and insight about what matters most. Offer yourself to God with the prayer of Teresa of Avila: "God, what do you want of me today?"

Sit prayerfully with this question as you review the day again. Be aware of images, thoughts, names, or actions that come to you. Ask for blessing to live this day responsibly and compassionately in the spirit of Christ.

Peace Covenant:

Today God, I will seek to bless someone, even as I have been blessed.

For more information about congregational blessings, visit *www.CofChrist.org/evangelist/congblessing1.asp.*

14
Friday
September

Through the Eyes of Love

By Lu Mountenay of Independence, Missouri, USA

...but Jesus said, "Let the little children come to me, and do not stop them; for it is to such as these that the kingdom of heaven belongs."

—Matthew 19:14

When I was about 10, my older sister, Judy, came home crying. I asked her what was wrong. She said some kids were making fun of her face. I asked, in all innocence, "What's wrong with your face?" It was as if I had said the cruelest words, and she ran crying from the room. She was hurt, and I was confused.

My oldest sister, Anita, heard all this and helped me understand. She asked, "Didn't you ever notice that Judy has a cleft palate?" I didn't know what that was, and no, I had never noticed. When I looked at Judy, all I saw was Judy. She was my sister, and I loved her just the way she was.

I felt bad that I had made her cry. Anita told a story to me about when Judy first was brought home from the hospital. Anita was about 4 and didn't know what a new baby should look like. When she saw Judy, she thought she was the most-beautiful baby in the world. Of course, at that new age, she hadn't had her initial surgery, and the cleft palate was prominent.

Anita greeted some visitors at the door and proudly took them to see the baby. They were all looking down with sad faces and shaking their heads. Anita didn't understand why they, too, didn't think she was beautiful.

Since then Judy has had surgery, and one hardly can tell anything ever was "wrong." Of course, Anita and I know nothing ever was *wrong*. It was only a physical perception, comparing her to what was considered "normal."

It would be great if people of all ages could adopt the innocent, accepting, mindset of children and see all humans through the eyes of love.

Prayer for Peace:

God of creation, clear our eyes of cynical cataracts, of blurring, shallow judgments, and of narrow vision. Let love and peace shine brightly in our eyes.

Spiritual Practice for the Week: Making Responsible Choices

Prayerfully seek God's guidance in your choices. Discernment invites us to orient our lives toward God. Review the responsibilities and opportunities in the day before you. Be aware of images, thoughts, names, or actions that come to you. Ask for blessing to live this day responsibly and compassionately in the spirit of Christ.

Peace Covenant:

Today, God, I will set aside preconceived ideas of "normal" and look at the worth of people as you see them.

15
Saturday
September

Dwell in Christ

By Karin Peter of Adrian, Missouri, USA

> *God is calling for a prophetic community to emerge, drawn from the nations of the world, that is characterized by uncommon devotion to the compassion and peace of God revealed in Jesus Christ. Through divine grace and wisdom, this faith community has been given abundant gifts, resources, and opportunities to equip it to become such a people. Chief among these is the power of community in Christ expressed locally in distinctive fashions while upholding a unity of vision, foundational beliefs, and mission throughout the world.*
>
> —Doctrine and Covenants163:11a

The South Miami Congregation sponsors a retreat at a campground in central Florida the last weekend of May each year. Expectations of seeing old friends and making new ones is part of the excitement as the event draws near.

Pastor Angela Moorman-Holguin and her multicultural congregation invite Hispanic congregations and groups from neighboring mission centers. The welcome and ministry offered by South Miami encourages participation, and attendance continues to grow.

The South Miami Congregation models "dwelling in Christ" as it welcomes new and old friends each year. The hospitality grows as people who attended the previous year's retreat invite new members and guests to join them for each year's celebration.

The Southern USA Mission Field is grateful for your contributions to World Mission Tithes. This financial support allows many individuals and families to take part in companionship, worship, and disciple formation at this event. Thank you for responding faithfully and generously.

Prayer for Peace:

God of revelation, we are ready to hear you. We are open and ready to be filled by your vision for our communities. Lead us with your grace and wisdom—lead us to peace.

Spiritual Practice:

One characteristic of the Restoration movement is ongoing revelation. We are a people always in process, becoming shaped by God's interaction with us. In prayer, listen deeply to the name, "Community of Christ." Write a prayer asking God to continue to form us through our name. Listen deeply to what it would mean to live in community, following and sharing the way of Christ.

Peace Covenant:

Today, God, I will prepare myself to be ready for whatever service I can offer.

16
Sunday
September

Follow Me

By Paul Davis of Kansas City, Missouri, USA

> *But turning and looking at his disciples, he rebuked Peter and said, "Get behind me, Satan! For you are setting your mind not on divine things but on human things." He called the crowd with his disciples, and said to them, "If any want to become my followers, let them deny themselves and take up their cross and follow me. For those who want to save their life will lose it, and those who lose their life for my sake, and for the sake of the gospel, will save it.*
> —Mark 8:33–35

I've never understood why Peter and Jesus get into it so angrily when they could have been enjoying a lovely retreat at "The Villages" of Caesarea Philippi, a spa center overlooking the sparkling Sea of Galilee. They've earned a rest, here at the halfway point of Mark, having ministered together for months throughout Galilee and now looking toward Jerusalem.

Peter has come a long way. He has come to believe Jesus is the Messiah and has said so out loud. Figuring out the Messiah has come—is standing right before you—and not running away deserves some praise. Jesus rewards Peter's brilliant, supremely courageous insight with a stern order to keep silent.

Instead of praise, encouragement, a celebration, Jesus delivers the most-shocking news. As Messiah, he is going to suffer, be rejected by the elders and priests, and be killed. Everyone knows that's not what messiahs are supposed to do. They do what Isaiah said; they deliver their people from suffering. Peter can hardly be expected to make sense of what Jesus was saying.

It feels like an act of concern for his friend when Peter takes Jesus aside to tell him this can't possibly be right. It's then that Jesus delivers his famous line, "Get behind me, Satan!"

Peter can't be expected to understand, but he's acting as the Tempter. He's inviting Jesus to give up the hard road he's on, to forgo the suffering, the sacrifice. What he can't imagine is that Jesus is about to ask him to come along, to get behind him, to follow.

Prayer for Peace:

God, our spiritual leader and guide, create in us strong hearts—willing to sacrifice and follow on the path of the peace of Jesus Christ.

Spiritual Practice for the Week: Embodying God's Shalom

Each day this week find a way to express and embody God's shalom. Begin by prayerfully listening to your longing for peace. Become silent and imagine you can hear the groaning of the Earth's peoples, nations, and creatures. Prayerfully open yourself to God's yearning for peace and the divine vision of shalom.

What images, feelings, and words come to you? What prayer for peace comes to you from your time of listening? Speak or write this prayer. What small act of justice, kindness, healing, or peacemaking is God inviting you to consider this day, this week?

Peace Covenant:

Today, God, I recognize Jesus as the Messiah. I accept my mission to follow.

17
Monday
September

The Fox, Robin, and Squirrels

By Shirley Remmenga of Fort Collins, Colorado, USA

> *Grace to you and peace from God our Father and the Lord Jesus Christ.*
> —1 Corinthians 1:3

I walked along a trail at dawn. I flung my arms wide, breathed deeply, and stepped with energy. I love to walk, especially early in the morning. This walk was a great one because it was full of surprises.

The leaves on the trees were just beginning to turn color. A mature fox ran across my path, and farther along a younger fox waited for me. He didn't trot away until I was within a couple of yards.

A robin, dressed in her bright red vest, was searching for worms and was not alarmed as I drew near. In fact, she never flew away as I passed her along the trail.

Before I reached home, I watched two squirrels playing tag on the grass, and then they scurried off to the treetops, where they continued to play. I was elated to have had such an energizing, delightful walk and was ready for whatever the day would bring.

God has created an awesome world that is so visible in nature. How blessed I am to have a place to walk, the time and the health to walk. Thank you, Creator God!

Prayer for Peace:

God of grace and peace, Creator of all we behold, pull us from our busy lives to rejoice in and appreciate your creation. As we enjoy peace of mind, may we share Christ's peace with the world.

Spiritual Practice for the Week: Embodying God's Shalom

Each day this week find a way to express and embody God's shalom. Begin by prayerfully listening to your longing for peace. Become silent and imagine you can hear the groaning of the Earth's peoples, nations, and creatures. Prayerfully open yourself to God's yearning for peace and the divine vision of shalom.

What images, feelings, and words come to you? What prayer for peace comes to you from your time of listening? Speak or write this prayer. What small act of justice, kindness, healing, or peacemaking is God inviting you to consider this day, this week?

Peace Covenant:

Today, Creator, I will use my senses to know your presence.

18
Tuesday
September

Tenacity

By Paul McCain of Oklahoma City, Oklahoma, USA

> *The wilderness and the dry land shall be glad, the desert shall rejoice and blossom; like the crocus it shall blossom abundantly, and rejoice with joy and singing.*
>
> —Isaiah 35:1–2

There is a spot in my front yard where I have seen, in my mind's eye, a beautiful redbud tree. I lost count of how many times my attempts to transplant a small tree to the spot failed, while hanging onto the idea there had to be life in that small plant. My daughter took pity on me and bought one from a nursery to replace the last lifeless set of twigs. I enjoyed its beautiful spring buds for several years until it started to get sick.

Each day it dwindled, my heart sank more. I kept getting questions from friends and family as to why I didn't pull the poor sapling out. I finally gave up.

As you might guess, it's not altogether about having a tree there; it's about not giving up. It's a statement about how life is lived—not giving up on programs too soon and not giving up on people who don't realize their own worth.

May we have the sense to move on when it's best to do so, but also the vision to see life in those around us. May we have the tenacity to work tirelessly, lovingly, to bring realization of God's love to those lives.

Now, on close inspection, many beautiful, tiny leaves finally are emerging from the small tree. The tree, like God's love, is also tenacious. I rejoice in the beauty of blossoms to come. To help the small tree in its determination to live, I am now watering it each day.

Prayer for Peace:

God of the giant sequoia and the tiny sapling, grow Christ's peace in us.

Spiritual Practice for the Week: Embodying God's Shalom

Each day this week find a way to express and embody God's shalom. Begin by prayerfully listening to your longing for peace. Become silent and imagine you can hear the groaning of the Earth's peoples, nations, and creatures. Prayerfully open yourself to God's yearning for peace and the divine vision of shalom.

What images, feelings, and words come to you? What prayer for peace comes to you from your time of listening? Speak or write this prayer. What small act of justice, kindness, healing, or peacemaking is God inviting you to consider this day, this week?

Peace Covenant:

Today God, I will share your living water with dormant lives.

19
Wednesday
September

Global Family

By Dawn Squires of Melbourne, Victoria, Australia

> *Heed the urgent call to become a global family united in the name of the Christ, committed in love to one another, seeking the kingdom for which you yearn and to which you have always been summoned. That kingdom shall be a peaceable one and it shall be known as Zion.*
> —Doctrine and Covenants 161:6b

Once a month I can get used postage stamps from a local university. I divide them to give to different charities—the Catholic Overseas Mission, the Uniting Church, and the Girl Guides.

I also give some to 11 children for their stamp collections. These stamps normally would be thrown away, but there are still uses for them.

I spoke with a woman who showed me what she did for charity. She makes boxes of jumpers (sweaters) for children whose parents are in financial need. Others help by giving her wool, or she buys it when prices are reduced. She also knits clothes for babies born to drug-addicted or struggling single women.

I thought of all the charities that people help without any trumpets heralding their work. These people have discerned God's call. It is lovely to see God at work in our global family.

Prayer for Peace:

Generous God, may we serve you by serving others. Expand our borders of concern to reach across the continents. Let us take delight in giving a helping hand. Let us find unity in our diversity. Let us pursue and share Christ's peace.

Spiritual Practice for the Week: Embodying God's Shalom

Each day this week find a way to express and embody God's shalom. Begin by prayerfully listening to your longing for peace. Become silent and imagine you can hear the groaning of the Earth's peoples, nations, and creatures. Prayerfully open yourself to God's yearning for peace and the divine vision of shalom.

What images, feelings, and words come to you? What prayer for peace comes to you from your time of listening? Speak or write this prayer. What small act of justice, kindness, healing, or peacemaking is God inviting you to consider this day, this week?

Peace Covenant:

Today, God, I will find a way to share Christ's peace globally.

20
Thursday
September

I Now Have a Testimony!

By Roger Hull of Carson City, Nevada, USA

> *Be of good cheer, O my people…If you will move out in faith and confidence to proclaim my gospel my Spirit will empower you and there will be many who respond, even in places and ways which do not now seem clear.*
>
> —Doctrine and Covenants 154:7a

I grew up in a Community of Christ congregation. When I was young we moved to Nevada, where I was the only child my age in the new congregation. I missed my old church friends and became lonely. I didn't want to go to church anymore. I stopped living the life God wanted me to live.

I married young and soon had four children. I was not a good husband and father. I committed some serious crimes and got divorced. I tried to go back to church, but I didn't fit in or feel welcome. I went to the only place I felt safe—home. The prodigal son returned.

I remarried, got joint custody of my children, and had one more. I still wasn't giving my whole being to God. This time I was accused of something I didn't do. I had no way to defend myself. The trial was meaningless to me. I am now in a Nevada state correctional center, again, far from my church family

In the 10 years I've been here, I go to the services of another denomination. A Community of Christ evangelist comes all the way from Texas to see me every three months. He serves me the sacrament of the Lord's Supper.

I've completed many Temple School classes. Until now, I never thought I had a testimony. I can say today that I know my Redeemer lives. I know God wants us to reconcile with one another and God. We are to forgive ourselves and one another. This is possible. This is my testimony.

Prayer for Peace:

God of grace, we confess the times we are not the people you would have us be. We ask your forgiveness and the forgiveness of those we hurt. As we open ourselves to your grace, may we forgive those who have hurt us. Help us share the cause of peace and justice.

Spiritual Practice for the Week: Embodying God's Shalom

Each day this week find a way to express and embody God's shalom. Begin by prayerfully listening to your longing for peace. Become silent and imagine you can hear the groaning of the Earth's peoples, nations, and creatures. Prayerfully open yourself to God's yearning for peace and the divine vision of shalom.

What images, feelings, and words come to you? What prayer for peace comes to you from your time of listening? Speak or write this prayer. What small act of justice, kindness, healing, or peacemaking is God inviting you to consider this day, this week?

Peace Covenant:

Today, God, I will seek the forgiveness of others I may have hurt.

21
Friday
September

United Nations International Day of Peace

By Brad Martell of Independence, Missouri, USA

You are the light of the world. A city built on a hill cannot be hid. No one after lighting a lamp puts it under the bushel basket, but on the lampstand, and it gives light to all in the house. In the same way, let your light shine before others, so that they may see your good works and give glory to your Father in heaven.

—Matthew 5:14–16

Looking out my living room window, I'm struck by the cross streets I live near. The white letters of North Union Street and West Truman Road against the signs' green background recall the history of both the USA Civil War and the Second World War.

As a peace and justice minister for Community of Christ I find it interesting that I have these daily reminders of times and places of great violence and challenge in our world. They not only reflect the past, but hold before me the wars, injustices, human-rights abuses, and environmental destruction of our world today.

I pray often as I walk to my office—the messages of the street signs behind me, and the spiraling Temple dedicated to the pursuit of peace, reconciliation, and the healing of the spirit, before me. I pray for the mission of the church. I pray for communities and individuals. I pray for a stop to violence and the overcoming of poverty and suffering. I pray for the peace of Jesus Christ to continue to transform lives and communities. I pray signal communities that uphold these values will one day shine before the world.

Today is the United Nations International Day of Peace (*www.internationaldayofpeace.org*). This "Peace Day" is an opportunity for people, organizations, and nations to take part in practical acts of peace around the globe.

I pray today and each day we as a community of Christ will continue to be transformed by Christ. I pray that as we live out the mission initiatives to Abolish Poverty, End Suffering and Pursue Peace on Earth our efforts will continue to multiply throughout the world.

Prayer for Peace:

Holy Parent, teach us the peace of Christ. Forgive our past and current wars. Forgive our destruction of your creation. May we reduce our consumption of Earth's resources and be better stewards of our planet.

Spiritual Practice for the Week: Embodying God's Shalom

Each day this week find a way to express and embody God's shalom. Begin by prayerfully listening to your longing for peace. Become silent and imagine you can hear the groaning of the Earth's peoples, nations, and creatures. Prayerfully open yourself to God's yearning for peace and the divine vision of shalom.

What images, feelings, and words come to you? What prayer for peace comes to you from your time of listening? Speak or write this prayer. What small act of justice, kindness, healing, or peacemaking is God inviting you to consider this day, this week?

Peace Covenant:

Today, God, I will work for justice and peace.

22
Saturday
September

Expanding the Capacity

By David Nii of Centennial, Colorado, USA

> *. . . when you are in the service of your fellow beings you are only in the service of your God.*
> —Mosiah 1:49

The Spokane Valley Congregation in Washington partnered with a nearby elementary school to launch a homework club that runs during the school year.

The program experienced overwhelming success in participation of students, teachers, and congregation members. Nine high-school volunteers joined the staff, which now totals 38 adults.

As a direct result of Spokane's homework club, three people were baptized in the first year. Seventy Claude Duty, the congregational missionary coordinator, set up an effective ministry for follow-up, phone calls, home visits, and side-by-side mentoring. New people attend services and prepare for baptism and confirmation of membership.

The congregation continues to expand its hospitality and community connections. Grants from World Mission Tithes expanded the capacity of the Homework Club. The program continues to bridge the educational needs of the community with the compassionate sharing of Christ's peace through congregational life. Thank you for responding faithfully and giving generously.

Prayer for Peace:

Thank you, God, for your presence. Thank you for opportunities to serve you by serving companions and strangers alike. We thank you for our mentors. We thank you for our volunteers. We thank you for the compassion of the community.

Spiritual Practice:

Remember or find a way to directly experience a fragrance you enjoy (scented oil, candle, fresh bread, pine trees, sea air, spices). Ask God to help you discern a situation to which you are called to bring reconciliation and healing. Pray that you might spread the peace of Christ as fragrantly and generously as the aroma you now experience. (See Ephesians 5:2.)

Peace Covenant:

Today, God, I will look for opportunities to serve you by serving others.

23
Sunday
September

Be Servants of All

By Art Smith of Independence, Missouri, USA

But they were silent, for on the way they had argued with one another who was the greatest. He sat down, called the twelve, and said to them, "Whoever wants to be first must be last of all and servant of all." Then he took a little child and put it among them; and taking it in his arms, he said to them, "Whoever welcomes one such child in my name welcomes me, and whoever welcomes me welcomes not me but the one who sent me."

—Mark 9:34–37

I can relate to the disciples in this text from the Gospel of Mark. They're made to look foolish again and again. I know I'm guilty of this one. Even when I think I've been doing better at not feeling superior to others, I realize I'm doing it again. Yikes!

What to do? Jesus seems to say that I'm not going to be able to cure myself of feelings of superiority just by giving myself a good talking to. Jesus says become a slave and welcome children. I know of one who emulates what Jesus is saying.

Not long ago I was visiting Simon's house in Sacaba, Bolivia. The building is made of adobe blocks, a humble structure indeed. Plaster on the living room walls was gouged off, patched, and gouged off again over the years. People scribbled on the paint with permanent markers. There's not much living room furniture, no sofa, no recliner, just stacks of little plastic chairs of many colors.

On this visit a new banner hung from the living room ceiling. It marked 10 years of hosting the Community of Christ Sacaba Congregation's children's church. Simon and his wife, Victoria, welcome dozens of kids every week.

Recently Simon retired from full-time church employment. As I talk with him about his retirement, I find, if anything, he has increased his congregational support, even without the church's financial backing. He still goes to Tiquipaya every Sunday and makes more trips to Collpa than ever before. In many ways, Simon chose the life of a slave.

I can't imagine Simon arguing with anyone about who's the greatest.

Prayer for Peace:

God, we would be humble like Jesus. Let us not concern ourselves with being greatest or first. Make us servants of peace as we serve others in the world.

Spiritual Practice for the Week: Welcoming Unity in Diversity

Meditate on unity in diversity. Prayerfully read Doctrine and Covenants 163:8c, which calls "the entire church to become a sanctuary of Christ's peace, where people from all nations, ethnicities, and life circumstances can be gathered into a spiritual home without dividing walls."

Create a large circle with your arms. See and feel the diverse people God invites inside this symbol of Christ's peace. Who is easy to welcome? Whom do you struggle to include? Ask God to forgive and heal barriers to Christ's peace.

Peace Covenant:

God, I will stand back and let others go before me, so they will be affirmed.

24
Monday
September

"Service Spirit Soon"

By Candy Brayton of Independence, Missouri, USA

But the wisdom from above is first pure, then peaceable, gentle, willing to yield, full of mercy and good fruits, without a trace of partiality or hypocrisy.

—James 3:17

I've had my 2005 car about six years. The top coat of paint is peeling, the front passenger window is sticking, and the "Service Engine Soon" light has come on.

The most-recent problem had me searching the owner's manual for answers. I learned a loose gas cap can trigger the "Service Engine Soon" light. The car's computer reads it as an *emission control failure*. In simpler terms, the car can tell when it's releasing an unacceptable level of pollution. The fix is either simple (make sure the cap is screwed on) or more involved (take the car to a service station).

What does car maintenance have to do with Christ's love? Good question.

When I think of "emission control," I think of the energy I project into the atmosphere. Do I pollute the environment with negativity, or do I enrich the environment with the positive energy brought by modeling my life on the example of Jesus? In this case, our virtual "Service Spirit" light should always be on. The spirit we emit needs a lot more formation than car care.

I try to set aside time daily for prayer and meditation. I try to be slow to anger. I'm trying to find positive ways to overcome sadness. I want to practice daily acts of kindness. It's not easy if one is stuck in a negative-emissions mode, but we can change that. It takes time, commitment, patience, and mostly prayer.

Prayer for Peace:

Creator God, fill us with your positive energy. Help us realize as we live the life you would have us live, we will emit a positive witness of you. Acts of kindness and sharing the peace of Jesus Christ will be our joy.

Spiritual Practice for the Week: Welcoming Unity in Diversity

Each day this week meditate on unity in diversity. Prayerfully read Doctrine and Covenants 163:8c, which calls "the entire church to become a sanctuary of Christ's peace, where people from all nations, ethnicities, and life circumstances can be gathered into a spiritual home without dividing walls."

Create a large circle with your arms. See and feel the diverse people God invites inside the sanctuary of Christ's peace represented by this circle. Who is easiest to welcome? Whom do you struggle to include? Confess the dividing walls between you and people too different or "dangerous" to invite into your spiritual home. Ask God to forgive and heal barriers that keep you and others from being one in Christ's peace.

Peace Covenant:

Today, God, I will be a positive witness for you.

25
Tuesday
September

The Gift of Friendship

By Lisa Soignier of Independence, Missouri, USA

> *Through divine grace and wisdom, this faith community has been given abundant gifts, resources, and opportunities to equip it to become such a people. Chief among these is the power of community in Christ expressed locally in distinctive fashions while upholding a unity of vision, foundational beliefs, and mission throughout the world.*
>
> —Doctrine and Covenants 163:11a

Shortly after the camping season I was following a conversation on the Internet with some friends. We talked about how much our first camp counselors meant to us. We compared the counselors to our first-grade teachers.

My first counselor was Dell at Camp Powderfork in Bald Knob, Arkansas. She was a wonderful teacher and mentor. Through the years, she sent me birthday cards, graduation cards, and kept up with the birth of my children.

When I moved to Independence, Missouri, several years ago, we reconnected and resumed our friendship. During the last few years of her life at a nursing home, she still wanted to know about every detail in my life. She was special!

During that same first youth camp, I met my best camp friend. We couldn't wait to see each other as summer camps came around each year. Last summer we again spent some time at that same campground. Thirty years had passed since we last saw each other. It was as if time had stood still!

The most-remarkable part of this story is that my friend is not a member of Community of Christ. Through the love and acceptance she felt from the campers, she continues to want to be a part of the companionship of this denomination. One never knows what God has in mind for us through friendship.

Prayer for Peace:

Generous God, we thank you for our teachers, mentors, and counselors. We thank you for lifelong friends. We thank you for the opportunities and resources of our community that enable us to reach out in pursuit of peace.

Spiritual Practice for the Week: Welcoming Unity in Diversity

Each day this week meditate on unity in diversity. Prayerfully read Doctrine and Covenants 163:8c, which calls "the entire church to become a sanctuary of Christ's peace, where people from all nations, ethnicities, and life circumstances can be gathered into a spiritual home without dividing walls."

Create a large circle with your arms. See and feel the diverse people God invites inside the sanctuary of Christ's peace represented by this circle. Who is easiest to welcome? Whom do you struggle to include? Confess the dividing walls between you and people too different or "dangerous" to invite into your spiritual home. Ask God to forgive and heal barriers that keep you and others from being one in Christ's peace.

Peace Covenant:

Today, God, I will look at my distinctive gifts and assess where I can best use them to share the peace of Christ.

26
Wednesday
September

Signal Community

By Stacey L. Keenan of Kansas City, Missouri, USA

May he judge your people with righteousness, and your poor with justice. ...May he defend the cause of the poor of the people, give deliverance to the needy...

—Psalm 72:2, 4

I am the treasurer of our school's Parent Teacher Association (PTA), and we often get requests from parents to spend funds for a charitable cause or needs of children. But because PTA is for educational purposes we needed to find other ways to meet the needs of the children and families in our school.

One mother came with the idea of a PTA-sponsored "Family Needs Committee." This committee takes requests from social workers, school counselors, nurses, and administrators to address specific needs in the district. The needs include shampoo, bedsheets, specific sizes of clothing and shoes, and backpacks.

Any PTA parent who wishes to be a part of this committee gives an e-mail address to the committee chair. The chairperson then sends an e-mail to all parents who signed up. Parents then bring the items to a pickup station. From there, they're delivered to the family by the social-service employee who made the request.

These items are not provided by PTA funds; rather the PTA committee acts as an e-mail transfer agency, and it's all based on volunteer parent donations.

Good problem: This program has been so successful, many parents have been frustrated. They want to help, but the typical response time to an e-mail is just five minutes, so one must act quickly to be able to donate.

In addition, our district set up a "closet" to supply families in need.

They receive essentials such as new underwear, socks, personal-hygiene items, coats, hats, and scarves.

At a "family night" my daughter's fourth-grade class collected more than 500 items for the necessities closet.

We have a responsibility as peacemakers and visionaries of justice to address human needs. It's great that our responses are needed...but we better hurry!

Prayer for Peace:

Gracious God, may we give what we can to help change lives. May we share the peace of Jesus Christ.

Spiritual Practice for the Week: Welcoming Unity in Diversity

Each day this week meditate on unity in diversity. Prayerfully read Doctrine and Covenants 163:8c, which calls "the entire church to become a sanctuary of Christ's peace, where people from all nations, ethnicities, and life circumstances can be gathered into a spiritual home without dividing walls."

Create a large circle with your arms. See and feel the diverse people God invites inside the sanctuary of Christ's peace represented by this circle. Who is easiest to welcome? Whom do you struggle to include? Confess the dividing walls between you and people too different or "dangerous" to invite into your spiritual home. Ask God to forgive and heal barriers that keep you and others from being one in Christ's peace.

Peace Covenant:

Today, God, I will act without hesitation to meet another's need.

27
Thursday
September

Leading the Way

By Don Richardson of Nauvoo, Illinois, USA

> *...and the scroll of the prophet Isaiah was given to him. He unrolled the scroll and found the place where it was written: "The Spirit of the Lord is upon me, because he has anointed me to bring good news to the poor. He has sent me to proclaim release to the captives and recovery of sight to the blind, to let the oppressed go free, to proclaim the year of the Lord's favor."*
>
> —Luke 4:17–19

When I was in basic training in the US military, a physical requirement was to run a "timed" mile. Recruits lined up on a quarter-mile track, 10 or 12 soldiers deep, about 15 yards behind another group.

I was placed close to the outside of the track. When we started, I sprinted to the inside and set a pace I thought I could keep up for the mile. After finishing, some others told me that when they saw what I did they thought I knew what I was doing, so they followed me.

If we are Christ's disciples, we will let God lead us in the way we should go. When we are baptized we commit to follow Jesus. We need to ask if our actions reflect our commitment. Or are we fair-weather friends of Jesus—following only when it's easy?

Let our words and actions show those around us who our leader is, who will release the captives and bring sight to the blind.

We might be ones who can lead others to Jesus.

Let us live our lives in a manner that others will want to follow us to Christ.

Prayer for Peace:

Tender Shepherd, may we keep our eyes on you as the one we would follow. Lead us on the path of peace that we may share with others.

Spiritual Practice for the Week: Welcoming Unity in Diversity

Each day this week meditate on unity in diversity. Prayerfully read Doctrine and Covenants 163:8c, which calls "the entire church to become a sanctuary of Christ's peace, where people from all nations, ethnicities, and life circumstances can be gathered into a spiritual home without dividing walls."

Create a large circle with your arms. See and feel the diverse people God invites inside the sanctuary of Christ's peace represented by this circle. Who is easiest to welcome? Whom do you struggle to include? Confess the dividing walls between you and people too different or "dangerous" to invite into your spiritual home. Ask God to forgive and heal barriers that keep you and others from being one in Christ's peace.

Peace Covenant:

Today, God, I will follow you and help lead the way for others to find Christ's peace.

28
Friday
September

Trust and Obey

By Mnqobi Ngwenya, of Bulawayo, Zimbabwe

> *...pursue righteousness, faith, love, and peace, along with those who call on the Lord from a pure heart.*
>
> —2 Timothy 2:22

A few weeks ago, early in the morning, a man cycled to town and went to the marketplace before it opened. A blind man sat by a fire with friends. The stranger came directly to the blind man and asked if he could pray for him. The blind man quickly agreed and prepared to receive his blessing.

The stranger prayed, and instantly the blind man's eyesight was restored. As the blind man and his friends were rejoicing, the stranger quickly got on his bike and cycled off without the crowd's notice.

I was humbled, not so much by the miracle that happened to the blind man, but by the humility and obedience of the man who performed the miracle.

Unlike Jonah's first response, he trusted the Lord and acted on what he was told to do. I imagined how far the man had cycled and what was going through his mind while on his way to the market.

I asked myself many questions and was convinced that if you trust the Lord and obey, God will be with you in fulfilling Christ's mission.

Prayer for Peace:

God, give us a receiving spirit and listening ears so we can quickly hear and obey your leadings. We would pursue righteousness and pure hearts. We would pursue peace.

Spiritual Practice for the Week: Welcoming Unity in Diversity

Each day this week meditate on unity in diversity. Prayerfully read Doctrine and Covenants 163:8c, which calls "the entire church to become a sanctuary of Christ's peace, where people from all nations, ethnicities, and life circumstances can be gathered into a spiritual home without dividing walls."

Create a large circle with your arms. See and feel the diverse people God invites inside the sanctuary of Christ's peace represented by this circle. Who is easiest to welcome? Whom do you struggle to include? Confess the dividing walls between you and people too different or "dangerous" to invite into your spiritual home. Ask God to forgive and heal barriers that keep you and others from being one in Christ's peace.

Peace Covenant:

Today, God, I will listen closely for your direction in my life.

29
Saturday
September

Go and Tell

By Rick Maupin, Council of Twelve Apostles

> *In Caesarea there was a man named Cornelius, a centurion of the Italian Cohort, as it was called. He was a devout man who feared God with all his household; he gave alms generously to the people and prayed constantly to God. One afternoon at about three o'clock he had a vision in which he clearly saw an angel of God coming in and saying to him, "Cornelius." He stared at him in terror and said, "What is it, Lord?" He answered, "Your prayers and your alms have ascended as a memorial before God.*
>
> —Acts 10:1–4

Organized in 1989, the church in Jamaica is in transition. The first generation of leaders is passing on, and a new generation is moving to the forefront.

For the future growth of the church in Jamaica and for the success of these new leaders, it is important that they have a strong connection with the church's identity, mission, and message.

Recently several of the current and potential leaders gathered for a weeklong leadership-training event.

It focused on educating and equipping young adults to go and tell—to be leaders and missionaries.

At the end of the week a young-adult leader challenged others by saying, "The key to the future is that we do not place what we have learned on a shelf. We need to take this back to our congregations and help them grow in their understanding of scripture and church mission."

Your contributions to World Mission Tithes made it possible to rent space and bring these leaders together for this important event. Thank you for responding generously.

Prayer for Peace:

Divine Listener, our prayers journey to you. We offer ourselves to help your children and therefore to honor you. In humbleness we ask you to accept what we offer toward sharing the peace of Jesus Christ.

Spiritual Practice:

Imagine or write a journal description of a banquet for your congregation and community. Envision rich sharing among diverse groups as people plan, cook, eat, share stories, and perhaps sing, or pray together. Prayerfully consider this question: "Is there a way for me to transform this vision into a real event?" What does the table ministry of Jesus look like in your personal and congregational life?

Peace Covenant:

Today, God, I will not take what I learn of you and place it on a shelf or hide it under a bushel. I will expand on it through my witness.

30
Sunday
September

Pray Faithfully

By Dave Schaal, First Presidency

> *...Have salt in yourselves, and be at peace with one another.*
>
> —Mark 9:50

When I reach for the salt, I give it little consideration. It's simply a seasoning that we use with little thought or reflection.

This would not have been the case in Jesus' time. More than just a seasoning, salt was a preservative necessary to sustain life in lean times. In addition, the Hebrew scriptures (Old Testament) show salt was to be used in some sacred rites. So when Jesus tells his disciples, "Have salt in yourselves," he was saying something about the spirit that needed to be "in them" to sustain their faith and the faith of others.

A mentor of mine went through many personal difficulties. At times his heart was broken. Still he insisted on praying each day, as often as he could remember. He also took time for his own healing, while making sure he continued to help people in need.

I became convinced this combination of constant prayer and care for hurting people caused him to uphold a powerful faith that sustained him and inspired others. He had "salt within himself."

How is your salt?

Prayer for Peace:

Faithful God, our tears roll down into the cracks of our broken hearts, and there your salty Spirit heals.

Spiritual Practice for the Week: Offering Blessings of Community

Each day this week receive and share blessings of community. Begin with a prayer of gratitude for the network of relationships in your life. See and feel connections with family members, spiritual friends, people in your congregation and community, people and creatures in God's sacred web of life. What blessings flow to you from these circles?

Reflect, pray, and write in your journal about the call to be "Community of Christ." Go deeper each day as you "discern and embrace" the "divine blessing" of this name that opens you to "become a blessing to the whole creation" (Doctrine and Covenants 163:1). What act of blessing are you invited to complete?

Peace Covenant:

Today, God, I will pray as often as I can remember.

1
Monday
October

Peace Colloquy…You Are Invited

By Nadine Stallbaumer of Independence, Missouri, USA

> *… and lift up an ensign of peace, and make a proclamation for peace unto the ends of the earth; and make proposals for peace…according to the voice of the Spirit, which is in you, and all things shall work together for your good; therefore, be faithful, and, behold, and lo, I am with you even unto the end. Even so. Amen.*
>
> —Doctrine and Covenants 102:11b–d

At the 2010 Peace Colloquy at the Temple in Independence, Missouri, a young woman from "Free the Children" was to speak. The planners asked if I could make an airport run to pick up Dalal Al-Waheidi and her assistant, Jenna.

Dalal is Muslim and wondered about the reception they might encounter. I told them this group would be open to hearing about their work for children, and we would be grateful for their presence.

Dalal made a wonderful presentation full of her personal story and excitement for the work of her organization. It was a miracle she was with us because she had moved throughout her life, facing war, and was forced to flee for safety more than once.

As we returned to the airport, they filled my ears with praise for the hospitality of the people at the Peace Colloquy. They felt embraced and wrapped in the arms of peace. It was exciting to hear how they responded to the love they had found within our community.

The 2012 Peace Colloquy is scheduled October 19–21. You are invited to check the details at *www.CofChrist.org/peacecolloquy/*.

Prayer for Peace:

Faithful God, we proclaim peace according to your Spirit, which is in us. Be with us in our mission of sharing the peace of Christ.

Spiritual Practice for the Week: Offering Blessings of Community

Begin with a prayer of gratitude for the network of relationships in your life. See and feel connections with family members, spiritual friends, people in your congregation and community, people and creatures in God's sacred web of life.

What blessings flow to you from these circles? Go deeper each day as you "discern and embrace" the "divine blessing" of this name that opens you to "become a blessing to the whole creation" (Doctrine and Covenants 163:1). What act of blessing are you invited to complete?

Peace Covenant:

Today, God, I will share Christ's peace as far as I can reach.

2
Tuesday
October

Responsible Choices

By Deb Crowley of Eaton Rapids, Michigan, USA

> *The path will not always be easy, the choices will not always be clear, but the cause is sure and the Spirit will bear witness to the truth, and those who live the truth will know the hope and the joy of discipleship in the community of Christ. Amen.*
> —Doctrine and Covenants 161:7

It's been a while since you drove this route. The *voice* from your Global Positioning System (GPS) tells you to "turn in two miles." But a road you just passed looked right.

So, ignoring the *voice*, you turn around and choose the direction that seems right. As you travel, the *voice* continues to direct you to turn around in half a mile.

The time to reach your destination has grown incredibly short! After a dozen or so ignored direction changes, you stubbornly turn the *voice* off, knowing you are correct.

Funny, now there are no familiar signs or landmarks. Time is running out. After 20 stubborn miles, you stop, find the paper map, and try to get your bearings. Drat! The GPS was right, after all! You turn the *voice* back on and decide to follow its lead, even if it seems illogical. Amazingly, you arrive at your destination—late, but forgiven.

Life is such a journey. God's *voice* through the Holy Spirit to your inner soul continually offers guidance.

Yet so often we think we know best and persistently choose our own path. We turn off the *voice* and continue to create our own road map. Sadly, too often, we find ourselves lost, alone, and frustrated.

When we finally listen to the *Voice* that penetrates our souls, we find healing, grace, and forgiveness. The voice of God has echoed across the ages and refuses to be stilled. God continually calls us to the work of Christ's mission—a journey familiar and unfamiliar, full of surprise and mystery. But if we listen and follow, we're in for an awesome life!

Prayer for Peace:

Revealing God, open our minds to your leadings. Open our hearts to your direction for sharing the peace of Christ.

Spiritual Practice for the Week: Offering Blessings of Community

Begin with a prayer of gratitude for the network of relationships in your life. See and feel connections with family members, spiritual friends, people in your congregation and community, people and creatures in God's sacred web of life.

What blessings flow to you from these circles? Go deeper each day as you "discern and embrace" the "divine blessing" of this name that opens you to "become a blessing to the whole creation" (Doctrine and Covenants 163:1). What act of blessing are you invited to complete?

Peace Covenant:

Today, God, I will get my bearings from the scriptures. I will listen to your Spirit in my soul before I make my choices.

3 Wednesday October

On Reflection

By Barrie Fox of Kirkby-in-Ashfield, Nottinghamshire, England

Here is my servant, whom I have chosen, my beloved, with whom my soul is well pleased. I will put my Spirit upon him, and he will proclaim justice to the Gentiles. He will not wrangle or cry aloud, nor will anyone hear his voice in the streets. He will not break a bruised reed or quench a smoldering wick until he brings justice to victory. And in his name the Gentiles will hope.

—Matthew 12:18–21

Saint Ambrose, a fourth-century bishop, is recorded as once saying the church is like the moon. It has no light of its own to give but only has light to reflect. The church is God's way of reflecting the gospel into the world around us. We need to continue to develop our trust in God, whose light *we* reflect. The word "hope" appears in our scriptures many times.

Jesus invites and encourages us to seek to bring his presence into the lives of others whenever we have the opportunity. I suppose it is true that I don't know as much about Jesus as I ought to, but I believe what I do know has made a positive difference in my life.

People can help or minister to others in many ways and places. When ministry is blessed by the power of the Holy Spirit, it reflects the hope and peace of Jesus Christ in our lives.

Prayer for Peace:

Source of hope and light, may we reflect you in all we do. May our ministry to others be blessed. May we share Christ's peace and bring hope to those who despair.

Spiritual Practice for the Week: Offering Blessings of Community

Begin with a prayer of gratitude for the network of relationships in your life. See and feel connections with family members, spiritual friends, people in your congregation and community, people and creatures in God's sacred web of life.

What blessings flow to you from these circles? Go deeper each day as you "discern and embrace" the "divine blessing" of this name that opens you to "become a blessing to the whole creation" (Doctrine and Covenants 163:1). What act of blessing are you invited to complete?

Peace Covenant:

Today, God, I will be a beacon of your light.

4
Thursday
October

A Frightened Joey

By Anne Loughran of Melbourne, Victoria, Australia

I lift up my eyes to the hills—from where will my help come? My help comes from the Lord, who made heaven and earth.

—Psalm 121:1–2

We watched and listened as a tsunami enveloped a country far from our shores. Then an earthquake hit one of our neighboring countries. Then it happened to *us*.

Devastating floods as we never had experienced came with cyclone Yasi. The storm cut a sweeping path of destruction and dumped unprecedented amounts of water onto already-sodden earth.

Amid the devastation, a joey (young kangaroo) was swept from its mother and was hurtling down a flooded river. A brave onlooker waded waist deep into the turbulent water and rescued the frightened animal, wrapping it around his shoulders and carrying it to shore.

Volunteers from all over the country were welcomed as they gave of themselves, helping to clear away the mud, water, and debris. Temporary shelter, food, clothing, and money poured in. Community of Christ made a large contribution.

I thank our compassionate God for those who give generously of their time, energy, and money in times of crisis. The Earth brings floods, and God sends help.

Prayer for Peace:

God of creation, we trust in you to send help in times of trial. We praise you for the generosity of others. We praise you for those who share justice and the peace of Jesus Christ.

Spiritual Practice for the Week: Offering Blessings of Community

Begin with a prayer of gratitude for the network of relationships in your life. See and feel connections with family members, spiritual friends, people in your congregation and community, people and creatures in God's sacred web of life.

What blessings flow to you from these circles? Go deeper each day as you "discern and embrace" the "divine blessing" of this name that opens you to "become a blessing to the whole creation" (Doctrine and Covenants 163:1). What act of blessing are you invited to complete?

Peace Covenant:

Today, God, I will do all I can to relieve suffering in crisis.

5
Friday
October

On-time Prayers

By Gary Piper of Fort Gratiot, Michigan, USA

> *For "Those who desire life and desire to see good days...let them seek peace and pursue it. For the eyes of the Lord are on the righteous, and his ears are open to their prayer."*
> —1 Peter 3:10–12

It's been about 10 years since I worked with a wonderful friend named Sue. I still can hear her thought-provoking, life-changing words: "Gary, God may not always answer prayers on *your* time schedule, but God is always on time!"

Since then those words have proven true. If I start to despair, God comes to my rescue.

As powerful and meaningful as my prayers are to me, not a day goes by that they don't conflict with my impatience with Jesus telling me to "endure." When I find myself surrounded by a life-storm I find myself praying, "God, we both know this storm will soon pass, so why not save me the anguish and end it right now?"

Almost immediately I recall Sue's voice, "Gary, God may not always come on your time schedule, but God is always on time!" Then it's as if someone or something lifts me above the storm, and from a safe distance I can see it swirling and blowing below me.

I remember the days before my myasthenia gravis (an autoimmune disorder) went into remission.

God always gave me the strength to give the ministry I was called to give.

Especially during times when I question my ability to give ministry, I endure and am blessed.

Prayer for Peace:

Listening God, give us patience. Help us endure. We have faith that you see and hear us. We will seek peace and share it with the world.

Spiritual Practice for the Week: Offering Blessings of Community

Begin with a prayer of gratitude for the network of relationships in your life. See and feel connections with family members, spiritual friends, people in your congregation and community, people and creatures in God's sacred web of life.

What blessings flow to you from these circles? Go deeper each day as you "discern and embrace" the "divine blessing" of this name that opens you to "become a blessing to the whole creation" (Doctrine and Covenants 163:1). What act of blessing are you invited to complete?

Peace Covenant:

Today, God, I will practice patience and faith when I pray.

6
Saturday
October

Good Problems

By Cathy Loving of Independence, Missouri, USA

> *...give, and it will be given to you. A good measure, pressed down, shaken together, running over, will be put into your lap; for the measure you give will be the measure you get back."*
> —Luke 6:38

The graceful, 20-inch-tall glass container sat on my desk. The jar had a large hole on the side and cracks radiating from a break.

How was I going to explain this minor tragedy to the person who put it under my care? One hour earlier, I could hardly wait to learn the total value of the coins it held. But now, the break held my vision, not the thousands of coins it contained.

Before and during the 2010 Peace Colloquy this glass container sat at the Temple foyer desk, serving as the deposit for the "Pennies for Peace" project. The coins collected would go toward building schools in Pakistan and Afghanistan.

The project was an overwhelming success. Old and young alike excitedly placed coins in the jar to the point we worried it would be too heavy to take to the bank.

But I couldn't get past the broken jar. Then it hit me: This is not a problem. This is a good predicament to be in. It was the joy of all those people contributing coins that broke through the jar.

Their generosity overflowed in expressing love for children in faraway countries. Just think of the possibilities if we overflowed church parking lots each week, if we overflowed our worship each week, or if we overflowed the offering basket each week.

Suddenly that glass container, in all its brokenness, beamed with God's love and the privilege of sharing that love with the people of the world.

Prayer for Peace:

Creator God, teach us not to worry. Teach us to have faith in you and our companions in the community. Help us raise our expectations of one another and give all we can in full measure, running over.

Spiritual Practice:

The psalms are prayers of honesty and trust. The psalmist trusts God's presence in times of fear and failure, joy and plenty, growth and change. Write a short psalm-prayer expressing to God the truth about your physical, emotional, and spiritual state. What are your deepest feelings, longings, and needs? What prayer of praise, intercession, or petition flows from you as you consider your life and the life of God's world?

Peace Covenant:

Today, God, I will examine so-called problems and see how they can be transformed and used for peace.

7
Sunday
October

Receive God's Blessing

By Wim van Klinken, director of International Headquarters

> *"Let the children come to me; do not stop them; for it is to such as these that the kingdom of God belongs. Truly I tell you, whoever does not receive the kingdom of God as a little child will never enter it." And he took them up in his arms, laid his hands on them, and blessed them.*
>
> —Mark 10:14–16

For several years a cat has been a joy since our family adopted it as a kitten. In our eyes it has been perfect: friendly, playful, wanting to be petted by all, and responsive when we call his name.

We addressed it as the little brother of our only child, Max, who was 11 when Smokey entered our family. Often, he would "cry" when Max left for school.

When my wife started to work outside the home, we were a little concerned that Smokey, who never was outside, would feel lonely.

We started considering adopting another cat, a new concept for us. After visiting the shelter we were told that bringing a new cat into another cat's multiyear territory has a certain risk.

We decided not to risk it, much to Max's disappointment.

After our decision, Max kept arguing and pointing to the advantages of having another cat. He kept taking us to the shelter whenever we were in the pet store. Although the caretakers at the shelter shared their negative experiences, they suggested bringing Smokey to see how he and a 2-year-old spayed cat would react to each other.

It was a perfect match, and we now are blessed with two friendly, playful, and responsive cats. We realize we would have done this long ago, if only we had listened to our child.

How often do we let our children come to us, listen to them, and make them part of our decision-making? How often do adults tend to look at the possible problems, afraid of losing what we have? What can we learn from our children who look at the world as a world of possibilities, a world full of God's blessing?

Prayer for Peace:

God of blessing, let us seek the innocent wisdom of children. May we emulate their positive nature and see the world as they see it. May we love as unconditionally as they love. May we learn peace from them.

Spiritual Practice for the Week: Connecting with God as Center

Each day this week connect with God through journal writing. Use a notebook, journal, computer, or any available paper. Prayerfully center on your intent to open yourself to God's presence and share what flows from your heart and mind.

Your "letter to God" might include thoughts, questions, feelings, needs, artwork, quotes, and scriptures, or it may take the form of a prayer, psalm, or poem. Try to write at least five minutes each day. What do you experience? Is this an effective way to connect with God? What surprises you? What images or questions from God emerge? What deepens or changes in your relationship with God, Christ, Spirit?

Peace Covenant:

Today, God, I will release my cynicism and doubts. I will adopt youthful and re-energized faith.

8
Monday
October

Wee Are Bells

By Lu Mountenay of Independence, Missouri, USA

> *You who are my disciples must be found continuing in the forefront of those organizations and movements which are recognizing the worth of persons…*
> —Doctrine and Covenants 151:9

I would identify Community of Christ's annual Peace Colloquy as one movement referred to in today's scripture. In 2010 we focused on children.

So go back with me two years. It is still fresh in my mind.

Greg Mortenson received the 2010 Community of Christ International Peace Award. He wrote *Three Cups of Tea* and *Stones into Schools*, describing how he coordinated the building of schools in the poorest parts of Pakistan and Afghanistan.

Greg participated in a grade-school assembly as part of the Colloquy. He shared the rostrum graciously with the children at the presentation ceremony.

For me, a highlight was the performance of Wee Bells. The children ranged in age from about 3–6. Among the songs they played was "Let There Be Peace on Earth." They rang their bells as the director held a card that matched the color of their bells.

One boy on the front row looked anxious until it was his time to ring. At that moment his face lit up, and he rang his bells for all he was worth. Then he waited on pins and needles until it was his time to ring again—back to enthused and joyous ringing.

We are bells waiting to be rung
we are songs waiting to be sung
we are words, we are ideas
longing to be heard.

We are tools waiting to be used
finely sharpened, ready and enthused
we are coals, we are embers
longing to be flames.

We are vessels waiting to be filled
we are soil waiting to be tilled
we are seeds, we lie dormant
longing to be sown.

Creator God, we give ourselves to you
let us know what you would have us do
we will listen, we are your people
longing to come home.

Prayer for Peace:

Creator God, help us take on the enthusiasm of your wee ones—ready and waiting to answer your call.

Spiritual Practice for the Week: Connecting with God as Center

Connect with God through journal writing. Prayerfully center on your intent to open yourself to God's presence and share what flows from your heart and mind. What deepens or changes in your relationship with God, Christ, Spirit?

Peace Covenant:

Today, God, I will be your peace-proclaiming bell.

9
Tuesday
October

A Covenant Remembered

By Lisa Soignier of Independence, Missouri, USA

> *But this is the covenant that I will make with the house of Israel after those days, says the Lord: I will put my law within them, and I will write it on their hearts; and I will be their God, and they shall be my people.*
>
> —Jeremiah 31:33

My baptism was beautiful. My grandfather baptized me and my uncle, who is three weeks younger than I. My uncle and I got into a little tussle. No, it was a *fight,* right there in the church.

My mom definitely was not pleased. Later I was ashamed. I was forgiven by all, and my walk with Christ has taken me on a wonderful journey.

My mom's family belonged to Community of Christ, and my dad's family went to another denomination. I had many opportunities to attend other churches with my friends. Because of relationships formed in my early years, I remained part of a small congregation in Louisiana, a state with only five Community of Christ congregations.

When asked why I stay a member of this church, my answer is simple: It's because my church is who I am. As our mission statement says, "We proclaim Jesus Christ and promote communities of joy, hope, love, and peace." I try to live this each day.

It wasn't easy for me to leave my family when I moved to Independence, Missouri, and went to work at International Headquarters. But then I remembered my covenant with Christ. As I came up from the waters of baptism, unsure of my surroundings, my grandfather pulled me to him and said, "It's OK. You're going to be OK."

Shortly after moving to my new home I had a dream. I was in a church friendship hall, and all was well. I glimpsed my grandfather, in his yellow cardigan sweater, smiling at me and saying those words again, "See, I told you. You're going to be OK." What a wonderful experience, since my grandfather has been dead for years. He reminded me of my covenant, which is written on my heart for life.

Prayer for Peace:

Covenant God, we are your people. We want to share your love with others. We want to share Christ's peace.

Spiritual Practice for the Week: Connecting with God as Center

Connect with God through journal writing. Use a notebook, journal, or computer. Prayerfully open yourself to God's presence and share what flows from your heart and mind. Try to write at least five minutes each day. What do you experience? What new images or questions from God emerge? What deepens or changes in your relationship with God, Christ, Spirit?

Peace Covenant:

Today, God, I will remember Christ's mission and promote communities of peace.

10
Wednesday
October

I Will Lift My Eyes

By Cindy Korf of North Platte, Nebraska, USA

> *Therefore my people shall know my name; therefore in that day they shall know that it is I who speak; here am I. How beautiful upon the mountains are the feet of the messenger who announces peace... Listen! Your sentinels lift up their voices, together they sing for joy; for in plain sight they see the return of the Lord to Zion.*
>
> —Isaiah 52:6–8

When I moved to Nebraska, I missed the mountains. In Colorado, I could gaze on them each day and at any moment. I purposely took the passage from Psalm 121, "I lift up my eyes to the hills" to be my inspiration to remember God. I saw the beauty and majesty of God's creation in the mountains.

But there are no mountains in Nebraska. I felt emptiness without their presence until one spring morning, when I heard a chortling noise in the sky. I lifted my eyes in curiosity and beheld a majestic sight. Like black silk ribbons drifting on the air currents, flocks of sandhill cranes flew across the heavens. How could I not hold my gaze heavenward and praise God for the beauty of creation?

In the days and weeks that followed, flocks of snow geese, Canada geese, and sandhill cranes constantly called me with their honking and chortling music. They called to me to lift my eyes to the heavens as they migrated south.

Wherever we find ourselves, there is always a reason to lift our eyes to behold God's majesty and beauty and to praise the Creator. I then can feel peace and share it with others.

Prayer for Peace:

God who speaks to us through birds and mountains, help us hear the messenger who announces peace. Assure us that it is you who speaks, you who blesses us with the beauty of creation and blesses us with peace.

Spiritual Practice for the Week: Connecting with God as Center

Each day this week connect with God through journal writing. Use a notebook, journal, computer, or any available paper. Prayerfully center on your intent to open yourself to God's presence and share what flows from your heart and mind. Your "letter to God" might include thoughts, questions, feelings, needs, artwork, quotes, and scriptures. Or it might take the form of a prayer, psalm, or poem.

Try to write at least five minutes each day. What do you experience? Is this an effective way to connect with God? What surprises you? What new images or questions from God emerge? What deepens or changes in your relationship with God, Christ, Spirit?

Peace Covenant:

Today, God, I will embrace the message of peace I find in nature.

11
Thursday
October

God's Spirit Will Accompany You

By Dawn Squires of Melbourne, Victoria, Australia

Do not be discouraged. You have not been promised an easy path, but you have been assured that the Spirit that calls you will also accompany you. That Spirit is even now touching alive the souls of those who feel the passion of discipleship burning deeply within. Many others will respond if you are persistent in your witness and diligent in your mission to the world.
—Doctrine and Covenants 162:3a–b

I didn't think I could afford to go to Women's Retreat last year. The handle on my lawn mower broke off. Having a large yard, I was afraid I would need to buy a new mower. Women's Retreat is in October, my most expensive month for household bills. Having to pay for a new mower would make attending Women's Retreat impossible. Life seemed difficult.

A generous person stepped forward and paid my way to the retreat. The retreat was a wonderful experience. My brother-in-law traveled several miles to take my mower home and weld the handle for me. He not only returned the mower, but he mowed the long grass for me.

Although I had several bills to pay on my pension day, they were not as costly as I had expected. In addition to attending the retreat, I could afford to go to family camp (reunion) in December.

How blessed I felt!

I have been assured I can leave aside my worries in life. I am in God's hands. God's Spirit will accompany me.

Prayer for Peace:

Generous God, we thank you for people who step up and help others. We thank you for events where we can renew our spirits and feel closer to you. Thank you for opportunities to share the peace of Jesus Christ.

Spiritual Practice for the Week: Connecting with God as Center

Each day this week connect with God through journal writing. Use a notebook, journal, computer, or any available paper. Prayerfully center on your intent to open yourself to God's presence and share what flows from your heart and mind. Your "letter to God" might include thoughts, questions, feelings, needs, artwork, quotes, and scriptures. Or it might take the form of a prayer, psalm, or poem.

Try to write at least five minutes each day. What do you experience? Is this an effective way to connect with God? What surprises you? What new images or questions from God emerge? What deepens or changes in your relationship with God, Christ, Spirit?

Peace Covenant:

Today, God, I will let my worries go, being assured of your presence.

12
Friday
October

There Are No Weeds in God's Garden

By Stacie Wittemyer of Toledo, Ohio, USA

> *For just as the body is one and has many members, and all the members of the body, though many, are one body, so it is with Christ. For in the one Spirit we were all baptized into one body—Jews or Greeks, slaves or free—and we were all made to drink of one Spirit. Indeed, the body does not consist of one member but of many.*
>
> —1 Corinthians 12:12–14

Every child knows the dandelion is the most beautiful of all flowers and is worthy of the finest vases. Later in life, a different sensibility develops in us, and dandelions become the outcasts of the flower kingdom. When gifted with a dandelion, we often stick it in a paper cup vase and throw it away as soon as the child isn't looking.

Sometimes that's how it is with people we see as outcasts. A stranger knows when hospitality is insincere, impatient, less than welcoming. At some level we *all* fear being outcasts of social systems. We spend a lot of energy hiding this feeling.

What blessings would reveal themselves if we shared authentically and walked side by side on journeys of poverty, numbing affluence, addiction, endless busyness, mental illness, violence, the deepest sorrows, and loneliness?

"Blessed are the poor in spirit, for theirs is the kingdom of heaven" (Matthew 5:3). We are claimed, and so are those we don't want to claim.

Like a dandelion pushing through crumbling concrete to find sunlight, nourishment, and a place to bloom so, too, does the spirit of our broken soul. Blessing the dandelions of our lives will call us into a sacred vulnerability with one another, a shared burden of companionship and healing.

The Spirit calls us to a pained awareness of the unnecessary suffering in our world. Together we can dedicate our energy and creativity to mutual well-being, justice, and peace.

Today, allow a cup of these least-loved dandelions to be the centerpiece of your table and your heart. For in their welfare we find our welfare.

Prayer for Peace:

God of the weeds and cultivated flowers, let us welcome all into the garden. In our diversity we will find unity and peace.

Spiritual Practice for the Week: Connecting with God as Center

Connect with God through journal writing. Use a notebook, journal, or computer. Prayerfully center on your intent to open yourself to God's presence and share what flows from your heart and mind. Your "letter to God" might include thoughts, questions, feelings, needs, artwork, quotes, and scriptures. Or it might take the form of a prayer, psalm, or poem. What surprises you? What new images or questions from God emerge? What deepens or changes in your relationship with God, Christ, Spirit?

Peace Covenant:

Today, God, I will welcome those who are thought to be "unwanted."

13
Saturday
October

All Are Called According to Their Gifts

By Evelyn Spence of Council Bluffs, Iowa, USA

> *. . . so we, who are many, are one body in Christ, and individually we are members one of another. We have gifts that differ according to the grace given to us: prophecy, in proportion to faith; ministry, in ministering; the teacher, in teaching; the exhorter, in exhortation; the giver, in generosity; the leader, in diligence; the compassionate, in cheerfulness.*
>
> —Romans 12:5–8

Our congregation has several programs devoted to youth ministry on weekdays after school. We offer the programs both to our membership and to the neighborhood.

One program, "The Community of Helping Hands," is designed to reach grade-schoolers.

On their arrival at the church, the children get snacks and have some free time to play in the gym. Recently, the congregation took a symbolic "walk to Jerusalem" at Eastertide. The children received the choice of walking or running around the gym to reach a congregational goal and work on fitness.

To fulfill the "helping" part of the program, the children collect inexpensive food for the pantry. Last month they collected peanut butter and jelly. This month it is cereal. All the members of the congregation donate food.

After snacks and exercise the children have a lesson and discussion time. This week the lesson centered on Matthew 6. They considered "the lilies of the field," how God cares for them, then segued into the idea that God loves all creatures as well as humankind. We should trust in God. Adults had the same lesson the previous Sunday during worship.

Next comes a craft time that connects with the scripture lesson. At 6:00 p.m., this group and the "Time for Teens" group join together to end the evening with a meal.

It takes the talents and gifts of many dedicated volunteers to run these programs, but they consider it part of their generous response.

Prayer for Peace:

Generous God, we marvel at your call to us and the gifts you give us to respond to that call. May we use our gifts to share your peace.

Spiritual Practice:

As you walk or drive today, notice the unlikely places where you see growth, life, color, beauty. Review your daily schedule. When and how do you attend to your spiritual center. How does beauty "color" new life growing from that center? How do you balance intimacy with God's Spirit with active ministries of discipleship? Journal your need to learn "spirit-centered balance" that allows you to live as an oak of righteousness, a repairer of ruins in God's world.

Peace Covenant:

Today, God, I will look for where there is need and respond with the gifts you have given for that purpose.

14
Sunday
October

Respond Generously to God's Grace

By Steve Jones, presiding bishop

As he was setting out on a journey a man ran up and knelt before him and asked him, "Good teacher what must I do to inherit eternal life?"...Jesus, looking at him, loved him and said, "You lack one thing: go, sell what you own and give the money to the poor, and you will have treasure in heaven; then come, follow me." When he heard this, he was shocked and went away grieving, for he had many possessions.

—Mark 10:17, 21–22

I have the most-wonderful ministry assignment in all the church. Almost each week I receive an envelope or visit by someone who is making a generous offering to World Mission Tithes. Here are two such moments:

"Dear Presiding Bishop, my name is Katy. I was baptized in August. I got money for Christmas from my grandma. I want to give 10 percent for my Mission Tithes. Thank you."

Fred and Martha (names changed) were passing through Independence and stopped to see the presiding bishop. Now retired, they had given years of service as caretakers at several of our campgrounds in North America."Our finances have been tight," they said, "but we have been blessed, and now in our retirement we want to continue our commitment to fund World Mission Tithes as best we can. It's not much, but we hope this $1,000 can help to provide ministry throughout the world."

God is generous. God is the giver of the first gift by giving us God's only begotten Son, Jesus Christ. Daily I receive the knowledge that people like Katy, Fred, and Martha are receiving God's grace and responding generously to the mission of Jesus Christ.

Prayer for Peace:

Gracious and loving God, we give you thanks for the grace and peace of the life and ministry of your Son. May we be a reflection of that grace and peace in the world.

Spiritual Practice for the Week: Growing a Gracious, Generous Heart

Each day this week open your heart to God's grace and generosity with a "breath prayer." Let your breath slow and deepen. Be aware of God's breath moving in and out of your heart. Spend several minutes focusing on breathing in God's generosity. With each breath, silently name one gift for which you are thankful. "God, I breathe in the gift of ______ with thanks."

Let your heart expand to contain God's gracious outpouring. With each breath out, name one gift you want to share from the overflow of your heart.

Eternal joy and peace await those who grow in the grace of generosity that flows from compassionate hearts.

—Doctrine and Covenants 163:9

Peace Covenant:

Today, God, I will not be shocked at Jesus' answer to the rich man's question. I will follow Jesus.

15
Monday
October

Have No Fear

By Eileen Turner of Portland, Oregon, USA

> *For the mountains may depart and the hills be removed, but my steadfast love shall not depart from you, and my covenant of peace shall not be removed, says the Lord, who has compassion on you.*
>
> —Isaiah 54:10

I took a temporary position as a nurse to fill in at short-staffed hospitals. One day I was assigned to an intensive-care unit (ICU). I acquainted myself with the unit, policies, and equipment. Then I introduced myself to the patient.

Though seriously ill, she was not as critical as others in the unit. But she was terribly frightened and anxious, probably because of the intravenous and chest tubes and the uncomfortable confinement they caused.

So the rest of the staff could attend to the more-critical patients without frequent interruptions, I spent the entire day caring for her. I was comfortable with all of her equipment and assured her we would have a good day together.

Once I'd completed the physical assessment and checked her vital signs, she began to relax. There was a large picture window in her room. It was a beautiful sunny day. As I looked outside, I was startled to find a peaceful cemetery stretching over the grounds.

My first thought was, "Why does a hospital have an ICU room overlooking a cemetery?" The implications seemed evident. But I laughed and asked her if she'd seen the view.

She hadn't, so I shared it with her, and it allowed us to talk more intimately about her fears.

Over the day, we had many moments of laughter, sharing, and a chance to relieve most of her anxieties as her condition improved.

This caused me to think there should be no fear in coming to the end of a life well-lived, because God's steadfast love will not be removed. God's compassion will be with us always.

Prayer for Peace:

Compassionate God, we thank you for your steadfast presence. Comfort us in our times of fear. Give us strength to share Christ's peace.

Spiritual Practice for the Week: Growing a Gracious, Generous Heart

Open your heart to God's grace and generosity with a "breath prayer." Let your breathing slow and deepen. Be aware of God's breath moving in and out of your heart. Spend several minutes focusing on breathing in God's generosity. With each breath, silently name one gift for which you are thankful. Let your heart expand to contain God's gracious outpouring. With each breath out, name one gift you want to share from the overflow of your heart.

Peace Covenant:

Today, God, I will leave my fears in your hands.

16
Tuesday
October

Though Many, We Are One

By Merna Short of Melbourne, Victoria, Australia

And will not God grant justice to his chosen ones who cry to him day and night? Will he delay long in helping them? I tell you, he will quickly grant justice to them.

—Luke 18:7–8

An Australian-born Greek woman was concerned about the isolation of some women of different nationalities. They could not speak English, the majority language of the country where they lived. It was difficult for them to vote or fully understand the justice system.

They weren't able to attend government language classes. She approached the staff of their children's school about teaching classes for these women.

The women became proud of their progress. They provided special morning teas to thank the staff. Each nationality provided food from its homeland and explained the dishes.

The sense of community blossomed. When grade reports for their children came in the mail, the women no longer relied on their husbands or children to read to them. A wonderful door of communication opened.

How like Community of Christ with its message of sharing throughout the world! We have learned much about and through our brothers and sisters from other countries and those who have traveled to minister among them.

We have grown together in love. Our congregations have people from diverse backgrounds with many abilities, and we are all richer because of what we can share. Although we are many, together we are one in Christ.

Prayer for Peace:

Creator God, may our rights not be limited by our differences. May we join as one community of joy, hope, love, and peace. May justice flow like a river.

Spiritual Practice for the Week: Growing a Gracious, Generous Heart

Each day this week open your heart to God's grace and generosity with a "breath prayer." Let your breathing slow and deepen. Be aware of God's breath moving in and out of your heart.

Spend several minutes focusing on breathing in God's generosity. With each breath, silently name one gift for which you are thankful. "God, I breathe in the gift of ______ with thanks." Let your heart expand to contain God's gracious outpouring.

With each breath out, name one gift you want to share from the overflow of your heart.

Eternal joy and peace await those who grow in the grace of generosity that flows from compassionate hearts.

—Doctrine and Covenants 163:9

Peace Covenant:

God of justice, today I will learn of other cultures to increase a sense of community.

17
Wednesday
October

Can You See? Are You Pedaling?

By Sally Walton of Walkersville, Maryland, USA

> *. . . Will you remain hesitant in the shadows of your fears. . . Or will you move forward in the light of your divinely instilled call and vision? The mission of Jesus Christ is what matters most for the journey ahead.*
>
> —Doctrine and Covenants 164:9e–f

One of my first assignments as a teacher of blind students was to be a rider-guide on a tandem-bike outing. Each staff member was to ride with a student to a park, where a picnic lunch awaited.

Terry, the girl riding with me, became quiet and did not want to go. After questions about *why* we were going, she made it clear she thought the outing was ridiculous.

Terry was afraid. After some coercing on my part, she agreed to think about it. She asked, "Do you really know where we're going?" After I assured her that I did, she asked another question, "Can you really see the road?" I assured her I could see the road and could navigate for both of us. She finally agreed to go.

From other staff members I heard "Keep pedaling back there." As soon as the students got comfortable riding, they tended to forget to pedal. If the road got bumpy, they got scared and forgot to pedal. As teachers we later chuckled about how little trust the students had in our ability to get them to the picnic.

Now, in mid-life, I find myself afraid to accept additional responsibilities. However, I have this nudging that God wants me to say "yes." During a morning of intense prayer (almost arguing with God about it), I heard myself saying, "Do you know the implications this has for my family?"

I suddenly was overcome by the memory of the bike ride years ago, realizing I was asking God the same questions my student asked me.

I realized I was God's blind child—a child who was scared and confused. I also knew God was telling me I didn't have to know the way or to even see the road.

God asked me only to get on the bike and start pedaling. I was reminded I will be led where God wants me to go. Now, if I can just remember to trust and keep pedaling on the journey ahead!

Prayer for Peace:

Tender Shepherd, we have faith that you will lead us. May we follow.

Spiritual Practice for the Week: Growing a Gracious, Generous Heart

Open your heart to God's grace and generosity with a "breath prayer." Be aware of God's breath moving in and out of your heart. With each breath in, silently name one gift for which you are thankful. With each breath out, name one gift you want to share from the overflow of your heart.

> *Eternal joy and peace await those who grow in the grace of generosity that flows from compassionate hearts.*
>
> —Doctrine and Covenants 163:9

Peace Covenant:

Today, God, I will pursue what matters most.

18
Thursday
October

Stuck in the Ice

By Willa Frey of Fairbanks, Alaska, USA

But seek the welfare of the city where I have sent you into exile, and pray to the Lord on its behalf, for in its welfare you will find your welfare.

—Jeremiah 29:7

Many of us get stuck in the mud at least once, but stuck in ice? I mean seriously stuck, as you feel the car sinking beneath you and grindingly come to a complete stop. I was not looking forward to a half-mile walk up the hill through the dark, in freezing ice and snow.

Ugh! Will spring ever come? Many thought it had come a few days ago with the arrival of warm weather and sunshine only to face another storm of ice and snow!

The wheel hubs were almost buried, but the engine gave its all, whirring and sputtering while trying to get traction. It worked! Slowly, the car began to crawl forward, and then it broke loose! Whew! Thank you, God!

My mind flashed back to times when I've felt the same panic and helplessness with day-to-day problems. With joy, I realized God was still with me and ready to supply other ideas or help when I took the time to ask. I've no doubt that God would have given me the energy I needed to walk up the hill, if necessary.

The times when I'm slow to ask and give in to panic or helplessness, God lets me struggle with various options until I'm ready to listen! I realize this is good for me at times. It helps me stretch my muscles—my praying muscles. I need to search for answers, but I also need to know God is always near to guide me, especially when I take the time to listen!

I hear God call me to promote the welfare down the road, in other places. I'm deeply grateful for God's kind and loving help in finding ways to get there. God is my compass!

Prayer for Peace:

Generous God, we call on you in our need. We pray for guidance to seek the welfare of others. Direct us that we may share Christ's peace.

Spiritual Practice for the Week: Growing a Gracious, Generous Heart

Each day this week open your heart to God's grace and generosity with a "breath prayer." Let your breathing slow and deepen. Be aware of God's breath moving in and out of your heart.

Spend several minutes focusing on breathing in God's generosity. With each breath, silently name one gift for which you are thankful. "God, I breathe in the gift of ______ with thanks." Let your heart expand to contain God's gracious outpouring.

With each breath out, name one gift you want to share from the overflow of your heart.

Eternal joy and peace await those who grow in the grace of generosity that flows from compassionate hearts.

—Doctrine and Covenants 163:9

Peace Covenant:

If I get stuck trying to serve others, God, I'll remember to pray for new ideas.

19
Friday
October

Doing Peace

By Shirley Remmenga of Fort Collins, Colorado, USA

> *You are a good and faithful people, but sometimes you fail to see the power that is resident in your own story and fellowship. Look carefully, listen attentively, and sense the Spirit among you...Be fervent in your witness, passionate in your discipleship, and vigorous in your labor on behalf of peace and justice. Where two or three such disciples form community, there will the Spirit be. Many will come to see.*
>
> —Doctrine and Covenants 162:8a–b

The 2010 Community of Christ Peace Award was given in honor of a project to build schools in Pakistan and Afghanistan. The Colloquy engaged the children and youth in the audience during the presentation and throughout the weekend.

The speaker, Greg Mortenson, told how he had been blessed by "doing" peace. I listened. I listened not only with my ears, but with my heart and soul. I sensed the Spirit among us. I heard his philosophy of how to promote world peace, one school at a time and one girl student at a time.

Jesus' message was peace—peace that affected and still affects people wherever and however they live. He was peace in action. This kind of peace effort takes faith and courage. Plus it takes a connection with the love and power of God, Allah, Yahweh, or the many other names we call this great Spirit of the universe. May each of us have the faith and courage, plus the connection to God, needed to "do" peace.

Prayer for Peace:

Creator God, send peacemakers to teach us. Help us learn of the far-off places where peace and justice haven't been found. May we support the efforts to share Christ's peace in those lands.

Spiritual Practice for the Week: Growing a Gracious, Generous Heart

Each day this week open your heart to God's grace and generosity with a "breath prayer." Let your breathing slow and deepen. Be aware of God's breath moving in and out of your heart.

Spend several minutes focusing on breathing in God's generosity. With each breath, silently name one gift for which you are thankful. "God, I breathe in the gift of ______ with thanks." Let your heart expand to contain God's gracious outpouring.

With each breath out, name one gift you want to share from the overflow of your heart.

> *Eternal joy and peace await those who grow in the grace of generosity that flows from compassionate hearts.*
>
> —Doctrine and Covenants 163:9

Peace Covenant:

Today, God, I will learn of places where I can promote justice and peace.

20
Saturday
October

Gratitude: The Orchid's Third Year

By Barbara Howard of Independence, Missouri, USA

The earth is the Lord's and all that is in it, the world, and those who live in it…
—Psalm 24:1

The orchid is blooming! This is the third year, and it promises more blossoms than ever. The plant, from a beloved friend, teaches me every day about the power of a disciple's generous response.

The plant each year has offered blossoms, reminding me of the wonder of God's creation. I have simply kept it moist through the non-blooming season.

It was gift, just as my life is gift. The abundance that surrounds me continually reminds me of God's grace, freely shared through creation and through community, offering me opportunity to respond, to keep alive by my response.

When the orchid first came into our home I hoped it would last until winter so the friend who gave it to us would not see how hard I am on plants. It defied my lack of horticultural skills, and in the second year new blooms smiled at my amazement.

It was if it were saying, "Look what I can do with so little." I said a prayer of thanksgiving, smiled back at the beautiful, blooming orchid, and resolved to be more generous.

Whenever we give, the gift transcends our intentions or imaginings. Some joyful offering may change a life, help start a community, bring a new sense of freedom. Any time we give in the spirit of thankfulness, whatever we give exceeds our fondest hopes.

I can nourish my orchid by keeping it moist, keeping it in the light, and acknowledging its beauty daily. I can nurture beyond the walls of my home by a grateful flow of diverse responses to God's grace at the heart of all life.

Prayer for Peace:

Lord of the Earth and everything in it—flowers and creatures, great and small—may we care for what you have given us and give back to you by being generous.

Spiritual Practice:

Inner transformation can take place amid daily activities and work. Try cultivating the spiritual discipline of grace and acceptance while weeding the garden (if you have a garden). As you pull each weed, offer a short prayer. Tug. (*God remove from my heart all prejudice and fear.*) Tug again. (*God, keep me from making unjust judgments.*) As you remove the weeds, continue praying. (*Plant in my heart the seeds of your love.*)

Try this kind of transforming prayer while engaging in repetitive activities or work (washing dishes, cleaning the floors, mowing the lawn).

Peace Covenant:

Today, God, I will be aware of the needs around me and make a joyful offering that may change a life.

21
Sunday
October

Serve in Community

By John Wight, senior president of seventy

> *. . . whoever wishes to become great among you must be your servant, and whoever wishes to be first among you must be slave of all. For the Son of Man came not to be served but to serve, and to give his life a ransom for many.*
>
> —Mark 10:43–45

As a child, I regarded the people who served as apostles with awe. I saw them as super-humans who somehow were better than everyone else and above doing menial tasks.

This view was shattered one summer when I was attending a family camp as a 15-year-old. I enjoyed working in the kitchen and was happy to help with KP duties. As I stood at a sink washing pots and pans one day, a gentleman walked up and asked, with a plain air of humble servanthood, if I needed help.

I was rather shocked when I looked up and found it was a guest minister—a man who had served as an apostle until the previous year. I was nearly speechless as I tried to answer his question, but I finally blurted out, "Sure, that would be great."

For the next hour, this boy and a former apostle stood side by side, scrubbing nasty, greasy pots and pans, and chatting. That was a pivotal moment in my life—a moment for which I am very grateful and one which I never shall forget.

It taught me in real and personal ways the lesson Jesus was trying to communicate in the story recorded in the 10th chapter of Mark. This man, who had served in the highest levels of church leadership, taught me the value of humility and how important it is "not to be served, but to serve."

Prayer for Peace:

Ground of our being, as humble servants we ask that our calling be made known to us. How can we serve you and our companions? How can we serve strangers? How can we share the peace of Christ?

Spiritual Practice for the Week: Caring for God's Sacred Creation

Each day this week choose a way to notice, give thanks, and care for God's sacred creation. Prayerfully consider one of the following suggested practices or create your own.

Walk in nature with a spirit of gratitude and "holy attention." Write a psalm of praise for the beauty of the Earth, or a prayer of healing and blessing for the wounds of the Earth. Learn about and engage in an act of Earth-keeping, such as recycling, simple living, fasting from over-consumption of resources. Notice the unique diversity of the planet's creatures and be gentle to plants, animals, trees, and people! Fall in love with the vast, intricate wonder of God's creation and give thanks.

Peace Covenant:

Today, God, I will not be above any task that I am asked to do for the cause of peace.

22
Monday
October

Each Faithful Step Taken

By Vera Entwistle of Forster, New South Wales, Australia

Collectively and individually, you are loved with an everlasting love that delights in each faithful step taken. God yearns to draw you close so that wounds may be healed, emptiness filled, and hope strengthened...Come before your Eternal Creator with open minds and hearts and discover the blessings of the gospel anew. Be vulnerable to divine grace.

—Doctrine and Covenants 163:10

Our 3-year-old grandson is having problems pronouncing certain words, and so "Grandpa" has become "Frumpa." Jaiden idolizes his Frumpa and has come to believe that whatever breaks, Frumpa can fix it.

On a recent visit to their home we were watching television when a news bulletin showed a plane crashing and bursting into flames. I must have looked shocked because Jaiden ran to me and patted my knee saying, "Don't worry Nanny. Frumpa fix it."

Later that day a dog owned by our grandson's family had puppies, and one died. Our son asked Jaiden if he wanted to help bury the puppy. "No!" he shouted. "Call Frumpa. He fix it."

The more I thought about Jaiden's faith in his "Frumpa," the more I was reminded of a similar faith I need to have in my heavenly Parent—that no matter how bad conditions may seem, we can ask God to fix it.

Concerns may not always be fixable, but we'll feel better for praying and being vulnerable to divine grace.

Prayer for Peace:

Eternal Creator, we open our minds and hearts to you. We place our faith in your healing care. We find peace in your divine love.

Spiritual Practice for the Week: Caring for God's Sacred Creation

Each day this week choose a way to notice, give thanks, and care for God's sacred creation. Prayerfully consider one of the following suggested practices or create your own.

Walk in nature with a spirit of gratitude and "holy attention." Write a psalm of praise for the beauty of the Earth or a prayer of healing and blessing for the wounds of the Earth. Learn about and engage in an act of Earth-keeping, such as recycling, simple living, fasting from over-consumption of resources.

Notice the unique diversity of the planet's creatures and be gentle to plants, animals, trees, and people! Fall in love with the vast, intricate wonder of God's creation and give thanks.

Peace Covenant:

I will take a faithful step today, God, and be vulnerable to your grace.

23
Tuesday
October

Freedom of Obedience

By Donna Boyd of Independence, Missouri, USA

For my yoke is easy, and my burden is light.

—Matthew 11:30

When I was a child I often said, perhaps like most children, "I'll be glad when I'm grown up and don't have to do anything I don't want." I thought when I became an adult there would be no one to tell me what to do, so I would be completely free.

In my teen years, I constantly rebelled against authority, straining for the freedom I craved.

Almost too soon it was mine. There was no one to tell me what to do. I soon discovered I must be my own boss and push myself through tasks others had once guided me through.

One day I decided to do nothing except what I wanted. As the day progressed I grew restless. The confusion and clutter resulting from ignored work made it impossible to accomplish what I wanted. Realizing that my work made a difference, I carried out my tasks with a new respect.

So I learned of the freedom that comes from attention to what matters most. When we do what we must with enthusiasm, we enjoy our work. We finish quickly and have more time to appreciate our blessings. We find Christ's mission is a light burden.

Prayer for Peace:

God of blessing, may we hear your call for us and respond with enthusiasm and without delay. May our yoke be Christ's mission, and may we willingly share his peace with the world.

Spiritual Practice for the Week: Caring for God's Sacred Creation

Each day this week choose a way to notice, give thanks, and care for God's sacred creation. Prayerfully consider one of the following suggested practices or create your own.

Walk in nature with a spirit of gratitude and "holy attention." Write a psalm of praise for the beauty of the Earth or a prayer of healing and blessing for the wounds of the Earth. Learn about and engage in an act of Earth-keeping, such as recycling, simple living, fasting from over-consumption of resources.

Notice the unique diversity of the planet's creatures and be gentle to plants, animals, trees, and people! Fall in love with the vast, intricate wonder of God's creation and give thanks.

Peace Covenant:

Today, God, I will exercise my freedom and choose to bear the burdens I am given with joy.

24
Wednesday
October

Eagles

By Evelyn Spence of Council Bluffs, Iowa, USA

...but those who wait for the Lord shall renew their strength, they shall mount up with wings like eagles, they shall run and not be weary, they shall walk and not faint.

—Isaiah 40:31

My husband and I are fortunate to live on a small lake that is part of a state park. On one side of our building lies an urban area. On the other side is the lake. The north side of our property connects us with the world with which we interact almost daily. The other side connects with nature.

A late-winter occurrence here is the presence of eagles. They perch in trees around the lake. As the lake begins to thaw, it becomes an expanse of ice floes and open water. It is thrilling to watch these mighty birds soar from a grove of trees across the lake to a lone tree, probably a quarter-mile distant.

Soon they swoop down to a floe of ice and watch for fish. They dip their heads into the water and bring up fish. Sometimes they sit on the ice and devour their prey.

If other birds are nearby, the eagles will carry the fish to the trees.

Eagles are highly admired. Friends ask us to call them when the birds are easily viewed. Watching wildlife is relaxing and meditative. Through the practice of patience, observing God's creation blesses us with inner peace. It assures us of the continuing cycle of nature and God's presence right in front of us, beside us, and within us.

Prayer for Peace:

Creator God, thank you for blessing us in nature with symbols of strength and endurance. May we always be aware of the Sacredness of Creation. May we be aware of ways to share Christ's peace.

Spiritual Practice for the Week: Caring for God's Sacred Creation

Each day this week choose a way to notice, give thanks, and care for God's sacred creation. Prayerfully consider one of the following suggested practices or create your own.

Walk in nature with a spirit of gratitude and "holy attention." Write a psalm of praise for the beauty of the Earth or a prayer of healing and blessing for the wounds of the Earth. Learn about and engage in an act of Earth-keeping, such as recycling, simple living, fasting from over-consumption of resources.

Notice the unique diversity of the planet's creatures and be gentle to plants, animals, trees, and people! Fall in love with the vast, intricate wonder of God's creation and give thanks.

Peace Covenant:

Today, God, I will take time to be aware of and appreciate your creation.

25
Thursday
October

Building Shalom

By Ron Dawbarn of Manchester, Tennessee, USA

> *Jesus Christ, the embodiment of God's shalom, invites all people to come and receive divine peace in the midst of the difficult questions and struggles of life. Follow Christ in the way that leads to God's peace and discover the blessings of all of the dimensions of salvation.*
>
> —Doctrine and Covenants 163:2a

How do you build a relationship with a God whose creative force extends for light-years throughout a universe of countless galaxies? Each galaxy contains stars we still cannot number.

How do you start the conversation?

I am fortunate to live in the countryside. On a clear night I can lie on the hillside in front of my house and look into space. On those occasions I experience a feeling of awe and wonder, a sense of closeness to God. As I lie there, I realize the awe and wonder is not *out there* at all, but deep *within* me.

We are blessed to have God's Spirit within each of us. It is unfortunate we often don't recognize the presence of the Divine within ourselves or in others.

We can read of many ways people have tried to build relationships with God. Most are valid and worthwhile. But we often overlook our most obvious, most tangible, and most available contact with God: our companion human beings, our brothers and sisters.

We are told wherever two or three gather in God's name, there will God be, also. We don't even have to ask God to be with us. We just need to be aware of the presence of God's shalom within us.

Prayer for Peace:

God of shalom, help us always be aware of your presence within us. Allow us to be aware of your presence in others. May we know the length and breadth of your shalom by sharing the peace of Jesus Christ.

Spiritual Practice for the Week: Caring for God's Sacred Creation

Each day this week choose a way to notice, give thanks, and care for God's sacred creation. Prayerfully consider one of the following suggested practices or create your own.

Walk in nature with a spirit of gratitude and "holy attention." Write a psalm of praise for the beauty of the Earth or a prayer of healing and blessing for the wounds of the Earth. Learn about and engage in an act of Earth-keeping, such as recycling, simple living, fasting from over-consumption of resources.

Notice the unique diversity of the planet's creatures and be gentle to plants, animals, trees, and people! Fall in love with the vast, intricate wonder of God's creation and give thanks.

Peace Covenant:

Today, God, I will start the conversation with others to build my relationship with you.

26
Friday
October

God's Care Given by Us

By Paul McCain of Oklahoma City, Oklahoma, USA

> *How precious is your steadfast love, O God! All people may take refuge in the shadow of your wings. They feast on the abundance of your house, and you give them drink from the river of your delights. For with you is the fountain of life; in your light we see light. O continue your steadfast love to those who know you, and your salvation to the upright of heart!*
>
> —Psalm 36:7–10

A co-worker fell and was taken to the emergency room (ER). Our administrator asked me to e-mail the worker's supervisor and then go to the ER.

When I arrived, the doctor was putting stitches in my friend's forehead. Shortly afterward someone came to X-ray her foot, on which I dutifully had kept an ice pack. My friend apologized for the inconvenience, but I told her I would stay as long as she needed.

After reading the X-ray, the doctor told her the foot was broken and he would have to give her a cast. My job was to talk to my friend, joke with her, and assure her whatever help she needed would be provided.

Soon a technician came and shaped the cast, wrapped it, and held her foot in the needed position while the material dried. A wheelchair was brought in, and I drove the car to meet the attendant and my friend at the ER door. When back at our workplace, I left her in the car while I found another worker to help us get her and her car home. The other worker also offered to help in any way needed, and we left my friend in her living room to rest.

As we went through the afternoon, I remember looking for ways to help, trying to be the hands and feet of God. We try to help so people do not feel alone in the world—to let them know they have a community that cares. We hope through us people will know of God's steadfast love. May we always be bringers of peace wherever the opportunity presents itself.

Prayer for Peace:

Steadfast God, we look to you for light. We look to you for a community of faithful servants. We would be faithful, too. We would share the peace of Christ.

Spiritual Practice for the Week: Caring for God's Sacred Creation

Notice, give thanks, and care for God's sacred creation. Walk in nature with a spirit of "holy attention." Or write a prayer of healing and blessing for the wounds of the Earth. Learn about and engage in an act of Earth-keeping, such as recycling, simple living, fasting from over-consumption of resources. Notice the unique diversity of the planet's creatures and be gentle to plants, animals, trees, and people! Fall in love with the vast, intricate wonder of God's creation.

Peace Covenant:

Today, God, I will be your hands and feet. Show me where I am needed.

27
Saturday
October

Share the Hope

By Karin Peter of Adrian, Missouri, USA

> *All are called according to the gifts of God unto them; and to the intent that all may labor together, let those that labor in the ministry and those that toil in the affairs of the people of business and of work labor together with God for the accomplishment of the work intrusted to all.*
>
> —Doctrine and Covenants 119:8b, adapted

"I look forward to Sunday morning. However, sometimes life's business can sap the joy from the day," Paula told me.

I was surprised because she had just described how she and others make multiple trips each Sunday to take children and young adults to and from church.

It is an awesome commitment that requires planning, time, and energy, all scarce after working all week at a full-time job. But Paula's face shone with joy as she described her Sunday rounds. "Then you drive up to a house, and three little bundles of energy come running at you full speed, shouting 'Pastor Paula! Pastor Paula! Are we going to church?' How can I not smile?"

Paula continued, "When we drive them home after church, we sing all the songs we sang during church. Their sweet voices touch my heart, and I am renewed. *I* am the one who receives ministry!"

Your contributions to World Mission Tithes help emerging congregations such as Paula's provide life-transforming ministry to children and young adults. Thank you for your generous giving.

Prayer for Peace:

Gather us in, God, as we welcome new friends. May we be open to receive their ministry, as well as to give them ministry. May we give ministry by sharing the peace of Jesus Christ.

Spiritual Practice:

A tree with superficial roots will wither during droughts or be uprooted by severe storms. A tree whose roots go deep is stable and draws from deep waters. Imagine yourself as a tree by a river or stream. Sense your roots extending deep into the earth in search of God's Spirit. Write a reflection or prayer about what you hope to find as your spirit searches for deeper identity in God. (See Jeremiah 17:7–8.)

Peace Covenant:

God, as I go about my work today, I will share the joy in my heart.

28
Sunday
October

Lord, Let Me See

By Dave Brock, presiding evangelist

> *...Bartimaeus son of Timaeus, a blind beggar, was sitting by the roadside. When he heard that it was Jesus of Nazareth, he began to shout out and say, "Jesus, Son of David, have mercy on me!"...Jesus stood still and said, "Call him here." And they called the blind man, saying to him, "Take heart; get up, he is calling you."...Then Jesus said to him, "What do you want me to do for you?" The blind man said to him, "My teacher, let me see again." Jesus said to him, "Go; your faith has made you well." Immediately he regained his sight and followed him on the way.*
>
> —Mark 10:46–47, 49, 51–52

The child turns to a parent or older sibling who has just unwrapped a box or opened an envelope and demands, "Let me see!" A teen watches her father trying to connect electric wires without injuring himself. In a combination of thinking out loud and some vague plea to the universe, the father mutters, "Let me see here!" An elderly woman with cataracts turns to the doctor just before surgery and says, "Let me see again, Doc!"

It is more dramatic when Jesus stops in his tracks to ask the blind man, "What would you have me do?" and Bartimaeus the beggar says, "Lord, let me see!" But, the tenor of the statement is the same as in the ordinary requests: petition, expectation, hope.

Why, then, if I'm honest, do I only infrequently and with considerable effort haltingly say, "Lord, let me see," and mean it?

I think it is because the blindness from which I need healing, but don't truly want, goes something like this:

"Lord, let me see where my actions are hindering the relationship with my colleague, Jennifer, at work." "Lord, let me see the positive traits and giftedness of Sam who, frankly, irritates me!" "Lord, let me see what gifts I have so I can say yes to the new priesthood call or the request to fill a tough leadership role in the community."

If I'm honest, much of the time I'd just as soon not hear Jesus ask, "What would you have me do?" Then I wouldn't have to confess that if it means blind spots will be revealed, new responsibilities may be added, other points of view to consider, I'd just as soon opt out.

God, give me the courage and the trust to say to you more often, "Please let me see."

Prayer for Peace:

Revealing God, we confess to having avoided your light many times. We have turned our eyes away from opportunities and challenges. Keep us centered on peace.

Spiritual Practice for the Week: Encountering Scripture as Continuing Revelation

Read and pray with the Doctrine and Covenants as continuing revelation of God's vision. Choose a favorite section or focus on recent counsel in Sections 156–164. Read a few selected paragraphs slowly three or four times. Pause to pray for deep understanding. Pray for opening of your heart to the text. Listen as fully and openly as you can. What sense of divine presence or invitation comes? What is revealed?

Peace Covenant:

God, I will expand beyond my blind spots and do what you would have me do.

29
Monday
October

Uplift

By Karen Porter of Liberty, Missouri, USA

...but with righteousness he shall judge the poor, and decide with equity for the meek of the earth...

—Isaiah 11:4

Jaeden, Charlott, Lori, and I went with Operation Uplift, a program to feed the homeless. Jaeden had been a few times before, so he was used to helping. One of our regular clients wasn't able to come to the truck for his food and toiletries. His friend came with a list of things needed for both of them. He told us his friend had just been diagnosed with cancer.

They needed many items. One person couldn't carry everything and the plates of hot food to the camp. Our driver offered to help. With their hands full, off they went to the camp.

Later we went out again on the same Uplift route. This time our original client came to the truck with the help of a cane. I called him by name. He was surprised we remembered him.

As he stood at the truck door, telling us what he needed, I got out and hugged him. I was about to leave when he asked me to wait so he could hug me back. As he left the truck, struggling with the cane to stay on his feet in the snow, he said, "God bless you."

On the way home we talked about how difficult life must be for those on the streets. We were cold even in our dry, heavy coats inside the truck. How can they possibly survive on the street? Surely he was one of the meek of the Earth and was able to express his appreciation for any blessing.

Prayer for Peace:

Compassionate God, hold before us the meek who are loved by you and will inherit your kingdom. May we respond to them with love and share with them the peace of Jesus Christ.

Spiritual Practice for the Week: Encountering Scripture as Continuing Revelation

Read and pray with the Doctrine and Covenants as continuing revelation of God's vision for the church and creation. Choose a favorite section or focus on recent counsel in Sections 156–164.

Pause to pray for deep understanding of meaning after the first reading. Pray for opening of your heart and emotions to the text. Prayerfully ask to hear the particular phrase or word that speaks to you or touches your life. Stay with this word or phrase. Listen as fully and openly as you can. What sense of divine presence or invitation comes? What is revealed?

Peace Covenant:

Today, God, the power of love will be my practice.

30
Tuesday
October

An Evangelist's Focus

By Bruce Crockett of Kirtland, Ohio, USA

> *...Vital to this awakening is the understanding that the Temple calls the entire church to become a sanctuary of Christ's peace, where people from all nations, ethnicities, and life circumstances can be gathered into a spiritual home without dividing walls, as a fulfillment of the vision for which Jesus Christ sacrificed his life.*
>
> —Doctrine and Covenants 163:8c

I'm preparing to give my first blessing as an evangelist. I have the privilege of getting to know someone, layer by layer, and hear their story. Sanctuary is a privileged role where trust makes up the pillars that support openness and vulnerability. The pillars support the expression of yearnings, needs, dreams, hopes, disappointments, and wounds. Sanctuary is a place of safety, and in that safety hope swells in the assurance of God's love.

Sanctuary is a place where we are reminded that we are past, present, and future, beloved of God. It is a place where we have great worth. We are reminded that though the path isn't easy at times, we learn lessons to share and reflect on for even-deeper wisdom.

Yes, I have the privilege to be with someone and to be open to the voice that will bless this person. So I must keep my focus and keep surrendering, listening, being vulnerable, confessing, and in the end, being affirmed and sent forth to love my neighbor, to express compassion, and to not judge or try to fix anyone.

We are called to represent Christ and provide *sacramental* opportunity for people to draw closer to God. We draw closer, not only in the moment of blessing, but in the days and weeks that follow as we engage in reflection and discernment. The evangelist blessing, as reminder and support, is an ensign of hope in times of doubt that God is near, that God cares, that God believes in us even in those times when our belief wanes.

Grace abounds. May I pay attention and observe its presence so grace may continue to mold me, shape me, and make me aware of the Spirit of blessing. This blessing swirls around us each day, perhaps unnoticed. Ah, the potential of that which awaits us, that which is possible. I must keep my focus!

Prayer for Peace:

Sacramental God, we await your blessing. Keep us focused on what matters most. Keep us focused on Christ's mission.

Spiritual Practice for the Week: Encountering Scripture as Continuing Revelation

Read and pray with the Doctrine and Covenants as continuing revelation of God's vision for the church and creation. Choose a favorite section or focus on recent counsel in Sections 156–164. Pause to pray for deep understanding of meaning. Pray for opening of your heart and emotions to the text. Prayerfully ask to hear the particular phrase or word that speaks to you or touches your life. Listen as fully and openly as you can. What sense of divine presence or invitation comes? What is revealed?

Peace Covenant:

Today, God, I will look for opportunities to bless as I have been blessed.

31
Wednesday
October

Dark Night of the Soul

By Peggy Michael of Cantonment, Florida, USA

The eyes of the Lord are on the righteous, and his ears are open to their cry... When the righteous cry for help, the Lord hears, and rescues them from all their troubles. The Lord is near to the brokenhearted, and saves the crushed in spirit.

—Psalm 34:15, 17–18

Do you ever feel like you're being pulled backward into a tunnel so long that you've lost your sense of time, direction, and feeling? Somewhere, are children laughing and friends greeting one another? Are mountains standing solid and secure?

If I ever believed in such ideas, I don't remember them now. I need God's grace, and yet I am afraid to make myself vulnerable.

Must I remain in this terrifying condition until death overtakes me, or will someone in the light show me a better way? They must search and pray, though, for I will be hard to find. I cannot find myself. If you have hope and tender mercy, call my name again and again, and I will try to follow your voice. For I do want to go out from this haunting prison. I do want to know my Lord again.

Are you the servant who can reach the hopeless with God's grace?

Prayer for Peace:

God of light, bring us from our dark places. Forgive us for our doubt. Encompass our broken hearts with your healing spirit. Then in wholeness, we can resume sharing the peace of Jesus Christ.

Spiritual Practice for the Week: Encountering Scripture as Continuing Revelation

Read and pray with the Doctrine and Covenants as continuing revelation of God's vision for the church and creation. Choose a favorite section or focus on recent counsel in Sections 156–164.

Pause to pray for deep understanding of meaning after the first reading. Pray for opening of your heart and emotions to the text. Prayerfully ask to hear the particular phrase or word that speaks to you or touches your life. Stay with this word or phrase. Listen as fully and openly as you can. What sense of divine presence or invitation comes? What is revealed?

Peace Covenant:

Today God, I will be the servant who shares love with one who is without hope.

1
Thursday
November

Sacredness of Creation

By Dorene Kilburn of Stratford, Ontario, Canada

For as the earth brings forth its shoots, and as a garden causes what is sown in it to spring up, so the Lord God will cause righteousness and praise to spring up before all the nations.
—Isaiah 61:11

Sometimes in the middle of winter, it's good to remember the new life of spring. When we look at the harmony and adaptation in the plant and animal world, we marvel at God's creation.

At a meeting of our local Field Naturalists Club, the guest speaker was a photographer and expert on butterflies and moths. He had a marvelous collection of photos and fascinating information.

One photo appeared to be only the trunk of a big tree, but he showed a moth was clinging to the bark. The moth was a mottled gray, blending perfectly with the tree trunk. Who but God could have created such stunning camouflage!

The speaker led us through a wonderful display of what is all around us in nature. We were overjoyed to hear his witness in statements like, "I see evidence in all the Earth of a Creator," and "My soul is...rejuvenated by close encounter with nature, and I often sense the Creator is interacting with me on some level through creatures with which I gambol."

What an affirmation of God's love for creation, a witness that has the potential to reach all the Earth's people. God loves us so much, and we can enjoy endless miracles in nature every day. Let us always give witness of our gratitude for divine presence in our lives and in the world.

Prayer for Peace:

O Great Spirit, whose voice I hear in the wind, whose breath gives life to the world, hear me. I come to you as one of your many children. I am small and weak. I need your strength and your wisdom. May I walk in beauty and peace...

—Chief Dan George

Spiritual Practice for the Week: Scripture as Continuing Revelation

Read and pray with the Doctrine and Covenants as continuing revelation of God's vision for the church and creation. Choose a favorite section or focus on recent counsel in Sections 156–164. Pray for deep understanding of meaning. Pray for opening of your heart and emotions to the text. Prayerfully ask to hear the particular phrase or word that speaks to you.

Listen as fully and openly as you can. What sense of divine presence or invitation comes? What is revealed?

Peace Covenant:

Creator God, I will walk in the cold with gratitude for the warmth of your spring to come.

2
Friday
November

Run and Not Be Weary

By Sally Walton of Walkersville, Maryland, USA

> *. . . but those who wait for the Lord shall renew their strength, they shall mount up with wings like eagles, they shall run and not be weary, they shall walk and not faint.*
>
> —Isaiah 40:31

I think about all the lessons I have learned from the people often considered the weakest of our society. I have been a special-education teacher for years, and I have worked with students who daily deal with assorted challenges.

I learned one outstanding lesson at the Special Olympics, an athletic competition for mentally and physically challenged people. I was standing near the course for the 25-yard walk. This is an event for athletes who have severe motor challenges.

Five athletes of assorted sizes and ages lined up. When the signal was given, they started walking, hobbling, and sliding toward the finish line. Many used canes and walkers.

The person who caught everyone's attention was a middle-aged gentleman who took a couple of steps and fell. With encouragement from his "coach-buddy," he got up, brushed himself off, and started again. He fell again after a few more steps. Again he got up, brushed himself off, and continued the race—for a few more steps.

He repeated this routine until he crossed the finish line and fell into the arms of his coach. He was far behind the other competitors. But he finished!

Everyone was so mesmerized by this gentleman that no one noticed who crossed the finish line first. In true Special Olympics spirit, all the finishers were declared winners and given medals.

This man's actions reminded me in a visible way of God's response to us. We run, we stumble, and we fall. God is always there, encouraging us to get back up and brush ourselves off. God then lets us start running again—usually only to stumble and fall. However, when we get to the finish line, God is there with open arms ready to declare us winners.

Prayer for Peace:

Thank you, patient God, for letting us start over when we fall—when we fail. Thank you for reaching out to us with open arms to catch us. Help us to transform the "arms" race into a "peace" race. May we all be winners.

Spiritual Practice for the Week: Scripture as Continuing Revelation

Read and pray with the Doctrine and Covenants as continuing revelation of God's vision for the church and creation. Choose a favorite section or focus on recent counsel in Sections 156–164. Pray for deep understanding of meaning and for the opening of your heart and emotions to the text. Pray to hear the particular phrase or word that speaks to you or touches your life. Listen as fully and openly as you can. What sense of divine presence or invitation comes? What is revealed?

Peace Covenant:

Today, God, I will be patient with myself and others.

3
Saturday
November

Sacramental Sharing

By Barbara Howard of Independence, Missouri, USA

For where two or three are gathered in my name, I am there among them.
—Matthew 18:20

We shared lunch with a young couple and went to a film about Hildegard of Bingen. As we left the theater we met a couple from our congregation, and the six of us returned to our home for a spontaneous evening together.

Throughout our meal of leftovers, stories were told, and joy abounded. We heard about each other's families, delighted in and pondered congregational issues, and laughed at embarrassing moments in church life. We struggled with difficult questions about contemporary culture and the role of the church in creative transformation of cultures We ate, rejoiced, and celebrated the intimacy of friendship.

The evening was sacred, and prayer seemed appropriate as we formed a quiet circle before parting. Throughout the remainder of the week the sense of God's presence seemed more intense, more vivid than it had before.

I've wondered since that evening if perhaps we limit the meaning of sacrament to ordinances in the church.

The presence of the living Christ is always with us. In a world where intimacy often is lost, the breaking of bread together, the sharing of lives is sacred.

I am grateful for our blessed community and the joy of sacramental sharing.

Prayer for Peace:

God of the individual, God of the community, let us come together to share our joy. Let us be blessed by one another's presence, and let us be transformed by the spirit of the table—food, story, laughter, and welcoming generosity.

Spiritual Practice:

Visualize or feel an empty vessel at the center of your being (a clay jar, a crystal vase, a metal bucket, or other container). Imagine wanting to draw something from the bucket to share with someone, but as you reach inside you find only a tiny pool of stagnant liquid. You are thirsty, dry, empty.

Then something clear and cool begins to pour over you. It splashes and tumbles into the vessel, filling it to the brim. The living water of Christ pours on and in you. Your vessel fills and runs over blessing your body and soul. Offer a prayer of thanksgiving and commitment to share living water with others.

Peace Covenant:

Today, God, I will seek others with whom to share your presence. I will respond with joy and generosity.

4
Sunday
November

Love the Lord

By Dave Brock, presiding evangelist

> *..."The first is, 'Hear, O Israel: the Lord our God, the Lord is one; you shall love the Lord your God with all your heart, and with all your soul, and with all your mind, and with all your strength.' The second is this, 'You shall love your neighbor as yourself.' There is no other commandment greater than these."*
>
> —Mark 12:29–31

Love God. Love your neighbor.

The rest is commentary. It is that simple. Almost all who walk the planet would say "yes" to those five words. Why then does it seem so difficult to live these two commandments?

Is God? If God *is*, what is God like? What does God want? How do I get to know God? Why do I sometimes feel like loving and connecting with God, and why do I at other times feel like I want God to leave me alone? Is loving God with *all* one's might, mind, and strength just a little too much to expect? Or is its practice my greatest joy and a gift to receive?

And who is my neighbor? With 6 billion people on the planet who is truly my neighbor and what is love supposed to look and feel like in the realities of my everyday life? What is doable?

Sometimes I can't get along with the kids next door. Other times I sense the deepest connection to a person of another faith who is praying for me. Who *is* my neighbor?

And what does it mean to love myself? Why does what passes for love so often not measure up or endure? How is it that I sometimes experience such deep love when I least expect it? Why am I surprised with a love beyond what seems humanly possible?

So, the questions lead to all the words and stories of faith that circle these two commandments. They are the guide on our path. Love is both a gift received, and it is the vulnerability that costs everything. Love is. Sometimes we stumble into it and out of it, and sometimes it comes to us unbidden like a fresh stream in the desert!

The key to the commandment, "Love the Lord," is the one great fact: "God is, and God loves you and me." If we know that fact—truly know it—then we fulfill the commandments!

Prayer for Peace:

God of eternal love, sometimes when we are distracted, your love *is* unbidden. When we open to it, we realize how thirsty for love we are.

Spiritual Practice for the Week: Honoring the Worth of All Persons

Read Psalm 139:13–18. After each reading sit quietly and let the deep meaning of the words sink into your mind, heart, and body. Sense the intimate knowledge God has of you. Ask God for an awareness of the sacred worth of each person on the planet. How are you being invited to notice, protect, heal, and affirm the spiritual identity of all?

Peace Covenant:

Today, God, I will take time to be still and feel your love wash over me. I will share your love with my neighbors.

5
Monday
November

Invest

By Melba Jean Dixon of Farwell, Michigan, USA

> *You are the salt of the earth; but if salt has lost its taste, how can its saltiness be restored? It is no longer good for anything, but is thrown out and trampled underfoot.*
> —Matthew 5:13

Our young adults are on fire! Two young women, Dana and Amber, are challenging our congregation in many ways. Together they plan services and encourage children and other young adults to utilize their gifts and talents.

Dana and Amber attended the 2010 World Conference. They attend young-adult gatherings and retreats in the mission center. They take part in the Studies and Advanced Leadership Training (SALT) classes. Each has made a three-year commitment to study and learn leadership skills. Amber has served as a summer youth camp director.

I am excited to see young adults take time from their busy lives to absorb the advanced training and worship experiences offered by the church.

Some may be reluctant to allow children and young adults to "do it their way." Those attitudes will result only in stale and dying congregations.

The youth may not do things in the traditional way, but the health of our congregations depends on them. Welcome and encourage them to be equal partners in congregational life. Invest.

Prayer for Peace:

Covenant God, help us grow with our young people. May we listen to their ideas and catch their enthusiasm. May we let our worship be flavorful and energizing for the sharing of the peace of Christ.

Spiritual Practice for the Week: Honoring the Worth of All Persons

Each day this week read Psalm 139:13–18. After each reading sit quietly and let the deep meaning of the words sink into your mind, heart, and body. Imagine God watching you grow in your mother's womb. What thoughts and feelings do you have about being "fearfully and wonderfully made" (Psalm 139:14)?

Sense the intimate knowledge God has of you and every child ever born. Ask God for an awareness of the sacred worth of each person on the planet. Weep with God over the soul-wounding forces and events that rob people of dignity and worth. How are you being invited to notice, protect, heal, and affirm the spiritual identity of all God's beloved people today? Pray for God's compassion.

Peace Covenant:

Today, God, I will place myself under the influence of young thinking and be open to your fresh Spirit.

6
Tuesday
November

Transformational U-turns

By Carole Walker of Lakeland, Florida, USA

He shall judge between the nations, and shall arbitrate for many peoples; they shall beat their swords into plowshares, and their spears into pruning hooks; nation shall not lift up sword against nation, neither shall they learn war any more.

—Isaiah 2:4

While riding with my sister on my first trip to Florida, she made a sudden U-turn. I instantly said, "I sure hope there aren't any police officers around." She calmly told me that U-turns usually are allowed in Florida. I thought back to a beautiful sampler that she gave me many years ago that says, "God Allows U-turns."

To me both of these represent experiences in life, the turns that must be taken en route to a final destination. Our routes along life's journey may have many turns, distractions, and troubles. Our gracious Creator watches over us at all times. Many times we go down an unsuitable road, and God may even carry us for a time.

The scriptures talk about beating swords into plowshares—turning instruments of war into tools of the garden. The direction, mission, and purpose of the weapon take a U-turn. The instrument has been transformed and will have a new life of nurture and service.

Watch for opportunities to make a U-turn to find the path of discipleship, the path of peace.

Prayer for Peace:

Guiding God, thank you for allowing U-turns in our lives. Thank you for your grace, which allows us to get on your path. Thank you for opportunities to turn around and get on the path to peace.

Spiritual Practice for the Week: Honoring the Worth of All Persons

Each day this week read Psalm 139:13–18. After each reading sit quietly and let the deep meaning of the words sink into your mind, heart, and body. Imagine God watching you grow in your mother's womb. What thoughts and feelings do you have about being "fearfully and wonderfully made" (Psalm 139:14)?

Sense the intimate knowledge God has of you and every child ever born. Ask God for an awareness of the sacred worth of each person on the planet. Weep with God over the soul-wounding forces and events that rob people of dignity and worth. How are you being invited to notice, protect, heal, and affirm the spiritual identity of all God's beloved people today? Pray for God's compassion.

Peace Covenant:

Today, God, I will study, learn, and follow you.

7
Wednesday
November

Harry and His Music

By Shirley Remmenga of Fort Collins, Colorado, USA

> *These are the things that you shall do: Speak the truth to one another, render in your gates judgments that are true and make for peace...*
>
> —Zechariah 8:16

I was listening to traditional Celtic music played by a four-person band while visiting in Clifden, County Galway, Ireland. Someone in the audience yelled, "Harry, sing for us!"

Harry, a Scotsman, thin as a reed, gaunt-faced, and elderly, was unable to walk without the use of two canes. He needed help to get to the stage. A chair was placed in front of the microphone.

He sat down, shut his eyes, and began to sing.

Everyone became quiet. From deep in his being he sang two familiar Scottish songs. Each word, sung in his native dialect, was clear, on pitch, and beautiful. I listened with awe and appreciation as tears filled the corners of my eyes. On first seeing him, I expected so little of his ability to sing.

My expectations were completely off target. Perhaps I should approach every situation with an open attitude, expectant of the best. I want always to be open positively to new experiences, to see the good in situations, to appreciate people without judgment. I thank God I don't have to do this growing alone. Will you grow with me?

Prayer for Peace:

Mystery God, we often wonder what will be on the table for us. May we always approach with positive expectancy and faith in your grace. May all our surprises teach us and grow us in peace.

Spiritual Practice for the Week: Honoring the Worth of All Persons

Each day this week read Psalm 139:13–18. After each reading sit quietly and let the deep meaning of the words sink into your mind, heart, and body. Imagine God watching you grow in your mother's womb. What thoughts and feelings do you have about being "fearfully and wonderfully made" (Psalm 139:14)?

Sense the intimate knowledge God has of you and every child ever born. Ask God for an awareness of the sacred worth of each person on the planet. Weep with God over the soul-wounding forces and events that rob people of dignity and worth. How are you being invited to notice, protect, heal, and affirm the spiritual identity of all God's beloved people today? Pray for God's compassion.

Peace Covenant:

Today, God, I will approach the unknown without prejudice.

8
Thursday
November

The Heavens Proclaim the Love of the Lord

By Cindy Korf of North Platte, Nebraska, USA

Rejoice in the Lord, O you righteous. Praise befits the upright. Praise the Lord with the lyre; make melody to him with the harp of ten strings. Sing to him a new song; play skillfully on the strings, with loud shouts. For the word of the Lord is upright, and all his work is done in faithfulness. He loves righteousness and justice; the earth is full of the steadfast love of the Lord.

—Psalm 33:1–5

It had been a dismal week of bitter cold. The morning was frigid, and more arctic cold was forecast. I was hurrying outside to take the trash to the garbage can when a marvelous thing happened! A small white fluff fell from the sky. Slowly it floated in front of me, calling to me.

I reached out and touched it! For a second it sat in my hand before disappearing. Another snowflake floated slowly and blissfully down from the sky. I felt a surge of happiness and reached to touch the fluff. It, too, sat magically for a moment in my hand.

Another wisp of whiteness descended lazily, and then another, and another. In that silent moment there was inexpressible joy—a oneness with God's creation. I felt I had reached out and touched a part of heaven. My little corner of the Earth would soon be full of snow. The Earth is full of the steadfast love of God.

Prayer for Peace:

Steadfast God, thank you for the circles of life. Thank you for the assurance we feel when your seasons continue, when your birds fly to warmth and return home, when your oceans ebb and flow and deposit your treasures on the shore. Thank you for water lifting to the sky, falling again as snow to thirsty earth and waiting mittens, muffling the sounds of traffic. Thank you for the completions that comfort us.

Spiritual Practice for the Week: Honoring the Worth of All Persons

Each day this week read Psalm 139:13–18. After each reading sit quietly and let the deep meaning of the words sink into your mind, heart, and body. Imagine God watching you grow in your mother's womb. What thoughts and feelings do you have about being "fearfully and wonderfully made" (Psalm 139:14)?

Sense the intimate knowledge God has of you and every child ever born. Ask God for an awareness of the sacred worth of each person on the planet. Weep with God over the soul-wounding forces and events that rob people of dignity and worth. How are you being invited to notice, protect, heal, and affirm the spiritual identity of all God's beloved people today? Pray for God's compassion.

Peace Covenant:

Today, God, I will wait with expectation and appreciation for the completion of circles in my life.

9
Friday
November

Prejudices of the Past

By Donna Boyd of Independence, Missouri, USA

Let no harmful talk come out of your mouths, but only what is useful for building up, as there is need, so that your words may give grace to those who hear... and live in love, as Christ loved us and gave himself up for us...

—Ephesians 4:29, 5:2, adapted

We lived in Louisiana during much of our children's formative years. Watching others struggle to free themselves from prejudices of their past, I wrote and expressed gratitude to my parents for teaching me to accept every person as an individual.

Mother wrote back, saying it had not been easy because wartime propaganda against the Japanese had twisted her thinking. Somehow she hid her prejudice as she outgrew it. Realizing how easily she could have taught me to hate, I thanked God for the blessing of an open heart to receive all humankind.

The problem the world faces in racial relations is an example of the chain with which we can bind our children. We may not realize the potential loss of liberty to their souls. How much better it is to give our children a compass of love to direct them into wholesome relationships with their fellow humans. We can limit them to association of our chosen friends or open for them the companionship of humankind.

The chains may be of race, religion, material wealth, education, culture, or family background. In the guise of protecting ourselves from undesirable influences we may be denying ourselves the kingdom of God. To share Christ's peace, we must take our companions by the hand and enter in.

Prayer for Peace:

Help us to realize, loving God, that all that blocks a person *out*, blockades us *in*. We will remember the worth of all people. Move us toward complete unity and the sharing of Christ's peace with all people.

Spiritual Practice for the Week: Honoring the Worth of All Persons

Each day this week read Psalm 139:13–18. After each reading sit quietly and let the deep meaning of the words sink into your mind, heart, and body. Imagine God watching you grow in your mother's womb. What thoughts and feelings do you have about being "fearfully and wonderfully made" (Psalm 139:14)?

Sense the intimate knowledge God has of you and every child ever born. Ask God for an awareness of the sacred worth of each person on the planet. Weep with God over the soul-wounding forces and events that rob people of dignity and worth. How are you being invited to notice, protect, heal, and affirm the spiritual identity of all God's beloved people today? Pray for God's compassion.

Peace Covenant:

Today, God, I will be mindful of my thoughts and words. A new generation is listening and learning.

10
Saturday
November

Guilt upon Guilt

By Lu Mountenay of Independence, Missouri, USA

> *Each of you must give as you have made up your mind, not reluctantly or under compulsion, for God loves a cheerful giver.*
>
> —2 Corinthians 9:7

It's only the beginning of November and already the bell ringers are out with their collection pots. They stand outside the entrances of stores, hard to avoid. I walk quickly past, keeping my eyes focused on the door. The clanging irritates me almost as much as the guilt I feel for not giving.

I want to say, "I'm sure yours is a worthwhile cause, but I give my charity dollars to other organizations." But they don't care, so I don't try to explain. Then I feel even guiltier when they wish me a merry Christmas. (Bah. Humbug.)

I finally get into the sanctuary of the store and start filling my cart with food. What's wrong with this picture? I know one purpose of the collection pot out front is to feed the hungry. I've been walking around in the nice warm store, and the collector has been standing in icy-cold weather.

I'm going to have to roll my food cart quickly past the bell ringer again on the way out. The guilt is building.

Here's the clincher. As I dash out the door, I see a woman in a wheelchair drop money in the collection pot. She has a big smile on her face. OK, OK. I get it.

I stop, dig in my purse, and put in some money. But that's not the way ("reluctantly and under compulsion") it should be done. I spend the rest of the day searching my soul for an attitude adjustment. I thank God for divine grace.

Peace for Peace:

Creator God, may we employ our enduring principle of Grace and Generosity under *all* circumstances with *all* people. May we learn from the humble and cheerful giver.

Spiritual Practice:

Praying for peace is a daily Community of Christ spiritual practice. Bring a small- to medium-size candle to your prayer space. If possible visit the church website, print the Daily Prayer for Peace, and bring it to your space. Greet God, light the candle, and sit quietly, looking at this symbol of God's Spirit and Christ's peace. Slowly read the Daily Prayer for Peace, silently or aloud. Sit in silence again. What images and desires for peace come to your heart and mind? Speak or write your own prayer for peace. Say amen and blow out your candle.

Peace Covenant:

At all seasons, God, I will give out of the joy of my soul, and I will bless the opportunity to do so.

11
Sunday
November

Give Your All

By Steve Hatch of Lee's Summit, Missouri, USA

He sat down opposite the treasury, and watched the crowd putting money into the treasury. Many rich people put in large sums. A poor widow came and put in two small copper coins, which are worth a penny. Then he called his disciples and said to them, "Truly I tell you, this poor widow has put in more than all those who are contributing to the treasury. For all of them have contributed out of their abundance; but she out of her poverty has put in everything...

—Mark 12:41–44

I was preaching at the Tecate Congregation in Baja California, Mexico. As part of the service the congregation took time to present each of us with a small bag of gifts. In my bag was a piece of candy, a new pair of socks, and a mug.

Small tokens, but the act of giving was immense. The Tecate Congregation is made of people without wealth, and the congregation does not have excess cash.

Regardless, the members wanted to honor those present and say thank you. I experienced that day abundant generosity expressed by those who had little to give. But the story does not end there. I enjoyed the sweets, and I have worn the socks many times. But I no longer have the mug.

At a gathering of World Church leaders we were asked to bring a mug or cup to give to a colleague. Each recipient was told that when we used our new mugs we needed to think about the person who gave the mug and to say a prayer for them.

I knew immediately which mug I was going to give—the mug I received in my bag at Tecate. I wanted to share the gift I had received with someone else.

The recipient of my mug is one of our ministers in the Netherlands. I was able to share the story of my mug with him.

The gift that was given to me by a congregation in Mexico is now in the Netherlands and continues giving.

Prayer for Peace:

God of generosity, we praise you for the overflowing companionship and hospitality found among your disciples. Where vessels are *empty* and these things have *not* been known, may we be the rivers by which your living waters flow. May we make peace flow.

Spiritual Practice for the Week: Examining God's Call to Me and to All

Each day this week reflect on God's call in your life. Begin by prayerfully asking to recall particular moments when you have experienced God's presence and invitation. Write in your journal or quietly reflect on images and insights that come.

When has God seemed most real in your life? How and when has God called you to use your energies and gifts? When have you felt most deeply connected and responsive to God's movement in your life? When have you felt disconnected or resistant to God's call? How do your gifts and callings connect with the call of God you notice in your family members, friends, congregation, or community?

Peace Covenant:

Today I will be a cup, God, either to catch the tears of another or to share a refreshing drink.

12
Monday
November

Light for the Journey

By Richard Howard of Independence, Missouri, USA

O send out your light and your truth; let them lead me…

—Psalm 43:3

All of us have known moments of truth and light. We also have experienced what is neither darkness nor light, but rather something akin to thick fog—old, faded signposts.

Someone near us—mentor, friend, spouse, son, daughter, father, mother—suddenly is gone. Uncertainty follows. A cacophony of voices crowds in. Our daily planner, filled with dates, places, numbers, and commitments, nearly splits us down the middle.

The cell phone rings, and we return-dial the number on the screen. But now we must leave a message in their voice mail. We've no sooner put away the cell phone than it rings again. And so the round continues, hour after hour. On we go, perplexed, wondering, at times empty. The fog settles in, a pesky reminder of clearer light that once graced earlier footsteps.

The memory and awareness of God's light holds us steady, gives us anchor; we are not overcome in dreariness. With growing conviction we sense we shall instead *overcome* one day. We shall overcome the drabness of routine, the steady diet of the mundane, and our false security in the familiar surroundings of the ordinary. Indeed, the memory of shining light, with surprising subtlety, now dawns and becomes a steady lamp unto our feet, for yet a new hour, a new day.

So it is that we move from darkness to gray to light. From haziness to clarity. From uncertainty to truth and the peace of Christ.

Prayer for Peace:

Transforming God, keep us moving toward your light and truth. Keep us sharing the peace of Jesus Christ.

Spiritual Practice for the Week: Examining God's Call to Me and to All

Each day this week reflect on God's call in your life. Begin by prayerfully asking to recall particular moments when you have experienced God's presence and invitation. Write in your journal or quietly reflect on images and insights that come.

When has God seemed most real in your life? How and when has God called you to use your energies and gifts? When have you felt most deeply connected and responsive to God's movement in your life? When have you felt disconnected or resistant to God's call? How do your gifts and callings connect with the call of God you notice in your family members, friends, congregation, or community?

Peace Covenant:

Compass God, even though I must pass through the fog, I will keep moving toward peace.

13
Tuesday
November

Faith or Fear

By Rose Peterson of Arkansaw, Wisconsin, USA

You have put gladness in my heart more than when their grain and wine abound. I will both lie down and sleep in peace; for you alone, O Lord, make me lie down in safety.
—Psalm 4:7–8

On a beautiful fall morning I was driving to work. As I entered a curve where the rural road cut into a hillside, a beautiful spotted fawn was standing beside the guardrail. The doe must already have leaped over the guardrail and into the long grass of the steep hillside.

I could see panic and fear fill the fawn as it began to run along the guardrail, looking for safety. I prayed the fawn would stay on the edge of the road and find its way to its mother.

At that moment the fawn darted into the middle of the road. I prayed no car was approaching around the blind curve from the opposite direction. Suddenly, the fawn ran toward the guardrail, jumped over, and disappeared into the long grass.

As I contemplated what I had seen, I began to ask God questions. Is that the way I react in a stressful situation? Do I react with panic and fear and try to handle my fear without turning to God? Or do I act with faith and prayer, relying on God to give me peace and strength through life's situations?

I believe God presented this interaction with creation for an opportunity to ponder these questions and help me to consciously rely more on God's help and comfort. We each have the opportunity to pray for safety and peace.

Prayer for Peace:

Tender Shepherd, in gratitude we call on you when we are in fear. We have faith you will help us make responsible choices and find safety and peace.

Spiritual Practice for the Week: Examining God's Call to Me and to All

Each day this week reflect on God's call in your life. Begin by prayerfully asking to recall particular moments when you have experienced God's presence and invitation. Write in your journal or quietly reflect on images and insights that come.

When has God seemed most real in your life? How and when has God called you to use your energies and gifts? When have you felt most deeply connected and responsive to God's movement in your life? When have you felt disconnected or resistant to God's call? How do your gifts and callings connect with the call of God you notice in your family members, friends, congregation, or community?

Peace Covenant:

God, today I will look for your lessons in nature and pray in faith.

14
Wednesday
November

I Am Standing, Waiting

By Peggy Michael of Cantonment, Florida, USA

Thus says the Lord of hosts, the God of Israel, to all the exiles whom I have sent into exile from Jerusalem to Babylon: Build houses and live in them; plant gardens and eat what they produce... But seek the welfare of the city where I have sent you into exile, and pray to the Lord on its behalf, for in its welfare you will find your welfare... For surely I know the plans I have for you, says the Lord, plans for your welfare and not for harm, to give you a future with hope.
—Jeremiah 29:4–5, 7, 11

I am touched by humble servants who sweat and toil for low wages...ignored, shunned, and demeaned.

They, too, dream noble dreams of peace and justice and then awaken to reality: war, poverty, and injustice. These laborers give so much and gain so little. I am deeply moved by humble servants who toil and dream, stand and wait.

The neighborhoods also are waiting. Clashing and crashing as culture merges into culture. Society churns in turmoil.

People run to and fro, confused and uncertain, denied rights. None is nurtured in this fermenting mass.

Are a few brave souls willing to go into the city and take the hopeful message of peace and justice to them, one at a time? With God's help, it can be done.

Prayer for Peace:

God of Israel and all exiles, bless our gardens that they will be bountiful. From this bounty may we share nourishment and hope with those who are alienated. May we embrace them as we do our own. May we end their waiting.

Spiritual Practice for the Week: Examining God's Call to Me and to All

Each day this week reflect on God's call in your life. Begin by prayerfully asking to recall particular moments when you have experienced God's presence and invitation. Write in your journal or quietly reflect on images and insights that come.

When has God seemed most real in your life? How and when has God called you to use your energies and gifts? When have you felt most deeply connected and responsive to God's movement in your life? When have you felt disconnected or resistant to God's call? How do your gifts and callings connect with the call of God you notice in your family members, friends, congregation, or community?

Peace Covenant:

Today God, I will put together the courage and go outside my comfort zone to share the hope of Christ.

15
Thursday
November

Joseph Smith Historic Site

By Evelyn Richardson of Nauvoo, Illinois, USA

The young man said to him, "I have kept all these; what do I still lack?" Jesus said to him, "If you wish to be perfect, go, sell your possessions, and give the money to the poor, and you will have treasure in heaven; then come, follow me." ... Then Jesus said to his disciples, "Truly I tell you, it will be hard for a rich person to enter the kingdom of heaven. Again I tell you, it is easier for a camel to go through the eye of a needle than for someone who is rich to enter the kingdom of God."

—Matthew 19:20–21, 23–24

Working at the Joseph Smith Historic Site in Nauvoo, Illinois, has been quite an experience for my husband, Don, and me. We started volunteering at the site, short-term, in the spring and fall of 2009.

Along the way, it didn't seem to be enough, and God's quiet, gentle nudge said, "Sell all and follow me" to the banks of the Mississippi River.

Early in 2011, we did just that. We sold our house in Osceola, Iowa, and became full-time volunteers in Nauvoo. Don is an interpretive guide, and I work at the Red Brick Store and Visitor Center.

We meet people from all over the world. We have opportunities to share the church's story and how it has been a part of our lives. Those from other faiths share their rich experiences with us, also. I have become more aware that we are all God's children and members of one family, regardless of individual backgrounds.

There is a sweet, sweet spirit in this place, and I know it is the Spirit of God flowing over beautiful Nauvoo.

Prayer for Peace:

God of our foundation, grant us the wisdom to learn of our heritage, experience your presence, and have faith in the future. Grant us the fortitude to follow the path of the disciple and the generosity to share the peace of Christ.

Spiritual Practice for the Week: Examining God's Call to Me and to All

Each day this week reflect on God's call in your life. Begin by prayerfully asking to recall particular moments when you have experienced God's presence and invitation. Write in your journal or quietly reflect on images and insights that come.

When has God seemed most real in your life? How and when has God called you to use your energies and gifts? When have you felt most deeply connected and responsive to God's movement in your life? When have you felt disconnected or resistant to God's call? How do your gifts and callings connect with the call of God you notice in your family members, friends, congregation, or community?

Peace Covenant:

Today, God, I will let go of what keeps me from following you.

16
Friday
November

You Have a Voice

By Eileen Turner of Portland, Oregon, USA

> *If you truly would be Community of Christ, then embody and live the concerns and passion of Christ. The challenges and opportunities are momentous. Will you remain hesitant in the shadows of your fears... Or will you move forward in the light of your divinely instilled call and vision? The mission of Jesus Christ is what matters most for the journey ahead.*
>
> —Doctrine and Covenants 164:9d–f

At one time in my career I was asked to represent my employer on a Clinical Investigation Committee. I would have to review enormous amounts of reading material to prepare for the monthly meetings.

Each clinical trial, if approved by the committee, would involve patients and staff for whom I held responsibility.

In preparing, I had to ask myself if what was being proposed was morally right, ethically sound, socially fitting, and safe. Essentially the question "What mattered most?" would answer for me how I would respond when it came time to vote. The difficult and pointed questions had to be asked. Doubt had to be erased before consensus and approval could be achieved.

Many clinical trials were rejected or sent back to the investigator for revision. The life and safety of the patient, as well as the professional status of the staff involved in the study, were in our hands.

We have a voice on many levels and in many life situations. Christ was that voice for those without a voice and for those who needed redirection. Can we listen to Christ's voice and speak out when the situation calls us to do so?

Prayer for Peace:

Revealing God, when we are under stress we need to listen for your voice. May we discern that voice and hear what matters most for the journey ahead.

Spiritual Practice for the Week: Examining God's Call to Me and to All

Each day this week reflect on God's call in your life. Begin by prayerfully asking to recall particular moments when you have experienced God's presence and invitation. Write in your journal or quietly reflect on images and insights that come.

When has God seemed most real in your life? How and when has God called you to use your energies and gifts? When have you felt most deeply connected and responsive to God's movement in your life? When have you felt disconnected or resistant to God's call? How do your gifts and callings connect with the call of God you notice in your family members, friends, congregation, or community?

Peace Covenant:

When I am in fear, I will not hesitate, God. I will speak up for what matters most.

17
Saturday
November

"Thankful for" List

By Marian Hassell of Richmond, Virginia, USA

> *Thus in their prosperous circumstances they did not send away any who were naked, or that were hungry, or that were athirst, or that were sick, or that had not been nourished. And they did not set their hearts upon riches; therefore they were liberal to all, both old and young, both bond and free, both male and female, whether out of the church or in the church, having no respect to persons as to those who stood in need.*
>
> —Alma 1:45–47

Prayer and thanksgiving are interwoven throughout the scriptures of the church. If we can look past the Christmas decorations in the stores, we are entering our season of thanksgiving in the USA. Canada celebrates this day in October.

For many, the season is synonymous with a family dinner, but there is much more to it than that.

For us as Christ's disciples, the question is not whether we observe a scheduled day of thanksgiving, but are we a thankful people? Many families have careers that take them in different directions during the week but allow for weekends together. An article I read recently talked about staying involved in each other's lives by keeping daily lists of "memorable moments and random thoughts" that occur throughout the day.

Would we deepen our relationship with God if we kept a "thankful for" list of the people, things, and ideas we encounter daily and then take that list to our times of personal worship? Our efforts to become purposefully thankful could become a spiritual practice. This would help us to cherish the world around us.

Our "thankful for" list could make us more aware of the blessings God continuously bestows on us. Also, we would be more aware of the ways we could be a blessing to others.

Prayer for Peace:

Generous God, we would be generous, too. May we take hospitality to all who stand in need.

Spiritual Practice:

Honoring and keeping the Sabbath is a spiritual discipline that nourishes persons, families, and congregations. Spend several minutes meditating on your plans for the day. Discern ways you can give intentional attention to God, the sacredness of life, and creation. Slow your pace, breathe deeper, see more clearly and compassionately, create spaces of quiet and solitude. Spend time in nature. Be alert for signs of beauty and divine presence. Cook and eat your food with keen awareness of color, taste, texture, fragrance. Listen to music, look closely at the face of a loved one, laugh and talk together. Pray over these Sabbath possibilities and enter the day with reverence.

Peace Covenant:

Today, God. I will make a list of how I can be more generous. I will begin to carry out items on the list.

18
Sunday
November

Help Us Remain Faithful

By Karin Peter of Adrian, Missouri, USA

As he came out of the temple, one of his disciples said to him, "Look, Teacher, what large stones and what large buildings!" Then Jesus asked him, "Do you see these great buildings? Not one stone will be left here upon another; all will be thrown down." When he was sitting on the Mount of Olives opposite the temple, Peter, James, John, and Andrew asked him privately, "Tell us, when will this be, and what will be the sign that all these things are about to be accomplished?"

—Mark 13:1–4

As a person who likes to plan and organize, I often prepare for assignments and events well in advance. Even vacation itineraries are laden with places to see and things to do, the route researched in detail, each stop carefully planned. I know exactly where we're going and what will happen next. It provides a sense of security and, dare I say, control.

I wonder if the disciples thought they had everything under control as they left the temple in Jerusalem? They were traveling with Jesus and came to expect the unexpected. They had seen the miracles and the crowds of followers. They even had sat with Jesus as he taught. But suddenly their world view turned upside down.

"Not one stone will be left standing." What could this mean? Jesus had their full attention!

Like the disciples, I want to know exactly what to expect, but through prayer and reflection I am learning to give up control. As changes come and difficulties arise I want to keep my full attention on Jesus.

I may not know exactly what is going to happen, but I know I am engaged in Christ's mission for God's purposes, and I know it is God who is in control.

Prayer for Peace:

Master Planner for the Earth, engage us in Christ's mission. Reveal to us your peaceful purposes and guide us on the road to their fulfillment.

Spiritual Practice for the Week: Making Responsible Choices

Each day this week prayerfully seek God's guidance in your choices. Discernment invites us to orient our lives toward God and God's vision for us and for creation. Begin by reviewing the responsibilities and opportunities in the day before you. Take these choices into prayer, asking God for wisdom and insight about what matters most.

Offer yourself to God with the prayer of Teresa of Avila: "God, what do you want of me today?" Sit prayerfully with this question as you review the day again. Be aware of images, thoughts, names, or actions that come to you. Ask for blessing to live this day responsibly and compassionately in the spirit of Christ.

Peace Covenant:

Today God, I will tear down walls of division and build up connections for peace.

19
Monday
November

In the Hands of God

By Louita Clothier of Lamoni, Iowa, USA

Peace I leave with you; my peace I give to you. I do not give to you as the world gives. Do not let your hearts be troubled, and do not let them be afraid.

—John 14:27

I was alone in my little red car, driving at night down Interstate 35 during a terrible Iowa blizzard. I cannot explain why my car kept going when others were in the ditch.

I believe we all are subject to the laws of nature. I could not justify that somehow I was kept safe by the will of God any more than I would hold God responsible for sending all those poor drivers into the ditch.

Nevertheless, I could not question the unmistakable calming and protecting presence riding with me that icy night. While the wind howled and tractor-trailers skidded, there was a sense I can describe only as being "in the hands of God."

Soon after turning from the interstate onto a narrow road, I slid into the other lane and became stuck in a snowbank. As another vehicle approached in my lane, my heart didn't beat any faster. Time seemed to stand still, and in that frozen second as I waited for the crash, I remember thinking, "It's been a good life, but this is probably the end."

I became aware that being in the hands of God didn't mean I wouldn't be injured. It didn't even mean I wouldn't be killed. I am still here, but in the illumination of that extraordinary moment of grace, I faced whatever would happen with the assurance that all would be well, no matter what.

That is the kind of peace Christ promised when he said, "Peace I leave with you; my peace I give to you." The peace that Christ gives comes not in the belief that our lives will always be protected from pain and disappointment—even death. Rather, it's in the assurance that whatever life may bring, we belong to God.

Prayer for Peace:

Comforting God, your presence brings us peace—peace in the assurance of your love. May we share the peace and love of Jesus Christ with the world.

Spiritual Practice for the Week: Making Responsible Choices

Each day this week prayerfully seek God's guidance in your choices. Discernment invites us to orient our lives toward God and God's vision for us and creation. Begin by reviewing the responsibilities and opportunities in the day before you.

Take these choices into prayer, asking God for wisdom and insight about what matters most. Offer yourself to God with the prayer of Teresa of Avila: "God, what do you want of me today?" Sit prayerfully with this question as you review the day again. Be aware of images, thoughts, names, or actions that come to you. Ask for a blessing to live this day responsibly and compassionately in the spirit of Christ.

Peace Covenant:

God, I will abide in your comforting peace of mind and pursue active peace, which requires me to work for justice.

20
Tuesday
November

Encouragement

By June Russell of Independence, Missouri, USA

> *....do good; seek peace, and pursue it.... The Lord is near to the brokenhearted, and saves the crushed in spirit.*
>
> —Psalm 34:14, 18

As I aged, I started feeling discouraged and useless. Then I received a letter from an old friend, expressing appreciation. She had just read an article I had written for *Daily Bread.* My spirits lifted. It was just what I needed to start writing again, not just for *Daily Bread*, but to anyone I felt needed encouragement.

John C. Maxwell, a public speaker and author, says encouragement changes everything. It makes us strive to do better, changes lives, and renews our hope. In his book, *Encouragement Changes Everything,* Maxwell writes of God's love: "God's love *for* us gives us the reason to encourage others. God's love *in* us gives us the ability to encourage others. God's love *through* us gives us the way to encourage others."

When I feel I can't do much or I'm not needed, perhaps I can reach out to others with loving words of encouragement by realizing how much God loves and blesses me. Perhaps I can be the pen that helps God save the crushed in spirit.

Prayer for Peace:

God of encouragement, we know you are near. We know through you our spirits can be made whole. Help us encourage others who need to be lifted. Help us realize we are blessed to be a blessing. Grant us the confidence and faith to share the peace of Christ.

Spiritual Practice for the Week: Making Responsible Choices

Each day this week prayerfully seek God's guidance in your choices. Discernment invites us to orient our lives toward God and God's vision for us and creation. Begin by reviewing the responsibilities and opportunities in the day before you. Take these choices into prayer, asking God for wisdom and insight about what matters most.

Offer yourself to God with the prayer of Teresa of Avila: "God, what do you want of me today?" Sit prayerfully with this question as you review the day again. Be aware of images, thoughts, names, or actions that come to you. Ask for a blessing to live this day responsibly and compassionately in the spirit of Christ.

Peace Covenant:

Today, God, I will pick up my pen, or the phone, or walk to a neighbor's to share words of encouragement.

21
Wednesday
November

Ikebana

By Carolyn Brock of Independence, Missouri, USA

Who is wise and understanding among you? Show by your good life that your works are done with gentleness born of wisdom. ...But the wisdom from above is first pure, then peaceable, gentle, willing to yield, full of mercy and good fruits, without a trace of partiality or hypocrisy. And a harvest of righteousness is sown in peace for those who make peace.

—James 3:13, 17–18

One rather-stressful day I wearily climbed the Worshiper's Path in the Temple in Independence, Missouri. I stopped for a moment of mindful attention at the ikebana arrangement and found myself slowly drawn into a space of healing and beauty.

It was as though I never had seen flowers before—their shapes, colors, and fragrances captivated me. I reverently touched petals and leaves and was drawn to wonder at the perfection of everything from the tiniest grain of pollen to the pebbles in the flat container of clear water. I wept as the flowers offered me their gift of grace and rest.

On several occasions I have watched the creation of an ikebana arrangement during a worship experience. Under the eyes and hands of the flower artist, the singular branches, pods, and blooms are cut and placed in a pattern meant to mirror harmony among sky, humans, and Earth. A community of color, form, and balance is created.

If only creating peace and justice in God's weary world were as elegant and easy. Perhaps it would help to think of ourselves as being held in the hands of God, who trims unnecessary "stuff" from our lives and places us in right relationship with one another. We do not stand alone. When we yield our separateness, our individual efforts, to the Spirit, we can be brought together in a community that mirrors harmony and justice in the manner designed of God.

Prayer for Peace:

God of flowers, sky, and earth, balance us in your living water. May we leave room in our arrangement of life for the eye to rest and the breeze to blow. May we trim the "stuff" that hinders us from sharing Christ's peace.

Spiritual Practice for the Week: Making Responsible Choices

Each day this week prayerfully seek God's guidance in your choices. Discernment invites us to orient our lives toward God and God's vision for us and creation. Begin by reviewing the responsibilities and opportunities in the day before you. Take these choices into prayer, asking God for wisdom and insight about what matters most.

Offer yourself to God with the prayer of Teresa of Avila: "God, what do you want of me today?" Sit prayerfully with this question as you review the day again. Be aware of images, thoughts, names, or actions that come to you. Ask for a blessing to live this day responsibly and compassionately in the spirit of Christ.

Peace Covenant:

Today, God, I will pause to learn from the flowers.

22
Thursday
November

The Kingdom among Us

By Barbara Howard of Independence, Missouri, USA

> ... *"Let the little children come to me; do not stop them; for it is to such as these that the kingdom of God belongs."*
>
> —Mark 10:14

A significant time in our congregational worship occurs early in the service: a focus moment, when the children often participate. It is a way of giving the children a chance to explore the meaning of the lectionary scripture passage. Eagerness and participation go hand in hand as the children respond.

As part of her sermon in a recent Thanksgiving service, the speaker suggested that Jesus grew up with the story of *sukkah*, a three-sided dwelling in which Jews meet to celebrate their journey from Egypt to Israel, feasting for seven days. Christian pilgrims in Colonial America, grateful for the safety of their journey and the harvest, might have drawn on that tradition as they established a season of thanksgiving.

The speaker invited the children to write and draw on a picture of a sukkah something for which they were thankful.

The children wrote or drew things about their families.

The children's gift that day, as they sat and worked quietly while the speaker preached, was a powerful ministry of presence.

Attentive silence, not usually associated with the children, was in itself an act of gratitude.

For several years we were primarily an adult congregation. To have the children bring ministry is a reminder of the ever-present Spirit of the kingdom that is in our community, opening us to futures beyond imagining.

Prayer for Peace:

Ever-present Spirit, we are thankful for the children among us. We are aware they can teach us so much. They will be our leaders to peace.

Spiritual Practice for the Week: Making Responsible Choices

Each day this week prayerfully seek God's guidance in your choices. Discernment invites us to orient our lives toward God and God's vision for us and creation. Begin by reviewing the responsibilities and opportunities in the day before you. Take these choices into prayer, asking God for wisdom and insight about what matters most.

Offer yourself to God with the prayer of Teresa of Avila: "God, what do you want of me today?" Sit prayerfully with this question as you review the day again. Be aware of images, thoughts, names, or actions that come to you. Ask for a blessing to live this day responsibly and compassionately in the spirit of Christ.

Peace Covenant:

Today, God, I will hold the children in my heart and listen to what they say.

23
Friday
November

Thanks-living

By Dorene Kilburn of Stratford, Ontario, Canada

> *...and you must give thanks unto God in the spirit for whatever blessing you are blessed with; and you must practice virtue and holiness before me continually. Even so. Amen.*
> —Doctrine and Covenants 46:9b, adapted

Thanking people and being thankful to God are important but often neglected. Even when I begin a day resolving to thank and be thankful, I find, when I look back at night, that I missed opportunities.

When a beautiful solo enhances worship service, how often do we thank the soloist for the contribution to the spirit of the service?

Do we thank the person who notices we're carrying several bags of groceries and opens a door for us? Do we nod or wave a "thank you" to the driver who lets us through a long line of cars to make a left-hand turn?

That "thank you," an acknowledgement of something that brought us pleasure, convenience, or encouragement, will be appreciated and might even brighten the other person's day.

We need to be thankful to God—intentionally thankful for the incredible world that has been created for us and the many people from whom we can learn and with whom we can share.

Let us be thankful for the beauty around us, often in unlikely places. It's easy to see the beauty in a lovely garden or the lush green of rolling hills. But we sometimes miss a single flower growing through a crack in a gray stretch of sidewalk. Let us be a thanks-living community.

Prayer for Peace:

Generous God, forgive us when we complain about what we don't have and forget to thank you for our many blessings. May we always remember to be aware of and express thanks for kindnesses. May we share gratitude and peace.

Spiritual Practice for the Week: Making Responsible Choices

Each day this week prayerfully seek God's guidance in your choices. Discernment invites us to orient our lives toward God and God's vision for us and creation. Begin by reviewing the responsibilities and opportunities in the day before you. Take these choices into prayer, asking God for wisdom and insight about what matters most.

Offer yourself to God with the prayer of Teresa of Avila: "God, what do you want of me today?" Sit prayerfully with this question as you review the day again. Be aware of images, thoughts, names, or actions that come to you. Ask for a blessing to live this day responsibly and compassionately in the spirit of Christ.

Peace Covenant:

God, I will take stock of my day and express gratitude to my community.

24
Saturday
November

Frugal, yet Full of Grace

By Jan Marshall of Independence, Missouri, USA

> *A poor widow came and put in two small copper coins, which are worth a penny. Then he called his disciples and said to them, "Truly I tell you, this poor widow has put in more than all those who are contributing to the treasury. For all of them have contributed out of their abundance; but she out of her poverty has put in everything she had, all she had to live on."*
>
> —Mark12:42–44

I spent many happy days on the farm with Grandpa and Grandma. Each had a different outlook about life, and each taught me lessons through actions and words.

They lived simply and frugally. I didn't know until after their death that they were "well off." You wouldn't have known it by the way they lived. They both valued saving and spending wisely, yet approached their decisions differently.

Grandpa valued being frugal. When he finally relented and bought a television, Grandma's joy was delightful. He wore the same shirts until they were too frayed to patch. The new shirts given as gifts remained unused. He shopped the grocery ads, yet didn't see the paradox (and humor) in driving 30 miles to save a few pennies on his favorite pancake syrup!

Grounded in her faith in God, Grandma saw life full of grace and blessing even in hard times.

She didn't give a second thought to sharing with someone in need. She canned fruits and vegetables from the garden for her family's needs all winter. She shared them with others as well.

Grandpa was generous, in his own way, and not as "hard-hearted" as this story might suggest. He feared loss; she saw bountiful blessings to share.

Grandma modeled an attitude toward generosity that provided a foundation for my life. Yet I admit sometimes Grandpa's attitude comes out in me, too. May I have the courage to continue to make choices guided by Grandma's wisdom and example.

Prayer for Peace:

Generous Provider, we would return to you an abundant portion of what you have lent us. We would use our resources to pursue peace.

Spiritual Practice:

Sit or lie in a relaxed posture. Imagine sitting or lying on a warm, sandy beach with waves rolling in and out near your feet. Listen to the waves as they "exhale" and "inhale." Begin to breathe in time with the waves. Become aware of the ocean as the presence of God, washing onto the shore to touch your body and spirit. With each breath receive what the ocean of God brings you. Let go of what is carried into the sea of God's presence. Give thanks.

Peace Covenant:

God, I will give, without thought to what I lose, but to the blessing and satisfaction of my soul.

25
Sunday
November

Testify to the Truth

By Barbara Borkowski of Lee's Summit, Missouri, USA

> *Pilate asked him, "So you are a king?" Jesus answered, "You say that I am a king. For this I was born, and for this I came into the world, to testify to the truth. Everyone who belongs to the truth listens to my voice."*
>
> —John 18:37

"Do you swear to tell the whole truth and nothing but the truth?" We hear that phrase on courtroom TV shows. What does it mean to tell the "whole truth"? Truth is subjective these days. My truth can be different from yours. And yet, Jesus brings to us a truth we can trust.

A few years ago at a family camp I talked with a woman who was struggling in her faith. She wondered who to trust, who to follow. She was influenced by a friend at home to think about her life and faith in a different way. She was afraid and anxious about her future and her relationships.

As we talked, we shared how important challenges to our faith can be. As we prayed we experienced the impress of the Holy Spirit. The Holy Spirit brings us truth in ways that go beyond words and language.

Experiencing the Holy Spirit is an important way to recognize "truth" in our lives. And yet, we need to take the next step as disciples who choose to listen and follow. Understanding Jesus as truth in our lives is meaningless unless we consciously choose to make changes in our lives that allow the Spirit to grow and flourish.

This is true: Following Jesus can bring freedom from anxiety and concerns that otherwise would overwhelm us.

Prayer for Peace:

God of truth, we listen for your voice. We want to be aware of your desires for us. We want to know the truth of what you would have us do.

Spiritual Practice for the Week: Embodying God's Shalom

Each day this week find a way to express and embody God's shalom. Begin by prayerfully listening to your longing for peace. Become silent and imagine you can hear the groaning of the Earth's peoples, nations, and creatures. Prayerfully open yourself to God's yearning for peace and the divine vision of shalom.

What images, feelings, and words come to you? What prayer for peace comes to you from your time of listening? Speak or write this prayer. What small act of justice, kindness, healing, or peacemaking is God inviting you to consider this day, this week?

Peace Covenant:

Today, God, I will be aware of your continuing revelation for my personal calling.

26
Monday
November

Christ at the Center of Christmas

By Lu Mountenay of Independence, Missouri, USA

And the peace of God, which surpasses all understanding, will guard your hearts and your minds in Christ Jesus.

—Philippians 4:7

This coming Sunday will mark the beginning of Advent. We will start preparing for and counting the days until the birth of Jesus. Or... we will start counting the days until the arrival of Santa Claus. But doesn't that compete with putting Christ at the center of Christmas?

Maybe we don't really need Santa Claus in our Christmas. First of all, promoting Santa implies to our children he is real—though he is not. Is it acceptable to lie, *sometimes?* Wouldn't our children wonder what else we lie to them about?

Secondly, supporting the Santa Claus fable gives children a shallow motive for being "good," rather than the right reason. We inadvertently might be teaching them to be good just for the rewards. And what about children in poverty who believe in Santa and are disappointed because they get few or even no gifts? Do they then believe they are "bad?"

After a few "Santa" Christmases, children begin to *expect* gifts—they may even think they have a *right* to them. Materialism is fostered. Materialism and generosity run counter to each other—we can't do both. We ask our children what they *want* for Christmas, but do we consider the *needs* of children around the world, or in our own cities and towns?

People might argue that taking Santa out of Christmas takes away the fun, the magic, and the mystery. I would answer: What about the kings riding camels? What about the bright star over the manger? What about the choirs of angels? What about the families coming home to be together? What about the children's pageants at church and the singing of carols? And what about the child in the manger, God's gift to all children? The story of Jesus' birth is filled with fun, magic, and mystery.

Let's put Jesus Christ at the center of Christmas, and not clutter Christmas with shallow distractions.

Prayer for Peace:

Divine Parent, help us prepare to celebrate Christ's birth with an eye single to your glory.

Spiritual Practice for the Week: Embodying God's Shalom

Express and embody God's shalom. Imagine you can hear the groaning of the Earth's peoples, nations, and creatures. What images come to you? What small act of justice, kindness, healing, or peacemaking is God inviting you to consider this day, this week?

Peace Covenant:

Instead of counting shopping days, God, I will count Advent days, and prepare for the Christ child.

27
Tuesday
November

Sacrament of Healing

By Carolyn Brock of Independence, Missouri, USA

> *"By the tender mercy of our God, the dawn from on high will break upon us, to give light to those who sit in darkness and in the shadow of death, to guide our feet into the way of peace."*
> —Luke 1:78–79

It started as a family conflict. The young woman exchanged words with her father. There was a hurried dash across the compound as he called a curse upon her, followed by her fall, resulting in a fractured ankle.

Months later the ankle had not healed well, even after treatment in the small hospital in northeast Kenya.

The girl asked for prayer, so we walked across the dry riverbed in the cool twilight. The story was told. The separation between father and daughter had not healed, and the girl no longer could walk. Anemic, she had given up eating and hope.

Under the deepening blues of the evening sky, Elkana and Dave knelt on a palm mat under the acacia tree where she had been placed. Consecrated oil was placed on her head. Prayers were offered in English and Swahili.

A sacred hush fell on the gathering of family and friends as the Creator named holy the girl, air, land, and life in that place.

She walked again and began eating. Restored to wholeness within her family, she remained joyful even when her leg later had to be amputated.

The lifting of the "curse" ended the conflict and brought a measure of healing.

Skillful conflict mediation might have changed the outcome of this story.

Dialogue might have prevented the broken bone.

We have much to learn about talking with each other, listening to each other. We are learning but not yet there. Our words may not carry power to curse, but they do wound and bring division.

When wounding occurs we still have avenues of healing and reconciliation. God's grace comes to us through the sacraments, through anointing and prayer, through our touch and healing presence.

These are the skills and gifts we are given as ministers of reconciliation.

Prayer for Peace:

Companion God, help us to know all the ways we can share your light with those who sit in darkness. May we share with them the prayers, our presence, and Christ's peace.

Spiritual Practice for the Week: Embodying God's Shalom

Each day this week find a way to express and embody Christ's peace. Begin by prayerfully listening to your longing for peace. Prayerfully open to God's yearning for peace and the divine vision of shalom. What small act of justice, kindness, healing, or peacemaking is God inviting you to consider this day?

Peace Covenant:

Today, God, I will be present for someone in need.

28
Wednesday
November

Reflections from the Refrigerator

By Deb Crowley of Eaton Rapids, Michigan, USA

Listen to the teachings (of your sacred journey) and discover anew its principles. Do not yearn for times that are past, but recognize that you have been given a foundation of faithful service, even as you build a foundation for what is yet to be.

—Doctrine and Covenants 162:2b, adapted

At first glance, one would judge my refrigerator door as unappealing, messy, or filled with *junk*.

As I stare at it, I ponder what I should take down. The picture of grandkids sledding in the snow, framed with jewels by a special kindergartener? The first handwritten, decorated letter with phonetically spelled words by the same child? Perhaps the photo of the Crowley clan and my niece's engagement photo should find their way into an album. Maybe Dustin's framed first-grade photo, which had been a gift to my mom and returned to me when she passed. A double memory.

If not the photos, then surely some magnets could go. But the teapot reminds me of the women I grew close to at a women's retreat. The Temple represents peace and the purpose for so much of my life efforts. The Haiti magnet from Outreach International speaks of human need and urges me to give generously.

So many memories clutter that door! Maybe a few nondescript magnets will disappear, but the majority of memories are staying for now.

Life gets cluttered and chaotic sometimes. *Junk* skews our vision. It interferes with our relationship with one another and God. It's time to step back, examine the pieces and parts of our life that are worth hanging on to and remembering why they are important.

Then, discard, change, or banish the rest! Once set in order, there will be room for experiences yet to be. A refreshed heart...it doesn't get any better than that!

Prayer for Peace:

Companion on our journey, we cherish and honor our memories. Help us find what matters most and let go of the rest. We look ahead to sharing peace yet to be.

Spiritual Practice for the Week: Embodying God's Shalom

Each day this week find a way to express and embody God's shalom. Begin by prayerfully listening to your longing for peace. Become silent and imagine you can hear the groaning of the Earth's peoples, nations, and creatures. Prayerfully open yourself to God's yearning for peace and the divine vision of shalom.

What images, feelings, and words come to you? What prayer for peace comes to you from your time of listening? Speak or write this prayer. What small act of justice, kindness, healing, or peacemaking is God inviting you to consider this day, this week?

Peace Covenant:

Today, God, I will set my life in order and make room for peace.

29
Thursday
November

Remembering with a Purpose

By Ward Serig of Pensacola, Florida, USA

And the peace of God, which surpasses all understanding, will guard your hearts and your minds in Christ Jesus.

—Philippians 4:7

One rich blessing God has granted us is memory. Remembering where we've been is an important part of our lives. We use many things as symbols to help us remember.

One way I remember is through my collection of cups. On a trip to Canada I bought a souvenir cup from the *Chi-cheemaun*, a native term meaning "big canoe." The Chi-cheemaun is the largest ferry boat on the Great Lakes.

The cup not only reminds me of the day my wife and I traveled to Manatoulin Island, it helps me remember the friends we traveled with. We visited those friends, high school classmates I hadn't seen in years. I remember where and what we ate, beautiful sunsets, morning walks along Lake Huron, and other people, places, and events we enjoyed during our vacation.

I have cups from places I have worked, traveled, and attended school. I have a reminder from the blood bank in recognition of being a donor. I have grandchildren who remind me that I am "the world's greatest grandfather."

We remember who we were and where we have come from so we will appreciate who we have become. Then we take our memories and set them on the shelf, where we easily can find them, and place the future in the front of us. It is a future of hope, promise, and peace. These will be our future memories.

Prayer for Peace:

God of wisdom, we place our hopes in you. We have faith in a future of peace.

Spiritual Practice for the Week: Embodying God's Shalom

Each day this week find a way to express and embody God's shalom. Begin by prayerfully listening to your longing for peace. Become silent and imagine you can hear the groaning of the Earth's peoples, nations, and creatures. Prayerfully open yourself to God's yearning for peace and the divine vision of shalom.

What images, feelings, and words come to you? What prayer for peace comes to you from your time of listening? Speak or write this prayer. What small act of justice, kindness, healing, or peacemaking is God inviting you to consider this day, this week?

Peace Covenant:

Today, God, as I keep memories in their cherished place, I will look to the future, where I can act in sharing Christ's peace.

30
Friday
November

Silver Linings

By Gena McDonald of Fayetteville, Tennessee, USA

> *For you shall go out in joy, and be led back in peace; the mountains and the hills before you shall burst into song, and all the trees of the field shall clap their hands.*
>
> —Isaiah 55:12

One day in 2011, we planned a small get-together with friends we had not seen or talked with in more than 10 years. They live in the Huntsville, Alabama, area. We were to meet for a few hours just to catch up.

That was the week tornadoes blasted Alabama. We were not able to get in touch with our friends until Saturday morning. They had been without electricity almost 72 hours.

The family has an autistic, 15-year-old son named Sam. Shortly after the family arrived at our home, beautiful Christian music was coming from our piano. I went into the family room, where Sam was playing with depth and grace.

He was so *into it* that chills went through me. I invited them to go to our small congregation.

The next morning our family went to church. Our friends were not there. During Sunday school our pastor mentioned we did not have anyone to play that day. During the final words of a heartfelt testimony, beautiful music came from the sanctuary. We assumed someone was playing a CD.

When we walked into the sanctuary, there was Sam, sitting at the piano, playing his heart out. Our pastor asked Sam's father if Sam would like to lead our congregation in music that morning. The congregation was overwhelmed. All the way home, I kept praising God for turning chaos into two wonderful experiences.

Do we believe God allowed the severe weather to take place just to bring us this experience? No. However, I believe in my heart it provided God an opportunity to demonstrate love for us.

Yes, bad things happen. But if we look for silver linings in God's world, then we can move forward and make the best of any situation.

Prayer for Peace:

Creator God, create in us hearts of music and joy. When we are in darkness, let us look for your light. When we are in in chaos, bring us your peace.

Spiritual Practice for the Week: Embodying God's Shalom

Each day this week find a way to express and embody God's shalom. Begin by prayerfully listening to your longing for peace. Become silent and imagine you can hear the groaning of the Earth's peoples, nations, and creatures. Prayerfully open yourself to God's yearning for peace and the divine vision of shalom.

What images, feelings, and words come to you? What prayer for peace comes to you from your time of listening? Speak or write this prayer. What small act of justice, kindness, healing, or peacemaking is God inviting you to consider this day, this week?

Peace Covenant:

Today, God, I will burst into song, even amid chaos.

1

Saturday

December

Let the Preparation Begin

By Lu Mounteray of Independence, Missouri, USA

> *You have already been told to look to the sacraments to enrich the spiritual life of the body. It is not the form of the sacrament that dispenses grace but it is the divine presence that gives life.*
> —Doctrine and Covenants 162:2d

Kneel, if you're able, toward the stable
heal, if you're able, at the table
see the quiver of the infant's lip
tiny fingers as they grip.
New eyes, so wise
they see past my face

see my need for grace
they reach into my heart
with healing art.
My Communion at the table
takes me back to the stable.
Who can separate the two?

Tomorrow we celebrate the sacrament of the Lord's Supper. How will Communion during Advent season be different from other Communion worships?

Throughout the year we prepare ourselves for the Lord's Supper with repentant hearts and through acceptance of God's grace. We try to reconcile any differences and conflicts in our souls.

We forgive ourselves and others, as Christ forgives us.

During the Advent season, how can we consider Christ's Earthly death on our behalf, as symbolized by the bread and wine, and at the same time think of him as a tiny, newborn life?

Cross and cradle, death and life, grief and gift, authority and innocence, loneliness and love, dark night of the soul and light of the manger star, tears and living water—what is our bridge?

Emmanuel!

Prayer for Peace:

Everlasting Giver of our cradle of love and Crafter of the grace-filled cross, hear our prayer. You are a light that hurts our eyes with exquisite pain. We behold the beauty and then are lost when it is hidden. Let us always seek, follow the light, bear the pain, and yet know the joy on the path to peace.

Spiritual Practice:

Spend a few moments remembering your experiences with the sacraments. Recall the details of the words, touch, prayers, rituals, symbols involved. How have these experiences brought healing and blessing to you and others? Offer a prayer of gratitude for the reconciling power of sacraments in Community of Christ and the worldwide Christian family.

Peace Covenant:

Today, God, I will hold the cradle and the cross in my heart as I prepare to kneel at your table tomorrow.

2
Sunday
December

God's Promise Will Be Fulfilled

By Kris Judd of Kansas City, Missouri, USA

The days are surely coming, says the Lord, when I will fulfill the promise I made to the house of Israel and the house of Judah. In those days and at that time I will cause a righteous Branch to spring up for David; and he shall execute justice and righteousness in the land.
—Jeremiah 33:14–15

Children long remember promises made to them. Our granddaughters remember promises. They eagerly await chocolate-chip pancakes for breakfast during sleepovers and feeding the birds in the backyard. They remember and believe in us to fulfill our promises because they know we love them, and they trust us.

When I was 5 years old, my parents promised to take me to Disneyland. Because I knew they loved me, I trusted them to take me there. I promptly found brown, paper grocery sacks and packed my toys. I placed the sacks on our back porch. These were important to take with me on the trip. Then I waited. When my parents found me with my toy-laden sacks, they asked what I was doing. I told them I packed and was ready to go to Disneyland.

Fifteen years later they took me, my sister, and two brothers to Disney World. I left my toys behind. They kept their promise, but the timing was theirs, not mine.

Our loving God has made promises to each of us, as well, because we are beloved children of God. The promises are fulfilled according to God's timing, not ours. Because we love God, we trust in the right way and at the right time the promises will be kept. God promises to love us always, to be with us constantly, and to hear our every prayer.

But often God's promises are fulfilled in ways least expected. We need to be open to all the surprising ways God enters our lives and calls us to be disciples of the One whose birth we anticipate this Advent season.

Prayer for Peace:

Loving God, we are thankful for your faithfulness. We thank you for your comforting words, which help us look to the future with joy. May we be at peace, trusting in your promises, trusting in *your* time.

Spiritual Practice for the Week: Welcoming Unity in Diversity

Meditate on unity in diversity. Prayerfully read Doctrine and Covenants 163:8c, which calls "the entire church to become a sanctuary of Christ's peace, where people from all nations, ethnicities, and life circumstances can be gathered into a spiritual home without dividing walls."

Create a large circle with your arms. See and feel the diverse people God invites inside the sanctuary represented by this circle. Who is easiest to welcome? Whom do you struggle to include? Confess the dividing walls between you and people too different or "dangerous" to invite into your spiritual home. Ask God to forgive and heal barriers that keep you and others from being one in Christ's peace.

Peace Covenant:

I will wait faithfully, God, for the fulfillment of your promise will surely be.

3
Monday
December

The Emmanuel Moment

By David Brock, presiding evangelist

"Blessed are the peacemakers, for they will be called children of God."

—Matthew 5:9

On January 20, 1986, in Nairobi, Kenya, I held Carolyn's and my newborn daughter, Emily, for the first time. I could not stop staring in wonder and amazement at this miracle from God. This flesh-and-blood incarnation of the "image of God" right there in my own arms—flesh of our flesh, bone of our bones.

Nurses reminded me of visiting hours, but I found ways to loiter in the lobby, then (with stealth and skill!) sneak back in during off-hours so I could have more Emily time!

I realized this human creature, who is ours and yet not ours, is the pinnacle of what defines "sacred" and "holy" for me. Possibly above all else, her life helps me understand the principles of God's love, the Worth of All Persons, and the Sacredness of Creation.

Her birth was the "meridian of time" moment that points me to the Christ event, the Emmanuel moment; the God with us, "pitching tent among us" event that is the lens through which I look to understand the nature of God and reality.

Or maybe, just maybe, it is the other way around.

Maybe I recognize Emily as sacred because of the story of another child born in the meridian of time in a cow's stall. Maybe it is because I understand God as one who is so committed to life, so in love with creation, such a believer in the "least of these" people and cultures, that I know how immeasurably worthy my daughter is...and *all* daughters and sons of the Earth.

Maybe I could look at her on the day of her birth and know as I'd never known before, the value of life, the need to make the world a place worthy of its children, because God became vulnerable and dwelt with us in Jesus. Maybe I understood how holy her birth was because of the holy night when Christ was born in that lowly manger...born to raise each child of Earth.

Prayer for Peace:

Mother and Father of each child on Earth, we see the sacredness of each one just as we see the sacredness of Christ. As much as we love our own, may we love all others. We pray all children may know the peace of Christ.

Spiritual Practice for the Week: Welcoming Unity in Diversity

Prayerfully read Doctrine and Covenants 163:8c, which calls "the entire church to become a sanctuary of Christ's peace, where people from all nations, ethnicities, and life circumstances can be gathered into a spiritual home without dividing walls." Create a large circle with your arms. See and feel the diverse people God invites inside the sanctuary of Christ's peace. Who is easiest to welcome? Whom do you struggle to include? Ask God to forgive and heal barriers.

Peace Covenant:

Today, God, I will be a peacemaker and thus be called a child of God.

4
Tuesday
December

Worship the Newborn Christ—All over the World

By Wendy Bacon of Brooktondale, New York, USA

For a child has been born for us, a son given to us; authority rests upon his shoulders; and he is named Wonderful Counselor, Mighty God, Everlasting Father, Prince of Peace.
—Isaiah 9:6

Now that I'm working on the next Christmas program for our little congregation, I'm remembering to send a "thank you" for the presentation made available on Community of Christ's website, "Nativity Pilgrimage."

Coincidentally, a member of our congregation collects crèches from all over the world. She assembled several on a table at the front of the sanctuary. I downloaded the video presentation. For our Christmas program each child in the congregation read the text on one picture while walking toward the front, dressed in the costume of another culture. The children placed the baby Jesus figurines with the matching crèche.

A few girls dressed to represent the "rich" visitors. Some boys were delighted to explain to their parents that they were to dress as homeless people—to be the "poor." The older kids enjoyed getting to say words like "inukshuk" and "asifiwe," from the international part of the video script.

One boy had been taking percussion lessons. At the photo in the video with the line "listen to the drums" he burst into a percussion solo that had jaws dropping all over the sanctuary.

When our tiniest child toddled to the front with a soft, baby Jesus doll and said, "Go ahead...play with it! You won't break it," tears rolled down faces.

At the end we sang joyous Christmas carols. Thank you so much for providing such a beautiful resource (*www.CofChrist.org/worship/a-z Worship.asp*). It inspired us to do something wonderful. I don't think we'll ever top it.

Prayer for Peace:

Holy Friend to every stranger—help us send the message of the newborn Prince of Peace the world around.

Spiritual Practice for the Week: Welcoming Unity in Diversity

Prayerfully read Doctrine and Covenants 163:8c, which calls "the entire church to become a sanctuary of Christ's peace, where people from all nations, ethnicities, and life circumstances can be gathered into a spiritual home without dividing walls." Create a large circle with your arms. See and feel the diverse people God invites inside the sanctuary of Christ's peace. Who is easiest to welcome? Whom do you struggle to include? Ask God to forgive and heal barriers.

Peace Covenant:

Today, holy Friend, I will continue to prepare for the coming of your Son.

5
Wednesday
December

Rejoice in the Coming of the Lord

By Craig Harper of Gilbert, Arizona, USA

> *Rejoice in the Lord, O you righteous. Praise befits the upright. Praise the Lord with the lyre; make melody to him with the harp of ten strings. Sing to him a new song; play skillfully on the strings, with loud shouts. For the word of the Lord is upright, and all his work is done in faithfulness. He loves righteousness and justice; the earth is full of the steadfast love of the Lord.*
>
> —Psalm 33:1–5

I remember one cold winter night I shared the organ bench with my mom. She was playing Christmas carols. Because I was old enough to read music, I was her page turner. She really didn't need the help, but she made me feel like I was needed. It was just for fun, for the season, and practicing for church.

The view outside, from the organ bench, included wind-driven snow and other images of harsh cold, but I was warmed by beautiful music, preparing for birth of Jesus. I was happy. Today, that memory fills me with love and powerful nostalgia.

My mom gave me music, and it continues in our home today. Often, Shari and I will hear the clarinet, the trumpet, or the guitar in a distant room. That would be Rachel and Austin now warming our home.

The gift of music is being passed on. I am thankful for music lessons my grandfather and grandmother gave my mom and for music lessons that have blessed each generation. Music in my house and music in God's house are great gifts to me. May they bless your life as well, whether you are the musician or the listening worshiper.

Prayer for Peace:

Great Musician, direct our humble songs, our modest melodies, our meek harmonies. Transform our lives to living instruments of praise and peace.

Spiritual Practice for the Week: Welcoming Unity in Diversity

Each day this week meditate on unity in diversity. Prayerfully read Doctrine and Covenants 163:8c, which calls "the entire church to become a sanctuary of Christ's peace, where people from all nations, ethnicities, and life circumstances can be gathered into a spiritual home without dividing walls."

Create a large circle with your arms. See and feel the diverse people God invites inside the sanctuary of Christ's peace represented by this circle. Who is easiest to welcome? Whom do you struggle to include? Confess the dividing walls between you and people too different or "dangerous" to invite into your spiritual home. Ask God to forgive and heal barriers that keep you and others from being one in Christ's peace.

Peace Covenant:

Today, God, I will sing, play, or listen to music that inspires me to prepare for the coming of the Lord.

6
Thursday
December

Hallelujah! I'm Singing!

By Elizabeth Else of St. Thomas, Ontario, Canada

> *How blessed are they! For they published peace; they published good tidings of good; and they declared to the people that the Lord reigns.*
>
> —Mosiah 11:207

Christmas is a time of whirlwind activities, tradition, and music. Unfortunately, the whirlwind often overshadows the joy of experiencing Advent, preparing the way for the newborn Christ. In the hustle and bustle we hear the familiar carols, but our minds may not be in tune with them.

For the last few years, I have celebrated Christmas in Australia. Northern snow and turkey have given way to beaches and picnics. One tradition I follow on Australian television is "Carols by Candlelight." One year I had the privilege of attending the live concert.

It was a perfect evening surrounded by dear friends. Thousands of people gathered in an outdoor stadium. A full moon shone with the Southern Cross in a sky filled with stars. The air was warm, and the mood festive. Hundreds of performers sang on stage, with the audience joining from time to time. I've always loved music and singing in the rafters of the soprano range. Since chemotherapy, my voice has changed considerably, but I sing anyway.

Then came the finale, Handel's "Hallelujah Chorus." Traditionally everyone stands with their candles and sings together. How I wanted to praise God with my voice again. "Hallelujah! Hallelujah!" The music seemed to soar to heaven and beyond—it was as if the whole world were singing to the Creator for the gift of Christ.

I felt lifted and sang once again in a way I had not for a long time. Then I realized I was part of a small miracle. The small miracle was happening to me personally; the larger one was the community experience, witnessing for a brief moment several thousand people singing, "Hallelujah."

May we join as a community to witness the miracle of Christmas. Hallelujah!

Prayer for Peace:

Generous God, we praise you with joy in our voices. Hallelujah! We praise you with the light of hope in our eyes. Hallelujah! We praise you with love in our hearts. Hallelujah! We praise you with the peace of Christ to share. Amen.

Spiritual Practice for the Week: Welcoming Unity in Diversity

Prayerfully read Doctrine and Covenants 163:8c. Create a large circle with your arms. See and feel the diverse people God invites inside the sanctuary of Christ's peace. Who is easiest to welcome? Whom do you struggle to include? Ask God to forgive and heal barriers that keep you and others from being one in Christ's peace.

Peace Covenant:

Today, God, I will sing a new song!

7
Friday
December

Jesus and Spirit

By Carolyn Brock of Independence, Missouri, USA

> *All this is from God, who reconciled us to himself through Christ, and has given us the ministry of reconciliation; that is, in Christ God was reconciling the world to himself…and entrusting the message of reconciliation to us.*
>
> —2 Corinthians 5:18–19

Jesus knew who he was. His experiences with God's Spirit gave him an unmistakable identity as the Beloved One. The name "beloved" accompanied the deep peace of Spirit resting on his body.

We cannot know what this experience meant for Jesus, but it was the transforming event resulting from his profound "yes" to God's call in the waters of baptism. Immersed, anointed, called by a new name, Jesus knew he was empowered to share living water, proclaim good news, perform acts of healing and justice.

We, too, can know our name by an anointing of the Spirit.

Our deep peace is found as God's beloved ones. It is from our experiences with God's Spirit that we take on a new identity.

God promises rivers of living water flowing from our hearts as a result of the Spirit's life in us.

What then becomes our profound "yes" to these gifts? What shall be our response to the Spirit's renaming, empowering presence as it invites us to live in new ways?

Prayer for Peace:

Reconciling God, we praise you for the gift of your Son. We praise you for your living water and new life. May we always be aware of the presence of the Spirit. May that awareness inspire us to share the living water and the peace of Christ.

Spiritual Practice for the Week: Welcoming Unity in Diversity

Each day this week meditate on unity in diversity. Prayerfully read Doctrine and Covenants 163:8c, which calls "the entire church to become a sanctuary of Christ's peace, where people from all nations, ethnicities, and life circumstances can be gathered into a spiritual home without dividing walls."

Create a large circle with your arms. See and feel the diverse people God invites inside the sanctuary of Christ's peace represented by this circle. Who is easiest to welcome? Whom do you struggle to include? Confess the dividing walls between you and people too different or "dangerous" to invite into your spiritual home. Ask God to forgive and heal barriers that keep you and others from being one in Christ's peace.

Peace Covenant:

Today, God, I will engage the ministry of reconciliation to heal relationships.

8
Saturday
December

Gratitude: One Key to Graceful Aging

By Richard Howard of Independence, Missouri, USA

> *You received without payment; give without payment.*
>
> —Matthew 10:8

A friend sent me a vertical string of five photos, each showing three dogs sitting together.

In the first, two tiny wolfhound puppies lean against a large cocker spaniel in the middle. Each successive picture shows the pups growing into large, powerful dogs, finally towering over the aging spaniel.

I have captioned this photo group, "Aging Gracefully." These images are graphic reminders of how, when we are vibrant and young and in prominence among our peers, we stand tall. We welcome newcomers into our congregational life, our work, and play.

The months fade into years. Gradually the new leaders find their pace, lending new strength to each mission focus.

They grow taller, stronger, and more responsible. The original spiritual mentors gradually settle into comfortable scenes. They make less noise, offer fewer suggestions, take more naps, and eat slower. They defer to their faith in God and emerging powers of the young.

A temporary sense of loss, bordering on resentment, invades the consciousness of those who just a few years ago had wielded power with poise and had been spiritual leaders.

But then something almost magical happens. As the "old dogs" recede from prominence into the quiet of gratitude, life takes on a splendid hue. There is more time to remember, reflect, breathe deeper, slowly soak up the sunshine, and find comfort in the strengths learned from their spiritual mentors of earlier years.

On the wings of one of those deep breaths comes a voice of encouragement and gratitude: "Life is good. We're surrounded by those whose vision goes beyond our own—surpassing what we thought we knew, growing closer to God and enabling us to give more than we receive. Hallelujah!"

Prayer for Peace:

God of the wise, God of the innocent, we take our turns in life gracefully. May we know when to lead, when to follow, when to give and receive, when to bless and be blessed.

Spiritual Practice:

Ask for God's healing and guidance as you enter this time of prayerful presence. Imagine you are floating in a beautiful sea of light. The golden light of this sea buoys you, so you float effortlessly. Waves of light carry and wash over you, bringing wholeness and peace. Rest in the sea of God's love.

Peace Covenant:

God, I will try to be a gracious mentor, and in turn, be gracious to my mentor.

9
Sunday
December

All Shall See God's Salvation

By Kris Judd of Kansas City, Missouri, USA

In the fifteenth year of the reign of Emperor Tiberius…the word of God came to John son of Zechariah in the wilderness. He went into all the region around the Jordan, proclaiming a baptism of repentance for the forgiveness of sins, as it is written in the book of the words of the prophet Isaiah, "The voice of one crying out in the wilderness: 'Prepare the way of the Lord, make his paths straight. Every valley shall be filled, and every mountain and hill shall be made low, and the crooked shall be made straight, and the rough ways made smooth; and all flesh shall see the salvation of God.'"

—Luke 3:1–6

During late 2010, many people became involved in or captured by the movement of random acts of culture taking place around the USA. This movement started as a flash mob in a Pennsylvania shopping mall at the end of October, with 650 people singing the Hallelujah Chorus from Handel's *Messiah*.

Later, the same chorus appeared in my city. While not all who were there were Christians, it was apparent the experience moved many. A reporter commented that at the end of the piece, he saw one woman cover her eyes and weep.

After attending a decade or more of *Messiah* performances at the Community of Christ Auditorium in Independence, Missouri, I had a powerful experience myself during the "Hallelujah Chorus." As we stood, I looked behind me and saw more than 3,500 people standing and singing, "And He shall reign forever and ever." I became aware of the scripture that "one day every knee will bow and every tongue confess" God.

My experience may not have been the experience of the other listeners. The experience of God's salvation can come to each of us in different ways, yet the source of salvation remains the same. I do believe that one day everyone will experience God's salvation. I dare not predict the manner in which it will take place, or the timing in another's life. I only trust the words of the prophet Isaiah and the Gospel writers.

They understood the power of Christ's love can transform anyone and everyone.

Prayer for Peace:

Transforming God, we kneel and confess our separation from you. Surprise us with random acts of diverse culture that unify us for peace.

Spiritual Practice for the Week: Offering Blessings of Community

Receive and share blessings of community. Begin with a prayer for your network of relationships. See and feel connections with family, spiritual friends, congregation, community, and God's creatures. What blessings flow to you? Go deeper each day as you embrace the call to bless and be blessed.

Peace Covenant:

In my life, God, I will prepare the way of the Lord. I will open my eyes to see your salvation.

10
Monday
December

...in Whose Name You Pray

By Donna Boyd of Independence, Missouri, USA

Hear, O my people of the church, I am Jesus Christ of whom you have sung and testified and in whose name you pray. I am the spirit of love and peace which is in the world and yet not known by the world.

—Doctrine and Covenants 157:11

Jesus prayed and taught his disciples to pray. Prayer is a hub of Christian life and growth. I would like you to journey with me through the maturing of our prayers. Remember the first prayers you heard, the first prayers you were taught. Who were some of those who made this investment in your spiritual formation?

You may recall some specific occasions when prayers were offered outside church gatherings. You may have some strong preferences about when and where to pray, whether alone or in public, whether a formal prayer or words that flow spontaneously from your heart.

How have our prayers changed from early childhood? Remember how in some prayers we followed the leader as we repeated phrases after our parents. Do you remember some "gimme" prayers that may have confused God with Santa? Do you remember bargaining with God as we promised everything—*if* our pet lived, we passed the test, we got the job, or we received a needed healing?

There were inspiring prayers that lifted us to fuller awareness of God's presence. There were lengthy prayers that seemed repetitive. There were tearful prayers as people poured out their hearts to God. We prayed, at times, without confidence, fearful of not having the right words. We may have stood silently with a friend or loved one overcome with grief when the prayer of presence was all we had to offer.

We grow and learn in our prayer lives. Prayers are conversations with the Divine. Have we learned to wait for God's response?

Prayer for Peace:

In Christ's name we pray. Amen.

Spiritual Practice for the Week: Offering Blessings of Community

Each day this week receive and share blessings of community. Begin with a prayer of gratitude for the network of relationships in your life. See and feel connections with family members, spiritual friends, people in your congregation and community, people and creatures in God's sacred web of life.

What blessings flow to you from these circles? Reflect, pray, and write in your journal about the call to be "Community of Christ." Go deeper each day as you "discern and embrace" the "divine blessing" of this name that opens you to "become a blessing to the whole creation" (Doctrine and Covenants 163:1). What act of blessing are you invited to complete?

Peace Covenant:

Today, God, I will listen for your response.

11
Tuesday
December

At the Mall, at the Stable

By Norma Cross of Independence, Missouri, USA

Agree with God, and be at peace; in this way good will come to you.

—Job 22:21

The shops in the mall
shine soft, fluorescent lights
call and pull you in.

The books, the balls, the beads, the baubles
draw in the hands that reach and touch…
and covet and buy.

But God offers blessings so quietly
in a barn, in a stall, in a manger,
in the arms of a young woman.

What God's gift brings is more precious
than gold, silver, beads, and balls.
Small babe, God's son, eternal life

Prayer for Peace:

Giving God, may we realize the gift of your Son is more precious than silver or gold. May we share the love of Christ with others. May we share the peace of Christ.

Spiritual Practice for the Week: Offering Blessings of Community

Each day this week receive and share blessings of community. Begin with a prayer of gratitude for the network of relationships in your life. See and feel connections with family members, spiritual friends, people in your congregation and community, people and creatures in God's sacred web of life.

What blessings flow to you from these circles? Reflect, pray, and write in your journal about the call to be "Community of Christ." Go deeper each day as you "discern and embrace" the "divine blessing" of this name that opens you to "become a blessing to the whole creation" (Doctrine and Covenants 163:1). What act of blessing are you invited to complete?

Peace Covenant:

Today, God, I will reconsider the gifts of Christmas. I will place Christ at the center.

12 Wednesday December

God's Patchwork Quilt

By Dorene Kilburn of Stratford, Ontario, Canada

For just as the body is one and has many members, and all the members of the body, though many, are one body, so it is with Christ. For in the one Spirit we were all baptized into one body—Jews or Greeks, slaves or free—and we were all made to drink of one Spirit. Indeed, the body does not consist of one member but of many.

—1 Corinthians 12:12–14

We attended a service at an Anglican church, where a friend of ours was the minister. Early in the service, his wife called the children to the front for the Children's Story.

I'll never forget it.

She held a beautiful crazy quilt, made from scraps of brilliantly colored fabric of all shapes and sizes. She explained it would not have been so beautiful if it had been just two colors arranged in squares all the same size, in nice straight rows.

The vibrant colors and various shapes and sizes made the quilt interesting. She pointed out that we, as God's creation, are like that quilt.

We are God's patchwork quilt, made more beautiful by our many differences. Our lives are enriched as we share God's world with people of many races, cultures, ages, and genders. Our ever-wise God has created diversity and calls us to focus on what we share in common, so that we can live in harmony.

Whose life will we touch today? Perhaps a stranger's, who needs to feel the love of Christ we can radiate by our caring.

Prayer for Peace:

Creator God, thank you for our varied and interesting world. We thank you even for that which we find strange. When we come across strangers, may we celebrate our differences and welcome them with the peace of Christ.

Spiritual Practice Practice for the Week: Offering Blessings of Community

Each day this week receive and share blessings of community. Begin with a prayer of gratitude for the network of relationships in your life. See and feel connections with family members, spiritual friends, people in your congregation and community, people and creatures in God's sacred web of life.

What blessings flow to you from these circles? Reflect, pray, and write in your journal about the call to be "Community of Christ." Go deeper each day as you "discern and embrace" the "divine blessing" of this name that opens you to "become a blessing to the whole creation" (Doctrine and Covenants 163:1). What act of blessing are you invited to complete?

Peace Covenant:

Today, God, I will stretch outside my life-box and celebrate what I find there.

13
Thursday
December

We Belong to God

By Merna Short of Melbourne, Victoria, Australia

Be merciful, just as your God is merciful.

—Luke 6:36, adapted

It was end of term at the primary school, and the children were excitedly preparing for the Christmas play.

We asked the "reindeer" to dress in brown. Kristy's mother couldn't afford to buy brown clothes for her, but that didn't worry the little actress. She took her place with the other reindeer.

"Where are your brown clothes dear?" asked the teacher. "My mother's color blind," answered Kristy (she was turning a truth to her best advantage). What could the teacher do? The parents would be there to see their little ones take part. How could she face this lovely mother if her little child was left out of the play? How could she disappoint the child?

It would just have to be the only year a "reindeer" would be yellow and green. The antlers were the evidence of where she belonged. The teacher granted that Kristy belonged with the other reindeers.

No matter how we appear to other people, we belong to God. Kristy wasn't going to let her lack of costume deny her a place in the community of actors. Nothing should deny us the place we belong—in God's world.

I'm thankful for the mercy the teacher showed this child of God.

Prayer for Peace:

Merciful God, teach us to be merciful. Open our minds that we may be shown the faith of a child—faith to share the peace of Christ.

Spiritual Practice for the Week: Offering Blessings of Community

Each day this week receive and share blessings of community. Begin with a prayer of gratitude for the network of relationships in your life. See and feel connections with family members, spiritual friends, people in your congregation and community, people and creatures in God's sacred web of life.

What blessings flow to you from these circles? Reflect, pray, and write in your journal about the call to be "Community of Christ." Go deeper each day as you "discern and embrace" the "divine blessing" of this name that opens you to "become a blessing to the whole creation" (Doctrine and Covenants 163:1). What act of blessing are you invited to complete?

Peace Covenant:

Today, God, I will make sure anyone I meet will have a place of welcome.

14
Friday
December

A Child's Gift

By Don King of Attleboro, Massachusetts, USA

> *The Lord make his face to shine upon you, and be gracious to you; the Lord lift up his countenance upon you, and give you peace.*
>
> —Numbers 6:25–26

When I was 10 years old, I lived on a small farm in southern Ohio. Down the road lived a middle-aged woman who maintained her own little farm. The only name I knew her by was "Omy." I always made it a point to stop my bicycle on my way home and chat with her. She was always alone.

She had a horse, a cow, a chicken, a pig, a dog, and a rifle. One night just before dark, I was pedaling past her house, and she was inside with her oil lamp burning. It was Christmas Eve, and she was all alone.

Feeling sad for her, I asked my mother if she could give me some money and take me to the store to buy her a gift. So with 50 cents I managed to get her a box of candy, and my mother wrapped it for me.

On Christmas morning I jumped out of bed and dressed. With the gift under my arm I walked right past our Christmas tree with all the gifts under it. I hopped on my bike and headed for Omy's house.

I knocked on the door. She opened it, and I said, "Merry Christmas, Omy!" She looked at me with such surprise and joy. I will never forget her shining face. As I rode home that morning a feeling of warmth came over me, and I did not feel the cold. I just felt the joy of giving.

Prayer for Peace:

Creator God, we thank you for the gift of children. We thank you for the greatest gift of all...the Christ child.

Spiritual Practice for the Week: Offering Blessings of Community

Each day this week receive and share blessings of community. Begin with a prayer of gratitude for the network of relationships in your life. See and feel connections with family members, spiritual friends, people in your congregation and community, people and creatures in God's sacred web of life.

What blessings flow to you from these circles? Reflect, pray, and write in your journal about the call to be "Community of Christ." Go deeper each day as you "discern and embrace" the "divine blessing" of this name that opens you to "become a blessing to the whole creation" (Doctrine and Covenants 163:1). What act of blessing are you invited to complete?

Peace Covenant:

Today, God, I will make it a point to stop by the place of a lonely person and be the gift of presence.

15
Saturday
December

My Life Overflows

By Jan Marshall of Independence, Missouri, USA

I lift up my eyes to the hills—from where will my help come?

—Psalm 121:1–2

I looked at my tithing statement and my financial records, wondering how to increase my giving. Misgiving gripped me when immediately my humble friend, Robert, came to mind. Generosity was one of his most outstanding traits. He testified often of God's grace and generosity.

Through his study of the scriptures, Robert felt he should live every day by looking for ways to share. And share he did—with his time, his money, his many talents, and most of all, his love for people. If you needed help, he was there. If he couldn't help, he would find someone who could.

Robert's practice of generosity came naturally to him. He lived his faith. Yet we saw the world differently. Robert saw life as a "half-empty glass." He looked first for the negatives to any new opportunity.

I see life as a "half-full glass"—full of more to come. His attitude puzzled me—how could someone so generous not see the positive opportunities first?

Perhaps his difficult childhood had something to do with it. Yet he didn't let his viewpoint stop him from giving with a generous heart. He loved people and the church community. So *others* might benefit, he gave without a thought how *he* might benefit.

My glass (life) is not half full or half empty. It is *overflowing* with God's generous Spirit. How can I not respond?

Prayer for Peace:

Generous Spirit, let us not concern ourselves about half-empty glasses. May we always respond generously to the overflowing blessings of the Earth. In this way, peace will follow.

Spiritual Practice:

The Jesus Prayer is an ancient spiritual practice from Orthodox Christianity. It is a way of connecting with the gracious spirit of Christ as we ask to receive his mercy.

The prayer comes from the scripture of the blind man calling Jesus to heal him. Silently enter prayer and let your breath become slow and even. Greet God and then take up the prayer phrase: *Lord, Jesus Christ* (as you breathe in)…*have mercy on me* (as you breathe out). Prayerfully repeat these words for several minutes (or 40 times). Breathe the presence of Christ into your mind, heart, and body. Be transformed as you receive the compassionate, peaceful heart of Jesus.

Peace Covenant:

I will be aware of blessings from you, God, from where my help comes.

16
Sunday
December

God Is among You

By Mikal Shedd of Independence, Missouri, USA

The Lord, your God, is in your midst, a warrior who gives victory; he will rejoice over you with gladness, he will renew you in his love…

—Zephaniah 3:17

Today is the third Sunday of Advent celebrated as joy! We find joy in the child with a first Christmas tree, in getting the gift we longed for, and in finding just the right present for someone. We find joy in Christmas carols and pageants, friends, family, and much more. I share now another kind of joy that comes in disguise.

My friend had slipped into a coma early the day before, her body devastated by illness.

The Intensive Care Unit is dark. Twelve people surround her bed: her roommate of many years, brothers, cousins, and many friends; too many for the ICU, but today the policies are relaxed. We are saying good-bye.

At first, the only sound is the respirator, working hard to force air into our friend's lungs. Then someone begins: "Did you know…" We listen as each tells a story: "Do you remember when…" "Always funny…" "We used to…" "How many dogs did she have, anyway?" We laugh together through our tears.

Her roommate has asked me to offer a prayer for them. When asked if we want a chaplain, she throws her arm around my shoulders and says, "No, we have our own chaplain."

Suddenly, a gentle warmth rests on my head and trickles through my body like an anointing oil, leaving a deep peace. My mind quiets. A great calmness fills me.

My friend turns to me, "We are ready." I stand quietly in that space made sacred by the loving presence of God.

I offer the prayer. It comes from a place deep inside me I did not know existed. Everyone in the room becomes restful. We are upheld, experiencing joy and pain as our dear friend is at last freed from her years of pain. We know the One she worshiped all her life has taken her home. Joy to the world!

Prayer for Peace:

Ever-present God, we cope with our struggles because of your love. We are ready to face dark nights of the soul when we know you are with us.

Spiritual Practice for the Week: Forgiveness

Sit in silence for a few minutes, releasing all thoughts. Think of an action you have not forgiven. As you hold that thought, breathe in deeply. With each breath, whisper "God, open my heart." Do this "breath prayer" seven times, remembering that Jesus asks us to forgive "seventy times seven." Throughout the day ask, "God, open my heart."

Peace Covenant:

God, even when remembering the absence of loved ones, I will remember your presence and be at peace.

17
Monday
December

The Gift of a Holy Child

By Barbara Howard of Independence, Missouri, USA

For the mountains shall depart and the hills be removed, but my kindness shall not depart from thee, neither shall the covenant of my peace be removed, saith the Lord that hath mercy on thee.

—III Nephi 10:18

Several years ago we went through a time of unusual pain and sorrow. We spent a weekend with dear friends who were separating after 25 years of marriage. They had moved to another state, so keeping our friendship fresh and alive was difficult. Their new marital status increased the difficulty.

Another friend was diagnosed with a terminal illness. A giant of a man, he was powerless to stop the disease ravaging his body. Death stalked our cherished relationships.

I went to church filled with anguish. Nothing penetrated the pain in my heart, the dreadful sense of loss, until I looked at the faces of the children in our congregation.

Some were youngsters I had known for years. One smiled, another gave the sneaky sanctuary wave that says, "See, I'm here, and I see you." Other children were new—I did not know their names, but they smiled, and their eyes welcomed me.

On that morning of grief, God spoke to me through the eyes of children. It was as though the Creator of the universe was aware of my private despair and was saying, "Look, here is hope. Right among this community is a promise for your future. Cherish these children. They are a gift to you."

At Advent I celebrate God's gift of hope in a particular child: Christ Jesus, whose birth, life, death, and resurrection are central meanings in my life. At the same time I celebrate the gift of children in my congregation—each a unique, irreplaceable gift.

Prayer for Peace:

Divine Comforter, only you can reach the depths of our pain. Thank you for the gift of children to be your vessels of love. Thank you for the gift of the Christ child, the greatest love of all.

Spiritual Practice for the Week: Forgiveness

Sit in silence for a few minutes, releasing all thoughts. At the end of the silence, say a silent prayer of gratitude. Now, think of something you have not forgiven, perhaps an action by a family member or a member of your congregation.

As you hold that thought, breathe in deeply. With each breath, whisper "God, open my heart." Do this "breath prayer" seven times, remembering that Jesus asks us to forgive "seventy times seven." Throughout the day take time to practice the exercise, always asking, "God, open my heart."

Peace Covenant:

Today, God, I will hold up each child in my congregation to your healing light. I will cherish them.

18
Tuesday
December

Stewards of Friendship

By Martha McKain of Lamoni, Iowa, USA

Learn of me, and listen to my words; walk in the meekness of my Spirit and you shall have peace in me.

—Doctrine and Covenants 18:2n

The Christmas Tea at Liberty Hall in Lamoni, Iowa, is one of the biggest events I help with during the year. It is a joy and a task to get that wonderful home ready for the holiday season. My artistic abilities are limited, so I need someone else's expertise to help decorate. Florence has come the last few years.

One day Florence and I were putting up the last decorations. She was working at the stair railing, and I was on a stepladder at the Christmas tree. Coming down, I missed the last step. I fell and went scooting across the floor. Nothing was hurt except my pride.

I finally came to my senses and realized Florence was sitting on the floor beside me. I said, "Oh Florence, why are you sitting there? I am so embarrassed." She said, "Don't feel that way. I am your friend. This is where I should be!" She probably will never know how much that meant to me. Real friendship is so important to our lives and is helpful in times of need, as well as times of joy.

This episode has caused me to do some thinking about others. I have been slow to do that. Friendship is a stewardship. As Jesus reached out to others, so I need to follow him. Bless us all as we reach out to our neighbors, making friends.

Prayer for Peace:

Companion God, your presence is a blessing to us. The presence of friends blesses us. When someone is on the floor in need, we will be there with them. When we are lifted in joy, we will share that joy. We will share the peace of Jesus Christ.

Spiritual Practice for the Week: Forgiveness

Sit in silence for a few minutes, releasing all thoughts. At the end of the silence, say a silent prayer of gratitude. Now, think of something you have not forgiven, perhaps an action by a family member or a member of your congregation.

As you hold that thought, breathe in deeply. With each breath, whisper "God, open my heart." Do this "breath prayer" seven times, remembering that Jesus asks us to forgive "seventy times seven." Throughout the day take time to practice the exercise, always asking, "God, open my heart."

Peace Covenant:

Today, God, I will be a friend to the lonely.

19
Wednesday
December

Love Your Neighbor as Yourself

By Cindy Korf of North Platte, Nebraska, USA

> *Jesus answered, "The first is, 'Hear, O Israel: the Lord our God, the Lord is one; you shall love the Lord your God with all your heart, and with all your soul, and with all your mind, and with all your strength.' The second is this, 'You shall love your neighbor as yourself.' There is no other commandment greater than these."*
>
> —Mark 12:29–31, adapted

My husband's company had a "Secret Giver" gift exchange for its Christmas party. After drawing the name of a person, we were to buy a $15 gift and then give it anonymously.

I was with my husband, shopping for the gift, when we saw an item that seemed perfect. And the item was on sale! We would be giving a $25 item and paying only $10! In my logic, I thought, this was generous (above the required $15). My husband thought differently.

I said, "It's normally $25."

"But, we paid only $10," he responded. "We need to find something more."

"What about tax, and the time we spent looking for it?"

"Then, it's a blessing for both of us. We're able to give more."

"Why?"

"Just think of the surprise and joy she'll have. She'll feel special. Wouldn't you like that to happen to you? Wouldn't you feel loved?"

That day, I learned from my husband about generosity—about giving to our true capacity to make someone else feel special, even with the knowledge that you'd never be recognized for the generosity.

Prayer for Peace:

Generous God, teach us about loving our neighbor. May we have generous hearts and think of more ways we can give and love. Teach us about sharing the peace of Christ.

Spiritual Practice for the Week: Forgiveness

Sit in silence for a few minutes, releasing all thoughts. At the end of the silence, say a silent prayer of gratitude. Now, think of something you have not forgiven, perhaps an action by a family member or a member of your congregation.

As you hold that thought, breathe in deeply. With each breath, whisper "God, open my heart." Do this "breath prayer" seven times, remembering that Jesus asks us to forgive "seventy times seven." Throughout the day take time to practice the exercise, always asking, "God, open my heart."

Peace Covenant:

Today, God, I will use my strength to show love to a neighbor in need.

20
Thursday
December

I Will Never Be the Same

By Stacie Wittemyer of Toledo, Ohio, USA

Finally, brothers and sisters, farewell. Put things in order, listen to my appeal, agree with one another, live in peace; and the God of love and peace will be with you.
—2 Corinthians 13:11

For the last several years caregiving had engulfed my life. Both my mother and grandmother had Alzheimer's disease. Over the years their care took over every facet of my life to the point I rarely went to church, which was some distance away. Nor did I have contact with the outside world.

I was losing my loved ones, *and* I was mourning the loss of *my* life, the one no longer filled with work, friends, church, hope, and purpose.

My mother passed away peacefully after several months of difficulties with breathing, eating, choking, and infections. I was spent.

She died the same week I turned 50 years old. I wondered if anything left of my 50 years of life was worth celebrating. There were no friends in my life to share it with, anyway.

A few days after telling my congregation about mom's death, I was asked to play the piano for the Communion service.

I looked up after the service and realized the entire sanctuary had emptied in just one minute. I guessed people had places to get to quickly.

I sat at the piano, sad that I would not have the chance to be with my church family for even a few minutes. I gathered my belongings and headed for the door. I rounded the corner, and there was my congregation, singing "Happy Birthday." They threw me a surprise party!

That moment of mutual tears, grief, and joy was sacred. God moved in their love, so I saw Christ's love, hope, belonging, and a future. Someone cared and shared love in my moment of need. I will never be the same.

Prayer for Peace:

God of love, thank you for our families. Give us strength to provide the care they need. Comfort us when they are gone. Thank you for our communities that "surprise" us through the tough times. Thank you for the ones who share the peace of Christ.

Spiritual Practice for the Week: Forgiveness

Sit in silence for a few minutes, releasing all thoughts. At the end of the silence, say a silent prayer of gratitude. Now, think of something you have not forgiven, perhaps an action by a family member or a member of your congregation.

As you hold that thought, breathe in deeply. With each breath, whisper "God, open my heart." Do this "breath prayer" seven times, remembering that Jesus asks us to forgive "seventy times seven." Throughout the day take time to practice the exercise, always asking, "God, open my heart."

Peace Covenant:

Today, God, I will surprise someone in need with a Christmas visit.

21
Friday
December

Giving

By Jeanne Davis of Kansas City, Missouri, USA

> *For he is our peace; in his flesh he has made both groups into one and has broken down the dividing wall, that is, the hostility between us. He has abolished the law with its commandments and ordinances, that he might create in himself one new humanity in place of the two, thus making peace, and might reconcile both groups to God in one body through the cross, thus putting to death that hostility through it.*
>
> —Ephesians 2:14–16

I'm thinking about Christmas and the giving we do. I think about the child who *gave* his lunch to Jesus for the seemingly impossible task of feeding everyone. Five or 5,000, it really doesn't matter…he gave all he had.

Perhaps because one person shared everything, others joined in…like a spontaneous potluck. Maybe someone else had a snack stuffed away, and every few people in the crowd kept sharing what they brought and *voilá!* Five thousand people are fed.

Because one boy shared, with Christ's blessing an enormous wave of generosity started! Everyone has to pass the food down the row to their neighbors. As they do, they can't be sure there will be enough for them, but sure enough, more food passes to them. Everyone shares! And then everyone feels connected to the group—they become community. One *new humanity* in place of individuals looking out for themselves. It's not what we share or how much we share, but that we offer. And so begins the generous wave of blessing.

I remember how I always gave my children money to put in the offering. It feels good to give; I knew this. My mom used to give me money to give. Giving is a blessing to the giver as much as to the receiver. It connects you to others. You become part of the community…of five or 5,000.

Prayer for Peace:

Generous God, we praise you for the gift of community. Inspire us to give to our true capacity and to bless where we can. We will be blessed to be a blessing. We will share Christ's peace.

Spiritual Practice for the Week: Forgiveness

Sit in silence for a few minutes releasing all thoughts. At the end of the silence, say a silent prayer of gratitude. Now, think of something you have not forgiven, perhaps an action by a family member or a member of your congregation.

As you hold that thought, breathe in deeply. With each breath, whisper "God, open my heart." Do this "breath prayer" seven times, remembering that Jesus asks us to forgive "seventy times seven." Throughout the day take time to practice the exercise, always asking "God, open my heart."

Peace Covenant:

Today, God, I will prepare a generous offering to help share the peace of Christ.

22
Saturday
December

Best Gift of All

By Michael Clarke of Clay Cross, Derbyshire, England

By the tender mercy of our God, the dawn from on high will break upon us, to give light to those who sit in darkness and in the shadow of death, to guide our feet into the way of peace.
—Luke 1:78–79

During Advent season, I was giving children a lesson about the meaning of Christmas. They were telling me the gifts they would like for Christmas. Some said they would like a new video-game system. Laptops and phones were mentioned.

We also talked about children who would not get such gifts because they live in a poor country.

We talked about a television show airing from a school, where children were trying out new toys. At the end of the show the host told the children they all would receive a gift. The following week, the host said the children gave all their gifts to a children's home.

We watched the children giving away their gifts with joy. We all could see the love in their hearts.

Back to our group discussion with the children. We talked about our best Christmas gifts. One girl in the class said her best gift was a gift from God. She said Jesus was the best gift. He never gets old or runs out of batteries, and he loves us all.

So at Christmas always think about the best gift of all—Jesus Christ: a gift we can all share.

Prayer for Peace:

Creator God, thank you for your gift of hope. May we share through our witness and generosity the light that guides our feet on the way to peace.

Spiritual Practice:

Hold (or imagine) a piece of patterned cloth. Examine it carefully. Notice the overlapping of threads, the mingling of colors to form the design. Write a journal entry about the threads and patterns of your life. What design do you see? How does the life pattern you are weaving create justice and wholeness in God's world? What new patterns is God calling you to weave?

Peace Covenant:

Today, God, I will think of the many gifts I have received and the many ways I can give.

23
Sunday
December

Rejoice

By Steven Shields of Lee's Summit, Missouri, USA

> *...And Elizabeth was filled with the Holy Spirit and exclaimed with a loud cry, "Blessed are you among women, and blessed is the fruit of your womb...For as soon as I heard the sound of your greeting, the child in my womb leaped for joy. And blessed is she who believed that there would be a fulfillment of what was spoken to her by the Lord."*
>
> —Luke 1:41–42, 44–45

Most everything about Jesus' birth was ordinary, simple, commonplace. Joseph and Mary were nobodies. Just an ordinary, working-class couple.

Joseph worked hard for a living and had no prospect of ever being rich. Mary, an unwed mother, had no hope for a life at all except for Joseph's grace and generosity to go through with their marriage.

Much is said of Jesus' humble birth, but the retrospective from a modern, economically developed cultural viewpoint assumes things that are not true. In Jesus' time, almost everyone was poor. In Jesus' time, almost all babies were born in abject poverty. Jesus' birth was no different from most other babies born that same day in Judea.

The only parts of Jesus' birth that were not commonplace were the angelic heralding to a ragtag band of shepherds and the prophetic messages given to those close to Mary. Even so, the guests were common, ordinary people.

Of course, who Jesus was and is gives us cause for great rejoicing. But what really makes it special is that everything about him was common, ordinary. Just like most of us. Jesus was born just like all of us. He grew up playing with the neighborhood children and learning to work; he never had wealth and status. Jesus is for everyone, regardless of any of the social trappings humans find so important and spend lifetimes seeking.

We rejoice because Jesus was and is one of us. Everyone has access to the Divine. That is precious in a world of status symbols. We can simply reach out and take all that Jesus offers. We rejoice in God's unconditional grace and generosity as revealed in Jesus Christ.

Prayer for Peace:

Generous God, we thank you for our poor yet powerful Jesus. May we not love power, but feel the power of love in our soul and use that power for peace.

Spiritual Practice for the Week: Joy of Gratitude

With arms outstretched, imagine God filling your arms with your family, friends, and possessions. Now, bring your arms across your body. Place your hand over your heart and thank God for the abundance.

Peace Covenant:

Today, God, I will seek peace above power.

24
Monday
December

Thank You, Isabella

By Norma Mercurio of Columbus, Ohio, USA

The wilderness and the dry land shall be glad, the desert shall rejoice and blossom; like the crocus it shall blossom abundantly, and rejoice with joy and singing. The glory of Lebanon shall be given to it, the majesty of Carmel and Sharon. They shall see the glory of the Lord, the majesty of our God.

—Isaiah 35:1–2

As a retired elementary teacher with 36 years of experience, I am aware of the truthfulness of "A little child shall lead them." Often I was led and taught by the many children I was privileged to teach. However, a powerful lesson also came from my granddaughter, Isabella, when she was 4.

It was Christmas, and every grandparent knows how special the holidays are when they can be shared with beloved, excited grandchildren. At the time, I lived about 150 miles north of my children, so I carefully packed my car with all the surprises I had prepared.

I left just before noon on Christmas Eve because we were going to attend church services together that evening. I was looking forward to the time and was excited about sharing the packages I had for Isabella and her little sister, Gabriela. Little did I know that waiting for me was a great gift.

I timed my arrival well, just as the children's naps ended. I left my car, walked up to the front door, and knocked. The door flew open, and there stood Isabella with a beautiful smile and a welcoming hug. In my excitement, I asked, "Isabella, who is coming tonight?" Without hesitation she joyfully replied, "Baby Jesus!"

"You are so right, Isabella. Baby Jesus is coming tonight!"

As you might have guessed, this wasn't the answer this humbled grandma expected. I'm sure Isabella isn't aware of the gift she gave me that Christmas Eve, but I will never forget. Thank you, Isabella. Thank you, God.

Prayer for Peace:

Holy Parent, may we always be open to learning from little children. May we follow them on the way to peace.

Spiritual Practice for the Week: Joy of Gratitude

Stand, if possible, with arms outstretched. Imagine God filling your arms with all that you have: family, friends, and possessions. Hold out your arms until they feel tired. Now, bring your arms across your body. Place your hand over your heart and thank God for the abundance that fills your life. Sit for a time aware of that abundance. Then ask God to help you open your heart in gratitude and share freely with others in deepest gratitude.

Peace Covenant:

God, I will keep Christ at the center of my Christmas.

25
Tuesday
December

Tidings of Comfort and Joy

By Peggy Michael of Cantonment, Florida, USA

Make a joyful noise to the Lord, all the earth; break forth into joyous song and sing praises. Sing praises to the Lord with the lyre, with the lyre and the sound of melody. With trumpets and the sound of the horn make a joyful noise before the King, the Lord. Let the sea roar, and all that fills it; the world and those who live in it. Let the floods clap their hands; let the hills sing together for joy at the birth of the Lord...

—Psalm 98:4–9, adapted

How can I help but worship the Creator? God has set me amid marvelous events. Daily I watch God display divine majesty in endless creation. God patiently weaves shifting sands with miles of rootlets; teaches oysters to turn irritants into shimmering pearls; creates billions of snowflakes, each one unique.

In a split second, divine lightning strikes and replenishes the nitrogen in the barren soil. Silently and ever so slowly, microscopic lichens dissolve giant stone mountains. A drip, a trickle of water carves deep canyons at their feet. I am borne away on the Sacredness of Creation.

After doing all this, is it any wonder the Divine has chosen to send us a Christ child to further our awe; to contemplate the mystery and to humble our existence; to give us joy, hope, peace, and the ultimate meaning of love?

Prayer for Peace:

O Creator of the Earth and of me, how can I help but worship you? In my mind's eye I gaze on the Christ child, and I praise you for such a gift. I hold him in my heart to know joy. I release him from my heart to share his peace.

Spiritual Practice for the Week: Joy of Gratitude

Stand, if possible, with arms outstretched. Imagine God filling your arms with all that you have: family, friends, and possessions. Hold out your arms until they feel tired. Now, bring your arms across your body. Place your hand over your heart and thank God for the abundance that fills your life. Sit for a time aware of that abundance. Then ask God to help you open your heart in gratitude and share freely with others in deepest gratitude.

Peace Covenant:

Today God, I will celebrate the birth of your son by singing songs of joy and sharing his peace.

26
Wednesday
December

Spiritual Practices

By Eileen Turner of Portland, Oregon, USA

> *And there came a voice to them, a pleasant voice, as if it were a whisper, saying, "Peace, peace be to you because of your faith in my well beloved, who was from the foundation of the world."*
>
> —Helaman 2:112

Most everyone has had a time when the stress of holidays "gets to you." It's often the same at my workplace. Over the years, as I moved from one position and location to another, I found I could fall back on a spiritual practice I learned at an earlier, stressful time: meditation.

I centered my thoughts on Christ, with the help of a mantra, twice a day for about 20 minutes.

This allowed me to free my mind of all activity, anxiety, and extraneous noise. Silently repeating any word can become a mantra, and joining it with rhythmic breathing in and out forms a pattern of relaxation.

I'd held a position where I was responsible for the clinical practice and staff education. The director was pressuring the leadership team, and meetings had become stressful and unbearable. I loved my job and was unwilling to let this atmosphere get in the way. By practicing meditation, I found I could contribute without fear of retaliation and become a stress-free, productive employee.

On another difficult day in another place and position, contentious problems seemed insurmountable. I took myself to a place in the hospital where I could look over a river and see a crew sculling with precision and grace. Its smooth, repetitive movements were a visual source of inner peace and calm.

God provides us with wonderful ways of dealing with everyday struggles, whether by prayer, meditation, or calming nature scenes. Our peace may depend on setting one more practice in motion.

Prayer for Peace:

Whispering God, we praise you for your gentle spirit. At this season, we will continue to center ourselves on Christ. We will share the teachings of the Prince of Peace.

Spiritual Practice for the Week: Joy of Gratitude

Stand, if possible, with arms outstretched. Imagine God filling your arms with all that you have: family, friends, and possessions. Hold out your arms until they feel tired. Now, bring your arms across your body. Place your hand over your heart and thank God for the abundance that fills your life. Sit for a time aware of that abundance. Then ask God to help you open your heart in gratitude and share freely with others in deepest gratitude.

Peace Covenant:

Today, God, I will continue Christmas with all its meaning in my heart.

27
Thursday
December

In His Name, We Will Hope

By Willa Frey of Fairbanks, Alaska, USA

> *Here is my servant, whom I have chosen, my beloved, with whom my soul is well pleased. I will put my Spirit upon him, and he will proclaim justice to the Gentiles. He will not wrangle or cry aloud, nor will anyone hear his voice in the streets. He will not break a bruised reed or quench a smoldering wick until he brings justice to victory. And in his name the Gentiles will hope.*
>
> —Matthew 12:18–21

I had the joyous experience of being invited to share in the sacrament of blessing my three new grandsons. The first one was Sebastian. Next were twin boys, Elliot and Sawyer. The sacrament of blessing of children is a wonderful experience!

As I prepared, I was impressed with the responsibilities I, the parents, and the congregation assumed. Christ commanded all of us to take these responsibilities seriously. That doesn't mean telling the parents what they should or shouldn't do. It means surrounding them with nurturing love, help, and consideration.

It is our responsibility to demonstrate Christ in our daily living—the most effective way for new parents to learn. This involves being good listeners, sensitive to their fears and mistakes. It's not as though we never have made any mistakes! They will learn from them just as we have. We will allow them room to grow.

God will always be with parents and those who set forth on this nurturing path, supporting one another. Embrace new parents with love.

They shoulder the hope of the world—God's children.

Prayer for Peace:

Tender Shepherd, nurture the parents who nurture the children. Protect these tender reeds that they may not be bruised. Let us look to them for our hope, as we look to Christ. May we share Christ's peace with the world's children.

Spiritual Practice for the Week: Joy of Gratitude

Stand, if possible, with arms outstretched. Imagine God filling your arms with all that you have: family, friends, and possessions. Hold out your arms until they feel tired. Now, bring your arms across your body. Place your hand over your heart and thank God for the abundance that fills your life. Sit for a time aware of that abundance. Then ask God to help you open your heart in gratitude and share freely with others in deepest gratitude.

Peace Covenant:

Today, God, I will support new parents without interfering.

28
Friday
December

Journey in Trust

By Heather Varner of Independence, Missouri, USA

Lift up your eyes and fix them on the place beyond the horizon to which you are sent. Journey in trust, assured that the great and marvelous work is for this time and for all time.
—Doctrine and Covenants 161:1a

God has accompanied me on a journey of patience and trust. My husband, Matt, and I had been married a couple of years and were ready to have a child. We thought within a year or so we would have a little bundle of joy. But after four years, it was still just the two of us.

We visited several doctors, including a specialist. There were tests, medicine, and procedures—but still no baby. I was confused, depressed, even angry with God. Why weren't we allowed to become parents? What had I done wrong? Did God hear my prayers for a child? It seemed other couples had children so easily. It wasn't fair.

Over time, my anger and frustration toward God lessened. Maybe we should choose a different way to bring children into our family. Certain that God must have a child for us somewhere, we began to explore adoption.

Then one day I was driving home from work. I looked at the blue sky and saw a white bird. It seemed to be circling over my car, following me, gliding on the breeze. Seeing the bird gave me a sense of peace, as if God was telling me everything was going to be fine. A few weeks later the doctor confirmed my pregnancy, and in 2009 I gave birth to our precious Emily Rose.

Through all this, I remain assured that God is always present—in our joys and in our sorrows. However life turns out, with patience and trust, I believe we can find goodness in God's grace. Lift up your eyes and journey in trust.

Prayer for Peace:

Co-creator God, give us faith for the journey. We thank you for our families. We thank you for sending your son to be our Prince of Peace.

Spiritual Practice for the Week: Joy of Gratitude

Stand, if possible, with arms outstretched. Imagine God filling your arms with all that you have: family, friends, and possessions. Hold out your arms until they feel tired. Now, bring your arms across your body. Place your hand over your heart and thank God for the abundance that fills your life. Sit for a time aware of that abundance. Then ask God to help you open your heart in gratitude and share freely with others in deepest gratitude.

Peace Covenant:

Today, God, I will lift my eyes to you in faith.

29
Saturday
December

Tradition

By Suzanne McMillan of East Sandwich, Massachusetts, USA

May the God of hope fill you with all joy and peace in believing, so that you may abound in hope by the power of the Holy Spirit.

—Romans 15:13

We had a tradition in our family. On New Year's Day we would start a jigsaw puzzle. However, for the last couple of years, we hadn't done one. But this year I thought it would be fun, so I bought a cheap puzzle.

That puzzle has frustrated us all. It's not cut precisely. The pieces are thin and don't fit well, even when you know they should. What used to be a source of enjoyment is increasingly a lesson in defeat. I keep wondering why I didn't spend a little more to get a good-quality puzzle. It would have caused much less trouble.

I have been meditating on the path of our discipleship being one of learning and growth. I compared it to our family's puzzle and wondered about the costs of discipleship. The more I "pay" in time, prayer, and study, the more truth I glean. I find that pieces somehow "fit right."

The same is true of trees. When I take on the "cost" of digging the hole the right size, preparing the soil, and watering, the trees thrive. When we don't pay the cost and plant haphazardly, the trees don't do well. I guess it comes down to the axiom, "If it's worth doing, it's worth doing right."

Let's be good stewards over our time and pay the cost for what matters most.

Prayer for Peace:

Generous God, may we be generous, too—with our time and our wealth. May we create traditions that strengthen what matters most. May we make time to share the peace of Jesus Christ.

Spiritual Practice:

Pray with a partner if possible. The heart is a center of compassion and spiritual connection. Stand or sit across from your partner with hands open and palms up. Invite your partner to place his or her hands, palms down, on your hands. Close your eyes and be aware of the connection between your heart and your partner's heart.

What needs, feelings, or longings do you sense? Invite God's presence to flow into you and move from your heart to the heart of your partner. Feel or see God's healing light and love flowing between your hearts. After a period of silent prayer, thank God and your partner. Say amen. (You also may pray this prayer by envisioning a particular person across from you.)

Peace Covenant:

Today, God, I will take the time and pay the cost to fit my life to you.

30
Sunday
December

Let Christ Be in You—A Good Fit

By Greg Clark of Independence, Missouri, USA

> *As God's chosen ones, holy and beloved, clothe yourselves with compassion, kindness, humility, meekness, and patience. Bear with one another and, if anyone has a complaint against another, forgive each other; just as the Lord has forgiven you, so you also must forgive. Above all, clothe yourselves with love, which binds everything together in perfect harmony. And let the peace of Christ rule in your hearts, to which indeed you were called in the one body. And be thankful. Let the word of Christ dwell in you richly…*
>
> —Colossians 3:12–16

I dragged myself out of bed this morning and, bleary-eyed, walked to my closet. I picked out blue slacks, a sweater, and a gray shirt. From my chest-of-drawers I grabbed some underwear and what I hoped were blue socks. Then I slowly dressed for work. That's so much easier than clothing myself the way God asks.

When I dress for work, I put on…well, clothes. When I dress for God, I'm told to clothe myself "with compassion, kindness, humility, meekness, and patience." And "above all, love."

When I dress for me, I'm pretty much the only person (except maybe my wife) who cares that my socks and slacks don't match. When I dress for God, every person I meet—and many I'll never see—might be affected if I don't do it right.

It's all about relationships. If I don't dress the way God wishes—the way Paul instructs the Colossians—I'm guaranteed to hurt others. Friends. Family. Co-workers. Virtually everybody I contact.

I also hurt those I never see. If I'm not clothed right, I don't act with the grace and generosity that can help others, even those in faraway places. I even hurt my relationship with myself. When I clothe myself with anger, apathy, and avarice, I'm assured of feeling grumpy throughout the day. More important, I provide a rotten example of the qualities a disciple should model, the same qualities with which Jesus wants me to clothe myself.

Then I not only hurt my relationship with other people, I hurt my relationship with God. I become less than God made me to be.

So next time I dress in the morning, I'll try to put on my best clothes first. And then I'll worry about picking out a shirt, sweater, and slacks.

Prayer for Peace:

Holy and loving God, we will put on love for you and our companions. We will don garments of compassion and patience. We will be kind. We will wear the peace of Christ in our hearts.

Spiritual Practice for the Week: Joy of Gratitude

Stand, if possible, with arms outstretched. Imagine God filling your arms with all that you have: family, friends, and possessions. Hold out your arms until they feel tired. Now, bring your arms across your body. Place your hand over your heart and thank God for the abundance that fills your life. Sit for a time aware of that abundance. Then ask God to help you open your heart in gratitude and share freely with others in deepest gratitude.

Peace Covenant:

God, today I will be mindful to show grace and generosity to others, knowing it will affect relationships.

31
Monday
December

Trust in God on High

By Linda Lyons of Kansas City, Kansas, USA

> *Those of steadfast mind you keep in peace—in peace because they trust in you.*
> —Isaiah 26:3

This morning I read the last devotional from *Daily Bread*, closing the volume for the year. As one day flowed into another and as one year melted into the next, I reflected on all that has happened in the last year.

Our son survived a life-threatening accident but lost his job. Our granddaughter died of cancer. For about three months we went to a funeral nearly every week. One daughter got a big raise, while others were laid off. My husband continues to work part-time at the age of 77. Our grandchildren are becoming more mature. We replaced our old furnace and air conditioner with the aid of a tax credit.

God's work continues in our community. I was ordained to the office of elder this last year. Many good—as well as sad—things have happened.

Then my thoughts turned to the comfortable feeling I have, knowing God was with me the entire year. What a blessing!

As I reflected on all this, my littlest dog jumped onto my lap and snuggled close. Her eyes seemed to say, "I trust you, and I will never let you down." I prayed, "I trust in you, God, and I hope I never let you down." This gave me a warm feeling. Just imagine the warm feeling God has when disciples trust and obey.

Prayer for Peace:

Comforting God, we thank you for being present in the dark and the light. Some moments would be hard to endure without you. We trust you to guide us as we share the peace of Jesus Christ.

Spiritual Practice of Gratitude:

Stand, if possible, with arms outstretched. Imagine God filling your arms with all that you have: family, friends, and possessions. Hold out your arms until they feel tired. Now, bring your arms across your body. Place your hand over your heart and thank God for the abundance that fills your life. Sit for a time aware of that abundance. Then ask God to help you open your heart in gratitude and share freely with others in deepest gratitude.

Peace Covenant:

God, I will thank you for your presence throughout the day and the year.

DAILY BREAD 2012

Author Index

DAILY BREAD 2012

Scripture Index

Old Testament

New Testament

Book of Mormon

Your Future Stories for Daily Bread

Your Future Stories for Daily Bread

New Hymnal
Coming October 2013

We Sing What We Believe

The new hymnal will include about 600 hymns—new and old—that reflect our identity, mission, message, and beliefs.

Watch for several "sneak peek" opportunities to see and sing new hymns in the coming months:

- A small selection of hymns for reunions in 2012
- Lyrics in the 2013 *Daily Bread* as poetry for reflection
- Shared hymns for the international church at World Conference 2013

The anticipated cost of each hardbound hymnal is less than $25!

Full details about the Hymnal Project are at *www.CofChrist.org/hymnal*.